Same-Sex Marriage
and Religious Liberty

Same-Sex Marriage and Religious Liberty: Emerging Conflicts

Edited by
Douglas Laycock,
Anthony R. Picarello, Jr.,
and Robin Fretwell Wilson

THE BECKET FUND FOR RELIGIOUS LIBERTY
AND
ROWMAN & LITTLEFIELD PUBLISHERS, INC.
Lanham • Boulder • New York • Toronto • Plymouth, UK

ROWMAN & LITTLEFIELD PUBLISHERS, INC.

Published in the United States of America
by Rowman & Littlefield Publishers, Inc.
A wholly owned subsidary of The Rowman & Littlefield Publishing Group, Inc.
4501 Forbes Boulevard, Suite 200, Lanham, Maryland 20706
www.rowmanlittlefield.com

Estover Road
Plymouth PL6 7PY
United Kingdom

British Library Cataloguing in Publication Information Available

Library of Congress Cataloging-in-Publication Data

Same-sex marriage and religious liberty: emerging conflicts / edited by Douglas Laycock,
Anthony R. Picarello, Jr., and Robin Fretwell Wilson.
    p. cm.
  Includes index.
  ISBN-13: 978-0-7425-6325-4 (cloth : alk. paper)
  ISBN-10: 0-7425-6325-1 (cloth : alk. paper)
  ISBN-13: 978-0-7425-6326-1 (pbk. : alk. paper)
  ISBN-10: 0-7425-6326-X (pbk. : alk. paper)
  ISBN-13: 978-0-7425-6564-7 (electronic)
  ISBN-10: 0-7425-6564-5 (electronic)
  1. Same-sex marriage—Religious aspects. 2. Same-sex marriage—Law and legislation.
3. Freedom of religion. I. Laycock, Douglas. II. Picarello, Anthony R., Jr. III. Wilson,
Robin Fretwell.
  BL462.S36 2008
  346.7301'68—dc22   2008019239

Printed in the United States of America

In memory of my sister, Martha
—Douglas Laycock

To my wife, Martha
—Anthony R. Picarello, Jr.

This is for my mother, Alice
—Robin Fretwell Wilson

Contents

Acknowledgments

We are indebted to the Becket Fund for Religious Liberty for sponsoring the conference that spawned this thought experiment and resulting book. The Becket Fund is a nonpartisan, interfaith, public-interest law firm dedicated to protecting the free expression of all religious traditions. The Becket Fund is frequently involved as counsel in cases seeking to preserve the freedom of religious institutions to pursue their missions without excessive government interference or entanglement.

The Becket Fund has dedicated significant resources to the neutral, academic study of the impact that changing the definition of the legal term "marriage" is likely to have on religious liberty. The Becket Fund has represented a wide range of clients—including Agnostics, Buddhists, Christians, Jews, Hindus, Muslims, Sikhs, Unitarians, and Zoroastrians, among many others—who take different positions on the same-sex marriage question.

We are also indebted to Washington & Lee University School of Law and the Frances Lewis Law Center for their support of this project, and to Joseph Mercer and Richard Schlauch for their painstaking assistance with the copy edit. We are grateful to Roger Severino, Eric Rassbach, and Benjamin Dougherty at the Becket Fund for their hard work and assistance. We also thank Professors Cole Durham and Robert Destro for their contributions to the conference that led to this book. Finally, we thank our editors at Rowman & Littlefield, Ashlee Mills and Krista Sprecher, for all their hard work.

Introduction
Anthony R. Picarello, Jr.

This is not a(nother) volume debating the pros and cons of same-sex marriage. Instead, it is a thought experiment in religious freedom carried out by seven outstanding legal scholars and practitioners. The experiment took place in December 2005 and was sponsored by the Becket Fund for Religious Liberty, a non-profit, public interest legal and educational institute dedicated to protecting the free expression of all religious traditions.

The authors gathered for this study represent a wide range of views on same-sex marriage. But they have been asked to avoid that underlying dispute and instead to take as a given that the legal definition of marriage has been expanded to include same-sex couples, and then to explore the religious freedom implications of that legal change.

The questions they explore in their chapters can be grouped into two broad categories. First, what kind of religious freedom conflicts, if any, are likely to emerge as a result of the change in marriage law? In what areas of the law will disputes emerge? Will the disputes be common or rare? Will these likely disputes fall into discernable patterns or categories that warrant distinct legal treatment?

The second set of questions relates to how these potential disputes, once identified, might be resolved. When the disputes come down to First Amendment litigation—whether under the Free Speech, Free Exercise, or Establishment Clauses—who will win, and why? Is it possible to avoid these conflicts altogether through the legislative or executive / regulatory process by fore-sightful accommodations of religious exercise, or is constitutional litigation inevitable? Are religious exceptions created by the political branches better or worse than, or as good as, exceptions created by the judicial branch? Could the disputes be resolved, in whole or in part, by the separation of religious and civil marriage?

Marc Stern's chapter traces out the scope of the problem. He identifies a wide range of potential church-state conflicts triggered by redefining legal marriage, some based on current experience where sexual orientation dis-crimination is prohibited, and some hypothetical. These include restrictions on speech against same-sex marriage in public employment and educational contexts, and elsewhere in the public square;[1] the withholding of licenses and accreditations from professionals and institutions that oppose same-sex marriage;[2] and civil rights laws that prohibit discrimination in employment, public accommodations, housing, and education.[3] Although he does not sys-tematically analyze how these conflicts have turned out to date, Stern notes the uneven and unpredictable character of the litigation outcomes, as well as the wide variation among legislative accommodations for religious exercise.[4]

Jonathan Turley draws a narrower focus, examining more closely two par-ticular anticipated conflicts. The first is the government's potential decision to deny religious organizations that oppose same-sex marriage the federal Section 501(c)(3)[5] tax-exempt status they would otherwise enjoy, just as that status was denied Bob Jones University[6] for its religious opposition to inter-racial marriage.[7] The second is the government's exclusion of opponents of same-sex marriage from state-sponsored charitable giving programs, just as the State of Connecticut recently excluded the Boy Scouts[8] from such a pro-gram for their opposition to same-sex conduct more broadly.[9] Turley explains that the Supreme Court's Free Exercise and Free Speech jurisprudence (in each case, respectively) is unfortunately muddled, and so fails to provide lower courts with clear guidance, allowing them to reach opposite results with near-equal justification.[10] He then argues that the Court should resolve the ambiguities strongly in favor of the freedoms of expressive association and religious exercise, in part to assure a genuine diversity in civil society of competing views on controversial questions.[11]

Robin Wilson draws on an analogous experience from the healthcare con-text, not only to predict the kinds of religious liberty conflicts that will arise out of same-sex marriage, but also to offer some constructive potential solu-tions to those conflicts. In particular, she discusses the history of disputes that have arisen where religious individual and institutional healthcare providers refuse to provide abortion or contraception services.[12] That history suggests that proponents of same-sex marriage may seek to harness the power of state and federal governments to withhold funding streams and tax exemptions. In this way, proponents would transform a negative right to be free from government interference in the controversial activity in question, into a positive right to support for that activity, from both government and objecting private actors.[13] That history also suggests that "conscience clauses" and other legislative and regulatory exemptions can go a long way toward reducing the number and severity of conflicts between same-sex marriage and religious liberty.[14] Wilson proposes, among other things, that legislatures grant objecting Justices of the Peace an exemption from having to perform civil same-sex marriages, so long as another willing Justice of the Peace is available to perform that service.[15]

Douglas Kmiec responds to the preceding chapters, recognizing the same range of potential conflicts, but identifying some considerations that could conceivably enable religious institutions to prevail in those conflicts, whether politically or judicially. He argues that the Internal Revenue Service's denial of federal tax exemption to Bob Jones University is based on reasoning that cannot easily be extended to religious institutions that oppose same-sex marriage, and that even if the exemption were denied, the Free Exercise Clause rationale of the *Bob Jones University* decision should be distinguished and ought not control.[16] However, he illustrates both the complexity and difficulty of defending religious doctrine that may soon be portrayed as antisocial. Should jurisdictions begin to follow the California Supreme Court's finding that sexual orientation is a suspect, highly protected classification, Kmiec predicts that state-level tax exemptions will be particularly vulnerable to attack, adding that they may be withdrawn not only through the regulatory process, but through direct challenge in court.[17] He joins Jonathan Turley in his strong critique of the Free Speech Clause reasoning of the United States Court of Appeals for the Second Circuit in *Boy Scouts v. Wyman*.[18] He also explores whether the participation of religious institutions in the government function of solemnizing civil marriages might subject them to the constraints of the constitution as "state actors," concluding that they would not.[19]

Chai Feldblum's chapter focuses on how to resolve these disputes when they arise, and more particularly what constitutional analysis should apply. She first emphasizes the importance of acknowledging both that there are genuine—and, in important respects, similar—liberty interests at stake on both sides of these disputes,[20] and that, nevertheless, one of the interests ultimately must prevail at the expense of the other.[21] She then argues that these mutually exclusive interests should be analyzed under the substantive Due Process protection of the Fifth and Fourteenth Amendments, as interpreted by Justice Souter in his concurring opinion in *Washington v. Glucksberg*,[22] rather than under the Free Exercise or Free Speech Clauses of the First Amendment.[23] On this analysis, claims of freedom to observe religious beliefs should not be treated any differently than those based on analogous secular beliefs and should rarely, if ever, prevail over claims of sexual liberty.[24] She concludes by proposing some narrow legislative exceptions that would describe the limited set of circumstances under which she believes that religious liberty interests should prevail.[25]

Charles Reid's chapter critically examines a proposed solution to some of these conflicts, which is to disjoin legal and religious marriage. He first provides a brief history of the institution of marriage in Europe and the United States, including its religious origins, and the deeply intertwined and occasionally indistinguishable roles of religion and the law within it.[26] This history suggests that any attempt at separating them completely would represent an extreme discontinuity with the past, creating confusion and alienation from the institution.[27] He adds that law has an inherently moral and religious dimension—as it both reflects the morality of society, which is most often religion-based, and instructs society in morality. Reid argues that the law of marriage is no different and, indeed, bears especially intimate ties with the moral and religious life, as it implicates ultimate questions and fundamental life experiences.[28] In this context, disjoining legal and religious marriage appears undesirable and unworkable, if not simply incoherent.[29]

Douglas Laycock's afterword wraps up this volume, first by dividing the conflicts between religious and sexual liberty into the avoidable (but, alas, unlikely to be avoided) and the unavoidable.[30] He then evaluates the contrasting approaches for resolving these conflicts offered by Feldblum (sexual liberty almost always prevails) and Wilson (religious liberty prevails if the same-sex couple can obtain services elsewhere), ultimately aligning with Wilson.[31] He also critiques Reid's opposition to the separation of religious and legal marriage—or, to use the refined vocabulary Laycock would propose, "religious marriage" and "civil unions"—and concludes that the separation is not only possible but desirable.[32] Although it would helpfully reduce the emotional intensity of the debate and correct a long-standing anomaly in American church-state law, this separation would not preclude or resolve entirely the conflicts examined in this volume.

For all its breadth and depth, this volume only begins to explore this new, exciting, and rapidly changing area of inquiry. It is my hope that it will stimulate a broader conversation about the relationship between religious liberty and the civil and legal definition of marriage, and so prompt others to examine these topics more deeply in the years to come.

CHAPTER ONE

Same-Sex Marriage and the Churches

Marc D. Stern[1]

California's legislative effort to legalize same-sex marriage, recently vetoed by Governor Schwarzenegger,[2] contained only one provision dealing with religion. Section 7 of Assembly Bill 849 provided:

> No priest, minister, or rabbi of any religious denomination, and no official of any nonprofit religious institution authorized to solemnize marriages, shall be required to solemnize any marriage in violation of his or her right to free exercise of religion guaranteed by the First Amendment to the United States Constitution or by Section 4 of Article I of the California Constitution.[3]

Modeled after the Canadian same-sex marriage legislation,[4] Section 7 deals with the official intrusion into religious liberty with regard to same-sex marriage that is least likely to occur. No one seriously believes that clergy will be forced, or even asked, to perform marriages that are anathema to them.[5] Nonetheless, this chapter argues that same-sex marriage would work a sea change in American law. That change will reverberate across the legal and religious landscape in ways that are unpredictable today. The most obvious will be in family law, a topic explored elsewhere in this volume.[6]

This chapter illustrates that the foreseeable collisions between religion and the reframed institution of marriage far exceed the narrow focus of Section 7 on solemnization. Part I examines the impact of same-sex marriage on the freedom to preach—in the church, public schools, or elsewhere in the public square. Parts II and III then consider how entities that require a license to operate or receive governmental funding will likely fare if they oppose same-sex marriage. Part IV assesses how recognizing same-sex marriage will push the existing boundaries of civil rights laws—from housing, to employment, to access to public property. Finally, part V briefly explores whether the Religious Freedom Restoration Act[7] or the Free Exercise Clause or state equivalents will insulate individuals objecting to the application of civil rights laws in ways that burden religious exercise.

I. The Freedom to Preach Against Same-Sex Marriage

First and foremost, religious institutions have the duty to spread the word, first to their own believers, and then to others. Faiths differ in the degree to which they feel obligated to "spread the faith," some being focused on reaching existing believers, and others being more outwardly directed. In today's mass media society, even believers are often addressed by their own faith leaders through widely disseminated newspapers, books, radio, television, and the internet, rather than only through in-church sermons or Sunday school classes.

Will speech against same-sex marriage continue unfettered? Under the American regime of freedom of speech, the answer ought to be easy. The First Amendment guarantee of freedom of speech protects speech that is highly critical of particular racial, religious, or ethnic groups, or religious ideas, even speech that crosses the boundary into raw bigotry.[8] It also protects speech that sharply criticizes existing law, so long as it falls short of direct incitement to imminent unlawful action and does not constitute fighting words.[9] There are signs that this robust vision of speech is eroding across Europe and elsewhere in the Western world, including the United States.

A. The Picture Abroad

Abroad, hate speech is illegal. Most European nations suppress hate speech in the name of protecting the equality rights of those defamed. European courts routinely uphold criminal convictions for racist speech, despite claims that these prosecutions impair freedom of speech. Great Britain recently considered government-sponsored legislation that would have made it a crime to incite religious hatred by criticizing a religion. The bill was defeated in the House of Lords.

Oriana Fallaci was prosecuted in Italy for defaming Islam by being sharply critical of its antimodern tendencies, a prosecution abated only by death. Upholding that complaint, a judge wrote that the complaint sufficiently alleged that Fallaci's published works were "unequivocally offensive to Islam."[10]

In Canada, a Protestant minister was fined by the Saskatchewan Human Rights Board of Inquiry for distributing bumper stickers with a circle and a slash together with a slogan categorizing homosexual behavior as sinful, quoting biblical verses condemning homosexuality.[11] The Queen's Bench of Saskatchewan upheld the administrative fine over the minister's free speech claim:

> The Board concluded that the stick figures combined with the biblical passages would expose homosexuals to hatred and ridicule.
> [T]he Board states:
>
>> Having reviewed all of the evidence, the Board accepts that the universal symbol for forbidden, not allowed or not wanted, consisting of a circle with a slash through it, may itself not communicate hatred. However, when combined with the passages from the Bible, the Board finds that the advertisement would expose or tend to expose homosexuals to hatred or ridicule, or may otherwise affront their dignity on the basis of their sexual orientation. It is a combination of both the symbol and the biblical references which have led to this conclusion.[12]

The court also held that prohibiting this speech was "a reasonable limit on the right to freedom of expression."[13]

This decision was reversed in a nuanced opinion four years later.[14] The Saskatchewan Court of Appeal held that the circle and slash and Biblical quotations did not violate the statute, at least in 1997, when equal rights for gays were newly established in Canada, same-sex marriage had not yet been legalized, and an active debate continued. The Court of Appeal also thought that the Biblical source of the quotations made them somewhat less offensive and less likely to be taken literally. But it did not say whether the same advertisement would be protected in 2006.

Canada's recognition of same-sex marriage and its addition of sexual orientation to Canada's hate speech law sparked fears that further prosecutions would be forthcoming.[15] And to some extent, that has happened. The Saskatchewan Queen's Bench has interpreted the Court of Appeal's decision not to preclude a proceeding for civil penalties against a defendant who distributed flyers accusing gays of desiring sex with children.[16]

Government authorities have attempted to regulate speech by religious groups with mixed success. In *Trinity Western University v. College of Teachers*, the Canadian Supreme Court considered the legality of the action of the teaching credentialing authority, the British Columbia College of Teachers (BCCT), to refuse to accredit a religious university's (Trinity) teacher training program.[17] As a condition of admission, Trinity students had to sign an acknowledgment that their conduct would comport with the school's policy that homosexuality was sinful. Despite this promise, there was no evidence that Trinity's students acted on their beliefs about homosexuality in their public school student teaching.

BCCT refused to accredit Trinity's program. It argued that Trinity-educated teachers would espouse anti-gay viewpoints in the public schools and that their mere presence would send a message of exclusion to gay students. The Canadian Supreme Court held that it was premature to deny Trinity's accreditation. It took note of Canada's commitment to equality, but also of its commitment to religious liberty. It also rejected BCCT's claim that Trinity's statement of faith illegally discriminated against homosexuals, who could not in good conscience sign it.

A dissent, however, would have upheld the decision of the BCCT:

> There can be no doubt that the attempt to foster equality, respect and tolerance in the Canadian educational system is a laudable goal. But the additional driving factor in this case is the nature of the educational services in question: we are dealing here with the education of young children. . . .
>
> The burden placed on expression is rationally connected to the . . . goal of ensuring a welcoming and supportive atmosphere in classrooms. The expression at issue, namely the signing of [Trinity's admission] contract, is itself the source of the . . . concern about the educational implications of teachers completing . . . training [under Trinity's auspices]. Therefore a burden on this expression is a rational response to the . . . mandate to protect the public interest. . . . [T]he [BCCT] had a reasonable apprehension of harm to the classroom environment; there is no need for scientific proof of cause and effect between the objective and the means.[18]

This last point may well be the dispositive one. Does one need actual proof of harm to justify silencing speech or is a "reasonable apprehension" of harm sufficient to carry the government's burden?

More recently, complaints have been filed with federal and provincial human rights commissions in Canada against a radio talk host and several websites, alleging that they violated Canadian human rights laws with broadcasts, a letter to the editor, and Web postings. The Alberta Human Rights panel recently decided that a minister violated Alberta's equality ordinance by sending a crude letter attacking homosexuals as "wicked" and calling for a "war" against their agenda, which included using tax funds to pay for schools to advocate that agenda. Although the individual parties sparred over whether the speech was political—and after the newspaper agreed never again to publish such a "hateful" letter—the hearing officer found that the letter written for publication violated Alberta's equality ordinance. "It is," she said, "in my view nonsensical to enact broad and paramount and remedial legislation . . . to protect the dignity and human rights of Albertans only to have it overridden by the expression of opinion in all forms."[19] Subsequently, the defendant was banned from further violations and instructed to request publication of an apology.[20]

In an earlier case, the Canadian Supreme Court upheld the firing of a teacher, Malcolm Ross, who expressed anti-Semitic sentiments in a letter to a local newspaper and in books, articles, and pamphlets. These had become the subject of local controversy:

> [T]he testimony of the students did not establish any direct evidence of an impact upon the school district caused by the respondent's off-duty conduct. Notwithstanding this lack of direct evidence, the Board concluded as follows:
>
>> Although there was no evidence that any of the students making anti-Jewish remarks were directly influenced by any of Malcolm Ross' teachings, given the high degree of publicity surrounding Malcolm Ross' publications it would be reasonable to anticipate that his writings were a factor influencing some discriminatory conduct by the students.[21]

In upholding the dismissal, the Canadian Supreme Court noted the central role of schools in communicating values:

> A school is a communication centre for a whole range of values and aspirations of a society. In large part, it defines the values that transcend society through the educational medium. The school is an arena for the exchange of ideas and must, therefore, be premised upon principles of tolerance and impartiality so that all persons within the school environment feel equally free to participate. . . . [A] school board has a duty to maintain a positive school environment for all persons served by it.
>
> Teachers are inextricably linked to the integrity of the school system. Teachers occupy positions of trust and confidence, and exert considerable influence over their students as a result of their positions. The conduct of a teacher bears directly upon the community's perception of the ability of the teacher to fulfill such a position of trust and influence, and upon the community's confidence in the public school system as a whole. . . .
>
> By their conduct, teachers as "medium" must be perceived to uphold the values, beliefs and knowledge sought to be transmitted by the school system. The conduct of a teacher is evaluated on the basis of his or her position, rather than whether the conduct occurs within the classroom or beyond. Teachers are seen by the community to be the medium for the educational message and because of the community position they occupy, they are not able to "choose which hat they will wear on what occasion;" teachers do not necessarily check their teaching hats at the school yard gate and may be perceived to be wearing their teaching hats even off duty.[22]

An American court has reached similar conclusions with regard to a teacher who belonged to the North American Man-Boy Love Association.[23] The teacher had not introduced the fact of his membership into the school, nor had he acted on his beliefs in school. Nevertheless, students knew of his membership in the association from the press. The courts upheld the discharge of that teacher for many, but not all, of the reasons given by the Canadian Supreme Court.

In Sweden, a pastor prosecuted for urging that homosexuality is sinful was convicted of a hate crime by a trial court. That conviction, however, was reversed by the intermediate court of appeals, and the Swedish Supreme Court upheld the dismissal of the charges.[24]

A document entitled *Yogyakarta Principles on the Application of International Human Rights Law in Relation to Sexual Orientation and Gender Identity*, published in 2007 by "distinguished experts in . . . human rights law," gives some sense of how far the scales are tilted against expressions critical of homosexuality. With regard to sexual orientation, these guidelines provide:

States shall:

A. Take all necessary legislative, administrative and other measures to ensure the right of persons, regardless of sexual orientation or gender identity, to hold and practice religious and non-religious beliefs, alone or in association with others, to be free from interference with their beliefs and to be free from coercion or the imposition of beliefs;

B. Ensure that the expression, practice and promotion of different opinions, convictions and beliefs with regard to issues of sexual orientation or gender identity *is not undertaken in a manner incompatible with human rights*.[25]

The right to speech to promote "different opinions," *i.e.*, critical views of homosexuality, is limited by the need not to be "incompatible with human rights," but no such restriction is applicable to speech in favor of equal treatment of homosexuals. While it is too early to know whether these guidelines will have any impact, Human Rights Watch has hailed the Yogyakarta Principles as a "milestone" for human rights.[26]

How do these cases translate to the United States? At first glance, not well. There are no hate speech laws on the books in the United States. The American constitutional regime of free speech is far sturdier than those in place overseas. Equality is less central to the American constitutional universe than it is in Canada or Europe.

A reflexive dismissal is, however, too glib a conclusion. There are recent efforts at American universities to judge the fitness of education students to become teachers on the basis of their moral attitudes.[27] So far, there is no evidence that these efforts extend to attitudes about homosexuality. It is reasonable to expect that they will. And, indeed, the Bush Administration's nominee for Surgeon General was recently sharply questioned about a paper he wrote fifteen years ago for a religious group debating its stand on homosexuality.[28]

The future course of events will partially depend on whether, and to what degree, American courts will be influenced by the decisions of foreign courts. The outlook for the long term is not certain. The prediction that opponents of same-sex marriage would be prosecuted under Canada's hate speech law did not come to pass when that very subject was debated across Canada. Still, the foreign cases are indications of a line of judicial thinking.

B. American Cases

There is nevertheless reason to worry now in the United States. Principles governing sexual harassment in the workplace could easily encompass expressions by religious institutions and persons that oppose same-sex marriage. Consider *Krell v. Gray*, a California decision upholding an injunction against a former teacher picketing in front of his former school with a sign identifying the principal as a racist.[29] Beginning with precedents on workplace harassment, the intermediate court found that the picketing interfered with the rights of school children because picketing would deny them a "safe, secure and peaceful" school environment.[30] It is no long jump from *Krell* to an injunction banning picketing in front of a school to protest a curriculum on same-sex marriage, on the theory that such picketing would deny some students a safe and peaceful environment.

Consider also a recent controversy at William Paterson University, a public university in New Jersey. The tenured head of an academic department at that public university sent an email invitation to fellow employees to view a film with gay/lesbian themes. A non-tenured member of the staff (not a faculty member) sent back an email asking not to be sent material describing "perversions." He threatened no one with exclusion from the university, called no one a name, and physically touched no one. The staff member was disciplined for threatening a tenured professor and engaging in harassment based on sexual orientation, in violation of state policy forbidding "derogatory or demeaning" remarks.[31]

A single "derogatory or demeaning" remark that does not seek immediate, actual sexual gratification, or threaten the loss of job security, will rarely constitute harassment under either state or federal law.[32] In a regime of free speech, no grown-up, not even a tenured faculty member, enjoys any legitimate expectation that the law will protect her against being exposed to disagreeable speech. Our entire regime of free speech depends on that principle. The United States Supreme Court has repeatedly refused to allow for hecklers' vetoes in the interest of communal peace, instead insisting that a thick skin is a requirement of democratic citizenship.[33]

The Attorney General of New Jersey took a different approach, however. The Attorney General found that William Paterson University was within its rights in disciplining the staff member.[34] Without analysis, and brushing past the question of whether the offending remark constituted workplace harassment in the first place, the Attorney General concluded that "clearly speech which violates a nondiscrimination policy is not protected." This was so "clear" to the writer that she cited not a single case or law review article in support, although she might readily have cited the California Supreme Court.[35] The case ultimately went to arbitration, and the arbitrator concluded that the sexual harassment charge was "not supported."[36]

The United States Supreme Court spoke to these questions in *Pittsburgh Press v. Pittsburgh Commission on Human Relations*, which ought to be controlling.[37] There a newspaper ran paid "want-ads" on a sex-segregated basis. The question was whether this practice violated an antidiscrimination ordinance. The Court upheld the application of the antidiscrimination ordinance, but concluded that:

> We emphasize that nothing in our holding allows government at any level to forbid Pittsburgh Press to publish and distribute advertisements commenting on the Ordinance, the enforcement practices of the Commission, or the propriety of sex preferences in employment. Nor, *a fortiori*, does our decision authorize any restriction whatever, whether of content or layout, on stories or commentary originated by Pittsburgh Press, its columnists, or its contributors. On the contrary, we reaffirm unequivocally the protection afforded to editorial judgment and to the free expression of views on these and other issues, however controversial.[38]

Presumably this view will preclude a hostile environment case based on a religious institution's spreading its message to outsiders and, perhaps, to employees generally (as opposed to targeting a single employee as a sinner). It likewise should have protected the employee in the William Paterson case and the picketer in *Krell*.

Employees in the private workplace have so far by and large fared poorly in asserting a right to express vocal opposition to the gay-rights movement and employers' celebration of sexual diversity. Those cases, discussed below,[39] are distinguishable, because they also raise questions of the employer's right to speak and act against intolerance in the workplace. Nevertheless, they are indicative of a general trend.[40]

What of the church as employer? And what of church-affiliated agencies, especially those offering primarily secular services, such as healthcare, to the general public? Could an employee or client of such an agency successfully assert a hostile environment claim because the employer actively campaigned against gay rights or same-sex marriage and asserted that these practices were irredeemably sinful? Would it matter whether the speech was not aimed at the workplace? Conversely, would an employee of a church-affiliated institution have a right to be accommodated in his religious beliefs in support of gay rights or same-sex marriage? Could an employee of, for example, Catholic Charities act on deep religious conviction by wearing a gay-rights t-shirt or by signing a newspaper ad in favor of abortion choice and then be denied religious accommodation?[41]

C. Exemption Statutes and Harassment – A Short Introduction

The answers to these questions will depend on the vagaries of state and federal statutes, discussed below. Some states wholly exempt religious institutions from the civil rights laws.[42] Others, following the federal model, permit only religious discrimination. These states allow religious identity discrimination (*e.g.*, "we hire believers only") but not religiously motivated discrimination (*i.e.*, the discharge of employees who engage in sexual relations the religious employer deems religiously unacceptable). Still other states expand the scope of exempted religious discrimination to permit discrimination when the employee has religious responsibilities.[43] And other states have no special exemption for religious institutions at all.[44]

Employment decisions about ministers are generally off limits to courts. But ministers often represent only a small percentage of the employees of church-affiliated institutions.[45] Thus, exemptions do not protect all religiously motivated speech by church-affiliated organizations critical of same-sex marriage, at least when that speech trenches upon interests protected by civil rights laws.

Moreover, substantial questions surround what sorts of religiously affiliated institutions fall within the scope of religious exemptions. The National Labor Relations Board and reviewing courts are "all over the map" in deciding what is a religious institution under *NLRB v. Catholic Bishop*,[46] a case which arguably rests on theories of the Establishment and Free Exercise Clauses that are no longer valid.[47] Some courts look to organizational documents, some to actual practices, and some to whether the institution has secular counterparts. Predictability is hard to come by.

Overarching all this is a pivotal question: does the exemption disappear when an institution accepts government funds? Professors Carl Esbeck, Stanley Carlson-Thies, and Ronald J. Sider assert that the answer is no in the employment context.[48] At least one federal district court has held that employers must choose between funding and an exemption.[49] The opinion of the United States Court of Appeals for the Second Circuit, in the child-care version of Dickens's *Bleak House*, *Wilder v. Bernstein*,[50] reached the same conclusion.

The Bush Administration has taken the position that acceptance of funds is not fatal to an assertion of religious exemption for employment discrimination, based in part on the Religious Freedom Restoration Act.[51] However, there is substantial political and legal opposition to that position (which may not survive the next presidential election).

The Administration's position is being challenged on constitutional grounds in a pending case with a gay-rights background, *Lown v. Salvation Army*.[52] There the United States district court issued a ruling mostly favorable to the Salvation Army, holding that receipt of government funds was not incompatible with asserting a Title VII exemption, although it left for further litigation the question of whether the Salvation Army could receive government funds in the first place. If the matter is not settled, an appeal is certain. No significant scholarly voice now argues that service providers that receive government funds ought to be able to discriminate against clients, but that issue is also sure to arise.

If the contraceptive insurance-coverage cases are any guide, only the house of worship itself can count on accommodation from the legislature or courts. In both New York and California, the courts upheld schemes that require church-affiliated social service agencies to provide contraceptive coverage, although churches themselves—defined as institutions in which a majority of employees (and clients and members) are of the same faith—need not do so.[53] These actions treat the church and its social welfare agencies as if they inhabit separate universes, a result at odds with other cases, notably the integrated-auxiliary tax cases.[54]

The media trumpeted the decisions as evidence that Catholic institutions could be compelled to provide contraceptives in furtherance of the state's compelling interest in sexual equality.[55] Of course, since employers were not seeking to discharge employees who used contraceptives, the real fight was over who paid. That payment was at stake should have undercut the states' claim to act in pursuance of a compelling interest, but it did not.

More worrying is a second aspect of both cases: that without breaching religious freedom or equal protection guarantees, the legislature may distinguish between the church as a place of worship and as a social welfare agency. It may also refuse to accommodate the latter's religious beliefs because of its greater openness to employees and clients of different faiths. Of course, there are decisions pointing decisively the other way in other contexts.[56] The message may be to stay small and intensely parochial if an institution wants to be absolutely certain of its eligibility for recognition as a religious institution.

D. Advocacy in the Public Schools

The picture in the nation's public schools is mixed. Schools generally have properly tolerated both a day of silence in support of harassed gay students, and counter-protests, mostly manifested in wearing t-shirts with relevant slogans or biblical verses. To judge from a representative sample of news clippings, schools have done a good job of applying the relevant free speech standards, although in one sample reviewed elsewhere, school officials were slightly more likely to suppress speech opposing gay rights than speech in support of them.[57] Obviously, results vary depending on where in the country the issue arises.

At least two cases discuss the free speech rights of students to oppose gay rights in the public schools.[58] In both cases, students wore t-shirts with citations from biblical verses indicating that homosexuality is sinful. In both, school officials told the students that they could not wear the shirts because they would interfere with the right of gay students to feel safe and secure. In neither was there actual evidence of disruption of education or harm to others.

The courts have reached conflicting results in these cases. In one, *Harper v. Poway Unified School District,* the court rejected the school board's motion to dismiss but gave substantial weight to its concerns about the safety and well being of gay students in avoiding "plainly offensive speech." The United States Court of Appeals for the Ninth Circuit upheld the refusal to issue a preliminary injunction protecting the wearing of the t-shirt. In the other case, *Nixon v. Northern Local School District*, a federal district court concluded that the speech on the t-shirt was fully protected. In yet another matter that never reached court, the Civil Liberties Union of Massachusetts urged school officials to permit students to wear such t-shirt messages.[59]

These courts disagree on two central points. The Supreme Court in its *Tinker, Fraser,* and *Kuhlmeier* trilogy allowed school officials to regulate student speech if it is "plainly offensive."[60] The *Poway* court refused to limit the "plainly offensive" category to sexual innuendo or racial epithets. It did not reach any final conclusion whether the phrase "homosexuality is shameful" is or is not "plainly offensive" in the public school context. The *Nixon* court, by contrast, limited the scope of the "plainly offensive" category to sexual innuendo and calls for drug use. It specifically excluded from that category "offensive" political and religious points of view.

The second point of dispute between these cases is whether the *Tinker* category of "harm to others" is implicated by anti-gay t-shirts. The *Poway* court thought it might be because the school district had an obligation to keep gay students safe.[61] The court reasoned that criticism of homosexuality might engender fear and feelings that homosexual students were unwanted. The court acknowledged, however, that the school could not allow t-shirts supporting gay rights while banning anti-gay ones. In *Nixon*, the court rejected outright the claim that "the silent, passive expression of opinion violated other students' rights." In the Supreme Court's most recent venture into these waters, *Morse v. Frederick* (also known as the "Bong Hits 4 Jesus" case), the Court considered the free speech rights of a student to display a banner that school officials reasonably believed to advocate illegal drug use.[62] The majority opinion acknowledged *Tinker*'s broad protection of student free speech, but did not explicitly decide whether it was still good law.[63] Two concurring justices, whose votes were crucial for the decision, indicated that they would reaffirm *Tinker*:

> During the *Tinker* era, a public school could have defined its educational mission to include solidarity with our soldiers and their families and thus could have attempted to outlaw the wearing of black armbands on the ground that they undermined this mission. Alternatively, a school could have defined its educational mission to include the promotion of world peace and could have sought to ban the wearing of buttons expressing support for the troops on the ground that the buttons signified approval of war. The "educational mission" argument would give public school authorities a license to suppress speech on political and social issues based on disagreement with the viewpoint expressed. The argument, therefore, strikes at the very heart of the First Amendment.[64]

These issues have been extensively canvassed in various court of appeals cases dealing with provocative speech in the public schools, including, for example, the display of confederate flags.[65] These cases often depend on the historic facts of each school, but also on the gray area between the Supreme Court's somewhat confusing precedents.

Lurking in both *Poway* and *Nixon* is the question of the extent to which a school must tolerate private student speech that undermines the substantive values the school seeks to inculcate. Consider just one illustrative case. In *Morrison v. Board of Education*,[66] a Kentucky school district had settled a lawsuit alleging that it allowed truly intolerable physical and verbal harassment of gay students. The settlement required diversity training for all students. In *Morrison*, evangelical Christian students sought (a) to be exempted from the portions of the diversity course that they found religiously offensive, a claim that faltered on *Mozert v. Hawkins County Board of Education*;[67] and (b) the right to express opposition to the points of view expressed by the school district in its diversity training.

Assuming the students' expression is respectful and non-disruptive, this latter claim ought to be easy, as students are not just passive recipients of points of view the school chooses to pass on.[68] Schools in a democratic society must educate, not brainwash. Indeed, school officials have an obligation to teach students to deal with, tolerate, appropriately respond to, and shrug off disagreements, even offensive disagreements.[69] How else will students learn to function as citizens of a democracy? Despite this duty, these cases suggest that school officials prefer to quash divisive speech rather than teach this essential skill of democratic citizenship.

Of course, children trigger special considerations. Children do not have the thick skin and self-confidence adults do or should have. True, students should be trained to accept the bruising give-and-take of a healthy democracy, but it is not a skill quickly or easily learned. In the meantime, schools have other important tasks to accomplish. Where criticism is aimed at children's identity and sense of self, it is natural that their sense of worth and their perception of being welcome in the school will be affected.

I would have trouble participating in a symposium if participants wore t-shirts announcing that all Jews were doomed to hell because they do not accept the lordship of Jesus. Not only am I an adult, but also a lawyer trained to trade in sharp disagreements without personalizing disputes. Most of us writing in this volume spend our lives grappling with the impact of religious differences. Children cannot be expected to have mastered these skills.

More clashes over speech about same-sex marriage in the public schools can be expected. In *Hansen v. Ann Arbor Schools*, a school district celebrated diversity day, delegating to a panel of students power to decide whom to invite to address the student body.[70] For a panel on religious attitudes toward homosexuality, the student planners invited only ministers who believed the Bible does not prohibit homosexuality. Students who held different views were rebuffed when they sought to add a dissenting minister. The federal district court found that in so doing, the school had impermissibly favored one faith over another. The court did not reach the obvious question of whether the panel was appropriate for a public school in the first instance. The judicial precedent is a helpful one, the underlying actions of school officials doubly disturbing.

There will also be clashes between schools and parents objecting to their children being taught the acceptability of same-sex relationships. Parents will assert that such instruction conflicts with their right to direct the moral upbringing of their children, interfering with their constitutionally protected right to do so. Such claims have been uniformly rejected.[71] However, it is not within the competence of public schools to overtly criticize church groups opposed to same-sex relationships.[72] It also remains to be seen how courts will react when students challenge in class what they are being taught.

E. Equal Access Act

The Equal Access Act[73] has been an effective tool for opening public schools to non-curriculum-related religious clubs. Gay-Straight clubs have also successfully invoked the Act to compel school officials to allow clubs urging tolerance of homosexual students and homosexuality. The Act embodies in statute the principle that in a designated public forum, content and viewpoint discrimination is impermissible.

Under the First Amendment, the heckler's veto is disfavored. The government cannot serve to silence speech unless all other means of keeping order will fail. This rule should carry over to the Act. The Act, together with the familiar features of the First Amendment, should protect clubs that speak out against same-sex marriage when it is legalized.

However, the Act does not provide blanket protection. Four provisions will likely be invoked to bar clubs that are organized to speak out for or against legalized same-sex marriage. The Act does not permit activities that "materially and substantially interfere with the orderly conduct of educational activities within the school,"[74] nor does it require schools to sanction meetings that are "otherwise unlawful."[75] Likewise, school officials need not sanction clubs that "abridge the constitutional rights of any person."[76] Finally, the Act provides:

> Nothing in this subchapter shall be construed to limit the authority of the school, its agents or employees, to maintain order and discipline on school premises, to protect the well-being of students and faculty . . . .[77]

Schools will undoubtedly argue that the well being of students whose parents are partners in a same-sex marriage is endangered by clubs devoted to opposing same-sex marriage. During the debate on the Act in Congress, it was proposed that one or more of these provisions could be used to bar a student Ku Klux Klan club. Claims that tolerating hateful speech endangers others or denies their constitutional right to attend school have been made by school officials in analogous cases involving private student speech (*e.g.*, confederate symbols). Sometimes these arguments have been accepted by courts applying *Tinker*,[78] on the theory that displays of these symbols generate fear on the part of minority students and deny them an equal right to an education.

It would seem that none of these sections could be invoked to block a club supportive or critical of same-sex marriage. There is nothing illegal about calling for a change in the law, even if it is a law that is credibly described as protecting equal rights or a law that reflects a broad moral consensus. And bare knowledge that some citizens oppose the school's own vision of the good society, or another person's moral judgments, should not be regarded as an "abridgement of the rights of any person" or an interference "with the orderly conduct of educational activities."

Only in a dictatorship should school officials expect to be free of dissenting points of view. One can, of course, imagine that a club critical or supportive of same-sex marriage would actually harass its ideological opponents in ways that would justify disciplinary action and, if egregious enough, even a decision to deny a club access to the school's forum. Since the entire theory of the Act is that tolerance by school officials does not transform private student speech into official speech, allowing a pro- or anti-gay club cannot be construed as official endorsement of its positions. Nonetheless, *Hsu v. Roslyn Union Free School District*, discussed below, accepted almost every one of these specious arguments to justify a ban on clubs that had religiously exclusionary membership policies.[79]

Additional cause for concern comes from the very problematic decision in *Caudillo v. Lubbock Independent School District*, in which a federal district court upheld a school's refusal to permit a gay-lesbian-straight club to meet on campus.[80] The club's website contained links to other websites that described same-sex sexual activity in apparently graphic detail, detail that the judge spared the sensitive reader. The judge found the links legally obscene, and hence grounds for excluding the club.

The court also reasoned that homosexual conduct was illegal. The school's denial of access came before *Lawrence v. Texas*[81] invalidated Texas's sodomy law, but the judicial decision came after. Incredibly, the district judge failed to note the significance of that decision.

The court offered several additional justifications for upholding the denial of access for the club. First, the court held that the school had closed its forum to all discussion of sexuality. The court regarded this as a permissible subject matter restriction, not an impermissible viewpoint- or content-based discrimination. No written policy laid out this restriction, however. Moreover, other groups at the school, like the Fellowship of Christian Athletes, at least asked their members about their views concerning heterosexuality, suggesting that enforcement of the rule against the Gay-Straight Alliance was raw viewpoint discrimination.

More to the point, in deciding the question of qualified immunity for school officials, the court invoked the Act's exception for maintaining order and protecting students.[82] (It made a similar point in its decision on the merits.):

> As stated above, schools may not discriminate on the basis of the content of the speech. However, the [Act] does not limit a school's authority to properly maintain order and discipline on school premises, protect the well being of the students and faculty, and assure that attendance of students at meetings is voluntary. 20 U.S.C. § 4071(f). . . . The relevant question is whether it should have been clear to Defendant . . . that denying the . . . group access to the bulletin boards, PA system, and meeting areas of the campus violated the [Act]. . . . Clemmons [a school official] stated in both his deposition testimony and in a sworn affidavit that he considered the then current criminal laws of Texas and determined that he could not allow a group to meet on campus that by its purpose and goals condoned directly or indirectly conduct that was classified as unlawful by state law. Such an assertion was made in reliance of [sic] the "maintaining order" exception of the [Act]. Upholding the law is in fact a form of maintaining order. Defendant Clemmons further contends that the safety of the students was considered, as well as the District's liability for establishing a situation allowing harassment and possible physical injury to a student. Clemmons also asserted that he believed the district's policy of prohibiting discussion of sexual activity or birth control other than abstinence fell within the "well being of the student" exception to the [Act].[83]

This reasoning founders on multiple grounds. First, while the school may itself teach abstinence-only-until-heterosexual-marriage, the school is not free to suppress dissenting views. Second, this reasoning confuses private student speech with school speech, the very ill the Equal Access Act was designed to cure. Third, the club did not practice homosexual conduct, which was illegal in Texas at the time the decision was reached by school officials, but fully legal by the time the court ruled against its request for injunctive relief. Instead, the club advocated for its legalization, a position ultimately vindicated by the United States Supreme Court. It is an elementary principle of free speech law that breaking the law and counseling its violation or repeal are two different things.

Fourth, there was no evidence that club members harassed other students. It would be positively perverse to allow the possibility of harassment of club members by students opposed to the club's agenda to silence its non-harassing speech, under the rubric of maintaining order. Fifth, only federal judges would believe that Lubbock was not engaged in viewpoint discrimination as a matter of fact when it tried to ban a Gay-Straight club. And sixth, it is, or ought to be, unconstitutionally paternalistic for a school to assert that allowing students to discuss an issue widely debated in society is harmful to them.

Caudillo is a threat to anti-same-sex marriage speech because it authorizes schools to selectively limit student speech. It is an ominous precedent. Those seeking to protect the right to speak out against the very thing the Lubbock club sought to advance, same-sex relationships, should have loudly criticized it. Unfortunately, the silence was deafening.

F. Elsewhere in the Public Square

Efforts to banish anti-gay religious messages from the public square are not limited to the workplace or the public schools. Consider *Okwedy v. Molinari*.[84] A pastor in Staten Island paid for a billboard announcing the Bible's opposition to homosexuality. The borough president then wrote the billboard company, saying he found the message "unnecessarily confrontational and offensive [and] that the message conveys an atmosphere of intolerance which is not welcome in our Borough."[85] The letter noted that the billboard company did business in Staten Island and invited the company to speak to the borough's anti-bias coordinator. The complaint alleged that, as a result of the letter, the owner of the billboard removed the postings.[86] In reality, the billboard firm made the decision to take down the offensive billboard prior to receiving the letter.

The federal district court first dismissed a free speech claim against the borough president on the ground that his letter was non-actionable protected speech. The United States Court of Appeals for the Second Circuit reversed:

> [T]he fact that a public-official defendant lacks direct regulatory or decision-making authority over a plaintiff, or a third party that is publishing or otherwise disseminating the plaintiff's message, is not necessarily dispositive in a case such as this. What matters is the distinction between attempts to convince and attempts to coerce. A public-official defendant who threatens to employ coercive state power to stifle protected speech violates a plaintiff's First Amendment rights, regardless of whether the threatened punishment comes in the form of the use (or misuse) of the defendant's direct regulatory or decisionmaking authority over the plaintiff, or in some less-direct form.[87]

However, the Second Circuit found no merit to the claim that the borough president was selectively suppressing unpopular religious views:

> [T]he facts alleged in the complaint do not support plaintiffs' Establishment Clause claim. Plaintiffs argue that [the borough president's] letter violated

their rights under the Establishment Clause of the First Amendment because it demonstrates the City's "official position of hostility toward the biblical viewpoint of homosexual practice and Okwedy's religious beliefs." Further, plaintiffs assert that, through his letter, [the borough president] violated the principle of "absolute equality before the law of all religious opinions and sects." Although [the borough president's] letter indicated he was aware of the biblical source of the quotations on the billboards, the letter did not "differentiate among sects," nor did it make "explicit and deliberate distinctions between different religious organizations." Thus, there was no violation of the "principle of denominational neutrality."

Moreover, after reviewing the allegations in the complaint, we are convinced that the district court correctly concluded that [the borough president's] conduct comports with the requirements of the test set forth in *Lemon v. Kurtzman*, which we apply in situations where a facially-neutral policy is challenged on Establishment Clause grounds. Because [the borough president's] letter did not create a denominational preference or violate the *Lemon* test, we affirm the district court's dismissal of plaintiff's Establishment Clause claim.[88]

On remand, plaintiffs dropped the claim against the borough president because his letter was not in fact the proximate cause of the billboard's removal. They continued to challenge the New York City ordinance banning sexual orientation discrimination as viewpoint discrimination. That ordinance's preamble recited the city's interest in suppressing prejudice and bigotry against gays—a *religious* view of the plaintiffs—and was cited by the borough president as justifying his letter.[89] The city's motion papers were ambiguous on whether the city believed that the discrimination ban authorized it only to jawbone those who spread intolerance or also authorized more muscular steps.[90]

The city was undoubtedly correct that it is not unconstitutional viewpoint discrimination for government to ban or campaign against sexual orientation discrimination, just as restrictive abortion laws that coincide with religious views do not constitute viewpoint discrimination. As the city pointed out, for some, miscegenation laws rested on a religious foundation. Yet, *Loving v. Virginia* was not wrong as a result:[91]

> The fact that some individuals or groups continue to disseminate messages rooted in bias and intolerance does not make laws seeking to eliminate such discrimination "content discriminatory." Nor does the fact that some individuals use the Bible, or other religious sources, to spread their messages of intolerance convert disagreement with their messages into "religious persecution." As this Court stated earlier in rejecting plaintiffs' Establishment Clause claim in the first instance: "Plaintiffs identified the biblical source of the quotes

across their billboard message, and The Borough President's reference to that fact cannot reasonably be interpreted as transforming his allowable commentary on plaintiffs' message into an impermissible display of official anti-religious animus."[92]

The ad in question did not call for violence, or even discrimination against gays. It attacked homosexuality as immoral, just as a Mennonite church might attack war as immoral. Presumably, the city would lack the authority to oppose the Mennonite reading of Scripture because it might incite anti-war advocates to acts of intolerance against the military. On the other hand, *Loving* makes clear that racial discrimination once enjoyed some religious support. It cannot be the case that, as a result, the President of the United States could not campaign against state anti-miscegenation laws. Nor would most of us think that a government of an Islamic country could not properly campaign against interpretations of Islam that urge holy war against non-believers.

What is the proper resolution of these issues? Two principles should guide here. First, that the unpopular message may not be officially suppressed, nor its dissemination impeded, by government. Second, government may not offer its own reading of Scripture at all, let alone describe some other reading as incorrect. (One has to ask who would have standing to enforce this latter rule?) Beyond this, religious groups may have to take their lumps. Religious groups have no right to silence government from advancing policies with which they disagree. When religious groups enter the market place of ideas, they necessarily accept the risk that they will be criticized.

II. Licensing and Registration of Entities Opposed to Same-Sex Marriage

A. Commercial Licenses

Businesses and not-for-profit organizations often must obtain state or local licenses before engaging in any of a wide range of activities. The most prominent of such licenses is the liquor license, but licenses also frequently are required to serve food, operate a child-care or mental-health facility, run a boiler, or hang an illuminated sign. Over a generation ago, licenses generated litigation on two constitutional fronts: whether the issuance of a liquor license to a club practicing race or sex discrimination constituted impermissible state action in support of discrimination in violation of the Fourteenth Amendment; and, conversely, whether a state ban on race or sex discrimination by licensees violated associational freedoms protected by the First Amendment.

1. State Action

Moose Lodge v. Irvis settled the first question.[93] The lodge held a liquor license. Pursuant to club rules, it served only whites. The United States Supreme Court held that the bare fact that a state license was issued to the lodge would not constitute illicit state action in support of racial discrimination:

> The Court has never held . . . that discrimination by an otherwise private entity would be violative of the Equal Protection Clause if the private entity receives any sort of benefit or service at all from the State, or if it is subject to state regulation in any degree whatever. Since state-furnished services include such necessities of life as electricity, water, and police and fire protection, such a holding would utterly emasculate the distinction between private as distinguished from state conduct . . . . Our holdings indicate that where the impetus for the discrimination is private, the State must have "significantly involved itself with invidious discriminations" in order for the discriminatory action to fall within the ambit of the constitutional prohibition.[94]

The three dissenting justices (Douglas, Brennan and Marshall) agreed that the bare fact that the state licensed and regulated a function was not enough to make the function state action. ("[T]he fact that a private club gets some kind of permit from the State . . . does not make it *ipso facto* a public enterprise . . . ."[95]). The dissenters insisted that liquor licenses were different either (or both) because of the extraordinarily high degree of accompanying state regulation or because the number of liquor licenses is limited, so that by issuing a license to a discriminatory licensee, the state would be restricting the availability of liquor to minorities. That rationale would not apply to purely regulatory licenses issued in unlimited numbers and without detailed regulation of a licensee's activities.

The *Moose Lodge* Court, however, unanimously invalidated a regulation requiring club licensees to strictly enforce membership rules. The effect of that regulation was to require the lodge to engage in racial discrimination.

The state action doctrine has become more restrictive since *Moose Lodge.*[96] Even if states legalize same-sex marriage, the bare fact that a group that refuses to recognize the legitimacy of such marriages holds a license would not make it vulnerable to a straightforward state-action-in-support-of-discrimination claim. As in *Moose Lodge* itself, however, the vagaries of regulation may produce isolated cases where state action will be present.[97]

2. Nondiscrimination as a Condition of Licensure

That a state is not required to bar discrimination by licensees does not mean that it cannot do so under its police powers. In the wake of *Moose*

Lodge, some state regulators prohibited alcoholic beverage licensees from engaging in racial discrimination. Licensees challenged these regulations in part on the ground that particular regulations were not authorized by statute. These challenges were mostly, but not inevitably, unsuccessful, as were constitutional challenges based on freedom-of-association rights.[98]

With respect to the constitutional claim, the reasoning of the Maine Supreme Court is typical:

> It is, therefore, rational—a regulation reasonably tending to promote the State's legitimate interest in preserving its own dignity and nobility before its citizenry—that the State, in a domain of activity in which it has the most plenary measure of police power available to the sovereign, should choose to formulate a public policy geared to avoidance of the image, or appearance, of acquiescence in, or condonation or encouragement of, practices which discriminate arbitrarily and invidiously on the basis of racial origin or color.
>
> Were we to hold that such effort by the State (regardless of whether it is constitutionally *compelled*) is constitutionally *prohibited* by the Fourteenth Amendment of the Constitution of the United States, we ourselves should be perverting and mocking the Fourteenth Amendment. In the language of Mr. Justice Frankfurter, concurring in *Railway Mail Association v. Corsi*:
>
>> To use the Fourteenth Amendment as a sword against such State power would stultify that Amendment. Certainly the insistence by individuals on their private prejudices . . . in relations like those now before us, ought not to have a higher constitutional sanction than the determination of a State to extend the area of nondiscrimination beyond that which the Constitution itself exacts.[99]

Fraternal lodges mounted more specific challenges to the regulations on the ground that they interfered with their freedom of association. Those challenges all failed. For example, the Utah Supreme Court reasoned that under Utah law, a lodge could set up its food and beverage service operation as a separate corporation, abiding by nondiscrimination requirements, while retaining exclusionary rules for the remainder of its operations.[100] However, the court held the lodge could not enter the public sphere of commerce, discriminate, and keep its license. Most of the courts considering these cases also referred to the plenary power of the states over liquor, a power reinforced by the Twenty-first Amendment, as sufficient ground to uphold antidiscrimination initiatives.[101] That latter ground of course is present only in challenges to liquor licenses.

These cases also considered whether relatively large clubs with active and unrestricted recruitment policies could assert claims of intimate association. Courts by and large concluded that they could not. Since the fraternal

organizations were not bound together by any discernable ideological purpose that would be adversely affected by enforcing a nondiscrimination
rule, claims of freedom of ideological association also failed.[102] Most of the
decisions predate the decision of the United States Supreme Court in *Boy
Scouts v. Dale*,[103] discussed below. *Dale*, however, will not help large, secular fraternal clubs. One outstanding question courts are likely to face is how
courts will classify clubs both fraternal and religious (or ideological) in nature, such as the Knights of Columbus.

Although the *Moose Lodge* decision involved a liquor license, the relevant
Maine antidiscrimination statute applied not only to liquor licenses but to
any license "for the dispensing of food . . . or for any service . . . ."[104] Whether
the court's decision upholding a nondiscrimination requirement, as a condition of licensure, would apply to a food service operation (*e.g.*, a church hall
used for weddings) with a food service license is unknown. Whether most
such operations could survive without a liquor license—except for groups
banning alcohol consumption altogether—seems doubtful.

The Maine antidiscrimination statute contained an exception for "organizations which are oriented to a particular religion or which are ethnic in
character." Secular fraternal clubs challenged the exception as a denial of
equal protection.[105] The challenge could equally well have been brought under the Establishment Clause.[106] The court was not persuaded:

> Since such organizations are formed to promote lawful objectives which their
> members share as common interests by virtue of their religious or ethnic iden-
> tities, their confining of membership to persons who bear the same religious or
> ethnic identity is a rational classification. It thus lacks the arbitrariness by
> which discrimination becomes invidious and which is outlawed by the "equal
> protection of the laws" clause of the Fourteenth Amendment of the Constitu-
> tion of the United States when it is the result of State action.[107]

B. Professional Licenses

Future conflicts over licensing are certain. Psychological clinics,[108] social
workers, marital counselors, and other groups or individuals must have licenses to run facilities offering their services, operate accredited educational
programs in keeping with their beliefs, or seek professional licenses. Some of
these licensees believe that same-sex relationships are, to use the Catholic
formulation, "intrinsically disordered."[109] Fifteen years ago, St. Cloud University School of Social Work demanded that all students accept the National Association of Social Workers ethics code as a condition of admission.[110] That code warned potential social work students that they could not

view homosexual behavior as a sin.[111] Students with conservative religious beliefs objected.

The American Jewish Congress (AJCongress) joined with the Christian Legal Society to successfully protest the requirement that students acknowledge that "the only legitimate position of the social work profession is to abhor the oppression that is perpetrated on gay and lesbian people and to act personally and professionally to end the degradation in many forms." The Supreme Court has held that "no official, high or petty, may prescribe what is orthodox"[112] in matters of morals; social-work-school administrators are "petty officials" in any test. Under legal compulsion, the University gave in.[113]

This can hardly be said to be the last word on this subject.[114] Indeed, one court upheld the American College of Obstetricians and Gynecologists' refusal to accredit a Catholic-affiliated medical school that did not teach abortion procedures.[115] Religiously affiliated law schools have so far unsuccessfully challenged as impinging on religious liberty American Bar Association (ABA) accreditation standards with regard to nondiscrimination and academic freedom.[116] The court in the medical school case emphasized its obligation to give deference to accrediting bodies. The law school cases foundered on problems of state action, as the ABA is not a state actor.[117]

However, an additional section of the ABA accreditation standards (hammered out as a result of the Oral Roberts University Law School's application for accreditation) provides:

(e) This Standard does not prevent a law school from having a religious affiliation or purpose and adopting and applying policies of admission of students and employment of faculty and staff that directly relate to this affiliation or purpose so long as (i) notice of these policies has been given to applicants, students, faculty, and staff before their affiliation with the law school, and (ii) the religious affiliation, purpose, or policies do not contravene any other Standard, including Standard 405(b) concerning academic freedom. These policies may provide a preference for persons adhering to the religious affiliation or purpose of the law school, but shall not be applied to use admission policies or take other action to preclude admission of applicants or retention of students on the basis of race, color, religion, national origin, gender, sexual orientation, age or disability. This Standard permits religious policies as to admission, retention, and employment only to the extent that they are protected by the United States Constitution. It is administered as if the First Amendment of the United States Constitution governs its application.[118]

This standard would ameliorate the problem of compliance with some secular standards. It allows a religiously affiliated school that is so-minded to admit or prefer in admission adherents who presumably are less likely to enter into same-sex marriages. It would not entirely address the problems facing religious law schools because it does not purport to permit other decisions—such as a refusal to admit persons in same-sex relationships even if exclusion is mandated by religious teaching. Nor does the standard address conflicts about the manner and content of instruction.

Conflicts between the helping professions and religious groups can be expected to increase. How will providers propose to deal with same-sex couples who come for marriage counseling? Will they refuse to provide counseling to such couples? Would a refusal violate public accommodation laws? Probably. Would religious professionals attempt to dissuade clients from same-sex activity? Would that be considered a breach of professional standards and therefore grounds for the loss of a professional license? The nearest analogy appears to be the case of pharmacists opposed to dispensing contraceptives and doctors opposed to abortion, issues taken up below.

These conflicts erupted in Massachusetts with regard to the licensing of Catholic Charities to place children for adoption. Catholic Charities refused to place children with same-sex couples as required by Massachusetts law.[119] The Massachusetts legislature refused to carve out a special rule for religious groups opposed to same-sex marriage. Opponents of such an exception labeled it unconstitutional.[120] The president of the Massachusetts Senate said he could not support a bill "condoning discrimination." The bill went nowhere.

III. Public Funding

There will also be substantial conflict over (1) eligibility for government funding for institutions that do not acknowledge same-sex marriage; and (2) conditions attached to government funds. There has not been much litigation about discrimination in funded programs, but there has been some. This part briefly summarizes that litigation.

In *Bellmore v. United Methodist Children's Home*, plaintiff Aimee Bellmore was denied employment by the Methodist Children's Home because she was a lesbian.[121] The home received substantial payments from the state. Before the court rendered a decision, the home essentially conceded to the plaintiff.[122]

At the regulatory level, the Bush Administration sought to permit faith-based recipients of federal aid to engage in discrimination, notwithstanding any local or state laws to the contrary. This stance largely responded to gay-rights ordinances and ignited a firestorm of criticism. The Bush Administration was forced to retreat. The President's subsequent Executive Order did not attempt to preempt state and local antidiscrimination laws.[123]

Questions of conditions have not yet been litigated directly in this context. However, courts generally have refused to apply the unconstitutional conditions doctrine to reasonable discretionary funding conditions, such as antidiscrimination laws.[124]

IV. Civil Rights Law

A. Introduction

1. The Scope of the Laws

Sharp clashes may be expected between civil rights laws that protect against discrimination on the basis of sexual orientation and marital status and the claims of religious institutions and individuals. The latter claims essentially maintain that when the government requires a religious institution or individual to treat same-sex couples as "married," the government is compelling them to violate their religious beliefs. This section limits its discussion to those cases in which the law requires an institution or a person to act in ways that are reasonably understood to relate to the same-sex marriage itself—for instance, by renting an apartment to the couple or providing "family benefits" to a same-sex couple—or to the nature of a religious institution as a sacred community.

This chapter does not analyze or defend bald claims that some persons do not want to associate with persons involved in same-sex marriages, or homosexuals generally. Neither does this chapter discuss the claim that in ordinary commercial employment involving a position that is not value laden, persons in same-sex relationships may offend some customers.[125] Such claims will have no chance of success in a legal regime that has accepted same-sex marriage. These claims may also crowd out cases with far greater chance of success by underscoring the importance of the government's interest in eliminating discrimination and strengthening the newly redefined family.

Civil rights laws bar discrimination in places of public accommodation, housing, and employment, and in admission to, and privileges in, educational institutions. Such laws exist at the federal level and in nearly all states, although details differ. Local equal rights ordinances also exist which, unless preempted by state law, may well go further than state law.[126] Some statutes are specific to one area and others, like California's Unruh Civil Rights Act,[127] offer general guarantees of equal protection in business establishments across a broad spectrum of activities.[128] Massachusetts extends constitutional rights to private actions[129] if accompanied by threats, intimidation, or coercion.[130]

In addition to general civil rights statutes, particular programs have "local" civil rights provisions. These often differ in scope from the general civil rights statutes. For example, Title VI of the 1964 Civil Rights Act bans racial discrimination in federally funded programs. By conscious design, there is no equivalent ban on religious discrimination in federally funded programs. But Head Start, the federally funded preschool program, contains its own such prohibition.[131] The result is a crazy quilt pattern of coverage.

Beyond formal statutory restrictions, there exists administrative civil rights activity. For example, nondiscrimination rules have been adopted for public- and private-university student clubs, rules the Christian Legal Society has actively challenged on numerous campuses. There are also employer rules, such as General Motors's policy of allowing gay affinity groups, but not religious affinity groups, on the strange ground that the latter, but not the former, will prove divisive.

The scope of these substantive prohibitions is measured in part by the exemptions to the civil rights statutes. These statutes include exemptions of various breadth for religious institutions. For example, such exemptions may have broad or narrow definitions of a religious entity. They may exempt only religious discrimination or exempt religious institutions generally. Some, such as the federal Fair Housing Act, are available only to churches that do not practice racial discrimination.[132]

In general, although both coverage provisions and exemptions are embodied in the same remedial statute, federal and state courts treat only the ban on discrimination as remedial. Hence, the ban is to be broadly construed. Exemptions are regarded as being in derogation of these salutary remedial purposes. Even though exemptions further the constitutional value of religious liberty, they are narrowly and grudgingly applied.[133] The disparate treatment between rights is a sign of our egalitarian times.

2. Intentional Discrimination and Adverse Impact

A word for those not conversant with civil rights laws—nondiscrimination statutes ban more than just intentional invidious discrimination ("No Jews, Catholics, or gays allowed."). At least under most federal civil rights statutes and the laws of many states and localities, the laws also ban practices that merely have the effect of excluding a protected class.[134] Thus, Yeshiva University's Albert Einstein College of Medicine, a school operating under Orthodox Jewish auspices, violated New York City's ban on sexual orientation discrimination when it excluded unmarried couples from married housing.[135]

Although New York did not recognize same-sex marriage, and hence the ban did not violate a ban on marital status discrimination, the married-only rule had the effect of discriminating against homosexuals who could not marry. Yeshiva did not raise any religious liberty defenses.[136] By contrast, some statutes, like California's Unruh Civil Rights Act, generally prohibit only intentional discrimination.[137]

Civil rights law accepts as a given that the law may be violated through the creation of a hostile atmosphere as well as by formal exclusionary acts. This is most appreciated with regard to employment, but it is true under almost all antidiscrimination statutes. The federal fair housing statute makes it explicit. It provides that it is illegal to make any "statement . . . with respect to [sale or rental of housing] that indicates any preference, limitation or discrimination."[138] As the United States Court of Appeals for the Second Circuit recently held, the fair housing statute protects against the "psychic injury" caused by discriminatory speech.[139]

3. Exemptions and Civil Rights

That clashes between religious liberty and the civil rights of participants in same-sex marriage are inevitable is shown not only by the cases discussed below, but by recent clashes over proposed legislation to protect religious liberty. Both clashes were won in a rout by those supporting unbending civil rights protection, chiefly gay rights. The continuing battle over employment discrimination in the charitable choice context reflects the same conflict.

Shortly after *City of Boerne v. Flores*[140] had been decided, and after revised federal legislation had been introduced to protect religious liberty to the extent Congress still had power to do so, the question arose of whether and how civil rights laws would be affected. Professor Douglas Laycock and I made the rounds of congressional offices to explain the legislation and respond to legislative concerns about civil rights. One of our appointments was with a liberal African-American member from the South, a man whose commitment to civil liberties I admire. The meeting was private—no press and only a few staff, all well versed in law.

The congressman could not be persuaded that religious exemptions from the civil rights laws, no matter how limited and how justified, would not quickly deteriorate into a general assault on the civil rights citadel. He was not playing to a crowd; there was none. Professor Laycock and I emphasized that the United States Supreme Court had held, in *Bob Jones University v. United States*, that the government had a compelling interest in uniform application of laws banning tax subsidies for racial discrimination, even as applied to religious institutions.[141] We argued to no avail that it was not likely that including religious liberty exemptions would lead to any substantial erosion of the ban on racial discrimination.

We walked out of the office knowing that we had failed to persuade. The point is not that we were inarticulate (I might have been; Professor Laycock certainly was not) or that we had no case to make. The point is that people who have been the victims of discrimination believe (sometimes correctly, sometimes not) that forces of bigotry remain strong and are barely contained by law. Consequently, they see any exemption or weakening of resolve as likely to erode hard-earned gains. That fear goes beyond substantive secular disagreements over whether equality claims ought to generally trump liberty claims where the two conflict. It also goes beyond claims that protecting the dignity of man trumps the legalistic and moralistic—and, for many, outdated and immoral—prohibitions of Leviticus.

Instead, the claim is that the search for exemptions is a back door effort to undermine equality rights generally. This claim is particularly acute in regard to gay rights. Much, if not almost all, of the opposition to the so-called "gay-rights agenda" comes from religious sources. Some of that opposition is hard to describe as anything other than raw bigotry (*i.e.*, unfounded accusations of child abuse and the like). When each side thinks that the effort is not about the resolution between a localized conflict but a skirmish in a take-no-prisoners war, it is hard to expect either side to allow the other any victories.

4. Civil Rights and the Private Sector

Constitutional lawyers are hard wired to focus on what the government does, and to think that the private sector should not be subject to the same constraints as the government. In its early decades, the African-American civil rights movement concentrated primarily on ending official segregation. By the 1960s it became plain that without equal access to private actors in the economic, social, and educational arenas, ending *de jure* segregation would not materially improve the situation of African-Americans. Thus, the 1964 Civil Rights Act targeted private employment and private places of public accommodation. The 1968 Fair Housing Act did the same for housing.[142] Subsequent laws dealing with discrimination against the handicapped follow the same pattern, as do existing laws and ordinances forbidding sexual orientation discrimination.[143]

Presumably, no one contributing to this volume would challenge the premise that the protection against bias and prejudice must extend beyond *de jure* discrimination to ensure meaningful equal participation in society. Evangelical Christians and Orthodox Jews (and atheists) are not about to agree that Title VII's requirement of accommodation in the private sector workplace ought to be repealed in order to avoid the problems raised for them in the workplace by same-sex marriage.

5. Overlapping Civil Rights Statutes

Some of the issues this part discusses have been litigated under civil rights in education statutes, some under fair housing statutes, and some under public accommodation statutes. The plaintiffs can invoke any of these statutes as applicable, or, as in the case of California, they can invoke a global civil rights statute such as the Unruh Civil Rights Act. The most obvious advantage of this choice of weapons is that plaintiffs get the advantage of the statute with the narrowest or even non-existent statutory religious exemption and the broadest remedies (that is, attorney's fees).

Although constitutional defenses and statutory ones, like the Religious Freedom Restoration Act,[144] are likely unaffected by which statute is invoked, the same is not true of statutory exemptions in civil rights statutes. Even if the Fair Housing Act's exemption for religiously sponsored housing applies to a particular housing development, this would not provide protection against a suit brought under 42 U.S.C. § 1982 (passed long before the Fair Housing Act), which contains no such exemption. If exemptions were to be conceived as affirmatively protecting religious liberty rights, not just as a shield against invocation of a particular statute, it would be possible to argue that the particular statutory right protected by the exemption ought to control more general civil rights prohibitions. For the moment though, the law is otherwise.

6. English Law

Before exploring the law in the United States, it is helpful to compare the law of Great Britain. The Equality Act of 2006 authorized the government to outlaw sexual orientation discrimination.[145] Prior to adopting regulations, the government conducted an inquiry into how to proceed. The relevant body (The Women & Equality Unit) posed the following questions about religious organizations and the scope of the proposed new administrative rules:

> Churches, mosques and many other religious organizations advance their faith or belief through activities such as worship, teaching and preaching, officiating in marriage, conducting baptisms and giving sacraments to members of their religious community. We recognize that there may be circumstances where the new regulations could impact on aspects of religious activity or practice in the light of the doctrines of some faiths concerning sexual orientation and the beliefs of their followers. We need to consider therefore the application of the regulations in these areas.

We are interested to hear views on the impact that the regulations may have in these areas, particularly where the regulations may impede religious observance or practices that arise from the basic doctrines of a faith. Any exceptions from the regulations for religious organizations would need to be clearly defined and our starting point is that these should be limited to activities closely linked to religious observance or practices that arise from the basic doctrines of a faith.

Religious organizations also have a role in providing wider services to the community with a social or welfare aspect such as organizing social groups for the elderly or for parents and toddlers. We do not see a case for exempting such services provided by religious organizations from the general prohibition on sexual orientation discrimination.

In line with the Equality Act of 2006 provisions in relation to discrimination on grounds of religion or belief, we are not proposing to exempt activities that are provided by an organization related to religion or belief, or by a private individual who has strongly held religious beliefs, where the sole or main purpose of the organization offering the service is commercial.

Similarly, we propose to apply the prohibition on sexual orientation discrimination to organizations—including churches, charities or other similar groups with a religious ethos—that are contracted by a public authority to deliver a service on its behalf.[146]

In the end, the Government took a narrow view of exemptions. The results were as follows:

The Government has listened to the many points of view offered in response to this question. In order to strike the right balance between the various interests, we will provide religious organisations and those acting under their auspices with an exemption from the Sexual Orientation Regulations provided they are:

- not operating on a commercial basis;
- not providing a service on behalf of and under contract with a public authority;
- and the aim of the discrimination is to comply with doctrine or avoid conflicting with the strongly held religious beliefs of a significant number of the religion's followers.[147]

In the wake of these new regulations, the Catholic Church in Scotland has threatened to close its adoption agency rather than facilitate adoption by same-sex couples, and a Catholic school has concluded that it cannot fire a headmaster in a same-sex civil union.[148]

B. Antidiscrimination in Education

Issues of same-sex marriage are likely to arise in the educational context in four ways: admissions to church-affiliated schools; employment; questions of housing; and regulation of school clubs. These may be raised either by a school insisting that student clubs abide by a principle of nondiscrimination in membership, or by religiously affiliated schools seeking to exclude student clubs advocating or supporting recognition of same-sex marriages.

1. Discrimination in Admissions

Statutes barring discrimination in education ban not only admissions discrimination, but discrimination in access to all facilities. No one would want it otherwise in regard to the more traditional categories of prohibited discrimination. *Bob Jones University v. United States* treated a ban on inter-racial dating as racial discrimination *simpliciter*.[149] *Bob Jones* is dispositive, if any citation were necessary.

Others in this volume will discuss tax exemptions.[150] This part notes only that there will inevitably be challenges to the federal and state tax-exempt status of institutions discriminating in admissions against same-sex couples. This follows from the rationale of *Bob Jones*—that the "charitable" element of Section 501(c)(3)[151] allows (perhaps requires) the government to deny exemptions to groups that violate fundamental public policy. Then-Justice Rehnquist may have been right that the *Bob Jones* Court was guilty of a fundamental misreading of the tax exemption statute. This is not a view to be expressed in polite company, and in any event was rejected by a majority of the Court.

A colleague at another Jewish organization reported that he was told by Carter Administration officials that the Internal Revenue Service was actively considering extending the rule against tax exemption for racially discriminatory schools to single-sex schools.

Admissions discrimination on the basis of a student's same-sex marriage is not likely to be a significant problem until college or graduate school. Still, a Christian high school in California is being sued under the Unruh Civil Rights Act for expelling two students in an allegedly lesbian relationship.[152] A trial court ultimately dismissed the action, but an appeal is pending. Schools training students to serve as ordained clergy are plainly free to reject students on this ground.[153] Beyond that, however, matters are less clear— even for religious schools that endeavor to create an enveloping religious environment. Discrimination on the basis of sexual orientation or membership in a same-sex couple is not "religious discrimination," which is the common formulation of exceptions to civil rights laws.

Even where the exemption is broader, as in New York,[154] it will be necessary to do two things: (1) actively invoke the exemption,[155] which may imperil a school's ability to be funded or receive a tax exemption; and (2) demonstrate that the use of discriminatory criteria furthers the religious mission of the school.[156] Even where this seems obvious, as in a Catholic university seeking a Catholic, not Jewish, vice president of student affairs, the New York exemption requires actual proof that the discrimination is "calculated by the institution to effectuate its religious mission."[157]

The issue of church-school admission policies regarding children with parents in same-sex marriages will also arise. Some schools will not wish to visit the sin of the parents on the children, but others will not wish to admit children from homes arranged in ways that are fundamentally at odds with the school's religious commitments and teachings.[158] At the very least, the presence of such children is likely either to generate self-censorship or to create tension between what a school teaches and what children know about their peers' homes. In an environment in which the state recognizes same-sex marriage, it will likely be perceived to be doubly incumbent on schools to teach their values on this issue, making the position of children from same-sex marriages particularly untenable.[159]

This issue is not purely hypothetical. To my knowledge, Orthodox Jewish schools in New York have been grappling with whether to admit children of single mothers who conceived with assisted reproductive technology. On the one hand, they feel obligated to educate all Jewish children; on the other, they are reluctant to do anything that would signal approval of these untraditional arrangements. (One has to ask what the result would be if a school decides to exclude such children and is sued under an ordinance barring marital status discrimination.)

Would it matter if a school generally insists on parental compliance with all of the school's religious norms or whether it singles out sexual orientation? In the former case, the exclusion will appear rooted in "religious" discrimination, in the latter, in "sexual orientation" or marital status. Paradoxically, this could mean that only the most insular groups, the ones most insistent on total student and parental compliance with religious norms, could avoid state coercion. This result occurred in *Wilder v. Bernstein*, which compelled non-Orthodox Jewish child-care institutions to function on a non-sectarian basis, but carved out an exemption for Orthodox Jewish homes because religion was all-pervasive in these homes.[160]

In the civil rights era, AJCongress discussed lawsuits seeking to either forcibly integrate Catholic schools or require them to accept non-Catholic black students.[161] This discussion never got far. The United States Supreme Court explicitly left open the question of the rights of sectarian schools to exclude on a racial basis in *Runyon v. McCrary*, holding that secular private schools enjoyed no such right.[162] The Court did note that associational rights could be overridden in the course of enforcing the Thirteenth Amendment, citing *Norwood v. Harrison*,[163] but it noted as well that there was no evidence that racial integration "would inhibit in any way the teaching in these schools of any ideas or dogma."[164] The IRS rules for tax exemption for all private schools do require proof that a school's curriculum is not tinged with racism, although these rules have not been challenged in court. (One has to ask: would the IRS in the future require suppression of teachings hostile to same-sex marriage as a condition of tax exemption?)

2. Married Housing—Dormitories

Levin v. Yeshiva University held that a "married only" rule had the effect of discriminating against same-sex couples on the grounds of sexual orientation, since such persons cannot marry.[165] A *fortiori*, a rule allowing only heterosexual couples into married housing will be illegal if same-sex marriage becomes legal.

Yeshiva's response to the adverse ruling was to drop the marriage rule and to allow any couple to reside in the dorm. Although in practice this meant that same-sex couples lived in Yeshiva's dorms, they did not enjoy Yeshiva's imprimatur on their relationship as marriage. This may be the best that could have been achieved. (One has to ask if Yeshiva lawfully could display a placard in its dorms expressing its own disapproval of same-sex relationships.)

3. Religious Clubs, Colleges, and Secondary Schools
a. Religious Clubs in Public Schools

Student clubs have raised civil rights questions both in public education and private schools. A much-mooted question is whether public schools may insist that student clubs seeking formal recognition not engage in discrimination that would violate the school's nondiscrimination policies. In *Hsu v. Roslyn Union Free School District*, the question was whether a student club must be recognized under the Equal Access Act even though it insisted that all members and officers be Christians.[166]

The United States Court of Appeals for the Second Circuit split the baby. It held that a public school could insist that membership be open on a nondiscriminatory basis, but that it could not insist that all elected offices be open to non-Christians. The court reasoned that admitting non-Christians to membership, and even permitting non-Christians to hold some offices, would not interfere with the club's desire to further Christian viewpoints, but that selection of other officers on a nondiscriminatory basis would:

> [T]here is no reason to believe, based on the present record, that the planning of a picnic or a service project must be done by a Christian in order to make it meaningful for Christian students. In the Walking on Water Club, the planning of these non-school activities is the only responsibility of the Activities Coordinator, who, according to the Hsus, must ensure that the activities do not "offend Christian sensibilities." But an agnostic with an understanding of "Christian sensibilities" might plan these activities as well as any other student. . . .
>
> The [students who wanted to form the club, Emily and Timothy Hsu] claim that all officers, including the Secretary and Activities Coordinator, must be prepared to "open or close a meeting with prayer . . . or to lead a Bible study" and that this duty justifies the exclusion of non-Christians from those posts. But this assertion has no limiting principle. Anyone in attendance at a religious meeting may be called upon for a benediction or to "lead a Bible study." There is thus no difference between (a) the Hsus' desire to discriminate in the selection of numerous officers of a small club, each of whom may be called upon to officiate briefly, and (b) a religious test for membership or attendance, which is plainly insupportable.
>
> The leadership provision is defensible, however, as to the President, Vice-President, and Music Coordinator of the Club, because their duties consist of leading Christian prayers and devotions and safeguarding the "spiritual content" of the meetings. Guaranteeing that these officers will be dedicated Christians assures that the Club's programs, in which any student is of course free to participate, will be imbued with certain qualities of commitment and spirituality.[167]

The court also noted that the club the Hsus sought to create was based on an affirmative desire to affiliate with like-minded people, and not some invidious prejudice against others. Were such animus present, the court suggested that a different result might obtain.[168]

> The fundamental values of "habits and manners of civility" essential to a democratic society must, of course, include tolerance of divergent political and religious views, even when the views expressed may be unpopular. But these "fundamental values" must also take into account consideration of the sensibilities of others, and, in the case of a school, the sensibilities of fellow students. The undoubted freedom to advocate unpopular and controversial views in schools and classrooms must be balanced against the society's countervailing interest in teaching students the boundaries of socially appropriate behavior.
>
> True, we analyze this case under the Equal Access Act, while the *Tinker* line of cases concerned the limits on the First Amendment rights in public schools. Nevertheless, the Equal Access Act strikes the same balance that the Supreme

Court has struck between First Amendment free speech rights and a public school's right to maintain order: the Act grants broad free speech rights . . . and restricts those rights . . . when club meetings "materially and substantially interfere with the orderly conduct of educational activities within the school."

Thus, a school may deny recognition to a student group that would otherwise be entitled to protection under the Equal Access Act, if there are grounds for concluding that recognition of the group would materially and substantially interfere with the school's overarching mission to educate its students . . . . Valid grounds may include a school's concerns that a club's discriminatory policies would disadvantage, subordinate, or stigmatize the excluded students, *debase the morals of students who practice the exclusion,* or frustrate the teaching of the "fundamental values necessary to the maintenance of a democratic political system." These values include "tolerance of divergent political and religious views, even when the views expressed may be unpopular," but also "disfavor the use of terms of debate highly offensive or highly threatening to others."[169]

Much of *Hsu's* reasoning ought to be suspect after *Hurley v. Irish-American Gay, Lesbian and Bisexual Group*.[170] It is likely, however, to result in decisions upholding the school if high school clubs insist that members make some sort of faith statement of opposition to same-sex marriage.

b. The College Campus

The Christian Legal Society (CLS) has been embroiled in a series of lawsuits with colleges insisting as a condition of recognition on CLS's openness to all students regardless of religion. The United States Court of Appeals for the Seventh Circuit held that that requirement impinges on CLS's freedom of association[171] Of particular interest is a now-settled lawsuit against Arizona State University, which excluded CLS because it would not promise to abide by the "sexual orientation" nondiscrimination provision of the school's code of conduct.[172] While that case settled, the university's role is likely a harbinger of things to come. Several additional cases[173] are pending in California, where a statute requires that campus programs and activities be "free from discrimination."[174] On its face, California's statute applies only to official activities, but school officials construe it more broadly.

CLS's defenses are rooted in the Constitution. Presumably, therefore, a private college could insist on a nondiscrimination rule for all clubs, as many schools do for fraternities. Although it might be possible to challenge such a rule by a private actor as religiously discriminatory since it would operate to exclude traditional faith groups, I doubt that such a challenge would succeed.

A final issue is whether, under either public accommodation statutes or statutes guaranteeing equal opportunity in education, religious universities need to allow clubs advocating gay rights to meet on their campuses, even if the clubs advocate positions at odds with a school's religious commitments concerning sexual morality. Every one of the Second Circuit's arguments in *Hsu* about the way in which discrimination thwarts a school's educational mission could be invoked in reverse by religious schools seeking to exclude clubs advocating gay rights. On the other hand, each of the arguments in *Hsu* would support the state's claim that it has a compelling interest in enforcing a rule granting access for clubs supporting same-sex marriage.

The results in the case law so far are mixed. In *Gay Rights Coalition v. Georgetown University*, the District of Columbia Court of Appeals held that the District's civil rights statute required that a gay club be given equal access to University affiliation, but that it was beyond the power of the District to compel the University to grant the club official recognition, *i.e.*, its blessings.[175]

The Gay Rights Coalition argued that since Georgetown "endorsed" other clubs at odds with Catholic teaching, it could have no plausible objection to extending the same endorsement to a gay-rights club. The court of appeals, however, rejected the claim on the ground that the intangible benefits that endorsement provides were not within the compass of the statute, and requiring an award of those benefits would trench on the University's First Amendment rights. Even in the days before *Employment Division v. Smith*,[176] the court rejected the school's free exercise defense to the portion of the ruling requiring more tangible benefits.[177] The court reasoned that that the law was narrowly tailored to further a compelling interest in eliminating invidious discrimination.

Two judges would have required official recognition of the club and denied Georgetown the right to label gay students as being in conflict with its moral views:

> Suppose, hypothetically, that a local private college religiously wedded to the views of the clergy who once offered a Biblical defense of slavery, or to the more recently expressed views of Bob Jones University, sought to limit black student groups to the tangible benefits of student activities by stressing that, because of their racial inferiority and/or their advocacy of racial intermarriage, they could not be officially "recognized" by the college on a par equal with other groups, such as a student chapter of the local Masonic lodge. Or, suppose that the same local college admitted self-acknowledged homosexuals to all degree-granting programs but carried them on all official college rosters, including the commencement program, under the exclusive heading "evil" students. I cannot imagine anyone seriously would contend that the Human Rights Act does not prohibit such second-class, restricted access to college facilities and services—that the Act tolerates such a "hostile environment."[178]

An intermediate appellate court in New Jersey reached a different result on essentially the same facts, in *Romeo v. Seton Hall University*.[179] Plaintiffs brought suit under New Jersey's antidiscrimination-in-education statute, which is inapplicable to an institution "operated by a bona fide religious . . . institution."[180] The court there rested on twin propositions: that the general nondiscrimination provision in a school handbook did not waive a statutory religious exemption and that an exemption was nonwaivable in any event.[181] The court was not troubled by the fact that Seton Hall also offered a full secular program, and was open to all, not just Catholics in good standing with the Church.

4. Employment Discrimination

The final issue likely to arise with regard to education is the hiring of faculty. This issue is best considered in the context of employment law, discussed below.

C. Places of Public Accommodation

Truly commercial enterprises owned by individuals with religious objections to serving same-sex couples will not succeed in challenging the applicability of public accommodation laws. A hotel chain's owners (Paris Hilton's parents, for example) might be religiously opposed to same-sex marriage. But even if they wanted to, the Hilton's owners would not be permitted to refuse to rent a room to a same-sex couple who identified themselves as a couple, and not just two people of the same sex sharing a room. In the case of hotels, this would probably follow in any event from an innkeeper's long-standing common-law duty to accept all (well-behaved) comers.[182]

What of other places of public accommodation such as camps, retreats, homeless shelters, and the like? In some cases, these will present issues of classification. Is one dealing with a place of public accommodation or a residence subject to a fair housing act? The differences may or may not be large, depending on the specifics of the statutes and especially their exemptions.

The federal public accommodation statute defines its coverage as follows:

> (b) Each of the following establishments which serves the public is a place of public accommodation . . . :
>
> > (1) any inn, hotel, motel, or other establishment which provides lodging to transient guests, other than an establishment located within a building which contains not more than five rooms for rent or hire and which is actually occupied by the proprietor of such establishment as his residence;
> >
> > (2) any restaurant, cafeteria, lunchroom, lunch counter, soda fountain, or other facility principally engaged in selling food for consumption on the

premises, including, but not limited to, any such facility located on the premises of any retail establishment; or any gasoline station;

(3) any motion picture house, theater, concert hall, sports arena, stadium or other place of exhibition or entertainment; and

(4) any establishment (A)(i) which is physically located within the premises of any establishment otherwise covered by this subsection, or (ii) within the premises of which is physically located any such covered establishment, and (B) which holds itself out as serving patrons of such covered establishments . . . .

(e) Private establishments

The provisions of this subchapter shall not apply to a private club or other establishment not in fact open to the public, except to the extent the facilities of such establishment are made available to the customers of patrons of an establishment within the scope of subsection (b) of this section.[183]

The coverage of the public accommodations law is typically quite broad. The most frequently litigated question concerns what is a "place" of public accommodation.[184] That issue generated substantial litigation over the Boy Scouts[185] until the Supreme Court resolved it on constitutional grounds.[186] Secular private schools are probably covered for at least some purposes, even if they are not covered under a separate education statute.[187] Summer camps are also within the scope of the statute,[188] as are YMCAs[189] and sports leagues.[190] So too, probably, are funeral homes,[191] cemeteries,[192] and in some states, professional practices such as dental offices.[193] The results are, however, sufficiently mixed that when faced with a complaint under a public accommodation statute in "places" not listed explicitly in the language of the act, counsel ought to give consideration to claiming that one's client is not a "place" of public accommodation.

Apparently no cases have held that the church is a place of public accommodation and therefore subject to the strictures of public accommodation laws. For federal disability law purposes, churches might have been thought to be such, but for an explicit statutory exclusionary clause.[194] At least one divided intermediate appellate court has found that parochial schools are not "places" of public accommodation under state law.[195] Georgetown University, however, was successfully sued under such a law and required to permit a gay-student club.[196]

Even though at the height of the civil rights era, eleven o'clock a.m. on Sunday was described as the most segregated hour in America, apparently no one brought suit to compel the integration of churches. Not long ago, however, I counseled a synagogue against which an administrative claim was brought under a New Jersey statute protecting the right of women to breastfeed in places of public accommodation. The complaint alleged that a member was precluded from breastfeeding in the sanctuary during services. The administrative agency charged with enforcement dismissed the complaint on the ground that the synagogue was not a place of public accommodation.

The New Jersey Civil Rights Commission is presently considering a public accommodation discrimination claim against a Methodist-owned camp meeting for refusing to rent a gazebo—sometimes used for church services—for holding a same-sex union ceremony.[197]

Whatever the scope of the public accommodation statute, it seems plain enough that the right to define standards for church membership is constitutionally beyond the regulatory authority of the states. It is at the heart of the church's autonomy. On the other hand, the fact that a for-profit place of public accommodation is owned by religious people or even a religious entity will not excuse violations of the statute.[198]

Public accommodation law has in fact been used as a weapon to force ideological change on organizations. In one case, Scientologists decided to "capture" an organization highly critical of its activities, the Cult Awareness Network, by invoking California's Unruh Law[199] to insist on full membership for Scientologists. The effort failed because the California courts ultimately saw the effort for what it was, an attempted ideological takeover of one group by another.[200]

D. Joint Commercial-Religious Endeavors

At least in the Orthodox Jewish community, many religious goods and supplies are provided not directly by the synagogues and not even by not-for-profit corporations wholly under religious auspices. Instead they are provided either by freestanding not-for-profits not formally owned or controlled by a religious institution[201] or by for-profit businesses acting in compliance with religious norms. I understand that the same is true of other churches. Communion wafers in the Catholic Church and temple garments worn by Mormons are not produced by the church itself, but by private companies under religious supervision. Consider the following issues, some of which are at this point theoretical, some of which have already occurred:

1. A for-profit restaurant or catering hall, operating under the supervision of an Orthodox rabbinical group to insure that the food served is kosher, is asked to cater a lesbian commitment ceremony conducted by a rabbi from a different branch of Judaism. The Orthodox rabbinic organization threatens to remove its supervision for that affair. The couple insists on a kosher affair with Orthodox rabbinic supervision.

(a) May the restaurant refuse the affair on the ground that the rabbinic group will not permit its name to be used in this connection, and without its approval the restaurant's business would be destroyed?

(b) Does the rabbinic group itself become subject to the public accommodation laws because of its symbiotic relationship with the restaurant, undoubtedly a place of public accommodation?

(c) Could the restaurant accept the catering job, but post signs on its premises saying that it (or its supervising agency, or both) found the same-sex ceremony offensive?

Fortunately for almost all concerned, the restaurant went bankrupt before the question had to be answered.

2. Could a summer camp operated in strict conformity with religious principles—and without which conformity parents would not enroll their children—refuse to accept children coming from same-sex marriages? Could it accept them on condition that the parents would not attend as a couple on visiting days? Should it matter if the camp is operated by a for-profit or not-for-profit corporation?

3. What would be the legal options for a cemetery (or a funeral home) asked to perform a funeral for a member of a same-sex couple when the funeral (or, for example, a grave marker) will indicate that the deceased was the loving partner of a person of the same-sex? The problem will be more acute for the cemetery than the funeral home, since the latter is generally not held responsible for what is said of the deceased (*i.e.*, no one blames a funeral home when the deceased is eulogized as generous and saintly, when he in fact was miserly and sybaritic). Would the result be different if, as in some faiths, funerals are regularly performed in the house of worship?

4. What of a church-affiliated community center (gym, Little League, etc.) that offers family programs? Must it enroll same-sex couples as families? What of a church picnic for families that is advertised in the local general circulation newspaper?

5. A religiously affiliated family service provider offers marriage-counseling services. Must it counsel same-sex couples in ways that facilitate or preserve the relationship? Would it matter if the service is advertised or is available only by referral of a minister? Would it violate the law to counsel partners to such marriages that their relations are sinful?

6. Would a printer be required to print invitations to same-sex marriages?[202]

We are not wholly without precedent on these questions. In two cases, one in Ohio,[203] and one in Massachusetts,[204] plaintiffs challenged arrangements under which Minister Louis Farrakhan rented an auditorium for black males only. These exclusionary arrangements were challenged as violations of public accommodation laws. In each case, the court rejected the claim on the ground that the exclusionary arrangement was protected by the freedom of association, since the meetings had a clear ideological purpose and the presence of women and whites would necessarily pressure the mosque to change the message:

> The record here establishes that the message sought to be conveyed at the meeting in question was one directed to the men's class, and sought to deal with issues of drugs, crime, and violence in the community, and the role the mosque perceived that the men of the community should play. According to the unchallenged testimony . . . , leaders of the mosque were of the view that Farrakhan might be able to "cure" some of the crime and violence occurring in the community with his words; their intention was to expose male members of the community, especially those males participating in crime and violence, to his message by holding the men's meeting. Forcing the mosque and its leaders to include women in the meeting would change the message. It would also be in direct contravention of the religious practice of the mosque. . . .
>
> To be afforded First Amendment protection, there is no requirement that an association exist for the particular purpose of disseminating a specific message. It must merely engage in expressive activity that would be impaired by the unwanted inclusion. . . . . The admittance of male members of the public to an otherwise nonpublic mosque meeting does not bring the event within the scope of Massachusetts public accommodation law. Holding otherwise would impermissibly burden the defendants' freedom of association under the First Amendment.[205]

The meeting at issue was the equivalent of a formal mosque service, and can be distinguished from less obviously religious endeavors, say, a church picnic or rental of an amusement park. Nevertheless these precedents are important because they suggest that there is no absolute ban on religious (or gender) discrimination in rental facilities that are not permanently part of the church or mosque. However, these precedents do not offer binding authority for church-affiliated groups, and do not reach the joint enterprise cases. Such decisions also underscore the importance of plainly articulating a rationale for an exclusionary policy.

It is important to note here the limits of the decision in *Hurley v. Irish-American Gay, Lesbian and Bisexual Group* (IAGLBG).[206] The question presented in *Hurley* was whether a St. Patrick's Day parade through public streets could exclude Irish gay and lesbian groups marching as such. The organizers had refused to allow IAGLBG members to march as a group in the parade for the purpose of expressing pride "in their Irish heritage as openly gay . . . individuals."[207] The organizers did not seek to exclude individuals who were openly gay. IAGLBG sued, alleging that the denial of group access violated Massachusetts's public accommodation law.

This discussion will leave aside the question of whether on the facts of the case there was state action—not a simple question on the facts there presented, but badly litigated by IAGLBG. The question confronting the Supreme Court was whether the state courts erred in enjoining the exclusion of the gay-rights marchers in light of the countervailing First Amendment rights of the parade's organizers.

The Supreme Court found that the state court had in fact erred. The state court order was tantamount to a requirement that the parade organizers "alter the expressive content of their parade."[208] Significantly, however, the Court prefaced its unanimous holding by noting that this case "does not address any dispute about participation of openly gay, lesbian or bisexual individuals in various units admitted to the parade," and whether the bare fact of such participation would have communicative content, *i.e.*, that such persons were respected members of the Irish-American community.[209] It is important to underscore that the parade organizers asserted a clear ideological message, unlike private social clubs whose freedom of association claims have repeatedly been rejected because they conveyed no identifiable ideological message.[210]

Boy Scouts v. Dale[211] fills in some gaps left by *Hurley*. The Scouts barred gay scoutmasters. The New Jersey Supreme Court held that that exclusion violated New Jersey's public accommodation law,[212] rejecting freedom-of-association claims on two grounds: that prior to the litigation the Scouts had not announced an explicit policy excluding gays; and that the state had a compelling interest in "eliminating the destructive consequences of discrimination."[213]

> When contrasted with its "all-inclusive" policy, Boy Scouts' litigation stance on homosexuality appears antithetical to the organization's goals and philosophy. The exclusion of members solely on the basis of their sexual orientation is inconsistent with Boy Scouts' commitment to a diverse and "representative" membership. Moreover, this exclusionary practice contradicts Boy Scouts' overarching objective to reach "all eligible youth." We are satisfied that Boy

Scouts' expulsion of Dale is based on little more than prejudice and not on a unified Boy Scout position; in other words, Dale's expulsion is not justified by the need to preserve the organization's expressive rights.

The invocation of stereotypes to justify discrimination is all too familiar. Indeed, the story of discrimination is the story of stereotypes that limit the potential of men, women, and children who belong to excluded groups.[214]

Note that the majority arrogated to itself the right to decide what message the Scouts should communicate. A concurring opinion argued that the exclusion was based on status alone and that status did not constitute speech.

A closely and sharply divided United States Supreme Court reversed, finding that the Scouts had clearly enunciated a policy of excluding gays, and that admission of gays would interfere with the inculcation of that policy. Surprisingly, the Supreme Court did not directly address the New Jersey court's suggestion that the state had a compelling interest in ending discrimination. I am not sure what to make of the silence, and whether that question remains open.

Since *Dale*, lower courts have rejected challenges to the Scouts' exclusionary practices relating to atheists and gays. Scout organizers have not been protected from other penalties, however, such as exclusion from a state's public employee charitable fund[215] or denial of preferential access to public places.[216]

Finally, it bears emphasizing that all successful invocations of a right to ideological association have come from not-for-profit organizations that exist to spread ideas. These cases almost certainly will not protect for-profit corporations. They say little with regard to social service providers whose primary purpose (at least from a secular perspective) is providing services, not spreading ideas.

One recurring issue regarding places of public accommodation, which has been particularly important for the gay community, concerns the prerogative of same-sex partners to visit their partners in the hospital or make healthcare or funeral arrangements for them. Often these cases arise when the parents or siblings object to the same-sex relationship. It is hard to imagine that a recognized right to same-sex marriage will not encompass such prerogatives, certainly in preference to other family members. Hospitals, even religiously based ones, will likely be required to acknowledge the decisions of same-sex partners. Perhaps they can rationalize their acquiescence on the ground that the partner ought to be treated as a *de facto* designated healthcare proxy. Funeral arrangements will not be able to invoke an implied proxy theory.[217] Here, too, family members will likely have to live with the implicit choice of the deceased that her partner will decide these matters.[218]

E. Access to Public Property

A special problem concerns access to public property. The leading case is *Gilmore v. City of Montgomery*, which arose out of the court-ordered integration of that city's schools.[219] The question was whether private "segregation academies" could be allowed access to publicly owned facilities such as parks, recreational facilities, and cultural attractions (*e.g.*, zoos and museums). The Court held that segregation academies were not constitutionally barred from facilities generally open to the public, but it indicated that they might be constitutionally barred from facilities where access was rationed:

> Traditional state monopolies, such as electricity, water, and police and fire protection—all generalized governmental services—do not by their mere provision constitute a showing of state involvement in invidious discrimination. The same is true of a broad spectrum of municipal recreational facilities: parks, playgrounds, athletic facilities, amphitheaters, museums, zoos, and the like. It follows, therefore, that the portion of the District Court's order prohibiting the mere use of such facilities by *any* segregated "private group, club or organization" is invalid because it was not predicated upon a proper finding of state action.
>
> If, however, the city or other governmental entity rations otherwise freely accessible recreational facilities, the case for state action will naturally be stronger than if the facilities are simply available to all comers without condition or reservation.[220]

The Court added a helpful summary that addressed the right of segregated clubs to use facilities generally open to the public:

> It should be obvious that the exclusion of any person or group—all-Negro, all-Oriental, or all-white—from public facilities infringes upon the freedom of the individual to associate as he chooses. Mr. Justice Douglas emphasized this in his dissent, joined by Mr. Justice Marshall, in *Moose Lodge*. He observed: "The associational rights which our system honors permit all white, all black, all brown, and all yellow clubs to be formed. They all also permit all Catholic, all Jewish, or all agnostic clubs to be established. Government may not tell a man or a woman who his or her associates must be. The individual can be as selective as he desires." The freedom to associate applies to the beliefs we share, and to those we consider reprehensible. It tends to produce the diversity of opinion that oils the machinery of democratic government and insures peaceful, orderly change. Because its exercise is largely dependent on the right to own and use property, any denial of access to public facilities must withstand close scrutiny and be carefully circumscribed. Certainly, a person's mere membership in an organization which possesses a discriminatory admissions policy would not alone be ground for his exclusion from public facilities. Having said this, however, we must also be aware that the

very exercise of the freedom to associate by some may serve to infringe that freedom for others. Invidious discrimination takes its own toll on the freedom to associate, and it is not subject to affirmative constitutional protection when it involves state action.[221]

This language should bar municipalities and other government agencies from excluding schools, church youth groups, and the like from generally accessible public property because of disagreements over same-sex marriage.[222]

F. Professional Practices

As noted, state courts are divided on whether professional practices are places of public accommodation. If they are, several problems will arise for affected professionals. These are readily illustrated by *North Coast Women's Care Medical Group v. Superior Court (Benitez, Real Party in Interest)*.[223] There (the plaintiff alleges), physicians in the practice refused to perform certain assisted reproductive technologies on a woman who was a partner in a same-sex relationship. The woman sued under California's Unruh Civil Rights Act,[224] alleging deliberate discrimination against her because she was a lesbian.

The physicians had a two-fold defense: (1) they would not perform this procedure for any unmarried person (a limitation legal at the time in California, but not now); and (2) interpreting the Unruh Civil Rights Act to prohibit a doctor's compliance with their religious beliefs would deny free exercise rights under the First Amendment and the equivalent provision of California's constitution. California has not recognized such religious liberty defenses to civil rights law under its fair housing laws,[225] so one must be skeptical of the physician's chance of success on this last claim. The case is presently pending after argument in the California Supreme Court.

Several points are worth noting. First, the plaintiff patient prevailed in the trial court even though the physicians were prepared to refer the patient to another physician in the same practice and to pay any additional expenses resulting from the referral. The objecting physicians were willing to treat the patient for all other purposes, including a pregnancy resulting from the procedure, so that the tangible burden on the patient was virtually nil. (These facts are disputed, but the case has been litigated so far as though this factual dispute were irrelevant.)

Second, this is not a case where physicians refused to treat a class of patients because they did not approve of their lifestyle and believed they were facilitating their *patients'* sins. The physicians are being asked to perform a procedure that they regarded as directly sinful.

Third, it is noteworthy that the California Medical Association filed two briefs. The first emphasized physician autonomy, but was withdrawn after creating an uproar. The association then substituted another brief, expressing horror at the thought that a physician might engage in "invidious" discrimination, but otherwise expressing support for the right of a physician to exercise professional judgment about performing particular medical procedures.

The American Medical Association's own ethical opinion on the subject is at war with itself. A recent opinion provides:

(1) Physicians must keep their professional obligations to provide care to patients in accord with their prerogative to choose whether to enter into a patient-physician relationship.

(2) The following instances identify the limits on physicians' prerogative: . . .

    (b) Physicians cannot refuse to care for patients based on race, gender, sexual orientation, gender identity, or any other criteria that would constitute invidious discrimination, nor can they discriminate against patients with infectious diseases. . . .

(3) In situations not covered above, it may be ethically permissible for physicians to decline a potential patient when: . . .

    (c) A specific treatment sought by an individual is incompatible with the physician's personal, religious, or moral beliefs.[226]

Fourth, if one is prepared to acknowledge a physician's right to refuse, one must be prepared to advance, in both publicly accessible and legal arguments, how this exception is different than one allowing a doctor to refuse to treat a patient because of race. How are these physicians differently situated than a physician religiously committed to the purity of the races being asked to facilitate the birth of a child to a mixed race couple?

Fifth, a professional's right not to participate in an abortion is protected by statute.[227] Absent such a statute, free exercise claims under Title VII's accommodation provision or the Constitution have not fared well. Thus the United States Court of Appeals for the Third Circuit refused to uphold such a claim in *Shelton v. University of Medicine and Dentistry*.[228] The court took it as settled that doctors and nurses cannot endanger patients' health because of their personal religious beliefs.

Sixth, the physicians in the pending California case were prepared to refer this patient to other physicians who were willing to perform the procedure. The *amicus* brief that the Christian Medical and Dental Association filed in the court of appeals urged the court to refrain from imposing such a requirement on physicians, because there will be physicians for whom such a referral is itself a violation of conscience.

This issue has arisen as well in the contraception context.[229] Advocates for a right of pharmacists to refuse to dispense insist not only on a right to refuse to personally dispense contraceptives, but also on a right not to tell patients of alternative locations where they may purchase them. In one extreme case, a pharmacist allegedly destroyed a prescription for contraceptives.[230] Such claims go well beyond anything courts will or ought to accept.

A patient has a legitimate expectation that a physician will inform him of available medical alternatives. Suppressing that information is a breach of that duty.[231] It will be difficult enough to pursue a right of conscience not to actually engage in sinful conduct. To extend it as far as the Christian Medical and Dental Association would is to endanger the entire enterprise. At best, one can insist that moral autonomy is not a right enjoyed exclusively by patients; that physicians also enjoy that right; and that it would disserve society to turn physicians into moral automatons. There are sufficient unhappy instances of physicians yielding to prevailing morality in the past century to give pause to those who would insist otherwise—Tuskegee, eugenics, Soviet psychiatry. But to value moral autonomy, one must value patient, and not just physician, autonomy.

North Coast will ultimately be a crucial precedent for the rights and duties of professionals confronted with the need to act in ways that reinforce same-sex relationships, and should receive the attention it deserves from the faith community. But civil rights laws and malpractice suits are not the only risks lurking. Licensing authorities may also exercise their authority to coerce religious conscience to yield to secular morality.

Some states, for example, protect a pharmacist's right of conscience by statute; others refuse to acknowledge any such right.[232] In California, legislation has been introduced to require pharmacists to dispense contraceptives.[233] The governor of Illinois has ordered the same result, a decision now being challenged in court. New Jersey, too, adopted such a law.[234] In a high visibility case, the Wisconsin Board of Pharmacy censured a pharmacist because he refused to fill a prescription *and* refused to refer the patient elsewhere.[235]

In general, professional groups—especially in the social services field—have been skeptical of religious claims for exemption. Marriage counselors, social workers, and psychologists can expect challenges under either public accommodation or licensure laws if they refuse to facilitate same-sex partnerships. The license challenges will be grounded on the proposition that the religious practice (say, attempting to persuade a homosexual to become heterosexual) falls below generally accepted secular standards of care, and hence is grounds for discipline, including loss of license. Opponents of professional conscience clauses make no bones about their ultimate aim. An opponent in Wisconsin, Fred Risser, was quoted as saying that "[i]f a healthcare worker does not want to support healthcare, then he or she belongs in a different line of work."[236]

In addition, regulatory bodies likely will be asked to prohibit therapies directed at same-sex couples (or homosexual individuals), such as so called "restorative therapy" on the ground that they lack a scientific basis. Such clashes will plunge the courts into treacherous ground.[237]

Religious practitioners who must be licensed will not easily escape such conflicts. Church groups may seek to avoid licensing themselves by claiming not to be offering mental health services, albeit at a price to any claims that their counseling is scientifically based. In Kentucky, the state has insisted that the services that one church group provides constitute mental health services; consequently, the group must obtain a license. One such battle recently settled.[238]

The results are mixed in the cases that have arisen out of these battles in the employment context. In one case, it proved to be an undue burden to accommodate a marriage counselor who refused to counsel gay couples.[239] The contraception cases are not clear-cut.[240]

G. Housing
The federal Fair Housing Act bans discrimination in the sale or rental of dwellings, defined as follows:

> (b) any building, structure, or portion thereof which is occupied as, or designed or intended for occupancy as, a residence by one or more families, and any vacant land which is offered for sale or lease for the construction or location thereon of any such building, structure, or portion thereof.[241]

Within the compass of the Fair Housing Act are institutions such as homeless shelters,[242] nursing homes,[243] residential care facilities,[244] drug rehabilitation centers,[245] children's homes,[246] battered women shelters, and AIDS facilities.[247] These cover the gamut of operations of church-affiliated organizations. Religious discrimination is barred in such places by the explicit terms of the statute.[248] Those who operate either low-income housing, homeless shelters, or senior citizen housing are affected by this statute. There is a limited religious exemption, discussed below.

H. Employment
The prohibition of the federal antidiscrimination law in employment, Title VII of the 1964 Civil Rights Act is broad and sweeping. It prohibits employ-

ment discrimination whether intentionally implemented or not. (While it does not presently reach discrimination on the basis of sexual orientation, I proceed on the basis that it will be so amended in the future. Some states already have such provisions.) Discrimination is prohibited not merely in hiring, but in all "terms, conditions, or privileges of employment,"[249] which includes fringe benefits (*i.e.*, refusing to pay for health benefits to same-sex partners), and, of course, creating or tolerating a "hostile environment" through harassment and the like.

In cases where the discriminatory act is intentional, the employer can justify it only by demonstrating a *bona fide* occupational qualification (BFOQ). A BFOQ requires a showing that an explicit exclusionary requirement (we do not hire persons involved in same-sex marriages) is one that goes to the essence of the business, and is the only way to achieve the purpose.[250] Customer preferences for heterosexuality (like supposed customer preferences for pretty stewardesses) will not sustain a BFOQ defense. In the present context, it is difficult to conceive of any BFOQ defense for a for-profit corporate enterprise that would sustain a blanket ban on hiring persons in same-sex relationships. Church and church-affiliated groups stand a better chance, but even this will likely be only on a case-by-case basis.

Where the practice is not intentionally discriminatory, but nonetheless has a discriminatory effect, a defendant seeking to defend itself must show that its challenged practice is "consistent with business necessity," a standard marginally easier to satisfy than BFOQ.[251]

What of not-for-profit agencies who insist that rules against hiring members of same-sex couples will destroy the essence of the employer's business or thwart some other business necessity? (I assume for the moment that the religious corporation exception is inapplicable.) The question is necessarily contextual. Notwithstanding *Corporation of the Presiding Bishop v. Amos*,[252] it will be hard to argue that the bare hiring of a member of a same-sex couple to be a janitor will destroy the essence of a business. Matters are more complicated where the employee in question has responsibilities to serve as a moral example.

In *Chambers v. Omaha Girls Club*, a club fired an unmarried black woman who became pregnant out of wedlock.[253] She had been hired to operate a program designed to discourage unmarried black girls from becoming pregnant. Given the distribution of out-of-wedlock births across the population when the case was litigated, a firing decision based on having an out-of-wedlock child had a disparate impact on blacks.

The United States Court of Appeals for the Eighth Circuit held that the club's desire for an appropriate role model was a sufficient business necessity to excuse the firing. Note, however, that Congress has narrowed the business necessity defense since *Chambers* was decided. Parochial schools firing unmarried pregnant female teachers have found a mixed reception in the lower courts in the face of allegations of sex discrimination because males engaging in extramarital sex are not discharged, if only because such activity by men is hard to prove.[254] Hard litigation can be expected over youth leaders and the like.

Terms, conditions, and privileges of employment include fringe benefits. The statute would thus prohibit a refusal to pay health insurance premiums for same-sex spouses, if an employer paid for benefits for heterosexual spouses. A religious employer could meet this problem by (a) not paying for spouses; (b) by allowing any employee to select any partner;[255] or (c) yielding to the commands of nondiscrimination law.

The statutory requirement of equal terms and conditions without regard to prohibited factors is the hook on which the law of workplace harassment has developed. Where an employer creates or tolerates an atmosphere under which an employee cannot comfortably perform, it denies an employee equal terms and conditions of employment.

It is now plain that employers have a two-sided obligation with regard to harassment. The employer may not itself engage in harassment and it may not allow employees or customers to create an intolerable environment for an employee based on one of the prohibited bases of discrimination. What of an employer who, under compulsion of law, hires people in same-sex relations and even provides them equal benefits as if they were a "traditional" married couple, but insists on noting in the workplace his strongly held opposition to such marriages?

Pittsburgh Press seems to hold that such expressions would be permitted.[256] Perhaps they would be. *United States v. Space Hunters*, however, suggests otherwise in the fair housing context.[257] Perhaps there is a difference between general statements of principles and statements directed at particular employees.

EEOC v. Townley Engineering[258] is instructive. There, the company mandated that all employees attend company-sponsored prayer meetings. The company was indifferent to whether employees prayed. Employees were, it claimed, free to use earplugs or quietly read. No one was penalized for not praying. Over Judge Noonan's powerful dissent bemoaning the second class status of religious freedom (here the rights of the company, not its atheist employee), the United States Court of Appeals for the Ninth Circuit held that the small company owned by deeply religious Christians and operated in keeping with their Christian beliefs could not compel attendance at prayer meetings. It did not, however, hold that the existence of company-sponsored prayer was itself improper or that it created a hostile work environment, as some urged. This appears to be a reasonable balancing of interests.[259]

From the point of view of the employee, both types of expression—that is, speech aimed at a specific individual on the one hand, and generalized religious speech on the other—may lead to discomfort, but from the view of the First Amendment there ought to be a substantial difference between them. One is analogous to fighting words; the other is not. Assuming an employer is uninterested in what happens in her workplace, the same distinction might be drawn when the contested offending speech comes from a fellow employee.[260]

This latter case is not likely to arise, as most employers, wary of the expense of defending a harassment lawsuit, are likely to enact their own rules on impermissible speech in the workplace. These are likely to suppress any speech that some other protected class of employee finds hurtful—a description that would likely ban any statements in the workplace objecting to same-sex marriage.

But what if employees are religiously bound to share their religious view with sinners? Among the duties that Title VII imposes on employees is the duty to accommodate religious practices, unless doing so imposes an "undue hardship,"[261] which the Supreme Court has interpreted to mean more than a *de minimis* hardship.[262] In a series of cases, the question has arisen whether an employer that supports efforts to welcome gays (and by extension same-sex partners) has a duty to allow employees with religious objections to voice those objections in the workplace. So far, most of the decisions say that the answer is no, at least for private employers.[263]

In the public workplace, the answer might be different if an employer allows (non-supervisory) employees to express themselves on political issues in the workplace.[264] In the private employment context, where the First Amendment does not apply to the employer's actions, the courts emphasize the right of the employer to control what is spoken in its own workplace. This principle would certainly apply to use of broadcast email over an employer's email network to oppose an employer's sexual orientation policy.

Further guidance on the subject came in an interesting case decided by the Seventh Circuit, in which evangelical Christian employees of General Motors protested the company's policy of recognizing affinity groups for gay employees, but not for persons with traditional religious viewpoints.[265] The district court held that the disparity in treatment did not violate Title VII. In its brief to the Seventh Circuit, GM argued that religious clubs would generate tension in the workplace not generated by racial or sexual orientation affinity groups. The Seventh Circuit accepted this argument, and affirmed.

The point is reminiscent of Bill Gates's explanation for Microsoft's support of a Washington State gay-rights bill—the need for Microsoft to create a welcoming environment for all. He did not explain, and nobody thought to ask, how it was that support for that bill would signal a welcome to those employees for whom it embodied a deeply offensive moral outlook.

It is, however, the case that employers may not ask employees to accept the legitimacy of any other person's sexual expression. The duty to accommodate would bar such a practice.[266] Neither can they single out for punishment from among those who do not take diversity training seriously only those religiously opposed to the legitimation of same-sex relationships.[267]

Courts have uniformly refused to require (or permit) accommodation where it in any way might be said to burden the equality rights of other employees. This explains the decision in the cases denying Catholic Charities an exemption from a law requiring employers providing health insurance to cover contraceptives—since any exemption would make female workers unequal. Similarly, courts have refused to require accommodation of over-the-road truck drivers whose schedules required them to work overnight shifts alone with female employees.[268] In any case in which an employer's request for excusal from Title VII or an employee's request for an accommodation would trench on another employee's equality rights, these cases, probably correct under *TWA v. Hardison*, would preclude relief.[269]

There is as yet no law addressing the question of whether public employees will have any right to accommodation if they seek to recuse themselves from performing or recording same-sex marriages. The Vermont Supreme Court has suggested that no such constitutional right exists.[270] Other courts in other contexts have been equally reluctant to allow public officials to invoke Title VII to pick and choose how they will enforce laws, even if others can fill in for them.[271] And, as noted above, Title VII has not provided much help for professional employees seeking to refuse to assist sinners with their services. Given the absence of First Amendment speech rights for public employees,[272] it seems very unlikely such rights of abstention will be recognized.

A New York trial court recently allowed a plaintiff alleging employment discrimination on grounds of sexual orientation to inquire whether the defendant harbored religious views against homosexuality.[273] The employer had expressed explicit anti-gay animus in the workplace and relied on the Bible for his alleged animus. The court allowed discovery on the ground that "no person should be permitted to use [religious liberty rights] as a cloak for discrimination . . . ." The court suggested that the evidence would be admissible at trial, although that would be an issue for the trial judge at trial. (Under New York's byzantine trial practice, the judge deciding discovery questions is not the trial judge.) The obvious lesson here for religious employers is not to talk anywhere about your views on homosexuality.

I. Exemptions

Exemptions from the civil rights laws follow a crazy quilt pattern. California, for example, wholly exempts religious institutions from its employment discrimination law, but refuses to allow an exemption for landlords refusing to rent to cohabitating couples.[274] Title VII of the 1964 Civil Rights Act exempts religious institutions from the ban on religious discrimination,[275] but other provisions of the Act, including that involving places of public accommodation, have no such exemption. The religious exemption in the federal Fair Housing Act is broad, but it is limited to religious institutions not discriminating on the basis of "race, color, or national origin," a limitation that does not appear in other exemptions.[276]

As noted throughout this chapter, the exemptions also differ in their description of the exempted entities. Is it only the church? Any religious organization? Any non-profit "operated, supervised or controlled by or in conjunction with a religious corporation," to use the language of the Fair Housing Act?[277] Differences in organizations may not materially distinguish between institutions as they appear in the real world, but they can make a world of difference in the availability of an exemption, as became clear with regard to the Federal Unemployment Tax Act,[278] under which some church schools were subject to the tax but others were not, based only on accidents of ecclesiastical and corporate form.[279] Careful attention must be paid to the precise language of any exemption, and, as noted above, whether it applies to all of the possible causes of action.

For reasons of space, I will focus on federal exemption statutes, touching on the states only in passing. They, and the resulting case law, illustrate the common problems that arise in this field.

1. Fair Housing Law

The exemption allows religious groups operating housing and not discriminating on the basis of race in membership to discriminate on the basis of religion in housing, but not, say, on the basis of race.[280] The exemption applies not only to a total exclusion, but also to preferences. That is, a nursing home might say that as long as we have beds we will take anyone, but if there is a shortage we will prefer members of our own faith. (One has to ask, could a covered entity invoke the exemption to prefer "more religious" members of its faith—i.e., those who observe strictures against same-sex marriage as opposed to those who do not—or, alternatively, insist that participation in same-sex marriage is inconsistent with one's status as a member of the faith?)

No state that I know of has an explicit statutory exemption for religiously based objections to cohabitating couples. Such cases have nevertheless been brought under constitutional provisions protecting religious liberty, with mixed results. Alaska[281] and California[282] rejected such claims; Massachusetts gave them limited recognition,[283] in those cases where accommodating the landlord would not work any hardship on potential tenants because other housing was readily available.

Some of the sting of the refusal to recognize the religion defense is ameliorated by the common "Mrs. Murphy's boarding house" exemption, which exempts owner-occupied buildings of (usually) four or fewer units from the statute.[284] These do not cover housing owned by investors not living in the building; but where such an exemption exists, it obviates the need to live in close quarters with people engaged in what the landlord regards as sinful behavior. However, the exemption usually protects only the landlord, not real estate or rental agents, or newspapers printing want ads for the rental of exempt housing.[285]

2. Public Accommodation Law

The public accommodation provisions of federal law have no specific religious exemptions. They also have a Mrs. Murphy exemption and do exempt activities that are distinctly private, which exempts clubs that remain small, carefully screen members, and do not indiscriminately recruit from the public. These provisions might protect smaller church-affiliated institutions, but they cannot protect hospitals and other large institutions, which by their very nature must be open to the undifferentiated broader public. Whatever the scope of the exemption, not-for-profit institutions that seek ideological conformity on religious grounds may have a defense under *Dale*.[286] These matters are being tested in Ocean Grove, New Jersey, where a Methodist group is refusing to rent space (a beach-side gazebo) that it owns—and uses for religious purposes, as well as for the general public—for a same-sex ceremony.[287]

3. Employment

The most litigated exemptions are found in Title VII. There are two overlapping exemptions: the first permits an educational institution to employ a person of its faith if it is "in whole or substantial part, owned, supported, controlled or managed . . . by a particular religious corporation, association, or society."[288] There is considerable uncertainty as to what criteria meet the "control or support" tests. A federal district court found that a Jesuit university, in which Jesuits did not command a majority of the board, did not meet the criteria.[289] But on not so dissimilar facts, the Eleventh Circuit found that a Baptist school was entitled to the exemption.[290] The Sixth Circuit also allowed invocation of the exemption by a medical school, noting that the school in question was "permeated with religious overtones."[291]

Both the Third and Sixth Circuits have held that the exemption reaches employment decisions based on conduct which, on religious grounds, "is inconsistent with [that] of [the] employer."[292] Thus, the protection offered by the statute to those covered by it is broad; its coverage, however, is limited to *educational* institutions "controlled . . . by a . . . religious corporation."[293]

A broader exemption is found earlier in the statute: "This subchapter (Title VII) shall not apply to . . . a religious corporation, association, educational institution, or society with respect to the employment of individuals of a particular religion to perform work connected with the carrying on by such corporation, association, educational institution, or society of its activities."[294] The number of organizations covered by the exemption is broader than the educational exemption. It is, however, limited to permitting "employment of individuals of a particular religion."

This statutory exemption has withstood constitutional attack even as applied to persons not engaged in actually transmitting religious values, including for example, a building engineer.[295] It has also been invoked successfully to allow the Christian Science Monitor to prefer Christian Scientists as reporters.[296] However, it is not sufficient that there be some historic connection to a religious denomination. The connection must be current, real, and tangible. Thus, a school established under a will creating a Protestant school was unable to invoke this section where there was little ongoing Protestant religious activity in the school.[297]

But this second section does not protect everything. It permits only religious discrimination, not, for example, religiously motivated sex discrimination. Thus, it did not exempt a school that provided health insurance only to single persons and married men (because it considered the husband to be the head of the household).[298] Would it exempt a school from a practice not intentionally discriminatory, but which has that effect—say a rule against extra-marital sex for parochial school teachers, given the relative ease of invoking the rule against pregnant teachers and the much greater difficulty of enforcement against men who engage in extra-marital sex?

Neither of these sections limits the judicially-created "ministerial exception." That exception precludes any judicial review of a church's decision to hire ministers. The ministerial exception has been applied to ministers,[299] music directors,[300] professors of theology at a Catholic university,[301] and hospital chaplains,[302] but not, for example, to the executive director of a synagogue.[303] Where it applies, it applies even to racial discrimination. The exemption has somehow survived *Employment Division v. Smith*.[304]

Finally, whatever the exact scope of the Title VII exemptions, they do not apply to for-profit corporations, even where the owners operate their businesses according to religious principles.[305] For that, individuals must look either to the Free Exercise Clause (unlikely to be of help) or the Religious Freedom Restoration Act (RFRA). The Bush Administration has expressed the view that RFRA will provide protection to permit employment discrimination by not-for-profit religious social welfare agencies, even where not protected by Title VII.

V. RFRA

This chapter has attempted only a sort of Cook's tour of likely conflict points. It has not addressed in detail the question of whether RFRA[306] or the Free Exercise Clause or their state equivalents will provide additional avenues of relief for those objecting to the application of civil rights laws in ways that burden the religious exercise of individuals. Obviously, the relevant parameters of RFRA and *Employment Division v. Smith*[307] will matter to these questions.

A familiar panoply of questions arises. For example, is a fair housing statute "neutral and generally applicable" if it exempts Mrs. Murphy's boarding house? If the point is that all have to comply with the law, then the exception undercuts the claim of general applicability; it allows secular reasons to be accepted for noncompliance but not religious ones. But other than Mrs. Murphy's boarding house, the rule against discrimination is neutral and generally applicable. The Third Circuit has read "generally applicable" strictly— if there is an exception, a compelling interest must be shown.[308] But other circuits are less literal about "generally applicable," and take it to mean that the statute covers the bulk of the relevant cases.[309]

Is there a compelling interest in enforcement of nondiscrimination rules on the basis of marital status (same-sex or heterosexual) in the case of religious organizations with profound differences over same-sex marriage? Of course, even if the compelling interest standard applies, it likely will not offer much comfort. By and large, courts have treated all civil rights issues as serving a compelling interest in equality. By and large, too, with the exception of Massachusetts,[310] the courts have not put teeth into the least restrictive means aspect of compelling interest analysis.

VI. Conclusion

Our charge is to imagine a world in which same-sex marriage is legalized. The conflicts explored here unfolded in a world without same-sex marriage. Because Americans may have little stomach for challenging couples the state treats as married, this exercise may well be more academic than real.

The legalization of same-sex marriage would represent the triumph of an egalitarian-based ethic over a faith-based one, and not just legally. The remaining question is whether champions of tolerance are prepared to tolerate proponents of a different ethical vision. I think the answer will be no.

Within certain defined areas, opponents of gay rights will be unaffected by an embrace of same-sex marriage. But in others, the impact will be substantial. I am not optimistic that, under current law, much can be done to ameliorate the impact on religious dissenters. If there is to be space for opponents of same-sex marriage, it will have to be created at the same time as same-sex marriage is recognized, and, probably, as part of a legislative package.[311]

CHAPTER TWO

An Unholy Union: Same-Sex Marriage and the Use of Governmental Programs to Penalize Religious Groups with Unpopular Practices

Jonathan Turley[1]

The debate over same-sex marriage has become for the twenty-first century what the abortion debate was for the twentieth century: a single, defining issue that divides the country in a zero-sum political battle.[2] With the long overdue decision to strike down statutes criminalizing homosexual relations in *Lawrence v. Texas*,[3] attention has shifted to the question of the positive rights of same-sex couples—and specifically their right to marriage. Various states have recognized civil unions and Massachusetts has recognized marriages for same-sex couples. This, in turn, has produced immediate questions of the recognition of same-sex marriage licenses in other states under the Full Faith and Credit Clause of Article IV, Section 1 of the United States Constitution. The intensity of this debate will only increase in the aftermath of the decision of the California Supreme Court in *In Re Marriage Cases*[4] that same-sex couples have a constitutional right to marry. Indeed, a new effort at passing a federal constitutional amendment has begun in response to the ruling.[5]

Just below the surface of this raw debate are fundamental constitutional questions that transcend same-sex marriage as a cultural issue. These questions concern the interaction of the government with organizations that discriminate on the basis of religious values. Inevitably, the government will have basic points of contact with any organized group—contacts that range from garbage collection to tax collection. In a free society, some of these groups will espouse or exercise values that conflict with majoritarian values. When these values are discriminatory, the government is caught between enforcing its principles of equality and protecting the principles of free speech, expressive association, and free exercise of religion.

In the last few decades, the government has abandoned a neutral position in its dealings with political or religious groups in favor of enforcing nondiscrimination policies. In doing so, the government has taken sides on religious or cultural controversies through such means as the denial of tax exemption or access to state-run charity programs. Same-sex marriage is only the latest public controversy forcing the government to address religiously based, discriminatory practices. As such, it may offer an opportunity for the United States Supreme Court to correct its own ill-conceived decisions in the area, particularly its decision in *Bob Jones University v. United States*,[6] where it allowed the government to withdraw tax-exempt status from a university due to its unpopular religious practices.

The Court's jurisprudence in this area is now hopelessly confused and contradictory. While the Court has allowed the government to punish groups for their religious practices through the denial of tax exemption, it has recently reinforced rights of speech and association in decisions like *Boy Scouts v. Dale*,[7] where it stressed that the right to association "is crucial in preventing the majority from imposing its views on groups that would rather express other, perhaps unpopular, ideas."[8] The cause for this confusion is due in large part to the Court's preference for creating insular or independent lines of jurisprudence. Thus, we have cases like *Roberts v. United States Jaycees*[9] where the Court allowed a state to force a private organization to abandon a gender-based membership policy and cases like *Dale* protecting the right of the Boy Scouts to exclude people on the basis of sexual orientation.[10] The result is a lack of internal coherence—a problem that has become something of a signature for the Supreme Court in the last few decades.

Same-sex marriage brings us once again to this inherent conflict between the exercise of First Amendment rights and the government's enforcement of a nondiscrimination policy penalizing discriminatory views. The merits of the same-sex marriage debate are largely secondary to the constitutional questions addressed in this chapter. In the interest of full disclosure, however, it is worth noting that I do not oppose same-sex marriage. To the contrary, I have been a critic of prior decisions, such as *Reynolds v. United States*,[11] that allow states to ban certain forms of marriage such as polygamy on moral grounds.[12] I have also advocated the elimination of the term "marriage" from governmental programs in favor of the more relevant term "civil union."[13] Despite these views, I believe strongly that the government should not use tax policy or charity funds to discriminate against groups on the basis of their religious views or practices.

Indeed, over the last few decades, we have seen an unholy union between gov-ernment programs and groups with majoritarian views that endangers the very basis of religious freedom and the rights of free speech and association.

The debate over same-sex marriage represents a coalescing of rights of free exercise, free speech, and expressive association. With the exception of abor-tion, same-sex marriage is almost unique in blurring neat divisions between these rights. Many organizations attract members with their commitment to certain fundamental matters of faith or morals, including a rejection of same-sex marriage or homosexuality. It is rather artificial to tell such groups that they can condemn homosexuality so long as they are willing to hire homosexuals as part of that mission. It is equally disingenuous to suggest that denial of such things as tax exemption does not constitute a content-based punishment for religious views. Many discriminatory organizations rely on tax exemption and state-sponsored charitable programs to survive. The denial of tax-exempt sta-tus presents a particularly serious threat to these organizations and puts them at a comparative disadvantage to groups with contrary views.[14] In both areas, the government has actively distinguished between groups based on their be-liefs—a role that troubles even those of us who support gay rights.

This chapter looks at restrictions on charitable giving as a perfect microcosm of issues in this area. It is also where a new and more consistent neutrality prin-ciple might be forged. Unlike direct government subsidies or grants, state re-strictions of charitable giving constitute a dangerous intervention into the rela-tionship between citizens exercising First Amendment rights and their chosen associations. As the Court has emphasized in campaign contribution cases, re-stricting money is often the same as restricting speech. The dangers of such in-tervention are magnified when the government imposes restrictions or barriers on some groups due to their faith-based practices while allowing other more popular or mainstream groups to reap the full benefits of tax exemption or ac-cess to donors. In the area of charitable giving, the Court should apply a strict neutrality principle that focuses on the status of the organization rather than its practices to determine questions of tax exemption or fund access. Absent such a neutrality principle, the public policy rationale (including a nondiscrimina-tory policy) for intervention places the government in the position of inhibit-ing the exercise of political and religious beliefs on a discriminatory basis.

As marriage or civil union licenses become more common, couples will in-creasingly and publicly identify themselves as gay and lesbian Americans. This will in turn increase the number of negative actions taken by private organiza-tions that view such status to be offensive or immoral. In this way, the self-iden-tification of couples will cause the self-identification of discriminatory organiza-tions. Courts will then have to decide what action, if any, governments can take against such organizations. It should be viewed as much as an opportunity for correction as for conflict. While the rivaling groups in the same-sex marriage debate have obvious differences on the merits, a neutrality principle in charity cases should be a common article of faith for Americans committed to a free and pluralistic society.

I. Taxing Religious Practices: The Use of Tax Exemption to Penalize Unpopular Religious Practices

The very lifeblood of American democracy is the concept of free and robust exchange of ideas and faiths. Obviously, the right to freely choose one's views and beliefs comes with the assumption that you may exercise those views and beliefs so long as you do not endanger or harm others. As the Court has noted, "'implicit in the right to engage in activities protected by the First Amendment' is a 'corresponding right to associate with others in pursuit of a wide variety of political, social, economic, educational, religious, and cultural ends.'"[15] To protect this right of free thought and free exercise, our Constitution forces a strict neutrality on the government, particularly in the free exercise of religion. Thus, we have strived to maintain a strict neutrality of government while using the power of the government to foster a pluralistic society of diverse views and faiths.

For much of our history, federal tax policy has reflected both ideals by maintaining strict neutrality while giving tax-exempt status to not-for-profit organizations. Indeed, before 1970 and the *Green v. Kennedy*[16] case, there was a reasonable assumption that tax exemption under Section 501(c)(3) was equally available to all charitable, religious, or public interest organizations regardless of their specific views. After all, tax exemption was viewed as an important public policy to encourage private donations and charitable conduct. The strength of the country has long been linked to the involvement of citizens in religious, public interest, and educational groups. By exempting money given to nonprofit organizations, the government removed financial penalties or barriers to the creation and maintenance of different groups. Without reference to the particular views or values, the government accepted that citizens should not be taxed a second time for seeking to express their beliefs in civil, cultural, political, or religious organizations. This approach was embodied in the language of Section 501(c)(3) of the Internal Revenue Code, which granted tax-exempt status to

> corporations, and any community chest, fund, or foundation, organized and operated exclusively for religious, charitable, scientific, testing for public safety, lit-

erary, or educational purposes, or to foster national or international amateur sports competition (but only if no part of its activities involve the provision of athletic facilities or equipment), or for the prevention of cruelty to children or animals, no part of the net earnings of which inures to the benefit of any private shareholder or individual, no substantial part of the activities of which is carrying on propaganda, or otherwise attempting, to influence legislation (except as otherwise provided in subsection (h)), and which does not participate in, or intervene in (including the publishing or distributing of statements), any political campaign on behalf of (or in opposition to) any candidate for public office.[17]

The sole concern of this section is that the organization does not work for the financial benefit of individuals or the political benefit of a candidate. To put it another way, the focus is on the nature—not the views—of the organization.

In the 1970s, there was a fundamental shift in the view of tax exemption. The government's change in policy toward discriminatory religious practices in part was due to a more general change in society and the law. Until 1954, most public education systems were racially segregated and the concept of separate but equal espoused in *Plessy v. Ferguson*[18] was the law of the land. With the rejection of "separate but equal" in its landmark decision in *Brown v. Board of Education*,[19] the Court correctly noted that discrimination itself produces great harm to both students and society. Thus, separate could never be truly equal in public education. In the decisions that followed, the Court enforced the Constitution's protections from discrimination in education, housing, and other areas. The nondiscrimination cases, however, inevitably took the Court closer and closer to private exclusionary policies.[20]

For the Internal Revenue Service (IRS), the issue came to a head in the case of *Green v. Kennedy*,[21] when a federal court granted an injunction against the Secretary of the Treasury to enjoin the IRS from granting tax-exempt status to schools that practice discrimination. This decision led to a new IRS policy embodied in a 1971 Revenue Ruling that required "[a]ll charitable trusts, educational or otherwise, [to be] subject to the requirement that the purpose of the trust may not be illegal or contrary to public policy."[22] Illegality is hardly a concern. However, when the IRS informed various organizations and schools that they would have to show that they do nothing that is "contrary to public policy," it sent a chilling message to many faith-based organizations, particularly non-mainstream organizations. First and foremost in these public policies was elimination of discrimination. Since many religions are based on distinctions between the faithful and the unfaithful, the pure and the impure, the chosen and the unchosen, discrimination is at the heart of many faiths. Central to the idea of purity is often the exclusion of individuals or practices viewed as impure. The adoption of the nondiscrimination policy as the touchstone of tax exemption put the government on an inevitable collision path with religious groups. Religious coherence and cohesion cannot be maintained without exclusion. Exclusion requires a form of discrimination between people who maintain principles of faith and those who do not.

The most significant collision point occurred in *Bob Jones University*.[23] The religiously based university had long maintained a policy against interracial relationships, denying admission to students in such relationships. It was an obviously repellent view for the vast majority of Americans, but the university insisted that it was a view directly linked to its religious mission. Thus, when the IRS denied the university tax-exempt status on public policy grounds, the university argued that to deny tax exemption is to severely punish the university for the exercise of its core religious views. Nevertheless, the Court held that the IRS could deny tax-exempt status in light of the nondiscrimination policies embodied in the Civil Rights Act of 1964, executive orders, and other legislative and executive sources.[24] The Court found:

> [A]n examination reveals unmistakable evidence that, underlying all relevant parts of the Code, is the intent that entitlement to tax exemption depends on meeting certain common law standards of charity—namely, that an institution seeking tax-exempt status must serve a public purpose and not be contrary to established public policy."[25]

Once neutrality was abandoned, the government was free to determine whether some forms of preferential treatment or exclusion are good or bad forms of discrimination. Thus, in a technical advice memorandum, the IRS decided that a charity could discriminate against people with inadequate Hawaiian ancestry. The Bishop Estate is a tax-exempt trust that maintains schools limiting admission to applicants who can show "at least one Hawaiian ancestor."[26] The IRS held that this form of discrimination was consistent with public policy and thus could continue with federal tax exemption for the trust.

Underlying the imposition of a nondiscriminatory condition is a view of tax exemption as essentially the same as a direct subsidy or grant. Many academics agree with the view that there is no cognizable difference between not taxing an organization and giving money directly to that organization. There is, however, a fundamental difference if you view tax exemption as serving a single purpose: fostering public participation in associations and groups regardless of their inherent views or policies. Tax exemption is the most direct way for the government to support the rights of free speech, free exercise, and association. Once tax exemption is viewed as a direct government subsidy of views or conduct, the government's role changes materially from facilitator to regulator of speech. In determining the eligibility for exemption, the government effectively divides the world into appropriate and inappropriate groups for the purposes of Section 501(c)(3). Indeed, the subsidy theory allows the government to impose an array of penalties on the operations of certain groups beyond exemptions. Thus, in California, the state supreme court in *Evans v. City of Berkeley*[27] upheld the denial of a marina berth in Berkeley for the Boy Scouts as a neutral application of a nondiscrimination policy. The court held that the city "did not purport to prohibit the [organization] from operating in a discriminatory manner; it simply 'refused to fund such activities out of the public fisc.'"[28] Nevertheless, while a line could be drawn that includes tax exemption with other such forms of claimed "subsidies," tax exemption remains a gateway barrier for many groups to have a substantial and sustainable organization.

The fact is that few organizations can thrive without tax-exempt status and fewer can effectively compete in the marketplace of ideas when outspent by mainstream groups with such status. If treated as akin to federal subsidies or grants, tax exemption offers the government universal influence in the composition and beliefs of political and religious groups. Not only does tax exemption give the federal government a role in a wide array of groups, it is a role that is highly intrusive. Federal subsidies or grants are often designed to impose controls or conditions on groups. In *Rumsfeld v. FAIR*, the Court held that Congress could place conditions on the receipt of federal funds that include the obligation to afford equal access to military recruiters on campus.[29] The government routinely "speaks" through funding of states and groups.

A clear line exists between federal funds and tax exemption, though the distinction has admittedly become more blurred with time and later decisions. The Court spoke most clearly in *Walz v. Tax Commission of New York*, where it noted that, while tax exemption necessarily "afford[s] an indirect economic benefit, . . . tax exemption is not sponsorship since the government does not transfer part of its revenue to churches but simply abstains from demanding that the church support the state."[30] Likewise, in *Trinidad v. Sagrada Orden*, the Court stated that "the [Section 501(c)(3)] exemption is made in recognition of the benefit which the public derives from corporate activities and is intended to aid them when not conducted for private gain."[31]

This clarity would be lost as the Court increasingly treated direct federal grants and exemption as a "practical similarity."[32] Yet, the Court was right in its effort to define a distinction in *Walz*. Tax exemption is less an agreement running between the government and the organization than it is an agreement running between the government and the taxpayer. With Section 501(c)(3), Congress assured taxpayers that they would not be taxed twice on the money: first, when they earned the money and then when they gave the money to a charity or not-for-profit. It is far more threatening for the government to single out organizations for penalties based on fluid concepts of public policy than it is to impose a national obligation to perform a specific precondition as in *Rumsfeld v. FAIR*.

While Congress may certainly deny all tax exemption to organizations, it has allowed for tax exemptions from the beginning of federal taxation. The Code, however, makes no mention of the public policy limitation in such exemptions. Congress has never given the IRS the authority to implement public policies through tax exemption denials—an authority that would allow any number of nondiscrimination, environmental, moral, or other policies to be imposed on private groups or corporations. The 1971 Revenue Ruling constituted a paradigm shift from a view of non-profit groups as inherently good for society as a whole without addressing individual views or practices.[33] Where the Court once distinguished between a subsidy and a tax exemption, it now viewed a tax exemption as almost indistinguishable from giving money directly to the organization. Indeed, in *Bob Jones*, the Court treated a tax exemption as part of a quid pro quo arrangement:

> When the Government grants exemptions . . . all taxpayers are affected; the very fact of the exemption . . . means that other taxpayers can be said to be indirect and vicarious "donors." . . . [T]o warrant exemption under § 501(c)(3), an institution must fall within a category specified in that section and must demonstrably serve and be in harmony with the public interest. The institution's purpose must not be so at odds with the common community conscience as to undermine any public benefit that might otherwise be conferred.[34]

It is hardly comforting that the Court wanted to "emphasize . . . that these sensitive determinations should be made only where there is no doubt that the organization's activities violate fundamental public policy."[35] The Court has emphasized that the agency is entitled to great deference,[36] and the level of scrutiny given such decisions seems often to depend on the inherently offensive aspects of the associational practice.

The decision erases any meaningful distinction between federal funding and tax exemption. There are a host of constitutional and legal distinctions between the two types of actions. Treating such exemptions as the equivalent of federal funding not only defies logic but it conflicts with other analogous cases. For example, in the area of tax deductions, the Court has already held that such indirect state support is not the same as direct funding of a religious organization. In *Mueller v. Allen*, the Court rejected such claims that a broad-based tax deduction that included private-school tuition had "the primary effect of advancing the sectarian aims of the nonpublic schools."[37]

The willingness to penalize some organizations based on their religiously based practices reinforces a dangerous dichotomy of protected views and unprotected exercise of those views. While the government can obviously prohibit illegal conduct by religious or political groups that harms others or society, there must be a clear distinction that allows for conduct that is viewed as merely abhorrent. Under the logic of *Bob Jones*, the government could strip tax-exempt status from Jewish organizations that refuse to hire a dedicated Nazi or a fundamentalist Islamic organization that refuses to hire a non-Muslim woman as an office assistant. Indeed, in *Christian Legal Society v. Kane*,[38] this is basically what the trial court ordered when it ruled that the CLS could not exclude people who rejected its religious beliefs under a nondiscrimination policy of the Hastings College of Law. While this was a membership case, the CLS had required agreement with its religious tenets after students joined who were opposed to its orthodox views. Yet, the court held that requiring the group to accept such members "targets conduct, *i.e.*, discrimination, not speech." The use of this distinction between conduct and speech ignores the obvious fact that the conduct is viewed as critical to fostering the speech. Moreover, once treated as "conduct," the courts can apply the generous standard under *United States v. O'Brien*,[39] which allows the incidental restriction of expressive conduct so long as the regulation (1) falls within the government's constitutional power; (2) furthers an important or substantial government interest; (3) that government interest is unrelated to the suppression of free expression; and (4) the incidental restriction on First Amendment rights is no greater than is essential to the furtherance of the governmental interest. It is a test that proves outcome determinative in nondiscrimination cases.

Gay rights and same-sex marriage are issues that promise to reignite this controversy over tax-exempt status. This area is a perfect microcosm of the confusion over the Court's ill-conceived cases. On one hand, the Court correctly found that the Boy Scouts of America could refuse to retain a gay scout leader due to its faith-based principles. However, this decision in *Boy Scouts v. Dale*[40] seems inherently at odds with the *Bob Jones* case. Presumably, while the Boy Scouts could dismiss Dale, the IRS could eventually strip the organization of tax-exempt status under the public policy rationale. Thus, the Scouts can constitutionally dismiss Dale but can be punished for that protected act with the massive financial penalty of the loss of tax exemption. While it cannot be said that there is a clear federal public policy against all forms of discrimination on the basis of sexual orientation, it is likely that such a policy will be recognized within the decade. Once that occurs, any organization that engages in discrimination as a matter of faith would be in a position similar to Bob Jones University. Indeed in its decision in *In Re Marriage Cases*, the California

Supreme Court found that denial of the recognition of marriage to same-sex couples was discrimination on the basis of sexual orientation.[41]

The Court once described direct federal subsidies of religiously based or discriminatory organizations as "a relationship pregnant with involvement and, as with most governmental grant programs, [one that] could encompass sustained and detailed administrative relationships for enforcement of statutory or administrative standards."[42] Indeed, with the advent of school vouchers and tax deductions for religiously based schools, such involvement is likely to increase despite the exclusionary practices of many religious schools. Tax exemption pales in comparison and offers an area where strict neutrality is possible and warranted.

There should be no question that discriminatory policies like Bob Jones's are bad for society. Likewise, there should be no debate that the views of groups like the American Nazi Party are bad for society. However, there is no way to foster the pluralistic ideals of our society if we cross the constitutional rubicon of content-based discrimination on the part of the government. The collisions between free exercise and equal treatment are already increasing. In 2001, New York's highest court ruled that Yeshiva University (founded on Orthodox Jewish beliefs) violated nondiscrimination laws when it banned same-sex couples from its married dormitory for the Albert Einstein College of Medicine.[43] Likewise, a Lutheran high school in California was recently sued for discrimination after expelling two alleged lesbians due to its religious view that homosexuality is a sin.[44] Such judicial determinations will inevitably trigger challenges to tax-exempt status and access to public funds. Society will then have to choose between the ideals of pluralism and equal treatment.

Just as the Court recognized that bad speech comes with good speech when it protected speech in New York Times Co. v. Sullivan,[45] the same is true for associations. Otherwise, in the name of nondiscrimination policies, the government must discriminate between organizations on the basis of their views. The same-sex marriage debate is likely to force these areas to collide. For example, it is doubtful that a fundamentalist Muslim or Christian school would retain a teacher who openly marries a gay or lesbian partner. The resulting termination will trigger the same issues as were raised in Bob Jones. Indeed, the impact is likely to be more significant in the area of sexual orientation than it was in the Bob Jones case. Thankfully, relatively few organizations follow racially discriminatory policies and those organizations tend to be fringe groups. It is far more common for mainstream religious and civil groups to discriminate on the basis of sexual orientation. The extent to which groups would be potentially disenfranchised under Section 501(c)(3) is quite large.

The cause of this coming storm is the failure of the IRS, Congress, and the Court to adhere to a content-neutral approach to tax-exempt status—returning to the pre-1970s treatment of organizations as qualifying based on their non-profit status and function rather than their internal views. Tax exemption on its face can be distinguished from other forms of governmental action like federal subsidies or conditional grants. There is far greater danger of content-based discrimination and a forced acquiescence of diverse groups to follow majoritarian values. Particularly given the silence of the Code on the use of non-tax policies to deny tax-exempt status, the Court should use this coming opportunity to change the path taken in *Bob Jones* and return to a neutrality principle in tax exemption cases.

II. Pre-Certification of Ideas: The Government's Barring Access of Unpopular Organizations to Publicly Funded Charity Sites

The denial of access to publicly sponsored charity sites offers a close variation of the tax exemption issue. Once again, the issue concerns the ability of the government to make it comparatively harder for unpopular organizations to reach citizens and secure funding for their activities. Again, federal courts appear willing to draw convoluted distinctions to maintain the right of governments to discriminate against certain organizations based on their beliefs while recognizing that their members have protected rights of association and speech in maintaining those beliefs. For example, in *Boy Scouts of America v. Wyman*,[46] the United States Court of Appeals for the Second Circuit held that the state of Connecticut could exclude the Boy Scouts from its publicly sponsored charitable campaign due to their discrimination on the basis of sexual orientation.

Notably, the nondiscrimination policy can be used to bar other aspects of an organization's activities, from the denial of a marina berth, discussed earlier, to the denial of a lease. In a recent controversy, the Boy Scouts were denied long-held leases under these nondiscrimination policies and subsidy theories in Philadelphia.[47] It may be possible to make a distinction between some collateral activities like the use of parks and marinas. However, as with tax exemption, losing equal access to donors can constitute a severe penalty for a group based on its religious or political views. Charity sites are meant to foster speech and association—as was tax exemption.

The Second Circuit structured its analysis in a frank assumption "that the removal of the BSA [Boy Scouts of America] from the Campaign was triggered at least to some extent by the BSA's exercise of what the Supreme Court has held to be a constitutionally protected right."[48] Nevertheless, the fractured cases left by the Supreme Court gave the Second Circuit ample basis to uphold the exclusion of the BSA. Despite the fact that the exclusion penalized the BSA alone and the state retained other organizations with discriminatory practices,[49] the court found that the state still maintained viewpoint neutrality. To buttress this decision, the court relied on the line of cases, including *Cornelius v. NAACP Legal Defense & Education Fund, Inc.*,[50] distinguishing public from nonpublic forums.

Notably, the Second Circuit narrowly construed the Supreme Court's decision in *Dale* to uphold the exclusion as simply not significant enough to qualify as "compulsion."[51] This is a signature of the Supreme Court's own cases, where difficult issues draw conclusory dismissals from the majority. Thus, in *Roberts v. Jaycees*, the Court faced an organization that had a long-standing gender-based membership rule that was tied directly to its stated purpose and identity. Yet, the Court simply held that "the Jaycees has failed to demonstrate that the Act imposes any serious burdens on the male members' freedom of expressive association."[52] It was entirely unclear how the Jaycees could show such a serious burden. The Court noted that they could engage in all of their customary acts, including meetings and civic events, with women. That is akin to saying that an organization can still speak so long as it does so in a state-sanctioned way. Clearly, the Jaycees wanted to do these activities on a gender-exclusive basis—a policy that may be obnoxious to many of us but a policy that was clearly valued by this organization, which litigated the issue to the Supreme Court.[53]

In reaching this conclusion, the Court endorsed a highly biased and uncertain role of courts in weighing the importance of unpopular characteristics of an organization.[54] Thus, in his dissent in *Dale*, Justice Stevens felt entirely comfortable dismissing references in the Boy Scout manual and claims of a religiously based opposition to homosexuality: "It is plain as the light of day that neither one of these principles—'morally straight' and 'clean'—says the slightest thing about homosexuality."[55] The Court has placed itself, and lower courts, as the ultimate arbiter of the importance of particular exclusionary principles to an organization and the significance of their denial to the organization's members. It is a role that is pregnant with dangers for judicial bias and that leaves core speech and associational rights uncertain and fluid.

The same type of analysis is evident in *Wyman* where the court simply held that the exclusion from the charity site was not as significant as the injury in *Dale* and "the effect of Connecticut's removal of BSA from the Campaign is neither direct nor immediate, since its conditioned exclusion does not rise to the level of compulsion."[56] This would suggest that, absent a denial of the right of exclusion, financial or administrative penalties can be im-

posed since they do not immediately cause a change—an artificial distinction since, absent funds, many of these organizations will have fewer positions to fill on an exclusionary basis.

It is difficult to accept the rationalization that "Connecticut has not prevented the BSA from exercising its First Amendment rights; it has instead
set up a regulatory scheme to achieve constitutionally valid ends under
which, as it happens, the BSA pays a price for doing so."[57] The actions
against the BSA didn't just "happen." In the company of other organizations
with exclusionary policies or practices, the BSA was singled out for this
penalty. The court did not question that there are many people in Connecticut who support the BSA in its religiously based mission.[58] Yet, the
court allowed the state to make contacts between the organization and citizens comparatively more difficult than with more popular organizations. Not
only do such efforts register the hostility toward these views, but also there
are clearly other means to advance nondiscriminatory policies.[59]

Nondiscrimination rules that are clearly compelling in some circumstances are not so compelling when used against a private organization exercising First Amendment rights. The constitutional rights in that context
should triumph, as the Court articulated in *Hurley v. Irish-American Gay,
Lesbian, and Bisexual Group of Boston*:

> The very idea that a noncommercial speech restriction be used to produce
> thoughts and statements acceptable to some groups, or, indeed, all people,
> grates on the First Amendment, for it amounts to nothing less than a proposal
> to limit speech in the service of orthodox expression. The Speech Clause has
> no more certain antithesis. While the law is free to promote all sorts of con-
> duct in place of harmful behavior, it is not free to interfere with speech for no
> better reason than promoting an approved message or discouraging a disfa-
> vored one, however enlightened either purpose may strike the government.[60]

The *Wyman* decision demonstrates how our constitutional doctrines in this
area have begun to resemble the formalistic use of canons of construction to
hide bias, as demonstrated by Karl Llewellyn in his famous table of "thrusts" and
"parries."[61] Llewellyn showed that for every canon of construction that said to
do A in a given circumstance, there was another that said to do the opposite
of A. Whichever canon the court selected, there was the appearance of neutrality but the bias was in the selection of the canon. The same can be said for
our current jurisprudence in this area. Courts can easily come to diametrically
different results in cases like *Wyman* by simply selecting from a variety of prece-
dential lines of authority. When the Court has structured its rulings in terms of
expressive association in cases like *Hurley* or *Dale*, it has protected First

Amendment rights to an extent that would have been difficult if it focused on public accommodation or nonpublic forum issues.[62] Thus, courts after *Dale* felt free to deny the BSA access to a city-run marina in Berkeley[63] and a park in San Diego.[64] Conversely, in cases like *Cuffley v. Mickes*, the United States Court of Appeals for the Eighth Circuit correctly barred the state from excluding the Ku Klux Klan from participation in a state "Adopt a Highway" program as a content-based form of discrimination.[65]

As shown below, while bringing these areas into complete coherence and consistency may be much to ask, the tax exemption and charity fund cases offer a clear and distinguishable area for a new approach.

III. Charity, Neutrality, and the Right to Discriminatory Associations

In *Boy Scouts v. Dale*, a slim five-justice majority appeared to finally give meaning to the right of association for discriminatory organizations. The Court noted that: "The forced inclusion of an unwanted person in a group infringes the group's freedom of expressive association if the presence of that person affects in a significant way the group's ability to advocate public or private viewpoints."[66] As post-*Dale* rulings have demonstrated, however, there remains confusion over the relative weight to be given such associational rights versus antidiscriminatory statutes or policies. Cases like *Roberts v Jaycees*[67] continue to suggest that some groups may be protected only in holding beliefs but not in the exercise of those beliefs.[68] There remains a failure to recognize that nondiscrimination policies are a compelling interest in some areas but not others. When applied in areas of public accommodation, for example, there is a clear compelling interest in the enforcement of nondiscrimination laws and such enforcement is the only effective means to accomplish these goals. However, when applied in the context of a private organization and directed at a matter of associational identity, the government interest is neither compelling nor permissible.

By focusing on the state interest—and applying it in both public and private contexts—the Court can engage in outcome-determinative logic, as it did in *Roberts*.[69] While recognizing the deprivation of associational values, the Court dismissed any injury in light of the state interest: The change was merely an "incidental abridgment of the Jaycees' protected speech, [and] that effect is no greater than is necessary to accomplish the State's legitimate purposes."[70] The Court made it sound like there was some spectrum of possible remedies. Yet, since the state interest is the end of discrimination, the prohibition of that discrimination will always be "no greater than is necessary."

Moreover, the significance of the value of equality to our society makes most deprivations—short of public management or termination—a lesser concern. This was apparent in the language of *Bob Jones*:

> [T]he Government has a fundamental, overriding interest in eradicating racial discrimination in education—discrimination that prevailed, with official approval, for the first 165 years of this Nation's constitutional history. That governmental interest substantially outweighs whatever burden denial of tax benefits places on petitioners' exercise of their religious beliefs. The interests asserted by petitioners cannot be accommodated with that compelling governmental interest and no "less restrictive means" are available to achieve the governmental interest.[71]

This type of heavily weighted analysis makes a mockery of any notion of a balancing of interests—nondiscrimination policies inevitably trump associational practices.

The alternative is to draw distinctions between public and private discrimination, recognizing state interests in the former but not always in the latter. The focus is on the speech and associational activity rather than the state interest in the private realm. A principle of neutrality in charity cases, including tax exemption cases, would significantly reduce the amount of state interference with acts of private discrimination or exclusion. It is an approach that seemed to be implied in the approach that the Court took in *Walz* when it noted:

> The course of constitutional neutrality . . . cannot be an absolutely straight line; rigidity could well defeat the basic purpose of [the First Amendment], which is to insure that no religion be sponsored or favored, none commanded, and none inhibited. The general principle deducible from the First Amendment and all that has been said by the Court is this: that we will not tolerate either governmentally established religion or governmental interference with religion. Short of those expressly proscribed governmental acts there is room for play in the joints productive of a benevolent neutrality which will permit religious exercise to exist without sponsorship and without interference.[72]

"Benevolent neutrality" must start with protecting associations from governmental interference with ability to raise self-sustaining charity. The tax exemption and charity cases offer an important opportunity to bring greater clarity in the application of public policies and specifically nondiscrimination laws to private groups. Such governmental contacts would be viewed as "mere passive" acts and "not the affirmative involvement characteristic of outright governmental subsidy."[73] It would further recognize the importance of fundraising to free speech and associational rights. Conversely, direct funding of, or involvement in, discriminatory organizations could still be barred under nondiscrimination laws. For example, in 2006, the Catholic Charities of Boston ended its work in arranging adoptions after the state notified it that, under Massachusetts law, it must offer the service to same-sex couples to maintain its license.[74] While the charity should be able to maintain a license while serving only couples with consistent religious views, it could legitimately be denied a state contract to handle adoptions due to such discriminatory practices.

This approach is diametrically opposite of the assumption in *Wyman*, where the court viewed the loss of access to be "neither direct nor immediate" enough to warrant protection.[75] In these cases, the government is imposing additional barriers for citizens trying to fund their First Amendment activities. Given the centrality of pluralism and open debate in our society, there should be a bar on the use of tax exemption or access to publicly run charity sites to enforce nondiscrimination policies. This will require that some of the Court's past rhetoric be made reality. As the Court stressed in a case involving private clubs in New York City, "[t]he ability and the opportunity to combine with others to advance one's views is a powerful practical means of ensuring the perpetuation of the freedoms the First Amendment has guaranteed to individuals as against the government."[76]

There is an obvious difference between penalizing discrimination in a public accommodation or restaurant and penalizing such discrimination in the hiring or membership of a discriminatory organization. We cannot maintain a pluralistic and free society unless our associations are free not just to speak but also to exercise their views. As Justice Sandra Day O'Connor noted in her concurrence in *Roberts*:

> [A]n association engaged exclusively in protected expression enjoys First Amendment protection of both the content of its message and the choice of its members. . . . Protection of the association's right to define its membership derives from the recognition that the formation of an expressive association is the creation of a voice, and the selection of members is the definition of that voice.[77]

The coming decade may force the Court finally to address the difficult decisions that it has long sought to avoid. If free speech, free exercise, and the right of association have true meaning in a pluralistic society, the government must be restrained in its imposition of some forms of content-based financial penalties. There is a distinction between tax exemption and direct government funding in the form of grants or scholarships. Tax exemption should be based on the simple notion that the government will not seek to tap the religious, educational, or charitable activities of its citizens. It is not a tool to be used to force such organizations to conform to majoritarian views. Likewise, the exclusion of groups from charitable listings invites the role of viewpoint discrimination that is anathema to a society based on notions of free, robust, and uninhibited speech and expressive association.

In both tax exemption and charitable listing cases, the ultimate choice of speech and association is left to individual citizens. The government should not "put a thumb on the scale" to make it relatively more difficult for these organizations to survive than those organizations that conform to popular views. The popularity of such groups should be left to the marketplace of ideas. This does not mean that the government can not distinguish between discriminatory and nondiscriminatory organizations in other respects. For example, while Bob Jones should not have had its tax exemption eliminated, the government should not have to pay for students to attend the school through grants or scholarships. In that case, the government is taking public monies from general revenues and directly assisting the school's educational recruitment and mission.

Of course, clarity requires an element of courage. We have to have the courage to remain faithful to our first principles even when they benefit the least popular organizations. Indeed, it means that racist and anti-Semitic citizens can form tax-exempt organizations that are run in conformity with their hateful ideals. However, the same-sex marriage debate should magnify the flaws in the Court's past jurisprudence. As states accept same-sex marriage and prohibit discrimination based on sexual orientation, conflicts will grow between the government and discriminatory organizations. There will be many religiously based organizations that will refuse to hire individuals who are homosexual or members of a same-sex marriage. If those individuals are holding a state license of marriage or civil union, it will result in a discriminatory act that was not only based on sexual orientation, but also on a lawful state-conferred status.

In my view, both sides in this debate will benefit from "greater room for play in the joints" for private discriminatory practices. First, both gay advocates and religious advocates are advantaged by a neutral government that does not interfere with charitable fundraising or access to donors. This is a cultural issue that is fit for national debate with well funded groups on both sides. Second, this debate will turn increasingly bitter and ugly if one side is viewed as suppressed in its efforts to raise charitable contributions or reach donors. I believe (and hope) that the nation will evolve toward a greater protection of homosexuals and greater recognition of civil unions. This evolution will not, however, occur if the government is viewed as unfairly trying to pre-determine the debate or harass one side. Finally, the progress made toward same-sex marriage and homosexual rights is due in large part to the protection of free speech and associational rights. The rights of gay citizens will be secured not simply with legal but also with cultural changes. The latter will depend on greater, not lesser, protection of speech and association on both sides of the same-sex marriage debate.

CHAPTER THREE

Matters of Conscience: Lessons for Same-Sex Marriage from the Healthcare Context

Robin Fretwell Wilson[1]

It is difficult to ignore the parallels emerging between same-sex marriage and the recently renewed debates about the limits of conscience in healthcare, sparked by refusals to dispense emergency contraceptives.[2] Both subjects are deeply divisive, and in both, persons of good will are saying "why should I have to give up my convictions so that you can have yours?"

Tensions over same-sex marriages and civil unions first erupted outside the United States in countries with longer experiences with same-sex relationships. In January 2006, a European human rights commission concluded that a clergy member's interest in not performing same-sex marriages must be subordinated to the couple's "right of access."[3] A year later in Spain, a powerful, socialist political figure, with the Prime Minister's backing, threatened to "establish[] a new status [for the Catholic Church], that puts her in her place," if the Church did not retreat from its opposition to a citizen education program that would teach children about same-sex relationships.[4] In Manitoba, Canada, twelve officials empowered to perform marriage ceremonies "quit because they refused to perform federal same-sex marriages as required by" provincial law.[5] This led to provisions in Canada's same-sex marriage legislation to insulate religious officials[6] from having to decide to go along or leave.[7] That legislation, however, did not resolve whether others authorized to perform marriages "have the right to choose to follow their religious beliefs."[8] In 2007, a 70-year-old marriage commissioner in Saskatchewan who refused to marry a homosexual couple, citing his religious beliefs, was forced to defend his decision before the Saskatchewan Human Rights tribunal.[9]

These struggles over whether there is a duty to assist or, conversely, a right to refrain have spilled over to the United States in the wake of *In re Marriage Cases* and *Goodridge v. Department of Public Health*, which recognized same-sex marriage for California and Massachusetts couples.[10] On the heels of the California Supreme Court's decision, the mayor of San Francisco, Gavin Newsom, derided San Diego County's decision to allow county clerks to exempt themselves from issuing marriage certificates to same-sex couples, "If you don't want to provide a marriage certificate and you've got a job that does that, then you should think twice about why you got the job in the first place and maybe you should get a new job."[11] Similarly, after *Goodridge*, the chief legal counsel for Massachusetts's governor told the state's Justices of the Peace that they must "follow the law, whether you agree with it or not."[12] Anyone who turned away same-sex couples could be held personally liable under the state's nondiscrimination statute, which provides for penalties up to $50,000.[13]

Clashes over same-sex relationships have also arisen in states that have embraced civil unions.[14] In 2008, in New Mexico—which has neither a statute nor a constitutional provision prohibiting same-sex marriage—the New Mexico Human Rights Commission found discriminatory the refusal of two New Mexico photographers to take pictures of a same-sex couple's commitment ceremony.[15] The Commission ordered the photographers to pay the complainant's attorney fees, which totaled more than $6000. In 2006, the New Jersey Department of Environmental Protection revoked the tax exemption of the Ocean Grove Camp Meeting Association (Ocean Grove), a Methodist ministry, after it refused to allow two same-sex couples to use its boardwalk pavilion for their civil commitment ceremonies.[16] The couples denied access to the pavilion also filed suit against Ocean Grove.[17] Thus, the sanction for refusing to assist same-sex couples extended beyond limited civil liability to losing valuable tax exemptions. Even before New Jersey's decision, bloggers and editorialists argued that states should force churches to marry same-sex couples by threatening to withhold the significant government benefits that churches receive.[18]

These clashes are not confined to disputes over marriage and civil commitment ceremonies. In 2004, Adoption.com, the largest Internet adoption site in the United States, refused to post the profile of a same-sex couple seeking to adopt. Adoption.com told the couple that it "allow[s] only individuals in an opposite-sex marriage to post profiles on the Web site."[19] The couple sued, claiming the refusal violated California's nondiscrimination law, which prohibits businesses from discriminating against customers on a variety of grounds.[20] The parties subsequently settled the private litigation between them. That settlement required in part that Adoption.com and its sister organizations, would not post profiles of Californians "unless the service is made equally available to all California residents qualified to adopt."[21] Put to the choice to make its services available to all or none, Adoption.com chose to leave the California market.

Healthcare providers have resisted morally-freighted procedures with equal vigor. In December 2005, the Catholic Action League of Massachusetts urged the state's Roman Catholic hospitals to defy Massachusetts's new emergency contraception law.[22] That legislation requires all hospitals, even private ones, to offer the morning-after pill to rape victims.[23] In July 2004, eleven Alabama nurses resigned positions at state clinics rather than provide emergency contraceptives against their moral convictions.[24] In 2006, a Chicago ambulance service fired a driver after she refused to transport a patient who was seeking an elective abortion.[25]

Although largely new to family law questions,[26] conscientious refusals in healthcare occupy well-trod ground, dating back before the United States Supreme Court's 1973 decision in Roe v. Wade.[27] In fact, nearly every state in the nation now has carved out a space for medical providers to continue in their professional roles without participating in acts they find immoral. States accomplish this with conscience clauses that authorize individual providers or entities to refuse to participate in certain specified procedures, usually abortion, sterilization, physician-assisted suicide, and, increasingly, the dispensing of emergency contraceptives.[28] Thus, even the very strong constitutional rights to abortion and contraception established in Roe v. Wade[29] and Griswold v. Connecticut[30] have yielded to the decision of others not to facilitate a woman's reproductive choices.

Before the advent of conscience clauses, however, the result was strikingly different. Although Griswold and Roe established only the right to noninterference by the state in a woman's contraceptive and abortion decisions,[31] family planning advocates worked strenuously to extend these noninterference rights into affirmative entitlements to another's assistance. This involved attempts both to force individual institutions to provide controversial services and to force individual healthcare providers to participate in them. The lever used in efforts to force public as well as private facilities to provide sterilization and abortion services was the receipt of public benefits. This argument had considerable success until Congress stepped in with the primogenitor of healthcare conscience clauses, the Church Amendment.[32] The Church Amendment prohibits a court from using receipt of certain federal monies as a basis for making an individual or institution perform an abortion or sterilization contrary to their "religious beliefs or moral convictions."[33]

The experience after *Roe* suggests where the next battle lines over same-sex marriage will likely be drawn: a concerted effort to take same-sex marriage from a negative right to be free of state interference to a positive entitlement to assistance by others.[34] It is likely that a stream of litigation is on the horizon designed to resolve competing claims of individuals who want to enter same-sex marriage and those who want to have nothing to do with facilitating this.[35] As the Parliamentary Secretary to the Minister of Finance in Canada, John McKay, commented during the debate on Canada's same-sex marriage legislation, "Were I a religious official or institution, I would be bracing for an onslaught of legal battering."[36] McKay appears to have predicted this well. Despite Canada's statutory accommodations, at least one gay-rights group is already contesting the charity status of religious institutions that refuse to support same-sex marriage. As the group explains, "We have no problem with the Catholic Church or any other faith group promoting bigotry. . . . We have a problem with the Canadian government funding that bigotry."[37]

As in Canada and other Western democracies, litigation is beginning to bubble up in the United States around a number of questions, including whether churches and religious groups must open their facilities to same-sex couples for their marriage or commitment ceremonies. As noted earlier, in 2006 two same-sex couples in New Jersey filed civil rights claims against a Methodist group for denying their request to use the group's boardwalk pavilion for their commitment ceremonies. A gay-rights group supporting the couple reasons that "the boardwalk has been used by the public without restriction, [and so] it's public."[38]

This chapter explores the dilemmas facing churches, clergy, state officials, and private individuals who, as a matter of conscience or religious conviction, feel that they can neither support nor participate in same-sex marriage unions. It argues that the demand for same-sex unions will result in a torrent of litigation, just as the assertion of abortion rights after *Roe* did, if legislatures fail to decide *ex ante* whether there is a duty to assist or, conversely, a right to refrain. Given the status of most churches and religious organizations as state nonprofits and federally tax-exempt organizations, public support arguments will surely be advanced to compel religious groups to participate in same-sex marriage. Thus, religious organizations in California and Massachusetts (and perhaps soon in other states that embrace same-sex marriage)[39]—as well as in states with domestic partnership or civil union laws—may reasonably worry that litigation will be required to defend their choice to refrain from participating in same-sex unions. This chapter argues further that legislatures should deflect this litigation with legislative accommodations as they ultimately did with fractious healthcare services. Indeed, legislative accommodations in medicine offer a number of approaches for resolving the clash between those who want a service and those who have moral objections to performing it. Many conscience clauses insulate providers from suit by patients, others from coercion by the government itself. Some provide unfettered discretion to refuse, while others provide an exemption only when it poses no hardship to the individual requesting the service.[40]

This chapter ends with a frank discussion about the trade-offs and costs of making any accommodations for conscientious objections over same-sex marriage. It concludes that clergy and churches cannot be required to participate in same-sex marriage for constitutional reasons. The issues are more difficult with respect to government officials, who are hired for a specific purpose. These officials stand as an entryway into marriage. While it remains an open question whether same-sex marriage will be treated as a fundamental right,[41] this chapter argues that to the extent it is, refusals by public officials should be accommodated only when their refusal would not pose a significant hardship for the couple trying to marry. Some may bristle at the idea that a public employee could refuse to perform a service for a certain class of people at all. But to be clear, this chapter argues that governments could permit public employees to refuse to perform a service *only if* that refusal does *not* stand in the way of exercising a fundamental right—when it does, a refusal would not be permitted.[42]

It is likely that clashes with representatives of the church or state over same-sex marriage ceremonies will occur infrequently. This is not true of refusals by private individuals. Here, it is not clear how policymakers should weigh the dignitary interests of same-sex couples and the moral and religious convictions of potential objectors. Because weighing competing moral values can be a "zero-sum" game,[43] perhaps the best we can hope for is a live-and-let-live solution, one that permits refusals for matters of conscience, but limits those refusals to instances where a significant hardship will not occur.

I. Matters of Conscience in the Healthcare Arena

Questions of conscience have great urgency in the healthcare context for a number of reasons. Religiously affiliated, denominational hospitals comprise the largest group of nonprofit healthcare providers in the United States.[44] Without conscience clause protection, healthcare providers have been unsuccessful in the lower courts in defending their choice to limit services on free exercise grounds under the First Amendment.[45] A law does not infringe on free exercise rights when it is neutral, generally applicable, and not targeted at religious practices.[46] For example, in *St. Agnes Hospital, Inc. v. Riddick*, the United States District Court for the District of Maryland upheld a state requirement that all accredited obstetrics and gynecology programs provide clinical training in family planning procedures.[47] The requirement did not violate the Catholic hospital's free exercise of religion because the court found a compelling interest in having every resident in obstetrics and gynecology trained in how to perform an abortion.[48] Further, the requirement "was not motivated by a discriminatory purpose" and applied equally to all facilities.[49] Congress ultimately overrode the requirement with conscience protection in the Danforth Amendment, as explained more fully below.[50]

St. Agnes is a prime example of the well-worn path that conscience clauses in medicine have followed: advocates file and sometimes win lawsuits seeking to compel the performance of services by individuals or facilities. Congress or the state legislature then steps in to provide a protected space for persons or facilities that might otherwise be compelled to provide such procedures. The history and development of these conscience clauses in medicine offer an important lens for examining how the strongly held beliefs of individual churches, clergy, or state officials opposed to same-sex marriage can be accommodated through legislation.

A. Protecting Providers from Coercion by Patients

Efforts to compel the provision of controversial medical services focused first on facilities. In this litigation, the bludgeon of choice against facilities was the receipt of public benefits or federal funds.[51]

Shortly before the United States Supreme Court's decision in *Roe v. Wade* in 1973, the United States District Court for the District of Montana in *Taylor v. St. Vincent's Hospital* enjoined a private, nonprofit, charitable hospital in Billings, Montana, from refusing to perform a tubal ligation.[52] In *Taylor*, the hospital had prohibited Mrs. Taylor's physician from surgically sterilizing her during the delivery of her baby by Caesarian section.[53]

Mrs. Taylor brought suit under 42 U.S.C. §1983, which prohibits entities acting under color of state law from subjecting "any citizen of the United States or other person within the jurisdiction thereof to the deprivation of any rights, privileges, or immunities secured by the Constitution and laws."[54] In denying the hospital's motion to dismiss for lack of jurisdiction, the court stated that "'the fact that the [hospital received] Hill-burton [sic] Act . . . funds is alone sufficient to support an assumption of jurisdiction . . . .'"[55] Hill-Burton funds are federal monies made available to hospitals to modernize and construct medical facilities.[56] The hospital's tax immunity and licensing by the state also established, in the court's view, a connection between the hospital and the state sufficient to support jurisdiction.[57]

Almost before the ink could dry on the injunction, Congress acted to tear it up with the Church Amendment.[58] The Church Amendment provided that:

(b) The receipt of any grant, contract, loan, or loan guarantee under the [act that created the Hill-Burton funds and other acts] by any individual or entity does not authorize any court or any public official or other public authority to require—

   (1) such individual to perform or assist in the performance of any sterilization procedure or abortion if [it] would be contrary to his religious beliefs or moral convictions; or

   (2) Such entity to—

      (A) make its facilities available for the performance of any sterilization procedure or abortion if [it] is prohibited by the entity on the basis of religious beliefs or moral convictions, or

      (B) provide any personnel for [such services] if [their performance] would be contrary to the religious beliefs or moral convictions of such personnel.[59]

Like many of the conscience clauses that have followed it, the Church Amendment protects both individual providers and facilities from compelled participation. Importantly, it not only provides protection in the *horizontal relationship* between the patient and individual facility or provider, but it also protects individual providers in *vertical relationships* against coercion from an employer or facility:

(c) No entity which receives [certain grant, contract, loan, or loan guarantees] may—

   (1) discriminate in the employment, promotion, or termination of employment of any physician or other health care personnel, or

   (2) discriminate in the extension of . . . privileges to [them], because he performed . . . a lawful sterilization procedure or abortion, [or] refused to perform [one due to] his religious beliefs or moral convictions, or because of his religious beliefs or moral convictions respecting sterilization procedures or abortions.[60]

After the Church Amendment's passage, the *Taylor* court dissolved its original injunction.[61] The court found that the effect of the Church Amendment was to prohibit courts and public officials from compelling individuals or institutions to perform or assist in abortions or sterilizations.[62] Consequently, the plaintiffs were denied all relief.

Despite the Church Amendment, litigation continued along the same lines for several more years. Family planning advocates continued to file suits to force hospitals to provide abortions and sterilizations, and the Church Amendment figured prominently in the rejection of these claims. For instance, in *Chrisman v. Sisters of St. Joseph of Peace*, a married woman sued for a writ of mandamus and injunction against a private, nonprofit hospital that refused to do a tubal ligation for her.[63] She alleged that the hospital acted under color of state law since it received Hill-Burton construction funds, enjoyed some state tax exemption, and was generally under state regulation.[64] In affirming the district court's dismissal, the United States Court of Appeals for the Ninth Circuit noted that "this argument has been seriously limited by [Congress's] action" in the Church Amendment, which "was clearly intended by Congress to prevent suits such as that advanced by Appellant."[65] Courts in many jurisdictions have held that receipt of Hill-Burton funds, and participation in other federal or state programs, cannot be used to compel private institutions to make their facilities available for the performance of abortions.[66]

Some courts believe that a different result should obtain when a public hospital refuses to provide abortion services. In *Nyberg v. City of Virginia*, the United States Court of Appeals for the Eighth Circuit invalidated a public hospital's ban on all nontherapeutic abortions in its facilities.[67] The court found that this ban would not serve the interest of the hospital or the state and that "the performance of abortions [would not] interfere with the normal hospital routine."[68] The court reasoned: "[O]nce the state has undertaken to provide general short-term hospital care, as here, it may not constitutionally draw the line at medically indistinguishable surgical procedures that impinge on fundamental rights."[69] Because the hospital would not have to hire new staff or establish new facilities in order to perform abortions, the hospital could not "arbitrarily preclude abortions from the variety of services offered which require no greater expenditure of available facilities and skills."[70] The decision rested in part on *Roe v. Wade*: the hospital's ban "unduly restricts what the United States Supreme Court has held to be a fundamental right."[71] Following *Nyberg*, both federal and state courts held that public medical facilities could not forbid elective abortions when the facility offered medically indistinguishable procedures.[72]

All of this ended with the Supreme Court's decision in *Webster v. Reproductive Health Services*.[73] There, the Court considered whether a hospital's refusal to provide abortion services infringes upon a woman's constitutional rights. The Court upheld a Missouri statute that prohibited public employees from performing abortions in public hospitals. The Court stated that, "[n]othing in the Constitution requires states to enter or remain in the business of performing abortions. Nor . . . do private physicians and their patients have some kind of constitutional right of access to public facilities for the performance of abortions."[74] The Court noted, however, that the case "might . . . be different if the State barred doctors who performed abortions in private facilities from the use of public facilities for any purpose," or if all medicine were socialized.[75]

In many ways, the result in *Webster* is not surprising. In *Doe v. Bolton*, the companion case to *Roe*, the Court recognized the need for protection against forced participation in abortions.[76] There, the Court struck down Georgia's criminal abortion statute that required, among other things, advance approval of abortions by a mandatory abortion screening committee.[77] The Court considered whether the committee was necessary as a means of protecting the rights of individual physicians and denominational hospitals.[78] Although this was an appropriate goal, the Court noted that it was unnecessary in light of Georgia's existing statutory protections for providers:

> Under [Georgia law] the hospital is free not to admit a patient for an abortion. . . . Further, a physician or any other employee has the right to refrain, for moral or religious reasons, from participating in the abortion procedure. These provisions obviously are in the statute in order to afford *appropriate protection* to the individual and to the denominational hospital.[79]

In a similar vein, lower courts have noted that the Church Amendment properly exempted denominational hospitals since "[t]o hold otherwise would violate the religious rights of the hospital."[80]

B. Protecting Providers from Government Pressure: The Second Wave of Conscience Protections

Receipt of benefits may be used as a wedge not only by private parties, but also by state, local, and federal governments to coerce participation in abortion and other controversial services. A favored tool of government for extracting certain behavior is the denial of participation in government programs.

After the Church Amendment, Congress expanded the scope of conscience clause protections in successive pieces of legislation, culminating most recently in the Weldon Amendment.[81] These enactments were designed to protect entities and individuals from punishments at the hands of the government. In 1996, for example, Congress in the Danforth Amendment prohibited federal, state, and local governments from discriminating against healthcare entities that refuse to (1) undergo abortion training, (2) provide such training, (3) perform abortions, or (4) provide referrals for training or abortions.[82] Specifically, it protected doctors, medical students, and health training programs from being denied federal financial assistance, certifications, or licenses they would otherwise receive but for their refusal.[83] This protection was not limited to refusals for religious or moral reasons but extends to refusals for any reason.

Congress put teeth into this protection against government coercion with the Weldon Amendment, which was tucked into a series of appropriations bills beginning in 2004.[84] The Weldon Amendment provides that:

> None of the funds made available in this Act may be made available to a Federal agency or program, or to a State or local government, if [it] subjects any institutional or individual health care entity to discrimination on the basis that the health care entity does not provide, pay for, provide coverage of, or refer for abortions.[85]

Significantly, the Weldon Amendment carved out certain abortions from application of this financial penalty, so that governments that make healthcare providers perform abortions in the case of rape, incest, or a life-threatening pregnancy do not risk their federal funds.[86] It also broadened significantly the kind of entities embraced by conscience protection. Under the Weldon Amendment, a "healthcare entity" includes an individual physician or other healthcare professional, a hospital, a provider-sponsored organization, a health maintenance organization, a health insurance plan, or any other kind of healthcare facility, organization, or plan.[87] The Weldon Amendment is the proverbial 800-pound gorilla. California alone stands to lose $49 billion in federal funds if it discriminates in this way.[88]

Just as family planning advocates have tried to force private hospitals to do abortions and sterilizations, advocates of same-sex marriage may bring similar challenges to refusals to preside over same-sex marriages. It is possible, of course, that such attempts would not succeed, but it would seem preferable to deflect this risk in advance. The healthcare context gives us a model for doing that. In fact, the Church Amendment itself influenced the outcome of that litigation in important and material ways, and presumably the Weldon Amendment will have a similar effect.

C. Dilemma Facing Tax-Exempt Churches and Religious Organizations in States That Legalize Same-Sex Marriage

As the second wave of conscience clause protections recognizes, the risk of coercion extends beyond private litigation. Churches and religious organizations that oppose same-sex marriage perceive a credible, palpable threat to their tax-exempt status, the benefits of which are substantial.[89] It is important here to distinguish between two different risks: the risk of losing one's state-level tax exemption and the risk of losing one's federal tax exemption.

The loss of a state-level tax exemption would be devastating for most churches and religious groups[90] since recognition as a charity under state law exempts an entity from *ad valorem* or property taxes, state sales tax, use tax, and income taxes.[91] Because only two state supreme courts have recognized same-sex marriage to date, there is little guidance about whether states would seek to withhold tax exemption from churches or, more likely, religious organizations if they refuse to facilitate same-sex marriages.[92] The Massachusetts Attorney General's Office has not issued an advisory opinion on this question since the *Goodridge* decision in 2003. But the Attorney General, Martha Coakley, has indicated that "[a]ccess to civil marriage for gays and lesbians is the law of the Commonwealth. . . . And as [the] Attorney General, charged with responsibility for upholding the law, I will do whatever I can to see that the rights of same-sex couples to marry is protected."[93] It is not clear whether such measures would extend to the tax treatment of churches or religious organizations,[94] but commentators have urged the denial of tax exemption for "private organizations incorporated under state law that discriminate based on sexual orientation."[95] Presumably because of their special status, the tax treatment of houses of worship as such would not be at risk; religious organizations, however, have historically not enjoyed the same umbrella of protection and may have more to fear.[96]

Risk also exists at the federal level. Although the Internal Revenue Service exercises considerable discretion in its enforcement priorities, the threat of losing federal tax exemption is not merely hypothetical, at least with respect to religious organizations. Like the state-level exemption, the benefits of federal tax exemption can be significant.[97] In order to be recognized as a tax-exempt organization under Section 501(c)(3) of the Internal Revenue Code, an organization's purposes and activities may not violate fundamental public policy. Under the public policy doctrine, a church or other tax-exempt organization may lose its tax-exempt status[98] even if it does nothing illegal and never violates the nondiscrimination provisions contained in Section 501.[99] Instead, the organization must only transgress the loose confines of "established public policy," a concept that neither the United States Supreme Court nor the IRS has fully fleshed out, as explained more fully below.

This public policy limitation has its genesis in *Bob Jones University v. United States*.[100] In that case, the IRS had revoked the federal tax exemption of two private schools: Goldsboro Christian Schools, which admitted only Caucasian descendants, and Bob Jones University, which prohibited interracial marriage and dating among its students and would not admit students who advocated interracial relationships or participated in them.[101] The Court upheld the IRS's decision, since the schools "prescribe and enforce racially discriminatory admission standards on the basis of religious doctrine" in violation of established public policy.[102] In reaching this decision, the Court found "Congress' intention was to provide tax benefits to organizations serving charitable purposes."[103]

This is important because, under the common law, "the purpose of a charitable trust may not be illegal or violate established public policy."[104] Thus the "purpose [of the organization] must not be so at odds with the common community conscience as to undermine any public benefit that might otherwise be conferred."[105]

Although the schools' admission standards were not illegal, they nevertheless violated an established public policy. The Court discerned this in (a) "[a]n unbroken line of cases following *Brown v. Board of Education* establish[ing] . . . that racial discrimination in education violates a most fundamental national public policy, as well as rights of individuals";[106] (b) Congressional actions that "testify to the public policy against racial discrimination," like the Voting Rights Act of 1965 and the Civil Rights Act of 1968; and (c) certain Executive Orders prohibiting racial discrimination in federal employment and Selective Service.[107] The Court made short work of the schools' claim that the prohibition on interracial dating was religiously grounded. Denying tax benefits to the schools, the Court noted, would not prevent them "from observing their religious tenets."[108]

Although Professor Kmiec correctly observes in this volume that "there have been very few true extensions of the *Bob Jones* public policy limitation outside the racial discrimination context,"[109] later IRS guidance sheds some light on the wide swath that "established public policy" cuts. In a General Counsel Memorandum, the IRS maintains that the *Bob Jones* decision "leaves little doubt" that racial discrimination, "whether in an educational context or *otherwise*," violates public policy in such a fundamental way as to justify revocation of an entity's tax-exempt status.[110] A court must therefore assess whether "there is a public policy against a particular activity and, second, whether that public policy is so fundamental as to require the denial or revocation of exempt status for organizations participating in that activity."[111] In a private letter ruling issued in 1988, the IRS likewise concluded: "Although applying on its face only to race discrimination in education, the implication of the *Bob Jones* decision extends to any organization claiming exempt status under Section 501(c)(3) and to any activity violating a clear public policy."[112] The United States Tax Court takes the same approach: "We believe the *Bob Jones* opinion unqualifiedly held that all organizations seeking exemption under 501(c)(3) must comply with fundamental standards of public policy."[113] Finally, tax guidance issued by the IRS suggests that conduct that would constitute a violation of law when performed by a state actor may be sufficient to revoke or deny a nonprofit's tax-exempt status.[114]

The public policy formulation in *Bob Jones* raises a number of threshold questions. First, what defines the contours of public policy? The Supreme

Court's decision in *Bob Jones* and tax guidance on this point variously describe the relevant yardstick as "'established' or 'fundamental' public policy,"[115] "fundamental national public policy,"[116] the "common community conscience,"[117] "fundamental standards of public policy,"[118] "clear public policy,"[119] and "national public policy."[120] One important question here is whether state or local law may shape or comprise public policy. Commentators have argued that "one can readily construct at least a superficially appealing case for looking to state law under the public policy doctrine."[121]

Thus, some commentators believe that the IRS could engage in "a type of analysis that considers a variety of sources—constitutional, nonconstitutional, federal and nonfederal"—in deciding whether a violation of established public policy exists.[122] Even those academics who question the applicability of state law to the public policy analysis concede that "[f]or now, it is sufficient to observe that state law should not be deemed entirely irrelevant in the quest for shaping the public policy doctrine."[123]

The possibility of a church (as opposed to a religious organization) losing its federal tax-exempt status may be remote in the current political climate.[124] The IRS generally takes a hands-off approach when it comes to churches themselves. For example, churches (although not religious organizations) automatically get tax-exempt status without filing anything with the IRS, are exempt from filing annual informational returns, and may only be audited for certain, limited purposes.[125] Moreover, it may simply be too difficult politically for the IRS to challenge churches over same-sex marriage practices.

Nonetheless, churches are not wholly exempt from the IRS's reach.[126] In 2005, the IRS threatened the tax-exempt status of All Saints Episcopal Church in Pasadena, California because of a 2004 sermon by the Reverend George Regas opposing the war in Iraq.[127] This was not an isolated threat, but part of a probe of "more than 100 tax-exempt organizations across the United States for allegations of promoting—either explicitly or implicitly—candidates on both ends of the political spectrum, according to the IRS."[128] Although none had lost their nonprofit status as of 2005, "investigations continued into about 60 of those."[129] While the prohibition against political activity is much clearer-cut than the public policy exception, the sheer size of the IRS's probe into the tax-exempt status of churches and religious organizations gives one pause.

In sum, although a church's or religious organization's risk of losing its Section 501(c)(3) characterization may be remote, it cannot be ignored. Anytime there is uncertainty, as there is within the loose confines of "established public policy," churches and religious groups have reason to worry. Much more than the threat to their federal tax exemption, however, churches or religious organizations reasonably may worry about risks to their state-level tax exemption.

While policymakers might conclude that these risks are not great, conscience clauses are useful in muting this risk, especially those patterned after the Weldon Amendment.

D. Degree of Protection Conferred by Conscience Clauses

The recognition of same-sex marriage also poses a second dilemma, this one facing individuals. While individual clergy presumably will not suffer repercussions for refusing to marry same-sex couples, at least if consistent with church tenets, individual clerks at state offices who refuse to complete a license for a same-sex couple may face real consequences.

Prior to the legislative accommodation in conscience clauses, healthcare providers who did not want to perform controversial services refused to do so at great risk to themselves. Thus, individual physicians and pharmacists have been disciplined, dismissed, sued, and retaliated against for not going along, either with their employer's demands or with patients' demands, to provide abortions or other services.[130] The legislative responses to these risks demonstrate the range of protections available to individuals and institutions and offer us one way to manage the clash between competing moral views.

Although nearly every state has a healthcare conscience clause encompassing some service, states vary dramatically in the strength of the protections given to objecting individuals and facilities. Some states provide no protection for the conscientious objector, as the appendix illustrates.[131] Others permit an objection only if the objector "shows proof" or states the reasons for objecting in writing.[132]

Some states ask very little of objecting providers, requiring only notice to the patient beforehand.[133] Some jurisdictions permit the invoker to object so long as they do not pose a "road block" to the patient's ability to access the desired service from another provider.[134] Other statutes require the doctor or institution to facilitate the patient's ability to get the service from another provider.[135] Some of these clauses simply parrot the protection afforded by the Church Amendment.[136] But many also insulate providers from punishment at the hands of the state and local government, as the Weldon Amendment does.[137]

Like the Church Amendment, many state conscience clauses address an individual's risk of coercion by her employer. Others recognize the burden that individual refusal can place on an employer. Thus, employees hired for the express purpose of performing a specific service are not exempted, nor are employees who work for facilities that exclusively provide abortions.[138] Other states limit this encroachment on individual consciences to employers that will experience an undue hardship as a result.[139] In contrast, yet other states prohibit employers from asking prospective employees about refusal to participate.[140]

Importantly, conscience clauses sometimes accommodate matters of conscience in both directions. Consider the physician who performs abortions outside a Catholic hospital but wants privileges within it. The "renegade" physician may worry that she is at risk for a denial of privileges at the Catholic hospital or other sanction. California's conscience clause removes this risk: a person associated with a medical facility that does not permit abortion "may not be subject to any penalty or discipline on account of the person's participation in the performance of an abortion" in another facility.[141]

Some states permit refusals on grounds other than religion or morality.[142] Some limit the ability to refuse only to denominational hospitals.[143] Others have expanded the right to refuse even to insurers and other healthcare entities.[144] Many states recognize the hardship that handing out the right to refuse may pose for patients in need of the service.[145] For this reason, some states limit the ability to refuse only to nonemergencies.[146]

All in all, states have structured legislative accommodations in a variety of ways to provide greater or lesser protection for persons who object to performing a service.

II. The Limits of State Conscience Clauses

Even though they provide important and real insulation for potential objectors, if the healthcare context is any indicator, state legislative accommodations may not be a panacea. As more and more professionals invoke them, courts, regulators, and policymakers have pushed back from this moral fault line.

A. State Constitutional Provisions Trump Legislative Accommodations

An Alaska Supreme Court case, *Valley Hospital Association, Inc. v. Mat-Su Coalition for Choice*,[147] demonstrates one important limit of state conscience clause protection: It must yield to the state constitution. Valley Hospital, a nonprofit corporation, prohibited abortions unless there was documentation that the fetus had a condition incompatible with life, the mother's life was threatened, or the pregnancy was the result of incest.[148] The lower court ruled this unconstitutional and the Alaska Supreme Court agreed. The court first found that Alaska's state constitution protects reproductive autonomy more broadly than the United States Constitution.[149] It then found that the hospital was "quasi-public"[150] and therefore could not infringe on a woman's fundamental right unless there was a compelling interest for doing so.

The court gave little weight to Alaska's conscience clause, which provided that "Nothing in this section requires a hospital or person to participate in an abortion, nor is a hospital or person liable for refusing to participate in an abortion . . . ."[151] The hospital's "sincere moral belief," the court wrote, could not outweigh the ability to procure an abortion.[152] In their view, constitutional rights "cannot be allowed to yield simply because of disagreement with them."[153] The court concluded that Valley Hospital, as a nondenominational hospital, had "at most a statutory right," which the legislature may not balance against the patient's "constitutional ones."[154] Thus, conscience clauses, the court held, are unconstitutional as applied to public entities.[155] Interestingly, the court rejected the notion that the hospital had its own constitutional rights: the hospital was "not affiliated with any religion" and therefore could not "raise a free exercise claim."[156]

The question then became whether Valley Hospital—a private, nonprofit community hospital—was sufficiently public to preclude application of the state's conscience clause. The court held that the hospital was quasi-public for a number of reasons: it was the only hospital serving the community;[157] the hospital's construction was funded in significant part by state and federal grants; and a substantial percentage of the funds received for hospital services came from governmental sources.[158] In addition, the hospital had a "special relationship" with the state through Alaska's Certificate of Need program,[159] and as a "community hospital," its "board [was] elected by a public membership."[160] This public status erased any opportunity for exercising a private conscience. Valley Hospital, the court concluded, must allow any doctor who is willing to perform an abortion to do so in its facilities.[161]

B. Discounting the Objections of Some
As healthcare conscience clauses are invoked with increasing frequency, regulators and policymakers have sought to cabin earlier, broader protections. For instance, an Iowa Attorney General Opinion concluded that Iowa's conscience clause exception did not extend to those not "recommending, performing, or assisting in an abortion procedure."[162] Consequently, nurses asked to provide comfort to patients receiving an abortion and pharmacists asked to make up the saline solution used in the procedures could not use the conscience clause to refrain from doing their jobs. The opinion emphasized the "slippery slope" that a contrary decision would create: "one could eventually get to the point where the man who mines the iron ore that goes to make the steel, which is used by a factory to make instruments used in abortions could refuse to work on conscientious grounds."[163]

The idea that some actions are too remote departs from the United States Supreme Court's treatment of conscientious objections about war. In that context, the Court has said that objectors get to decide how offensive a task is, not the rest of the world. In *Thomas v. Review Board*, the Court found that Indiana's denial of unemployment compensation benefits to the plaintiff violated his First

Amendment right to the free exercise of religion.[164] Thomas, a Jehovah's Witness, resigned from his position at the Blaw-Knox Foundry & Machinery Company when he was transferred to a department that fabricated turrets for military tanks.[165] Thomas maintained that his religious beliefs prevented him from participating in the production of war materials, although he previously worked in another department making sheet steel for industrial use.[166] He was denied unemployment compensation under Indiana's Employment Security Act. Both the Review Board and the Indiana Supreme Court concluded that Thomas made a personal choice rather than a religious choice and, consequently, that his termination was not based upon "good cause arising in connection with his work."[167] The Indiana court gave "significant weight to the fact that another Jehovah's Witness had no scruples about working on tank turrets; for that other Witness, at least, such work was 'scripturally' acceptable."[168]

Reversing, the United States Supreme Court noted that it is not the Court's role to "dissect religious beliefs because the believer admits that he is 'struggling' with his position or because his beliefs are not articulated with the clarity and precision that a more sophisticated person might employ."[169] Although the Indiana compensation statute did not compel a violation of conscience, the Court concluded that even a facially neutral regulation may offend the constitutional requirement for government neutrality if it "unduly burdens the free exercise of religion."[170] Here, the Court found that Thomas was left with no alternative but to resign.[171]

III. What Do Healthcare Conscience Clauses Offer in Navigating the Moral Clash over Same-Sex Unions?

What can these healthcare statutes tell us about how to navigate the impending collision over same-sex unions? This part first canvasses a number of lessons that policymakers should draw from the experience of healthcare providers after *Roe v. Wade*. It then offers some thoughts about resolving first order conflicts in those states that adopt same-sex marriage—namely, how states should treat clergy members and public officials who decline to solemnize same-sex marriages. This part also considers how to approach second order conflicts, which are likely to be much more common—that is, what to do with private individuals who refuse for religious or moral reasons to provide services to same-sex couples in a wide range of contexts.

A. Lessons from the Healthcare Context

What can these healthcare statutes tell us about how to navigate the unfolding collision over same-sex marriage? First, like abortion, the issue of same-sex marriage is deeply divisive. It has already raised, and will surely continue to raise, horizontal claims between same-sex couples and those who object to performing same-sex marriage ceremonies, just as abortion did.[172] Vertical clashes are also conceivable between individual clerks or clergymen and their parent institutions, the state, or the church.[173]

Second, until the legislature acts, it is likely that churches, clergy, state clerks, and private individuals will face litigation designed to resolve the question of their participation in same-sex marriage or, conversely, their right to refrain. In this volume, Professor Feldblum argues that "an inevitable choice between liberties must come into play. . . . If the government tolerated the private exclusionary policies of . . . individuals in the commercial sector, such toleration would necessarily come at the cost of gay people's sense of belonging and safety in society."[174] Now, it is certainly true that legislative accommodations necessarily would come at the expense of same-sex couples in those unusual situations where no other providers are reasonably available and there is a real barrier to access. As explained in part III.B. below, however, a live-and-let-live solution will in most situations allow both sides to live their lives while maintaining their values.[175] Nonetheless, in the rare case, there will be winners and losers. How society responds to the question of which person's claim should take precedence reflects how committed society is to safeguarding the dignitary interests of same-sex couples or the religious and moral convictions of conscientious objectors. For instance, when the Alaska Supreme Court held that a private, nonprofit hospital could not burden the ability to procure an abortion under state law,[176] it was saying to the provider that the right to abortion matters more than an objector's interest in not participating. That decision was tantamount to saying that "not only does the patient deserve an abortion, but you, the provider, are going to perform it." Legislatures that enact conscience clauses are, by definition, valuing more heavily the moral and religious convictions of the objectors; and legislatures that refuse to enact conscience clauses are valuing more heavily the dignitary interests of same-sex couples—not to be embarrassed, not to be inconvenienced, not to have their choice questioned.

Third, as with abortion, where litigation arose in contexts that were inconceivable at the time that *Roe* was handed down, there is almost no end to the number of contexts in which this clash of competing moral values will arise—and, hence, almost no end to the coming wave of litigation. In New Jersey, two same-sex couples filed civil rights complaints against a Methodist ministry for denying their request to hold a civil union ceremony in the group's boardwalk pavilion.[177] A physician in Great Britain is campaigning the Health Minister for an opt-out on religious grounds for doctors who do not feel comfortable serving as medical references to same-sex couples wishing to adopt.[178] In California, an unmarried lesbian woman sued doctors who refused to artificially inseminate her.[179] Christian, Jewish, and Muslim leaders in the United Kingdom and elsewhere fear that new laws "aimed at stopping businesses from discriminating against gays . . . will force religious believers to act against their consciences."[180]

Fourth, legislative accommodations can affect the outcome of litigation, as the Church Amendment illustrates. Now, it may be that an exemption will be ultimately unnecessary with respect to churches or individual clergy since the Constitution already provides considerable insulation.[181] For example, courts have refused to reach a determination on the merits in a lawsuit over a pastor's claims regarding her appointment and discharge because they were "fundamentally connected to issues of church doctrine and governance and would require court review of the church's motives" for discharge.[182] Here, one can easily imagine clashes between a same-sex couple and a church or individual clergyman who refuses to marry the couple. Any claim against the church or clergy presumably is doomed to fail since it would put the court in the position of squarely controlling and directing a religious function. No one has tried such an audacious thing before and so there appears to be no precedent that says it cannot be done. Yet, if it is not unconstitutional to order a clergy person to administer a sacrament against his will, it is hard to imagine what would be unconstitutional. In this instance, a legislative accommodation may accomplish little more than the protection the Constitution already provides. But state clerks are a different matter entirely. For them, legislative accommodations are crucial to the ability to refuse to complete the necessary paperwork or to solemnize marriages, as clerks do in some states.[183]

Fifth, legislative accommodations affect not only the outcome of litigation, but its likelihood as well.[184] Here is the real value of legislative accommodations even for churches and clergy. An accommodation that encompasses not only clerks, but churches and clergy, may forestall individual suits against individual churches or clergymen premised on the notion that they receive public benefits or serve a public function—solemnizing marriage—and so must provide access to a public good. Broad legislative accommodations may also forestall efforts by state and local governments to pressure churches into performing same-sex marriages, using the same "public benefits" club. Moreover, a federal Weldon-like legislative accommodation would make it more expensive for state and local governments to punish churches, clergy, or (more likely) state clerks that refuse to participate in same-sex marriage.

Sixth, legislatures cannot dodge the question of whether conscientious refusals should count, at least in those jurisdictions with nondiscrimination laws in place. As Professor Feldblum correctly points out, nondiscrimination laws in many states place a big thumb on the scale against the right to refrain from facilitating same-sex marriage.[185] Nondiscrimination laws have already figured prominently in a related context, adoption. In 2006, the Catholic Bishops of Massachusetts sought permission from the state to exclude gay and lesbian parents from adopting children through Catholic Charities, their social service agency.[186] Catholic Charities originally allowed a handful of lesbian and gay parents to adopt,[187] then ceased to place children with lesbian and gay parents in violation of state law prohibiting discrimination on the basis of sexual orientation.[188] The Catholic Bishops approached counsel to seek an exemption from the statute, only to be informed by the Governor of Massachusetts that any exemption would have to come from the legislature or through a judicial ruling.[189] Rather than bending to the state's will, the Catholic Bishops got out of the adoption business entirely. After June 30, 2006, Catholic Charities stopped placing children for adoption in Massachusetts.[190] Thus, states with nondiscrimination laws may be effectively deciding the question when they remain silent about the ability to object.

Seventh, even if states have passed antidiscrimination statutes, the possibility of legislative accommodation is not foreclosed.[191] In countries that have a longer experience with same-sex marriage than the United States, some argue that the question of whether one can refuse is easily resolved by reference to existing law. For instance, one Canadian official "compared marriage commissioners to police officers, whom she said cannot pick and choose what laws they are going to uphold, but are required to uphold all laws."[192] At least in the United States, states historically have given judges and other authorized celebrants considerable discretion to choose whether or not to solemnize a marriage.[193] More fundamentally, however, whether the law now requires authorized celebrants to marry all comers begs the question of whether it *should* require them to do so. For instance, the New Jersey Attorney General recently addressed whether state law permits authorized celebrants to decide whose relationships they will solemnize—in that case, by presiding over a civil union. Interpreting the laws of the state as they are, the Attorney General held that government officials who make themselves available to perform marriage ceremonies generally must also make themselves available to perform civil unions for same-sex couples. The opinion relied on New Jersey's public accommodation statute.[194] Because New Jersey has already prohibited discrimination on the basis of sexual orientation and lacks a legislative accommodation, it is difficult to imagine the Attorney General deciding this question any other way. But, again, the question posed here is whether the refusal *should* be illegal—not whether it is.

Eighth, the power of state legislatures is not unlimited. Any legislative effort will necessarily yield to the state and federal constitutions. The lesson of *Roe* and *Griswold* is that the individual's right to be free from the state's interference with reproductive and contraceptive choices is just that—the right to be free from government interference. It does not translate directly into a right to assistance, a fact that legislatures have chosen to make clear by statute. Now it may be that the nature of marriage is different from these noninterference rights,[195] given the fact that the state holds a monopoly on marriage. Unlike abortion, where the state does not have to be in the business of performing abortions, the state *is* in the business of performing marriages. Because they stand as an entryway into legal marriage, clergy and clerks who refuse to solemnize a marriage may infringe on the right to marry since the couple cannot secure this good in any other way. This, then, takes us to the crucial question: Can we really say that a clerk's or a clergy member's refusal is likely to erect a barrier to entering marriage? We turn to this question in the next subpart.

B. Toward an Imperfect Solution

How states should approach questions of conscientious refusals to facilitate same-sex unions necessarily depends on the status of the objector and the nature of the function they would perform. The first order question for states presumably will be whether to provide a space for those who represent the church or the state to refrain from facilitating same-sex marriages or civil unions. The second order question will be whether other persons, who represent neither the church nor the state, should receive a legislative accommodation for a range of choices—from refusing to provide the reception hall for a same-sex marriage to refusing to do a psychiatric review or home study for a same-sex couple wishing to adopt. This subpart first discusses first order conflicts involving clergy and clerks, then offers some tentative observations about second order conflicts between private individuals.

1. First Order Conflicts: The Right to Marry

The first site of friction over same-sex marriage is likely to be around the ability to marry itself and will involve representatives of the church and the state, both of whom have the power to marry couples. As to churches and members of the clergy, the state cannot easily affect the choices to perform, or to refrain from performing, same-sex unions because of constitutional doctrines limiting their control of religious functions (and neither *should* the state be able to reach these decisions).[196]

For clerks and other state officials, the operative question is whether, as noted above, a refusal would erect a significant barrier to a couple's ability to

obtain and enjoy all the privileges and benefits of marriage. It does not necessarily follow that permitting conscientious refusals will bar access to marriage. This is so because so many different parties in any given state can
marry a couple. Moreover, protections for conscience need not come at the
expense of access to marriage. Information-forcing rules—that is, rules that
require refusing parties to direct couples to others who will perform the service—allow protection for matters of conscience without sacrificing access or
humiliating same-sex couples. States have capitalized on this approach with
emergency contraceptives. For example, Illinois requires pharmacies that do
not carry emergency contraceptives to post a sign directing patients to other
pharmacies that do.[197] Clerks' offices likewise can take steps to avert collisions over same-sex marriage with good information and good practices.
These offices should ask existing and prospective employees whether they
would anticipate a moral or religious objection and keep appropriate lists.
Same-sex couples who present could then be directed to a willing clerk with
little inconvenience. One virtue of this information-forcing approach is that
it respects matters of conscience without inconveniencing same-sex couples,
and is much less draconian than requiring all clerks to serve all comers. It is
also much less draconian than deciding that no clerk will be placed in the
position of having to choose, which effectively resulted when several counties in California decided for "administrative and budgetary reasons" that the
county would no longer solemnize marriages.[198]

Although information-forcing rules may be an obvious solution, they may
not be a complete one. Same-sex couples may still face hardships in trying to
tie the knot. It is not inconceivable that in remote parts of a state, where
there are only one or two clerks, the ability of a clerk to object may frustrate
a same-sex couple's exercise of its right to marry. Likewise, in locales where
every clerk in a given office wants to claim a moral objection, foreseeable
hardships would arise.[199] In such instances, these predictable denials would
clearly pose a hardship for the couple. But whether they would bar access to
the institution of marriage is a different question. The answer to this question depends on the function that the objecting party is actually performing.
Here, it is important to distinguish between clerks who would merely process
paperwork for a license from those who would solemnize the marriage.

When a clerk is merely issuing a license to the couple, it seems unlikely
that an individual refusal will bar entry into marriage. Marriage licenses
nearly always require a waiting period of a day or several days.[200] Thus, if a
clerk refuses to process an application, another clerk may be able to process
it before the waiting period would have elapsed. Because the couple could
not marry in any event until satisfying the requisite waiting period, there is
no direct sense in which the clerk's refusal denies the couple the privileges

and benefits of marriage. The couple is still able to marry if another clerk provides the necessary license.

Of course, one clerk's refusal may push back the timing of a couple's ceremony if another willing clerk cannot readily be located. The possibility of slight delay while locating a willing clerk can be addressed with a modified timing rule. States could simply have a different timing rule for same-sex couples than they do for other couples, placing them in the same position in term of access to marriage.[201] Information-forcing rules would also assist to avoid such delays.

Because the clerk's refusal to process paperwork does not frustrate a couple's ability to marry, the constitutional dimension of the refusal falls away,[202] leaving a straight-up contest between two sets of competing moral claims. It is not self-evident how policymakers should weigh the dignitary interests of same-sex couples and the moral and religious convictions of potential objectors. Some people would find it offensive simply to be directed to another willing clerk, at least where the reason for the redirection is apparent. And as taxpayers, same-sex couples would likely be indignant to learn that their taxes support employees who will not provide them a service to which they are entitled. Same-sex couples likely would not be alone in this view: many citizens believe that while we can exercise our religions in our private capacities, we should not do so in our government jobs, and, as a consequence, state workers should be required to provide all the services the office provides to all who present. On the other side of the ledger, some find it offensive to facilitate acts that they find immoral. Clerks and other celebrants may also have a reliance interest in their professions and jobs; many started at a time when they never would have imagined they would be asked to issue licenses to, or to marry, same-sex couples.[203] For them, being redirected from one clerk to another, while not a trivial burden, simply pales in comparison to the burden of having to quit one's job. As discussed more fully in part III.B(2) below, one way to balance competing moral claims is to limit the ability to refuse to instances where a hardship will not occur.

When an objector refuses to solemnize a marriage, however, this poses a harder problem. Here, an objector would actually be choosing to marry or not to marry the couple and so is, in some immediate sense, deciding whether the couple *can* marry. In contrast to clergy, whose choices the state cannot easily affect, the question of refusals by judges and clerks poses additional challenges. Clerks and judges are employed by the state and perform a public function. Their denial, then, may operate as a denial by the state itself.[204] The question then becomes, can this couple marry if the celebrant refuses to do the ceremony? States may conclude that if there is another celebrant in a specified time period or geographical area who will marry the couple,[205] the objecting celebrant should be permitted to refuse. But if the objector is the only celebrant available, the denial is tantamount to a denial of access to marriage. Because of the unique constitutional status of marriage, states then face a choice—bar conscientious refusals entirely or provide a hardship exception to the ability of the objecting clerk to refuse. Here, too, states can exploit information-forcing rules to minimize this win-lose outcome. States can simply require all authorized celebrants (other than clergy) to indicate their willingness to perform ceremonies for same-sex couples, and direct couples at the time of application for a license to these willing providers.

2. Second Order Conflicts: The Opportunity to Be Treated as Any Other Couple

Second order conflicts are those in which one private individual, who does not represent a church or the state, says to another, "I would prefer not to facilitate your marriage or relationship" by providing the reception hall or the cake or the flowers or any number of other things. The conflicts among private individuals are likely to be more common and pervasive than first order conflicts. Indeed, these refusals are likely to crop up not just in the marketplace, but in the workplace and nearly every other setting imaginable. It is easy to foresee an employer denying spousal leave or other benefits to a same-sex spouse/employee, citing religious or ethical objections;[206] or a hospital that will not extend spousal visiting privileges to legally married same-sex spouses or registered domestic partners. Massachusetts has already felt ripples through its adoption system, as have other countries.[207]

Although an exhaustive treatment of these second order conflicts is beyond the scope of this chapter, a few observations are in order. In one sense, these second order conflicts are easier to resolve, because neither party represents the church or the state, and the refusal does not bar access to a good guaranteed by the Constitution, marriage. In this sense, they parallel the disputes between private physicians who do not want to perform abortions, and private patients who want one. In the abortion context, states have variously chosen to give the physician unfettered discretion to refuse to participate in the procedure; or to require the physician to transfer the patient to another provider (and thus preventing the physician from hobbling the patient's ability to secure the abortion); or to require the physician to provide an abortion in an emergency or when medically indicated.

Legislatures will likely have to tease out on a case-by-case basis how the state will want to approach various refusals. With some predictable disputes, such as those over reception halls and bakeries, it is difficult to imagine dire consequences flowing from the refusal of a particular facility or bakery. But it is much easier to imagine hardships resulting from the denial of benefits that other married couples enjoy, such as hospital visitation. Even where hardships do not result, being turned away can inflict damage which should not be lightly dismissed—the harm to one's dignity. In this way, discrimination on the basis of sexual orientation inflicts the same harm as racial discrimination does. For some states, this precise concern for a person's dignity will anchor the state's policy choice. Many states, although not all, now bar discrimination on the basis of sexual orientation in public accommodations, as they do with race and other impermissible grounds.[208] While the parallels between racial discrimination and discrimination on the basis of sexual orientation should not be dismissed, it is not clear that the two are equivalent in this context. The religious and moral convictions that motivate objectors to refuse to facilitate same-sex marriage simply cannot be marshaled to justify racial discrimination.

In another sense, some second order conflicts are trickier to resolve because marital status is tied to the receipt of so many goods in our society. Indeed, marriage is the touchstone for receiving a host of government-provided or government-mandated benefits that married couples simply take for granted: receipt of family medical leave from certain large employers; benefits for spouses of civil service employees; special treatment under estate and gift tax laws; exemptions from loss-gain valuations for property transfers between spouses; the ability to file joint tax returns; evidentiary privileges; protection under state inheritance, community property, and deferred community property laws; standing to recover for loss of consortium; ability to hold property in a tenancy by the entirety; and other state-level benefits.[209] For these government-mandated goods, states may be constrained in the ability to grant the right to refuse, since those refusals would mean that one couple's marriage carries less value than another's—with the state's blessing.[210]

However, where a refusal concerns a matter not linked to government-mandated benefits flowing from marriage, policymakers are left with the straightforward, but thorny task of weighing two sets of interests: the dignitary interests of same-sex couples and the moral and religious convictions of potential objectors. In this enterprise, both parties cannot win. The ability of the baker to refuse to provide a cake irreducibly comes at the expense of the disappointed and inconvenienced couple; and the ability of the couple to demand a cake of the baker comes necessarily at the baker's expense. Perhaps the best we can hope for is to create statutorily a live-and-let-live solution, one that provides the ability to refuse based on religious or moral objections, but limits that refusal to instances where a significant hardship to the requesting parties will not occur.

Many will see this live-and-let-live approach as a lose-lose situation: religious adherents will receive little comfort from the fact that they only have to serve same-sex couples in *rare* circumstances. For these adherents, the duty *not* to facilitate is an absolute—it will be no less repugnant if they are compelled to facilitate same-sex relationships only when a significant hardship would otherwise result (although a hardship approach should reduce greatly the number of times when this would occur). Likewise, same-sex couples may take little comfort from the fact that others must serve them only when a hardship would result. States, of course, have two other choices: take the win-lose approach, and elevate the interests of one private party over the other; or do nothing. Of these, the worst result would be to do nothing given the looming tide of litigation.

The controversy over adoption services in Massachusetts provides a nice case study of the trouble with a win-lose approach. As a private adoption agency, Catholic Charities operates as a separate legal entity from the church, albeit one that is identified with the church. As a separate legal entity, Catholic Charities represents neither the church itself, nor the state, and so for this purpose its refusal is a second order conflict.[211] Arguably, a sensible approach would have been to carve out an exemption for Catholic Charities, allowing the agency to place children only with heterosexual, married couples. This solution would have had little practical cost to same-sex couples. Adoption placements by Catholic Charities comprised only 4 percent of the adoptions in the state.[212] Same-sex couples, therefore, had access to the services of other agencies handling the great bulk of the state's placements. Yet by failing to create an exemption, the state prodded Catholic Charities to cease providing adoption services altogether, forcing other agencies to absorb the placement of those children and likely lengthening the placement process.[213] A legislative accommodation would have permitted Catholic Charities to continue to perform the important work that it did do for more than 720 children over the span of two decades. In this win-lose situation, Catholic Charities lost, prospective adoptive parents lost, and so did many children in Massachusetts.[214] Sadly, an all-or-nothing stance led the Roman Catholic Church in parts of the United Kingdom to unwind their association with "three of its top adoption agencies." The Church could not comply with both its religious tenets and England's Sexual Orientation Regulations.[215]

IV. Conclusion

The decision in *Roe* did not force anyone to perform abortions. Despite this, the question of a duty to assist was revisited repeatedly in lawsuit after lawsuit. Even after the Church Amendment, private, nonprofit hospitals were forced to defend their choice not to make their facilities available for the performance of abortions. Although courts turned back a number of these claims, the history of litigation after *Roe* provides a convincing prediction about the trajectory that litigation after *Goodridge* and the *Marriage Cases* is beginning to take. States can deflect this litigation, as they have with abortion and other deeply divisive questions in healthcare, by deciding now whether issues of conscience matter.

CHAPTER FOUR

Same-Sex Marriage and the Coming Antidiscrimination Campaigns Against Religion

Douglas W. Kmiec

In recent proceedings before the United States Supreme Court,[1] law schools sought to keep military recruiters off campuses in retaliation for the military's "don't ask, don't tell" policy against overt homosexual identity or conduct. These law schools simultaneously sought to avoid being penalized pursuant to a federal spending condition for treating military and other potential employers unequally. The schools claimed that losing federal subsidies for refusing to give equal access to military recruiters would be an unconstitutional infringement of their rights of speech and association. The argument re-opened the debate on whether it was proper for the Court, some twenty-five years earlier, to deny the tax-exempt status of a religiously affiliated university that drew racial distinctions among its students as a matter of scriptural understanding.[2] As Justice Breyer asked during the referenced oral argument, if law schools could exclude "anti-gay" military recruiters without losing their federal subsidies, shouldn't Bob Jones University have had the "same right . . . because they disapprove of social mixing of the races" on religious grounds?[3] Mr. Rosenkranz, counsel for the law schools, argued that in *Bob Jones University v. United States* the government could demonstrate a compelling need to eradicate racial discrimination.[4] The proffered answer left some justices unconvinced. The government has other needs of "immense national importance," Justice Scalia said, referring to recruiting top candidates for the military.[5] Those other needs led to a unanimous judicial endorsement of the power of Congress to condition the receipt of federal subsidy on equal access for military recruiters notwithstanding the claim that doing so would threaten a school's freedom of association and speech.[6]

The above colloquy and result in the law school case frame a possible coming difficulty for churches that remain steadfast in their defense of traditional marriage. Were federal equal protection or substantive due process to be construed to require states to license same-sex marriage, those who have profound moral or religious objection to the social affirmation of homosexual conduct would be argued to be the outliers of civil society, and for that reason, to be ineligible for a tax exemption or other public benefit. The Court's unanimous confirmation of the power of Congress to condition the receipt of the federal benefits of law schools with which it disagreed—as a logical extension of its earlier ruling denying Bob Jones University a tax exemption for maintaining religious practices the Internal Revenue Service found to be contrary to public policy—is of specific interest to the present chapter.

It poses this question: were the social antipathy directed toward Bob Jones for its religiously inspired racial segregation to be newly aimed at the religious defenders of traditional marriage between a man and a woman, how conceivable is it that churches would be targeted for similar legal penalties and disadvantages? This is hardly a far-fetched inquiry, as apparently one of the main aspirations of the homosexual movement is retaliation against the defenders of traditional marriage. Professor Eugene Volokh, a noted libertarian scholar and advocate of same-sex marriage, writes:

> The gay rights movement has long involved three related goals. One has to do with liberty from government repression—freedom from sodomy prosecutions, from police harassment, and the like. A second has to do with equal treatment by the government: The movement to recognize same-sex marriages is the most prominent recent example. A third has to do with delegitimizing and legally punishing private behavior that discriminates against or condemns homosexuals.[7]

Other gay advocates put the matter more bluntly, describing their objective as wanting to "discredit[] and force[] to the margin"[8] religious practices that honor traditional marriage.

Whether racial discrimination and the differentiation of traditional and same-sex marriage are not analogous remains disputed.[9] Nevertheless, for the purpose of a thought experiment, this chapter assumes such analogy to have gained popular acceptance, and then asks the further question: what penalties may accrue to churches or related religious entities that adhere to religious doctrine that is unaccepting of same-sex marriage?

To be realistic, the "punishment" of a church or religious entity for not accepting or performing same-sex marriages would not occur in a single step.

The first step would be to make a successful political case for government to add sexual orientation to generally applicable nondiscrimination laws. That is being actively pursued in legal journals and legislative assemblies. Were that advocacy effort successful, it could then be argued that a religious organization that excludes gays or lesbians from its marital rites could be denied its tax exemption. The rub, of course, would be explaining why denying the exemption would not violate a religious organization's rights of organizational and expressive association, free exercise of religion, and free speech. Arguments dismissing these rights are being advanced in legal writing and they deserve to be taken seriously.[10] The Supreme Court has not addressed this issue directly, but it has sustained the denial of tax-exempt status to a charitable organization that engaged in lobbying activity.[11] Of course, refusing to publicly subsidize political lobbying is more viewpoint neutral than denying a tax exemption to a church whose theology is claimed to be substantively at odds with public policy.

That said, it should not be thought that a religious organization would have significant *constitutional* protection under the Free Exercise Clause. Under the Court's jurisprudence, religious organizations would have no greater constitutional ability to draw sexual orientation distinctions than any other entity, provided the government's nondiscrimination requirement was applicable to all nonprofit organizations and did not single out religion generally for disadvantage or a particular religion for disfavor. This is the teaching of *Employment Division v. Smith*,[12] which leveled the "free exercise" of religion by making it subordinate to any governmental objective so long as it was nominally rational and evenhanded. Professor Volokh raised the possibility of unconstitutional IRS entanglement in monitoring the discriminatory practices of religious organizations, but he and others believe this Establishment Clause concern can be met by giving exemption to a "church," narrowly defined, so that say, Catholic churches would not be obligated to hire gay clergy.[13] By this reasoning, however, there would be no need to supply constitutional exemption to religious schools, social services, or other "auxiliaries" for their hiring decisions.

As a *statutory* matter, the federal Religious Freedom Restoration Act (RFRA)[14] should require the *federal* government to justify any withdrawal of a federal tax exemption that substantially burdens religious belief or practice. The justification would need to survive strict scrutiny and be the least restrictive means of advancing the government's nondiscrimination objective. It is not clear that this standard could be met under the Court's present jurisprudence. Some states have enacted similar RFRA-like protections, which would also block the imposition of a *statutory* sexual orientation nondiscrimination requirement.[15]

So what does this mean for our thought experiment—can the government punish churches or other religious bodies that refuse to accept or perform same-sex marriage or not? The answer varies widely by jurisdiction and is multi-faceted and the subject of much guesswork. As more fully discussed in the balance of this chapter, if the punishment consists of a denial of state tax-exempt status, the answer in a state like California is "almost certainly, yes." If however, unlike California, the state has a statutory RFRA-like protection of religious exercise, and sexual orientation has not been found to be a protected classification equivalent to race under the state constitution, the answer is "more than likely, no." If the state protects against sexual orientation discrimination by statue, rather than by state judicial construction of the state constitution, and the state has statutory protections of religious freedom as well, the answer is, "it's anyone's guess," since we have no univocal jurisprudence determining what happens when two statutory rights collide. Indeed, everything from the precise wording of the competing statutes to their chronology of enactment would need to be assessed.

If the question is asked with reference to the practically and economically important federal tax exemption, and the punishment would be applicable to any nonprofit that differentiates on the basis of sexual orientation, the answer is "plausibly yes." The plausibility of the federal conclusion increases greatly if lower court federal precedent begins to mimic the California prohibition against sexual orientation discrimination in marriage, and the game would be over with a United States Supreme Court determination to that effect. Any conclusion wherein the prohibition of sexual orientation discrimination trumps religious freedom cannot be assumed, and it should not be seen as easily achieved. Despite the writings of Professors Volokh and Nicholas Mirkay that reach or advocate this result, present law is still some distance (albeit shortening) from this conclusion.

However, the formal argumentation here may mean less than public consensus. The drive for same-sex marriage had appeared stalled until the California ruling. Massachusetts was the lone state to require it, and based upon a requirement of reciprocity, it did not make Massachusetts's same-sex license available to non-residents. Moreover, multiple states have rejected same-sex marriage within their own states by constitutional referendum. Yet, political tides may be shifting.

Now, California has kicked the door marked "inter-state implications" wide-open. Unless California voters amend the state constitution by ballot initiative to overturn the judgment of the California Supreme Court, state residents and non-residents will continue to have unfettered access to California same-sex marriage licenses, which, as people migrate or return home, will put political and litigation-induced pressure on sister states to accept them.

National political tides may be shifting as well. While the presumptive Democratic and leading presidential nominee, Barack Obama, opposes same-sex marriage (favoring instead civil unions), he also has called for repeal of the federal Defense of Marriage Act as an unwarranted congressional interference with state sovereignty. He almost assuredly would see sexual orientation as a classification worthy of heightened protection, and would be likely to seek the repeal of the "don't ask, don't tell" sexual orientation limitations that apply to the military.[16]

In light of these developments, the number of steps before it would be seen to be publicly acceptable to punish outlier churches or religious bodies might well be fewer in number than first anticipated when a draft of this chapter was discussed at an important conference of the Becket Fund for Religious Liberty in 2005 in Washington, D.C.[17] Nonetheless, putting political speculation aside, let us turn in the balance of this chapter to the detail of the argumentation in as objective a fashion as possible.

I. Loss of Federal Tax Exemption?

Section 501 of the Internal Revenue Code (IRC)[18] provides an organization an exemption from federal income taxation, provided that organization meets several criteria.[19] Qualifying organizations must be "organized and operated exclusively for religious, charitable, scientific, testing for public safety, literary, or educational purposes, or to foster national or international amateur sports competition, . . . or for the prevention of cruelty to children or animals . . . ."[20] Beyond this, net earnings may not accrue "to the benefit of any private shareholder or individual,"[21] and the entity may not be engaged in political campaigns or substantial lobbying. Parallel provisions in Section 170 of the IRC permit taxpayers to deduct contributions to a qualifying organization.[22]

Bob Jones,[23] however, stands for the proposition that the statute is only part of the story. After all, Bob Jones University was unquestionably an educational institution organized on a nonprofit basis. This was insufficient, reasoned the Court, since "underlying all relevant parts of the Code, is the intent that entitlement to tax exemption depends on meeting certain common law standards of charity—namely, that an institution seeking tax-exempt status must serve a public purpose and not be contrary to established public policy."[24] The Court discerned that "Congress' intention was to provide tax benefits to organizations serving charitable purposes,"[25] and the meaning of charity was then derived from common law trust doctrine. The trust doctrine would acknowledge the "public benefit" of education, but this doctrine, according to the Court, also contained within it the proposition that no trust or charity can be formed to advance an illegal purpose.[26] This implied qualification was thought to be especially important in order to keep the government from indirectly supplying assistance to antisocial hateful groups like schools for training terrorists.[27]

The implied corollary was broadened further, such that exemption would be denied if "there [is any] doubt that the activity involved is contrary to a fundamental public policy."[28] As already noted, the focal point of public policy in *Bob Jones* was the elimination of racial discrimination in education. It was relatively easy for the Court to locate this fundamental policy goal in precedent such as *Brown v. Board of Education*,[29] the legislative enactment of the Civil Rights Act of 1964, and "numerous Executive Orders."[30]

The Court noted that Bob Jones defended its racial distinctions on what the University claimed was "a genuine belief that the Bible forbids interracial dating and marriage."[31] Recurring to the belief-conduct distinction, however, the Court found that practice unprotected by the Free Exercise Clause. Relatedly, the Court viewed the governmental interest in racial neutrality to be "compelling" and "substantially outweigh[ing] whatever burden denial of tax benefits places on [Bob Jones's] exercise of [its] religious beliefs."[32] Finally, the Court rebuffed an Establishment Clause argument that through its selective exemption decision the government was favoring one religion over another. Not so, said the Court; "a regulation does not violate the Establishment Clause merely because it 'happens to coincide or harmonize with the tenets of some or all religions.'"[33] Having a singular rule against racial discrimination kept the government from becoming entangled in assessing claims that particular discriminatory practices were genuinely religious. Thereafter, the task of determining whether an organization's activities violate such a public policy would rest squarely with the IRS, as part of its responsibility for making the initial determination of whether the organization is charitable.[34] The Court upheld the IRS's determination that Bob Jones University violated the federal policy against racial discrimination in education and thus did not provide a public benefit justifying its tax exemption as a charity.[35]

II. *Bob Jones* Is Not a Direct Precedent for Denying a Tax Exemption to Churches That Refuse to Perform Same-Sex Marriages

Professor Robin Wilson, in a thoughtful chapter, notes that the IRS has taken the position in a private letter ruling that while the decision in *Bob*

Jones related only to race discrimination in education, "the implication of the *Bob Jones* decision extends to any organization claiming exempt status under Section 501(c)(3) and to any activity violating a clear public policy."[36] As a general matter, letter rulings are no longer entitled to *Chevron*[37] deference; rather, under the decision in *United States v. Mead Corporation*,[38] these more informal interpretative directives will be accorded deference by a reviewing court only if they draw on the agency's specialized expertise and are well-reasoned. In the tax area, however, letter rulings and temporary regulations are sometimes given full *Chevron* deference normally reserved for formal rules issued after notice and comment rulemaking, on the theory that IRS letter rulings represent the studied and unified policy of the Department of the Treasury.[39] As noted immediately below, there have been very few true extensions of the *Bob Jones* public policy limitation outside the racial discrimination context by either regulatory means.[40]

Before *Bob Jones*, for example, the IRS denied exempt status on public policy grounds to organizations believed to be violent.[41] After *Bob Jones*, the IRS took a dim view of granting an exemption on public policy grounds to the Church of Scientology, which it found to be "imped[ing] the IRS in performing its duty to determine and collect taxes from petitioner and other Scientology churches."[42] The activities alleged were egregious, including "fil[ing] false tax returns, burglariz[ing] IRS offices, st[ealing] IRS documents, and harass[ing], delay[ing], and obstruct[ing] IRS agents who tried to audit the Church's records."[43]

Bob Jones has been administratively extended to include racial discrimination in any 501(c)(3) context, not just education. For example, exemption was denied to a trust maintained for impoverished white citizens of a particular city.[44] Discrimination on the basis of race was stated to be a violation of a "public policy so fundamental as to justify denial of charitable status to any organization otherwise described in section 501(c)(3)."[45] But the IRS has refused explicitly to push *Bob Jones* beyond the topic of race.[46] For example, when a support program for teaching the literature and history of the Bible was challenged as an impermissible establishment of religion, the IRS determined that, based on precedent, the objection was without merit, and cautioned against finding *Bob Jones* like violations of public policy premised on other individual rights.[47] Somewhat confusingly, the IRS also noted that it could "think of no more fundamental federal public policy than the Bill of Rights."[48]

Extension of the *Bob Jones* principle to same-sex marriage should not be assumed. First, the Court's description in *Bob Jones* of the "consistent" efforts to eliminate racial discrimination—even by military force[49]—has no counterpart with same-sex marriage. Second, the Court found *Bob Jones* to lack all public benefit insofar as it was in violation of "fundamental" public policy. The Court expressly left open "whether an organization providing a public benefit and otherwise meeting the requirements of Section 501(c)(3) could nevertheless be denied tax-exempt status if certain of its activities violated a law or public policy."[50] Applying this framework, the positive social good of a church should not be wholly disregarded. Third, the *Bob Jones* court emphasized that a "sensitive determination [of whether particular activities are 'charitable'] should be made only where there is *no doubt* that the organization's activities violate fundamental public policy."[51]

Bob Jones found a common law public policy against racial discrimination in education. There is no comparable common law base supporting same-sex marriage. The absence of common law support for same-sex marriage can be discerned in *Lawrence v. Texas*.[52] *Lawrence* may have overruled *Bowers v. Hardwick*,[53] but that overruling could not revise the common law, which, even the *Lawrence* majority had to concede, did not affirmatively protect homosexual sodomy, at least as that conduct was a subset of nonprocreative sexual activity that was generally prohibited. The *Lawrence* majority simply chose not to be bound either by common law or democratic definition of immorality. As such, *Lawrence* is a precedent built solely upon judicial will—or in Justice Kennedy's words, the Court's "obligation . . . to define the liberty of all . . . ."[54] This is a troubling exercise of judicial hubris. Nevertheless, by its own terms, the right of intimacy discovered in *Lawrence* does not have a common-law lineage, and it has nothing to do with public policy derived from the "common law standards of charity." For this reason alone, *Bob Jones* in light of *Lawrence* is not fairly seen as a precedent relevant to tax-exempt status and same-sex marriage.

The most recent IRS thinking is to confine *Bob Jones* to its racial context. In finding no basis to revoke an exemption on public policy grounds for an over accumulation of income,[55] the IRS commented that "[c]urrently the sole basis for revocation of exemption on public policy grounds is engaging in racial discrimination."[56] Were it otherwise, Professor Wilson nicely illustrates the range of difficult questions that would demand answers by an unthinking expansion of the *Bob Jones* ruling, including most basically: what defines the contours of public policy; what makes a public policy fundamental; and how many acts would demonstrate a disregard of public policy?

Professor Wilson nevertheless writes that "[c]hurches and religious organizations that oppose same-sex marriage perceive a credible, palpable threat [of loss of tax exemption]."[57] "Threat" is an appropriate word to capture the ideological goal of the gay and lesbian community to delegitimize or marginalize those who adhere to a religiously based, traditional concept of marriage. The invalidation of a state law that had criminalized homosexual sodomy in *Lawrence v. Texas*,[58] or the Massachusetts decision in *Goodridge v. Department of Public Health*,[59] or the consolidated California cases finding a state-constitutional requirement of same-sex marriage,[60] cannot be taken lightly. Yet these form an insufficient foundation upon which to claim a fundamental public policy basis for exemption denial under *Bob Jones*. States overwhelmingly prohibit same-sex marriage,[61] with many recent reaffirmations of marriage being between a man and a woman.[62] Beyond that, the federal Defense of Marriage Act absolves states from recognizing same-sex marriages under another state's law.[63] In addition, the United States Supreme Court held in *Boy Scouts of America v. Dale* that a scout troop could exclude an openly gay scoutmaster on the grounds that, as a private entity, the scouts' right of association trumped a state public accommodations law prohibiting such discrimination.[64]

III. Tax Exemptions Are Not Subsidies

One possible strategy for churches seeking to differentiate *Bob Jones* is to advocate a return to an earlier understanding of tax exemption that is both an aspect of tax theory, and an important limit upon government control in constitutional jurisprudence. Quite simply, tax exemptions are not subsidies. As a matter of tax policy, an exemption is a recognition that nonprofit organizations, like churches, do not realize taxable income. Moreover, to liken an exemption to a subsidy makes it too easy to confuse the two in constitutional jurisprudence, as Justice Brennan's concurring opinion observed in *Walz v. Tax Commissioner*.[65] There Justice Brennan noted that an exemption is less support than the simple abstention "from demanding that the [entity] support the state."[66] Exemptions and subsidies are "qualitatively different."[67]

Confusion between exemption and subsidy brings with it the unwarranted consequence of associating spending conditions with government control.[68] In *Rumsfeld v. Forum for Academic and Institutional Rights (FAIR)*, the Supreme Court held that Congress may require a law school that accepts federal money to observe a federal spending condition requiring equal access for military recruiters.[69] While Justice Breyer, judging by his comments during oral argument, appeared to believe that this flows directly from the holding in *Bob Jones*, as a matter of tax theory, it does not. The law schools in *FAIR* are bound by a condition on a direct cash subsidy—and it should not be surprising that the government gets to decide how to spend its own resources.[70] There was no

similar expenditure of resources in *Bob Jones*; there was only a tax policy decision that the income benefit imputed to the beneficiaries of the services of
a nonprofit university was simply too diffuse to administratively and effi-
ciently capture.[71] As Professor Bittker writes:

> [t]he federal income tax of current law, then, "exempts" nonprofit groups; and
> this quite naturally leads, on a quick glance, to the conclusion that they have
> been granted the "privilege" of "immunity." Once this characterization is ac-
> cepted, it is only a short step to such pejoratives as "loophole," "preference,"
> and "subsidy." Unless blinded by labels, however, one can view the federal in-
> come tax instead as a tax on income that inures in measurable amounts to the
> direct or indirect personal benefit of identifiable natural persons. So viewed,
> the Internal Revenue Code's "exemption" of nonprofit organizations is simply
> a way of recognizing the inapplicability to them of a concept that is central to
> the tax itself.[72]

Viewed in this manner, a tax exemption of a nonprofit organization is not
the equivalent of a subsidy that, under existing spending power doctrine, can
support a control condition. Professor Jonathan Turley nicely elaborates why
tax exemptions and subsidies should be treated differently in terms of free
speech theory, noting that with a tax exemption "the ultimate choice of
speech and association is left to individual citizens. The government should
not 'put a thumb on the scale' to make it relatively more difficult for these
organizations to survive than those organizations that conform to popular
views."[73] Professor Turley's observation thus echoes a point made by Justice
Powell in his concurring opinion in *Bob Jones* itself. Justice Powell noted
that, apart from race, Section 501(c)(3) should not be interpreted in a fashion that "ignores the important role played by tax exemptions in encourag-
ing diverse, indeed often sharply conflicting, activities and viewpoints."[74]
Powell thus recognized that, unlike a subsidy, "the provision of tax exemptions to nonprofit groups is one indispensable means of limiting the influence
of governmental orthodoxy on important areas of community life."[75]

Assuming, however, that the Court is no longer capable of differentiating
a subsidy from an exemption, the very language used to justify the nondiscrimination or control condition on the tax exemption in *Bob Jones* simply
does not transfer to the same-sex marriage context. First, the Court in *Bob
Jones* sought to maintain the imperfect analogy between subsidy and exemption in order to exclude "Fagin's school for educating English boys in the art
of picking pockets," or closer to the present era, "a school for intensive training of subversives for guerrilla warfare and terrorism . . . ."[76] The public policy limitation was a fail-safe mechanism to avoid underwriting extremism, or

at least, those social institutions which "violate deeply and widely accepted views of elementary justice."[77] In a civilized society, such a fail-safe mechanism is inapposite to entities like churches[78] which, the debate over same-sex marriage aside, are generally conceded to have an unquestioned role of positive good.[79]

IV. The "Public Benefit" Conferred by Churches to Merit Tax Exemption Does Not Make Churches into State Actors

The common law justification for tax exemptions specified in *Bob Jones* was "that the exempt entity confers a public benefit—a benefit which . . . supplements . . . the work of public institutions already supported by tax revenues."[80] By its own terms, a church officiating at traditional, but not same-sex, marriage supplies a public benefit. Yes, the public registry—rather than a church—will have to fulfill any demand for same-sex process, but any continued officiating at traditional marriages still supplements and is to the public benefit.

While supplying a public benefit through the partial performance of a public function is yet another reason to find the church's tax exemption to be somewhat resistant against a *Bob Jones* attack, it may raise a more profound difficulty. In particular, does officiating at marriage ceremonies, in lieu of the state, mean that the church has been delegated a public function[81] in such a way as to now be subject to the more stringent application of constitutional precepts applicable to a state actor? In all states, religious personnel are given authority to "solemnize" a marriage, provided they do so within the parameters of civilly issued licenses.[82] Determining when religious solemnization falls within acceptable civil regulation, however, can result in awkward interplay between church and state. Consider, for example, the question put to the California Attorney General of whether a resigned priest may satisfy the state solemnization requirement. After surveying a good deal of theological information, albeit duly noting that it was not the role of the Attorney General to take sides in internal religious matters, the state's chief law enforcement officer reached this conclusion:

> Thus, in order to fall within the category of "priest" under [state law], one must be authorized by his denomination to solemnize marriage, and act within the scope of that authority in the solemnization of marriage; i.e., the authority of an individual other than a judge or commissioner to solemnize marriage depends upon the duly constituted authorization by the religious denomination of such person, whether or not ordained, to act *in that capacity*. An individual who is not duly authorized by his religious denomination to solemnize marriage, such as a person who, by virtue of resignation, is not authorized to engage in active

ministry, does not satisfy the criteria of [state law]. It may be noted in this regard that [state law] makes no reference, as in the case of a judge, to a resigned
or retired priest, minister, or rabbi.

It is concluded accordingly that a priest who has resigned from active ministry within the official Roman Catholic structure, who is recognized by the
church as a priest but is not allowed by the church to perform marriages without a bishop's authorization, may solemnize marriages under [state law] only as
authorized by the bishop.[83]

Likewise, numerous judicial decisions have opined on the sufficiency or
insufficiency of particular religious credentials to solemnize a marriage.[84]
These church-state interactions are of some relevance in determining
whether a church is a "state actor" under either the United States Supreme
Court's public function or entwinement tests. These tests inquire as to the
joint participation and private involvement in state activity. A classic case
involved the lease of parking space by a discriminatory private restaurant,
which facilitated the retirement of public debt obligations. The Court
found a sufficient "symbiotic relationship" to attribute the racial discrimination of the private entity to the state.[85] So, too, the Court found the selection of a jury by private civil counsel to be the equivalent of a state personnel selection exercise.[86] In deciding this type of public function
delegation case, Justice Kennedy elaborated several factors that might be
argued to make the church a state actor in its solemnization function. For
example, Kennedy highlighted the extent to which the private actor is performing a traditional governmental function and employing the incidents
of government authority.

Mitigating against a finding of a delegation of public function, however,
would be the fact that marital licensing could hardly be said to be now, or
historically, the exclusive province of the state, a factor that, if absent, has
influenced the Court not to find state action.[87] Exclusivity is important in
public delegation analysis since it is far easier to justify imposing stringent
constitutional requirements where the state empowers a private entity and
then leaves no choice but to patronize it.[88] This, however, is not the modern
circumstance of the church. Even as church officials may solemnize a marriage, they hardly have a monopoly on this function. Moreover, as a historical matter, public involvement with marriage is relatively modern, and this
fact cuts as well against finding even the existence of a public function.[89] In
the middle ages, marriage was a private contract between families. In America, well into the nineteen century, marriage was recognized as a contract
valid under common law until superseded by statute.[90] Indeed, common law
marriage—whereby a couple consent to live together and hold themselves

out as husband and wife—remains possible in a dozen states, even as the practice has been abolished in many other states.

The alternative entwinement test seems even less applicable. This standard was first announced in *Brentwood Academy v. Tennessee Secondary School Athletic Association*, where the Court found a private athletic regulatory body to be so dominated by public officials in its inner workings that fairness demanded the observance of constitutional limitations.[91] The state action inquiry, said the Supreme Court, was fact-bound and could be outweighed by a "countervailing reason against attributing activity to the government."[92] In *Brentwood*, the association was populated largely (84 percent) by public institutions, state officers were *ex officio* members of its board, and the employees of the association were participants in the state retirement system. None of these facts are truly present vis-à-vis solemnization, other than the already noted evaluation by public legal officials of legitimate or "approved" religious actors. Such approval determinations may press the free exercise boundary, but they also supply a "countervailing reason"—keeping church and state separate—for the judiciary to be highly reluctant to find the church to be a state actor. The notion that churches are state actors, merely because their ceremonies are accepted in lieu of a civil one, is an insufficient symbiotic relationship/public delegation or entwinement to satisfy existing Court precedent that defines the outer boundary of state action.

More plausible is not that the church is a state actor in its marriage solemnization function, but that following constitutional approval of same-sex marriage—the hypothetical thought experiment assumed here for purposes of analysis—the state, itself, will be argued to be precluded, as a matter of equal protection, from assigning any part of the licensing to a discriminatory private actor that subscribes only to traditional marriage. This claim would likely be premised upon *Norwood v. Harrison*,[93] which held that the Equal Protection Clause prohibited the government from providing textbooks to private schools that engaged in racial discrimination. But *Norwood* is an oft-cited, yet seldom applied precedent. There are no cases applying the holding of *Norwood* to organizations that discriminate on the basis of religion. Indeed, the *Norwood* Court distinguished the case before it from others in which the government extended aid to religious schools because, unlike discrimination on the basis of race to which the Constitution ascribes no value, discrimination on the basis of religion may stem from the constitutionally protected right to free exercise. The Court specifically noted that "the Constitution . . . places no value on [racial] discrimination as it does on the values inherent in the Free Exercise Clause."[94] An Equal Protection claim against government support of the Salvation Army was rejected by the federal trial court in New York for just this reason.[95]

Of course, any state government approving of same-sex marriage may decide on its own to withdraw the authority of the church to solemnize marriage for civil law purposes. Government may structure its own programs, even as it may not punish a private speaker for the exercise of constitutional rights.[96] It is not always easy to differentiate these cases, a matter that gets murkier when a tax exemption is wrongly characterized as a subsidy. As already discussed, government may not condition the continuation of *federal* tax exemption on the church's discontinuation of its support for traditional marriage. A *state* tax exemption may be different.[97]

V. Jurisdiction Over the Church?

There is a general "ministerial exemption" under the First Amendment, which, on occasion, precludes civil courts from inquiring into disputes or application of religious doctrine. Arguably, a lawsuit seeking to compel some manifestation of church acceptance of same-sex marriage might fall within this exemption. As the Supreme Court has noted,

> civil courts are bound to accept the decisions of the highest judicatories of a religious organization of hierarchical polity on matters of discipline, faith, internal organization, or ecclesiastical rule, custom, or law. For civil courts to analyze whether the ecclesiastical actions of a church judicatory are in that sense "arbitrary" must inherently entail inquiry into the procedures that canon or ecclesiastical law supposedly requires the church judicatory to follow, or else into the substantive criteria by which they are supposedly to decide the ecclesiastical question. But this is exactly the inquiry that the First Amendment prohibits . . . .[98]

In *Rockwell v. Roman Catholic Archdiocese of Boston*,[99] a federal district court referenced and applied the ministerial exemption in a gender discrimination challenge to the all-male priesthood. Priestly selection and retention is based on faithful observance of religious teaching, and thus, is outside the purview of nondiscrimination laws. This is true even if such laws are deemed neutral and generally applicable in accordance with *Employment Division v. Smith*.[100] Several appellate decisions confirm that the ministerial exemption survives *Smith*,[101] and *Rockwell* followed this reasoning, finding the gender complaint to fail to state a claim. The court in *Rockwell* also found the woman's challenge to the tax-exempt status of the church to be without standing. The court reasoned that the woman could show no factual nexus between the tax-exempt status and church teaching that makes women priests impossible in Roman Catholicism. Relatedly, the court observed that redressability was also absent. Just as revoking a tax-exempt status could not modify church doctrine regarding ordination, it can be reasonably argued that it could not alter (and thereby redress) the church's fidelity to marriage solely between a man and a woman.

While the standing objection to an individual suit seeking the revocation of a church tax exemption is premised upon well-settled Supreme Court precedent,[102] not too much comfort should be drawn from either a defense premised on standing or the ministerial exemption. The latter is often limited to employment questions. For example, in a case upholding a subpoena in a criminal prosecution of clergy sex abuse, a California appellate court reasoned that "the ministerial [exemption] doctrine is based on the notion a church's appointment of its clergy, along with such closely related issues as clerical salaries, assignments, working conditions and termination of employment, is an inherently religious function because clergy are such an integral part of a church's functioning as a religious institution."[103] Finding the matter to be "not an employment case," the court held the ministerial exemption doctrine to have no application and enforced the process against the church. While it is possible to argue that a nondiscrimination law or judicial decision favoring same-sex marriage raises a middle question, insofar as it implicates the sacramental or liturgical practices of the church, the prospect of a court readily accepting the analogy to the ministerial exemption seems too close to call.

VI. Learning from the Boy Scouts: Undermining the Church's Tax Exemption from Below

The Boy Scouts of America (BSA) maintain a policy comparable to church teaching in opposition to homosexual conduct, and by implication, same-sex marriage. For reasons coinciding with the analysis made in this chapter, gay-rights advocates have conceded that it would be futile or unrealistic to anticipate removal of the BSA's *federal* tax exemption.[104] In addition, the BSA is conceded not to be a state actor since "the courts have yet to accept the argument that tax exemption rises to the threshold level of 'state action.'"[105] Moreover, *Bob Jones* is inapposite insofar as sexual orientation, unlike race, is not a suspect class. Notwithstanding these points that support the freedom of both the BSA and the church, gay-rights advocates argue that state law will prove to be friendlier to a lawsuit challenging a state or local tax exemption. State standing doctrines, for example, are often premised simply upon ownership of property and the contention that an exemption contrary to public policy raises an objecting owner's tax. Such generalized taxpayer standing is not available in federal court.[106]

Once in state court, pursuant to relaxed state-level standing, a complainant would likely point to state law protecting against discrimination on the basis of sexual orientation. As this is written, sexual orientation is not a protected category under federal civil rights laws, though there have been several attempts to add it. This more expansive state nondiscrimination provision would then be argued to be a compelling justification equivalent to that recognized in *Bob Jones* and sufficient to overcome BSA's defenses of free speech and association. We know, of course, that the United States Supreme Court has protected the BSA's speech and associational rights from direct state mandate under a public accommodation law to include active homosexuals in its leadership ranks.[107] But to date, there is no high court precedent securing those same speech and associational rights from the burden of tax exemption loss. Recognizing this, homosexual advocates have launched a retaliatory strike from below against the BSA—successfully precluding it from various local public resources, such as parks and marinas.[108] The next step, say gay-rights activists, is removal of BSA's state-level tax exemption.

VII. Retaliation from Below as an Unconstitutional Condition: The Denial of Viewpoint Neutrality

The church obviously enjoys comparable rights of speech and association to that of the BSA, as well as the added constitutional protection of free exercise. But as with the scouts, same-sex marriage proponents could seek to make the exercise of these rights subject to retaliatory penalty at the local level. Arguably, revoking a state or local tax exemption in response to the constitutional exercise of speech, association, and (in the church's case) religion, amounts to an unconstitutional condition. Government may not condition government benefits on the relinquishment of constitutional rights. Government may prohibit speech or associational rights only where it has a viewpoint-neutral basis for doing so—as, for example, in the evenhanded preclusion of political activity by all nonprofit organizations[109]—or in pursuit of a compelling interest.

Unfortunately, this textbook legal doctrine has not always been observed, and the BSA has already suffered an inscrutable and questionable loss in a federal circuit court,[110] which should have prompted the assistance of the church community, and should certainly merit its attention now. Specifically, the United States Court of Appeals for the Second Circuit asserted that a nondiscrimination law covering sexual orientation does not suppress viewpoint, but rather merely avoids "immediate harms" such as economic discrimination. Aside from its *non sequitur* quality, the court's reasoning seems to amount to the proposition that the government can suppress the BSA (or a church) from maintaining the view that same-sex marriage is doctrinally impossible because otherwise there would be "harm" from not obtaining a same-sex marriage. This tautological logic cannot be squared with existing constitutional principle. It is intended to fit the government's suppression of viewpoint into the legal rubric that posits that "nonverbal expressive activity can be banned because of the action it entails."[111] But this rubric is ill-fitting, as all it means is that government must have a viewpoint-neutral justification to ban what could be, but is not always, expressive or symbolic conduct. Flag-burning, after all, can be banned for fire risk, though not because it gives political offense. When the government's only plausible justification for denying the BSA access to a charitable campaign (or a church a local tax exemption) is to prevent the expression of the idea that homosexual conduct is immoral, or that marriage can only exist between a man and a woman, a viewpoint-neutral justification is constitutionally wanting. Penalizing churches for adhering to religious teaching supporting traditional, but not same-sex, marriage is either facially viewpoint-based or, at a minimum, premised upon viewpoint in application.

Nor does the case law supporting the unique suppression of abortion protest allow local tax exemption retaliation against the church. The abortion protest injunction cases have permitted the imposition of an injunction only where it was *not* directed at the protesting message.[112] Revoking the church's local tax exemption for unwillingness to preside at or otherwise affirm same-sex marriages is unquestionably directed at making the church pay a price for fidelity to religious principle. Moreover, it cannot be excused by the abstract suggestion that it is directed not at content or viewpoint, but a psychological injury akin to sexual harassment or hateful, race-based conduct.

Revoking a local tax exemption for maintaining the traditional view against same-sex marriage should be unconstitutional, absent compelling justification. At present, since sexual orientation is not (yet) a *federal* suspect classification and same-sex marriage is not a fundamental liberty (even as *Lawrence* has found substantive protection against interference with homosexual intimacy in a home), there is no compelling justification for abridging speech, associational, and religious freedom rights. However, push *Lawrence* to support same-sex marriage as a fundamental right, and the church is then in a similar position to the BSA, seeking to defend one fundamental liberty (religious exercise) against another (same-sex marriage). The church may be more inclusive of homosexuals than the BSA, provided there is adequate assurance of chastity,[113] but the church can ill-afford to let the BSA fight its membership battles alone. The effort to deprive the BSA of state and local tax exemption gives momentum to ill-conceived, but often very costly, private retaliation, such as BSA's exclusion from local United Way chapters.[114] The same fate awaits the church.

Overall, the denial of state or local tax exemption strategy is premised upon compounding its initially smaller impact into a larger, and ultimately, federal one. As one proponent of this strategy commented:

> The effect of revoking state-level tax-exempt status is potentially exponential. As the other states that prohibit sexual orientation discrimination follow . . . sending a similar message of disapproval, corporate donation . . . will grow even less attractive. In the best case scenario, the IRS could use a multi-state revocation of state-level tax-exempt status as the basis for a Revenue Ruling denying federal § 501(c)(3) tax-exempt status and § 170 donor deductibility to [the church]. . . . At that point, [the church] could still theoretically maintain its [policy against same-sex marriage]; however, such a stance would be fiscal suicide.[115]

Employment Division v. Smith[116] will make more difficult any Free Exercise limitation upon governmental retaliatory acts, whether at the federal or local levels. Establishment Clause jurisprudence, however, might permit the church to argue against the government's establishing a minimum floor or minimally acceptable public theology in order to qualify for tax exemption or a public benefit. To deny a tax exemption because a church refuses to sanction same-sex marriage is to prescribe under force of law a qualifying theology. While this results in preferring some religions over others, it also gives rise to a claim of discrimination or religious preference that may answer *Smith* itself.

VIII. Why Religious Freedom Should Prevail over an Assertion of Legal Equivalence Between Traditional and Same-Sex Marriage

First, any right to same-sex marriage assumes that which remains deeply disputed—namely, seeing same-sex and traditional marriage as the same. The claimed equivalence mistakes equal protection of the law for a guarantee of undifferentiated equality. Like cases—not unlike ones—are to be treated alike. Nothing in equal protection history or original understanding suggests an identity between same-sex and traditional marriage.

Second, it is illogical to impose a penalty for unwillingness to perform a same-sex marriage (*e.g.*, denial of licensure or solemnization authority, denial of tax exemption, civil fines) where those seeking the performance of such service have ready secular alternatives (*e.g.*, a judge, city clerk, or local justice of the peace).

Third, and relatedly, those who join a church do so with implied consent to the church government. As Douglas Laycock has written, so long as there is no question about the voluntariness of consent, there is little justification for interference with internal church affairs.[117]

Fourth, the limited nature of the *Bob Jones* ruling suggests that outside racial discrimination, and predominantly in the education context (where unconsenting students may be present), "[m]atters belonging to the spiritual core, or epicenter, such as church membership or employment of clergy, are insulated from state regulatory processes."[118] Ultimately, in contemplating how to reconcile new antidiscrimination claims premised upon sexual orientation and a deeply embedded civil liberty such as religious freedom, it is appropriate to recall the intrinsic importance of freedom of religion as put by Madison:

> It is the duty of every man to render to the Creator such homage and such only as he believes to be acceptable to him. This duty is precedent, both in order of time and in degree of obligation, to the claims of Civil Society. . . . We maintain therefore that in matters of Religion, no man's right is abridged by the institution of Civil Society and that Religion is wholly exempt from its cognizance.[119]

To render "such homage" as only a particular citizen believes "acceptable," there must be freedom to choose a religious community that reflects that choice. Nondiscrimination laws limit choice, and it has been the practice of American law only to limit freedom of choice in extraordinary circumstances,[120] for example, when necessary to place off-limits morally irrelevant considerations like race. To use the coercive power of government to impose same-sex marriage by means of loss of tax exemption or public benefit is quite simply a legally and morally dubious denial of freedom.[121]

CHAPTER FIVE

Moral Conflict
and Conflicting Liberties
Chai R. Feldblum[1]

Imagine that you and your same-sex male partner got married last year in Massachusetts and are now planning a delayed honeymoon in Tennessee. You search the Web and find a lovely guesthouse in your price range. Nothing about the guesthouse's description on the website makes you think you will not be welcome there. You make reservations through the website.

The two of you arrive at the guesthouse, sporting your wedding rings and calling each other "honey." The owner of the guesthouse asks if you are gay. You answer that you are and explain that this is your delayed honeymoon. The owner is very gracious and courteous, but explains that you cannot stay in his guesthouse unless you agree to sleep in separate rooms and also agree not to engage in any sexual activity during your stay. He explains that his religion requires that he "love the sinner, but hate the sin." For this reason, you are welcome to stay at his guesthouse, but only if you do not use his facilities to carry out sinful activities.

The owner also gives you a list of guesthouses in town that do allow gay couples to stay in the same room. And, he quickly assures you, he has checked and there is no law that prohibits him from treating you in this way.

Let us assume all the other guesthouses are full and you decide to stay at the original guesthouse and abide by the owner's rules. No one can claim that the guesthouse's rules have prohibited you from "being gay." Your identity as a gay person has not disappeared simply because you have been precluded from having sex with your partner during the weekend. But, presumably, you have experienced some dignitary harm. And, indeed, your identity as a gay person would have little real meaning if you were *consistently* precluded from having sex with your same-sex partner. This identity—or "identity liberty," as I describe it below—is necessarily curtailed by the *absence* of a law prohibiting public accommodations from discriminating against gay people.

Now imagine that you and your opposite-sex wife have decided to open a Christian bed and breakfast. You view your guesthouse as a haven for God-fearing, evangelical Christians. You do not advertise generally on the Web, only on Christian sites. You make it very clear in all your advertisements that you run a Christian business and that you will not rent rooms to cohabiting, homosexual couples (married or not) or to cohabiting, heterosexual couples who are not married. One day you are sued because your state has a law prohibiting discrimination based on marital status and sexual orientation. The court rules that the law places no burden on your religious beliefs because your religion does not require you to operate a guesthouse. You are ordered to change your guesthouse's rules.

No one can claim that the court order has prohibited you from "being religious." As the court has explained, you may continue to hold whatever beliefs you want about sexual practices. You simply may not impose those beliefs on others. But you feel that your beliefs and identity as a religious person simply cannot be disaggregated from your conduct. Your religious belief—your "belief liberty" interest, as I term it below—is necessarily curtailed by the *existence* of a law that prohibits you from discriminating on the basis of sexual orientation or marital status.

We tend not to think of these conflict situations in the language of conflicting liberties, and certainly not in the language of liberties that have something in common, even as they conflict. Those who advocate for laws prohibiting discrimination on the basis of sexual orientation tend to talk simply about "equality." Those who seek to stop such laws from coming into existence, or who seek religious exemptions from these laws, tend to talk about "morality" and/or "religious freedom." And these groups tend to talk past each other, rather than with each other.

My goal in this chapter is to surface some of the commonalities between belief liberty and identity liberty and to offer some public policy suggestions for what to do when these liberties conflict. I first want to make transparent the conflict that I believe exists between laws intended to protect the liberty of lesbian, gay, bisexual, and transgender (LGBT) people so that they may live lives of dignity and integrity and the religious beliefs of some individuals whose conduct is regulated by such laws. I believe those who advocate for LGBT equality have downplayed the impact of such laws on some people's religious beliefs and, equally, I believe those who have sought religious exemptions from such civil rights laws have downplayed the impact that such exemptions would have on LGBT people.

Second, I want to suggest that the best framework for dealing with this conflict is to analyze religious people's claims as belief liberty interests under the Due Process Clauses of the Fifth and Fourteenth Amendments, rather than as free exercise claims under the First Amendment. There were important historical reasons for including the First Amendment in our Constitution, with its dual Free Exercise and Establishment Clauses.[2] But the First Amendment should not be understood as the sole source of protection for religious people when the claims such individuals raise also implicate the type of liberty interests that should legitimately be considered under the Due Process Clauses of our Constitution.[3]

My argument in this chapter is that intellectual coherence and ethical integrity demand that we acknowledge that civil rights laws can burden an individual's belief liberty interest when the conduct demanded by these laws burdens an individual's core beliefs, whether such beliefs are religiously or secularly based. Acknowledging that these liberty interests exist and can be burdened by civil rights laws does *not* necessarily mean that such laws will be invalidated or that exemptions from the law will always be granted to individuals holding such beliefs. Rather, as I hope to demonstrate below, Justice Souter's concurrence in *Washington v. Glucksberg*[4] offers us a useful approach for engaging in an appropriate substantive due process analysis that provides us with a means of seriously considering the liberty interest at stake without necessarily invalidating the law burdening that interest.

Finally, I offer my own assessment of how these conflicts might be resolved in our democratic system. I have no illusions that either LGBT rights advocates or religious freedom advocates will decide I have offered the correct resolution. But my primary goal in this chapter is simply to argue that this conflict needs to be acknowledged in a respectful manner by both sides, and then addressed through the legislative processes of our democratic system. Whether my particular resolution is ultimately accepted feels less important to me than helping to foster a fruitful conversation about possible resolutions.[5]

I. Impact on Belief Liberty When Protecting LGBT Liberty

A. Postulating an Age of LGBT Liberty

In 2008, the most pressing question for LGBT people probably is not, "How can we be sure that we are adequately considering and taking into account the beliefs of those who believe we are immoral and sinful?" At the moment, it seems that people who hold that point of view are prevailing in any number of states, at the direct expense of LGBT people's liberty. Over the past decade, forty-one states have passed statutory Defense of Marriage Acts, defining marriage as solely between a man and a woman.[6] Twenty-six states have amended their constitutions to restrict marriage in a similar fashion.[7] In thirty states, a person can be fired from a job, thrown out of his or her apartment, or refused service in a restaurant simply because he or she is gay, lesbian, or bisexual.[8]

Given the current state of affairs, I believe the primary focus and energy of the LGBT movement must be directed at fighting for legislation and judicial outcomes that will allow LGBT people to live lives of honesty and safety in today's society. Indeed, I have spent a fair portion of the last twenty years of my professional life engaged in that struggle and I expect to do more of the same in the future.[9]

But I also believe it is only a matter of time before the world around us changes significantly. In some number of years (I do not know how many), I believe a majority of jurisdictions in this country will have modified their laws so that LGBT people will have full equality in our society, including access to civil marriage or to civil unions that carry the same legal effect as civil marriage. Or perhaps federal statutory changes, together with federal constitutional decisions, may result in LGBT people achieving full liberty across all states. At the very least, I believe it is worth postulating this outcome and considering now, rather than later, the impact that the achievement of such liberty might have on employers, landlords, and others whose moral values (derived from religious or secular sources) cause them to believe that same-sex sexual conduct is sinful for the individual and harmful to society.

Why do I believe an era of full LGBT liberty is simply a matter of time? A large part, I am sure, is due to my being an optimist who believes that simple truth and justice often win out in the long run and that truth and justice demand full liberty for LGBT people.

But my conviction also comes from observing changes in our society over the past twenty years and from reading opinion polls. The polling numbers indicate that an increasing number of people in this country simply do not believe homosexual orientation and conduct are as big a deal as they once were. These individuals may not particularly *like* homosexuality, nor do they believe that homosexuality is morally equivalent to heterosexuality. But they do not seem as agitated about homosexuality as they have been in past decades.

No poll that I have seen asks the question directly: "Do you think homosexuality is a big deal?" But a reduced anxiety about homosexuality is the overall gestalt that emerges upon reviewing the myriad polls that have asked members of the American public about their views on homosexuality over the past thirty years. Karlyn Bowman, a resident scholar at the American Enterprise Institute (AEI) who specializes in polling data, has done a Herculean task of reviewing and compiling information from over 200 polls, conducted from 1972 to 2006, that have asked questions about the American public's attitudes towards homosexuality.[10] Bowman's report is both illuminating and intriguing.

Bowman begins her report with a section called *Acceptance* and notes the following:

> In 1973, when the National Opinion Research Center at the University of Chicago [NORC] first asked people about sexual relations between two adults of the same sex, 73 percent described them as "always wrong" and another 7 percent as "almost always wrong." When the organization last asked the question in 2004, 58 percent called them always wrong and 5 percent almost always wrong. NORC interviewers have asked the same question about extramarital sexual relations over the period, and they find no liberalization in attitudes.[11]

The Roper Center at the University of Connecticut, together with AEI, did a subgroup analysis of the NORC cohort data. Their analysis showed that in the age cohort of 30–44, there was an even more significant reduction in the percentage of respondents who believed homosexual relations were "always wrong." In 1973, 74 percent of respondents in that age cohort believed homosexual sexual relations were "always wrong."[12] In 2002, only 48 percent of respondents in that age cohort answered that homosexual sexual relations were "always wrong"—a reduction of 26 percent.[13]

Bowman's compilation also indicates that an enduring half of the American public continues to believe that homosexuality is not morally acceptable, although that number appears to decrease slightly if respondents are asked about "homosexual relationships" or homosexuality as an "acceptable alternative lifestyle," rather than about "homosexual behavior."[14] The number of people who say they personally know a gay person, however, or who say they have become more accepting of gays and lesbians over the past few years, has increased significantly over the past fifteen years.[15]

Of particular note is the number of people who seem to have discovered gay people in their own families. In a 1992 Princeton Survey Research Associates

(PSRA)/*Newsweek* poll, 9 percent of respondents said that someone in their family was gay or lesbian, while 90 percent reported that there was no one in their family who was gay or lesbian.[16] In 2000, 23 percent of respondents said that someone in their family was gay or lesbian, while only 75 percent reported there was no one in their family who was gay or lesbian.[17] Given that the number of gay people probably did not increase 14 percent between 1992 and 2000, one must presume that more gay people told their families about their sexual orientation during that time period.

Perhaps because of the greater familiarity that members of the American public are beginning to have with gay people (including their own family members), purging homosexuality from our society does not appear to be a huge priority for a significant segment of our public. What is particularly interesting about Bowman's polling compilation is the number of people who do not think homosexuality is a moral issue at all,[18] and the significant percentage who do not think it would matter that much if there was greater acceptance of gay people in society. For example, in a 2003 PSRA/Pew Research Center survey, respondents were asked the following question: "Do you think more acceptance of gays and lesbians would be a good thing or a bad thing for the country—or that it would not make much difference either way?"[19] Only 31 percent of respondents said that more acceptance of gay people would be bad for the country.[20] Twenty-three percent thought it would be good for the country and 42 percent felt it would not make much difference.[21]

In considering these poll data, it is useful to identify three possible views of gay sexual activity. The first view is that such activity is morally harmful (and/or sinful) both for the individual and for the community. In light of that view, gay sexual activity must be discouraged to the greatest extent possible in order to advance the moral health of these individuals and of the communities in which they reside. The second view is that gay sexual activity is not good, but is also not inherently harmful; it is more akin to an unfortunate, abnormal health condition that one does not wish for oneself (or for one's children), but is not a harmful element that must be purged from society. The third view is that gay sexual activity has the same moral valence as heterosexual activity and that gay people are basically similar to straight people.

To me, these various polls taken together indicate that there is a significant number of people (but substantially less than a strong majority of people) in this country who hold the first view of gay sexual conduct and who believe homosexuality is morally problematic and society must therefore do whatever it can to discourage, disapprove of, and reduce the incidence of homosexual behavior. There is also a much smaller group of people who hold the third view and who believe that homosexuality is as morally acceptable as heterosexuality.

And, finally, there is a significant group of people in the middle. These people adhere to the second view of gay sex and therefore hold conflicting views about public policy and homosexuality. They do not feel homosexuality is morally equivalent to heterosexuality and therefore they are not interested in conferring civil marriage on gay couples.[22] But they also do not believe it would be terribly harmful to society if gay couples were acknowledged and permitted to have equal rights.[23] Thus, when given the choice between marriage or civil unions for same-sex couples, and no legal recognition for same-sex couples at all, support for "no legal recognition" never goes above 50 percent and, in most cases, hovers between 35 percent and 40 percent.[24] Conversely, when one combines the small public support for gay marriage with the more substantial support for civil unions, there is consistently a majority of support for some legal recognition of gay couples.[25]

What this means to me is that the second view of gay sex holds significant sway in our society today. For example, I presume many parents today would prefer that their child not be gay. But if their child were gay, these parents may no longer believe they must desperately seek out professional "help" for the child. The large number of well-adjusted, happy, and successful gay people living openly and honestly in today's society reinforces the medical profession's current judgment that there is nothing psychologically wrong with being gay.[26] It is also possible that the horror value of discovering one's child is gay has subsided. Although the majority of parents today may not want their child to be gay, they may be less horrified to find out their child is gay than they would be if they discovered their child were having sex with his or her sibling, having sex with a child, or having sex in public.

And, at bottom, these parents do not want their children discriminated against "just because they are gay." Parents may not like the fact that their child is gay, but they also do not want American society to penalize their child unduly for that fact.[27]

For purposes of this chapter, therefore, I am postulating that the coming decades will see a rise in legislation and judicial opinions that favor full liberty for LGBT people. Assuming that is the case, how should we think about the fact that granting such liberty to gay people might put a burden on people who feel that if they rent an apartment to a gay couple, allow a gay couple to eat at their restaurant, or provide health benefits to a same-sex spouse, they are aiding and abetting sinful or immoral behavior?

B. Impact of LGBT Liberty on Belief Liberty

To consider the question I pose above as even worthy of consideration, one must believe that a civil rights law that protects the liberty of LGBT people by prohibiting discrimination based on sexual orientation or gender identity (or by conferring civil union or marriage status on same-sex couples) might place a burden on the liberty of some people regulated by the law. This belief is not self-evident. Many people assume that since such laws merely regulate the *conduct* of individuals governed by the law, they have little or no impact on such individuals' beliefs or identities.

But I believe such laws might, in certain circumstances, burden what I call "belief liberty."[28] What I mean by "burden" is that the law will require an individual to engage in conduct that he or she believes is inconsistent with his or her most deeply held beliefs.

From a liberty perspective, whether such beliefs stem from a religious source or from a secular source would be irrelevant. Certainly, in America today, religious people of certain denominations may hold more negative views of homosexuality and may feel more of a burden from such laws.[29] But we miss the mark, I think, if we analyze this burden solely as a burden on religious liberty, writ narrow, rather than as a burden on belief liberty, writ large.

Obviously, as a practical matter, the United States Supreme Court's decision in *Employment Division v. Smith*[30] limits the reach of the Free Exercise Clause's protection for religious beliefs from broadly applicable civil rights laws. But, as a theoretical matter, I believe it is more appropriate in any event to analyze these belief claims as liberty claims and not to elevate religious beliefs over other deeply held beliefs derived from nonreligious sources. From the perspective of a person holding a particular belief, the intensity of that belief may be as strong regardless of whether it has a religious or a nonreligious source.

What should be relevant for a liberty analysis is whether such beliefs form *a core aspect of the individual's sense of self and purpose in the world*. An individual may be able to meet this standard whether his or her beliefs are religiously based or secularly based.

Fully acknowledging the existence of a burden that may be imposed by civil rights laws (including marriage equality laws) requires two independent steps. First, we must consider what moral values are inherent in civil rights laws and whether these values might conflict with the deeply held beliefs of some individuals who are regulated by the law. Second, we must consider whether forcing someone to act (or not to act) in a certain way can burden a liberty interest in a manner that should be protected under the Due Process Clause.

1. The Moral Values in Civil Rights Laws

A major strand of liberal political theory postulates that "morality"—in the sense of a moral, normative view of "the good"—is not the proper object of governmental action. According to this view, individuals living in a pluralist society will inevitably hold divergent normative and moral beliefs, and the role of law and government is to adequately safeguard the rights necessary for each individual to pursue his or her own normative view of "the good life"—not to affirmatively advance one moral view of "the good" over others.[31]

In a recent short comment on why government should not be involved in recognizing any marriages (for either same-sex couples or opposite-sex couples), Tamara Metz nicely captures this viewpoint. Metz posits that the goal of marriage as an institution is to have a couple's relationship supported by an ethical authority outside the couple itself. And the "liberal state," argues Metz, is "ill-suited to serve as an ethical authority."[32] Why? As Metz explains: "Ideally, the liberal state is relatively distant, more legal than moral, and more neutral than not among competing worldviews so as to protect individual freedom and diversity."[33]

I do not disagree that a liberal state must have, as its highest priority, the protection of pluralist ways of living among its citizens, subject to such ways of living not harming others in society. My argument is simply that when government decides, through the enactment of its laws, that a certain way of life does not harm those living that life and does not harm others who are exposed to such individuals, the government has necessarily staked out a position of moral *neutrality* with regard to that way of living. And that position of moral neutrality may stand in stark contrast to those who believe that the particular way of living at issue is morally laden and problematic.

I have both documented and personally watched as supporters of a gay civil rights bill have gone to great lengths to argue that they are not taking a position on the morality of homosexuality or bisexuality by supporting such a law.[34] I agree that supporting such a law does not necessarily convey a message that "gay is good." But it is disingenuous to say that voting for a law of this kind conveys *no* message about morality at all. The only way for the state to justify prohibiting private employers, landlords, and business owners from discriminating against gay people is for the state to have made the prior moral assessment that acting on one's homosexual orientation is not so morally problematic as to justify private parties discriminating against such individuals in the public domain. To return to the three possible views of gay sex, supporting a law that prohibits discrimination based on sexual orientation requires that the supporter hold, at a minimum, the second view of gay sex—even though it does not require that the supporter hold the third view.

For example, we do not have laws today that protect those who engage in domestic violence or pedophilia from employment, housing, or public accommodation discrimination. We do not ask about these groups of individuals: "Well, but can they type? Can they do the job?" I do not believe the lack of such laws is due solely to the lack of an adequate "pedophile lobby" or "domestic violence abuser lobby." Rather, I believe society (as reflected in its government's public policy) has determined that actions of this kind hurt others and are thus morally problematic. For that reason, a private actor who uses the fact that an individual has engaged in these actions as grounds for exclusion is not viewed as engaging in unjustified discrimination.

This analysis works equally well to explain and describe the status quo in which LGBT people currently remain vulnerable to private and public discrimination. When the government *fails* to pass a law prohibiting nondiscrimination on the basis of sexual orientation, in the face of documentation that such discrimination is occurring on a regular basis, or *fails* to allow same-sex couples access to civil marriage when the practical need for that access is documented for scores of families, the government has similarly taken a position on a moral question. The state has decided that a homosexual or bisexual orientation is not morally neutral, but rather may legitimately be viewed by some as morally problematic. It is precisely that determination which provides the justification for legislators to continue denying full liberty to those who act on their homosexual or bisexual orientations and who are open and honest about their actions.

Granted, the issue is often framed in these cases as a question of "equality." That is certainly true. The existence of civil rights laws, as well as the absence of such laws, certainly determines how much equality LGBT people will enjoy in our society. But let us be clear: the fact that this is a question of equality should not obscure the fact that this is *also* a question about morality. And that is because moral beliefs necessarily underlie the assessment of whether such equality is *justifiably* granted or denied.

Once we acknowledge how moral assessments necessarily underlie civil rights laws, it becomes easier to understand how a law prohibiting discrimination based on sexual orientation might shock the system of some members of society. For those who believe that a homosexual or bisexual orientation is not morally neutral, and that an individual who acts on his or her homosexual orientation is acting in a sinful or harmful manner (to himself or herself and to others), it is problematic when the government passes a law that gives such individuals equal access to all societal institutions. Such a law rests on a moral assessment of homosexuality and bisexuality that is radically different from their own. Such a law presumes the moral neutrality of homosexuality and bisexuality, while those who oppose the law believe homosexuality and bisexuality are morally problematic.

Conversely, for those who believe that any sexual orientation, including a homosexual or bisexual orientation, is morally neutral, and that an individual who acts on his or her homosexual or bisexual orientation acts in an honest and good manner, it is problematic when the government *fails* to pass laws providing equality to such individuals. The failure to pass such a law rests on a moral assessment of homosexuality and bisexuality that is radically different from their own. Such failure presumes homosexuality and bisexuality are morally problematic, while those who desire the law believe homosexuality and bisexuality are morally neutral.

This is why then-Professor (now Judge) Michael McConnell is correct to observe that disputes surrounding sexual orientation "feature a seemingly irreconcilable clash between those who believe that homosexual conduct is immoral and those who believe that it is a natural and morally unobjectionable manifestation of human sexuality."[35] McConnell believes that the debate over sexual orientation is best approached by the government extending respect to both of these positions, without taking sides on either position. Thus, using an analogy to the respect people seek from government for their religious beliefs, he urges the following:

> The starting point would be to extend respect to both sides in the conflict of opinion, to treat both the view that homosexuality is a healthy and normal manifestation of human sexuality and the view that homosexuality is unnatural and immoral as conscientious positions, worthy of respect, much as we treat both atheism and faith as worthy of respect. In using the term "respect," I do not mean agreement. Rather, I mean the civil toleration we extend to fellow citizens and fellow human beings even when we disagree with their views. We should recognize that the "Civil Magistrate" is no more "competent a Judge" of the "Truth" about human sexuality than about religion.[36]

But what McConnell fails to appreciate in his analysis is that the government *necessarily* takes a stance on the moral question he has articulated every time it *fails* to affirmatively ensure that gay people can live openly, safely, and honestly in society.

Note, for example, how McConnell characterizes possible governmental actions (and inactions) under his recommended approach:

> Under this approach, the state should not impose a penalty on practices associated with or compelled by any of the various views of homosexuality, and should refrain from using its power to favor, promote, or advance one position over the other. The difference between a "gay rights" position and a "First Amendment" approach is that the former adopts as its governing principle the idea that homosexuality is normal, natural, and morally unobjectionable, *while the latter takes the view that the moral issue is not for the government to decide.* Thus, the government would not punish sexual acts by consenting gay individuals,

nor would it use sexual orientation as a basis for classification or discrimination, without powerful reasons, not grounded in moral objections, for taking such action. On the other hand, the *government* would not attempt to *project this posture of moral neutrality onto the private sphere*, but would allow private forces in the culture to determine the ultimate social response.[37]

It seems apparent from McConnell's writing (although, for some reason, he fails to state so explicitly) that the "gay rights" position is one that calls for government intervention in the private sector through laws that make discrimination on the basis of sexual orientation illegal or that make civil marriage available to same-sex couples. I gather that is what McConnell is referring to when he argues that the government should not "project this posture of moral neutrality onto the private sphere."[38]

But if that is the case, McConnell is simply wrong to assume that a government's failure to pass such laws rests on the view "that the moral issue is not for the government to decide." The government *is* taking a position on the moral question when it fails to extend access to civil marriage to same-sex couples. It is precisely because some people hold the view that homosexuality is immoral that gay people have been *denied* equal protection under the law up until this point. Government has not simply been sitting on the sidelines of these moral questions during all the time it has failed to pass laws protecting the liberty of LGBT people. Government has quite clearly been taking a side—and it has not been taking the side that helps gay people.

McConnell correctly diagnoses the opposing moral viewpoints, but his proposed solution is no more satisfying than the solutions proposed by gay rights leaders who characterize gay civil rights laws as simple "neutral" prescriptions of equality that have no impact on a person's religious or moral beliefs. Both McConnell and these gay rights leaders are trying to deal with the conflict by simply wishing it away. That is neither possible nor intellectually honest.

2. The Burden on Liberty

Passage of a law based on a moral assessment different from one's own can certainly make an individual feel alienated from his or her government and fellow citizens. But that is a far cry from accepting that such a law burdens one's liberty in a way that might require further justification by the state. I might disagree with my government's foreign policy or economic policy and think on some days that I would be happier living in some other country. But without something more, it is hard to argue that my liberty—even something as broad as my "belief liberty"—has been burdened.

The "something more," from my perspective, is a legal requirement that an individual *act*, or *refrain from acting*, in a manner that the individual can credibly claim undermines his or her core beliefs and sense of self. Without such a trigger, a claim that one's liberty has been burdened cannot legitimately be maintained. Explicating this point requires a discussion of both belief liberty and the interaction between conduct and belief.

a. Three Forms of Liberty

It is way past time to get over the *Lochner* era's[39] baggage and embrace the full scope of our Due Process Clause's liberty interest. Numerous scholars over the past thirty years have produced compelling and thoughtful analyses of the liberty interest embodied in the Fifth and Fourteenth Amendments.[40] I have no such grand schemes here. My goal in this part is more limited: I want to focus on Justice David Souter's concurrence in *Washington v. Glucksberg*[41] and suggest that we apply the lessons of his concurrence to thinking about belief liberty more generally.

In his *Glucksberg* concurrence, Justice Souter is clear that he believes the *Lochner* line of cases was incorrectly decided. But that is not because a person's "right to choose a calling" is not an essential "element of liberty."[42] Rather, it is because the Court's decisions in the *Lochner* line of cases "harbored the spirit of *Dred Scott* in their absolutist implementation of the standard they espoused."[43] In other words, it is not that living and working where one will is not an essential part of liberty. But the government must have the ability to regulate that liberty in a reasonable manner in order to carry out its important interests.[44] The Court's failure in the *Lochner* line of cases was its failure to properly judge and apply the government's important interest in protecting the social and economic welfare of its citizens. It was not a failure in judging the importance of work as an element of liberty.[45]

But Justice Souter's main priority in his *Glucksberg* concurrence is not to revive the importance of contract as a liberty interest. His main objective is to attack the Court's approach, over the past fifty years, of focusing almost exclusively on whether a proclaimed liberty interest is a "fundamental right," and then almost invariably invalidating any legislation burdening such a right. To Justice Souter, this approach not only represents a wrong turn from earlier substantive due process jurisprudence, but it also elides the key point that liberty interests naturally fall across a spectrum. Thus, many interests can be "liberty" interests and still be *justifiably* burdened by the government because of the needs of society.[46]

Justice Souter finds guidance for this approach in Justice Harlan's dissent from dismissal on jurisdictional grounds in *Poe v. Ullman*:

> [T]he full scope of the liberty guaranteed by the Due Process Clause cannot be found in or limited by the precise terms of the specific guarantees elsewhere

provided in the Constitution. This "liberty" is not a series of isolated points pricked out in terms of the taking of property; the freedom of speech, press, and religion; the right to keep and bear arms; the freedom from unreasonable searches and seizures; and so on. It is a rational continuum which, broadly speaking, includes a freedom from all substantial arbitrary impositions and purposeless restraints, and which also recognizes, what a reasonable and sensitive judgment must, that certain interests require particularly careful scrutiny of the state needs asserted to justify their abridgment.[47]

For Justice Souter, the types of interests that would require particularly careful scrutiny would presumably be those described in *Planned Parenthood of Southeastern Pennsylvania v. Casey*, an opinion written jointly by Justices O'Connor, Kennedy, and Souter:

> These matters [personal decisions relating to marriage, procreation, contraception, family relationships, child rearing, and education], involving the most intimate and personal choices a person may make in a lifetime, choices central to personal dignity and autonomy, are central to the liberty protected by the Fourteenth Amendment. At the heart of liberty is the right to define one's own concept of existence, of meaning, of the universe, and of the mystery of human life.[48]

Drawing from a historical overview of substantive due process cases and Justice Harlan's dissent in *Poe*, Justice Souter articulates two basic guidelines for courts engaging in a substantive due process analysis. First, a court "is bound to confine the values that it recognizes to those truly deserving constitutional stature"[49]—an approach that enables a court to avoid engaging in piercing scrutiny of every conceivable burden on liberty that may arise across the spectrum.[50] Second, a court may not intervene "merely to identify a reasonable resolution of contending values that differs from the terms of the legislation under review."[51] As Justice Souter articulates the standard,

> It is only when the legislation's justifying principle, critically valued, is so far from being commensurate with the individual interest as to be arbitrarily or pointlessly applied that the statute must give way. Only if this standard points against the statute can the individual claimant be said to have a constitutional right.[52]

Justice Souter never directly repudiates the strict scrutiny standard requiring that governmental restrictions on fundamental rights be narrowly tailored to fit a compelling government interest.[53] But his emphasis that a court must consider whether a "legislation's justifying principle, critically valued" is "*commensurate* with the individual interest"[54] appears clearly designed to argue that a court has flexibility in its substantive due process analysis. That is, in order to be true to what Justice Souter sees as the spirit and design of the constitutional protection of liberty, while at the same time ensuring that government is able to regulate effectively in a complex world, he calls for an almost dialectical valuation of the government's interest against the particular liberty interest at stake.[55]

Of course, Justice Souter's opinion in *Glucksberg* was only a concurrence. Justice Rehnquist's majority opinion offered a very different view of substantive due process. Under the majority approach in *Glucksberg*, there are a limited number of "fundamental rights" that can be clearly named and found, based on objective, historical facts, to be rooted in our nation's tradition.[56] With regard to legislative burdens on this very limited set of "fundamental rights," courts will apply strict scrutiny (not dialectical balancing) and will almost invariably invalidate the legislative burden.[57]

But the Supreme Court's deployment of a liberty analysis to invalidate Texas's sodomy law in *Lawrence v. Texas*[58] opened the door to a revival of Justice Souter's more capacious understanding of substantive due process. Professor Robert Post observes that Justice Kennedy's "extravagant and passionate" opinion in *Lawrence* "simply shatters, with all the heartfelt urgency of deep conviction, the paralyzing carapace in which *Glucksberg* had sought to encase substantive due process."[59] And Professor Larry Tribe notes that the "*Glucksberg* gambit" to "collapse claims of liberty into the unidimensional and binary business of determining which personal activities belong to the historically venerated catalogue of privileged acts and which do not" could well have succeeded, had future cases followed its trajectory.[60] Instead, as Tribe notes, even the briefest examination of the *Lawrence* opinion makes plain that the Court steadfastly resisted a "reductionist procedure" that reduces the liberty interest to "flattened-out collections of private acts."[61]

Indeed, the Supreme Court's opinion in *Lawrence* triggered a revival of writing on liberty, much of it from people who had been writing and thinking about liberty for a long time. Among these scholars, Professor Nan D. Hunter was one of the first to explicitly connect the Court's analysis in *Lawrence* with Justice Souter's concurrence in *Glucksberg*, and to suggest that *Lawrence* may "mark[] the beginning of a substantive due process jurisprudence that examines negative liberty limits on state power before, or instead of, articulating a specific standard of review."[62]

In her analysis, Hunter does not speculate on whether she thinks this move by the Court is a positive development for liberty jurisprudence; she is agnostic on that question. I have noted elsewhere that I believe Hunter is correct with regard to her prediction of how the Court may proceed with substantive due process analyses in the future.[63] My point here is to argue that Justice Souter's approach is also the appropriate one for the Court to adopt.

I recognize that some might view Justice Souter's approach as a death knell for important fundamental rights, while others may view it as a simple and necessary correction to earlier substantive due process jurisprudence. But on its merits, Justice Souter's approach seems to me to properly reflect the reality of our complex society while staying consistent with the plain meaning of the Fifth and Fourteenth Amendments. Governmental laws constantly burden liberty, and to decide that only laws that cross a magic line called "fundamental rights" should ever be subject to claims of redress seems rigid and inappropriate. Justice Souter's approach permits courts to recognize realistically and honestly the myriad ways in which laws might burden the liberty interests of those subject to the laws, while not necessarily invalidating the laws.

In 2002, Professor Rebecca Brown offered a comprehensive and sophisticated analysis of the liberty interest embodied in the Fifth and Fourteenth Amendments, complete with a vigorous defense of the courts' responsibility to protect such liberty, an explanation of how such judicial review is consistent with, not destructive of, democracy, and a framework for considering liberty claims.[64] In explaining why protecting liberty interests is as important a constitutional goal as protecting equality interests, Brown observed:

> [I]n a world of increasingly diverse personal and moral values, supporting very different notions of the good life, the communion of interests between representatives and represented can degrade even when laws nominally operate evenhandedly. For example, laws that provide that "no one may [blank]" can exploit difference as effectively as a classification, when the blank is an activity that "we," the political ins, have no wish to do, but that "they," the outs, claim a profound need to do in pursuit of personal fulfillment.[65]

Brown uses laws prohibiting sodomy or assisted suicide as principal examples of the need to question a legislature's reasons for burdening liberty.[66] But the same framework that Brown proffers to scrutinize such prohibitions should apply as well to a legislature's prohibition of discriminatory conduct that might adversely impact a regulated person's liberty. The fact that we might need to be concerned in the coming decades with the potential liberty burdens imposed by a sexual orientation nondiscrimination law or a marriage equality law (rather than with the liberty burdens posed by a criminal sodomy law or a law that excludes same-sex couples from civil marriage) simply reflects the reality that moral values are beginning to shift in this country—as I believe they should.

Finally, in thinking about the types of liberties that rise to the level of requiring more searching government justification, I believe it is helpful to group the spectrum of liberty interests into three broad categories: bodily liberty, identity liberty, and belief liberty.

There is nothing magical about these categories, and I do not contend they are the only ones that make sense. But I believe this three-part categorization is an intellectually coherent manner in which to think about the spectrum of liberty interests that the Supreme Court has protected over the decades.[67]

"Bodily liberty" is the easiest one to describe: the state should not invade the integrity of our bodies without a good reason for doing so.[68] Protecting members of the public from contagious diseases is a good reason to force someone to have his body invaded through a vaccination; fighting drug crime is not a good enough reason to force someone to vomit by pumping an emetic solution through a tube into his stomach.[69]

"Identity liberty" is the term I would use to describe the liberty that the *Casey* plurality sought to capture in its "mystery of human life" description, a description repeated by Justice Kennedy in the *Lawrence* majority:

> These matters [personal decisions relating to marriage, procreation, contraception, family relationships, child rearing, and education], involving the most intimate and personal choices a person may make in a lifetime, choices central to personal dignity and autonomy, are central to the liberty protected by the Fourteenth Amendment. At the heart of liberty is the right to define one's own concept of existence, of meaning, of the universe, and of the mystery of human life.[70]

Despite Justice Scalia's scoffing at this description as meaningless for purposes of law,[71] I think it accurately captures a set of liberty interests that go to the core of a person's identity. This may be a person's identity as a parent (including the decisions whether to have a child and how to raise the child), a person's identity as a spouse or a lover (deciding what form of sexual intimacy one wishes to engage in), a person's racial, ethnic, or religious identity, or a person's gender identity. As I have previously observed,

> Not that many personal decisions rise to the level of "defin[ing] one's own concept of existence, of meaning, of the universe, and of the mystery of human life." We should not let the lofty rhetoric mislead us to the conclusion that these words can mean everything and anything. They do not. The examples provided by the *Lawrence* majority give meaning to the type of personal decisions at play here—the choice to marry, the choice to have a child (or not have a child), the choice to have sexual intimacy with a partner, the choice to raise

a child in a certain fashion. These are not small decisions. These are those big decisions in life that go to the core, essential aspects of our selves.[72]

Moreover, while the phrasing of the "mystery of human life" sentence reflects a twenty-first century language of human self-awareness, a similar sentiment regarding the importance of self-identity seems to underlie one of the Court's earliest descriptions of the liberty interest, in *Meyer v. Nebraska*:

> While this court has not attempted to define with exactness the liberty thus guaranteed, the term has received much consideration and some of the included things have been definitely stated. Without doubt, it denotes not merely freedom from bodily restraint but also the right of the individual to contract, to engage in any of the common occupations of life, to acquire useful knowledge, to marry, establish a home and bring up children, to worship God according to the dictates of his own conscience, and *generally to enjoy those privileges long recognized at common law as essential to the orderly pursuit of happiness by free men.*[73]

What was recognized at common law as essential to the "orderly pursuit of happiness by free men"[74] is no doubt different from what would be recognized as such today. But the underlying objective of the standard is the same— identifying an area of core identity for which the government needs a good reason before it may infringe upon it.

Finally, I use the category "belief liberty" to refer to the liberty to possess deeply held personal beliefs without coercion or penalty by the state. Belief liberty presumably could be subsumed under identity liberty, since our beliefs are very often constitutive of our identities. But I believe it is worth identifying this type of liberty separately because it is so often conflated with First Amendment rights to free speech, free expression, and free exercise of religion. That conflation is understandable; most cases dealing with "beliefs" naturally arise under the First Amendment. But is it necessary that such beliefs be protected *solely* under the First Amendment? Certainly, the ability to believe what one will seems "essential to the orderly pursuit of happiness by free men [and women]."[75]

The First Amendment right to free speech necessarily protects any speech, no matter how trivial. The First Amendment right to free exercise necessarily protects (within the limits of current Supreme Court doctrine) any religious belief, no matter how trivial. By contrast, I believe it is appropriate that the belief liberty protected under the Due Process Clause be limited to those beliefs that occupy a position of significant importance to the individual. Even if those beliefs are not so constitutive of the person's identity as to be protected under "identity liberty," the "mystery of human life" description of identity liberty offers us some guidance as to the type of beliefs that should demand more searching scrutiny when a burden on such beliefs is alleged.

Obviously, we all have many beliefs. If the government had to justify every burden on every belief caused by every law, it would presumably have little time to do anything else. But, certainly, we are capable of placing these beliefs in some sort of hierarchy. For example, I believe that heterosexuality and homosexuality are morally neutral characteristics (similar to having red hair or brown hair), and I believe that acting consistently with one's sexual orientation is a morally good act. I also believe that flowers are necessary to happiness and that *Star Trek* is a great contribution to our culture. But I would rank my beliefs regarding sexuality as much more significant to my sense of self than my beliefs regarding flowers or *Star Trek*. Thus, in order for belief liberty to be situated at a point in the spectrum that requires greater government justification for infringement, such beliefs must constitute an important core aspect of the individual.[76]

Analyzing belief liberty under the Due Process Clause (and not simply under the First Amendment) also serves to equalize deeply held beliefs that may derive from religious sources, from purely secular sources, or from spiritual sources that are not traditionally viewed as religious. If these beliefs are an integral part of the person's sense of self, my argument is that they are protected by belief liberty. The particular source of the individual's beliefs is not the barometer of their importance for due process purposes. For belief liberty, the source of the beliefs (be it faith in God, belief in spiritual energy, or a conviction of the rational five senses) has no relevance. A belief derived from a religious faith should be accorded no *more* weight—and no *less* weight—than a belief derived from a nonreligious source.

As the Supreme Court reflected on a somewhat related question in 1944:

> If by this position appellant seeks for freedom of conscience a broader protection than for freedom of the mind, it may be doubted that any of the great liberties insured by the First Article can be given higher place than the others. All have preferred position in our basic scheme. All are interwoven there together. Differences there are, in them and in the modes appropriate for their exercise. But they have unity in the charter's prime place because they have unity in their human sources and functionings. Heart and mind are not identical. Intuitive faith and reasoned judgment are not the same. Spirit is not always thought. But in the everyday business of living, secular or otherwise, these variant aspects of personality find inseparable expression in a thousand ways. They cannot be altogether parted in law more than in life.[77]

b. Burdening Belief by Regulating Conduct

To understand the burden that an LGBT equality law might place on some people's belief liberty, one must start by acknowledging that a state necessarily takes a position of moral neutrality on sexual orientation when it passes such a law. For that reason, the logical underpinning of such a law will be at odds with the belief systems of some individuals who are subject to the law.

But, obviously, such a law does not require individuals subject to the law to change their beliefs. An employer who is required to hire a gay person or a hotel owner who is required to rent to a gay couple may continue to believe whatever he or she wishes about the immorality or sinfulness of homosexuality. To grasp the full impact of such laws, therefore, it is necessary to explicate and acknowledge the logical intertwining that many people (including religious people) experience between their conduct and their beliefs such that compliance with a neutral civil rights law may burden their belief liberty.

Obviously, in a complex society, conduct must be regulated in a way that belief need not be. That is a truism. From the Supreme Court's ringing protection of belief in *West Virginia v. Barnette*[78] to its consistent refrain that religious beliefs will be protected in a manner that religious conduct will not be,[79] the logical distinction between conduct and belief has been clear.

But it does not follow from that truism that conduct should always be viewed as completely and wholly distinct from belief. Certainly, courts have recognized that particular conduct may be used to communicate an expressive belief.[80] Why should it be so difficult to accept that engaging in certain conduct (or being precluded from engaging in certain conduct) might burden an individual's strongly held beliefs?

Indeed, I would argue that gay people—of all individuals—should recognize the injustice of forcing a person to disaggregate belief or identity from practice. For years, gay people have been told by some entities that they should separate their status from their conduct. In the religious arena, this has been framed as "loving the sinner, but hating the sin." That is, gay people have been told that their *status* as individuals with homosexual orientation is not inherently sinful—but that if they *act* in a way consistent with that orientation, then they are engaging in sin.

In the legal arena, this approach to a gay person's identity and being has been framed as the "status/conduct" distinction. Particularly as a means of dealing with the holding in *Bowers v. Hardwick*,[81] some legal advocates had argued that their clients should not be discriminated against for the *status* of being gay, although they deliberately failed to claim equal nondiscrimination rights for their clients' rights to engage in gay *conduct*.[82] From the moment I became aware of this legal approach, I have detested it and argued against it.[83] It seemed to me the height of disingenuousness, absurdity, and indeed, disrespect to tell someone it is permissible to "be" gay, but not permissible to engage in gay sex. What do they think being gay *means*?

I have the same reaction to those who blithely assume a religious person can easily disengage her religious belief and self-identity from her religious practice and religious behavior. What do they think being religious *means*? Of course, at some basic level, religion is about a set of beliefs. But for many religious people across many religious denominations (Catholic, Protestant, Jewish, and Muslim—to note just the ones I have some personal understanding of), the day-to-day *practice* of one's religion is an essential way of bringing meaning to such beliefs. And while religious beliefs on homosexuality may seem the most familiar to us, there may be people with strongly held secular beliefs who feel just as strongly on the issue.

Given this perspective, it makes sense to me that three born-again Christians who run a chain of sports and health clubs would feel that "[t]heir fundamentalist religious convictions require them to act in accordance with the teachings of Jesus Christ and the will of God in their business as well as in their personal lives," and hence mandate them to hire only employees who conform to their views about proper sexual behavior.[84] It also makes sense to me that these same owners would feel their religion compels them to have these employees "talk[] to homosexuals about their religious views and sexual preference and [tell] them homosexuality [is] wrong."[85] And I can well understand the elderly Christian woman who believes "God will judge her if she permits people to engage in sex outside of marriage in her rental units and that if she does so, she will be prevented from meeting her deceased husband in the hereafter."[86]

Whether such conduct should legitimately be permitted in a workplace or a public accommodation is a separate question. But at this stage of the analysis, we should be concerned solely with whether a burden on belief liberty *exists*, not with whether the burden is nevertheless *justified*. The relevant question at this stage is how a court or a legislature should respond to an allegation that engaging in certain conduct, in compliance with a neutral law, *burdens* an individual's beliefs that constitute a core aspect of that individual's sense of self.

My argument is that we should err on the side of accepting the person's allegation for purposes of deciding whether a burden on liberty *exists*. (Again, this is different from the subsequent step of deciding whether the burden on liberty is ultimately *justified*.) In erring on the side of the person making the allegation, there must of course be some basis to the person's claim that will situate the belief-liberty interest on the upper end of the liberty spectrum.

That is, the person must demonstrate that he or she holds a particular belief that is core to his or her sense of self and must make a credible claim that engaging in certain conduct would be inconsistent with that belief. But beyond that, I do not believe the government acts appropriately when it second-guesses the individual and concludes, for example, "Really, this isn't such a burden on your belief."

Many judges have been unsympathetic to religious individuals' claims that a neutral law burdens their religious beliefs. As I describe below, sometimes judges wrap their justification for the burden into their analysis of whether a burden exists in the first place. Sometimes judges creatively construe a law so as to result in the absence of a burden and sometimes judges simply dismiss the religious person's allegation that a burden exists.

For example, in *Smith v. Fair Employment & Housing Commission*, the Supreme Court of California considered whether a housing law that prohibited discrimination based on marital status imposed a "significant burden" on a religious landlady who did not wish to rent to an unmarried, heterosexual couple.[87] The court concluded that no such significant burden existed because the landlady could invest her capital in an enterprise other than housing.[88] The court also noted that the landlady's religious beliefs did not "require her to rent apartments; the religious injunction is simply that she not rent to unmarried couples."[89] In light of that fact, the court concluded: "No religious exercise is burdened if she follows the alternative course of placing her capital in another investment."[90]

A similar analysis was advanced by a dissenting judge in *Donahue v. Fair Employment & Housing Commission*,[91] a state court ruling in California that also concerned a religious couple who did not wish to rent to unmarried, cohabiting heterosexual couples. In concluding that the burden on the couple's religious conduct was slight, the dissenting judge first observed that the couple "d[id] not contend that refusing to rent to unmarried cohabitants is a central tenet of their religious belief," nor did they "contend that the burden imposed by the statute prohibits them from practicing their religion."[92] Rather, the couple's only contention, observed the dissenting judge, was that "if they are compelled to rent to unmarried cohabitants, they would be—in effect—aiders and abettors in the commission of sin by others in violation of their own religious beliefs."[93]

The dissenting judge was unsympathetic to this concern. As the judge concluded:

> The Donahues are the owners of a five-unit apartment building which they rent to members of the general public. They are engaged in secular commer-

cial conduct performed for profit. There are no religious motivations for their conduct. The statute does not require the Donahues to aid and abet "sinners," it merely requires them "to *act* in a nondiscriminatory manner toward all prospective [tenants]. 'A legal compulsion . . . to refrain from discriminating against [prospective tenants] on the basis of [marital status] can hardly be characterized as an endorsement'" or the aiding or abetting of sin.[94]

In the case involving born-again Christians who owned and operated a chain of sports and health clubs in Minneapolis, a Minnesota court found no burden on the owners' religious beliefs by offering a creative interpretation of the state's gay civil rights law. The court observed that "based on his understanding of the Bible, Owens [the owner of the clubs] (the other principals agree with him) clearly is opposed to homosexual *acts.*"[95] For example, quoting from the trial transcript, the court noted that Owens had emphasized that, with regard to homosexuals, he has "a love, a heartfelt love for them, but not for the activity. The same way I would have a heartfelt love for anybody; but as God says in his word, we can hate the sin but we love the sinner."[96]

But, the court observed, the Minneapolis ordinance prohibited discrimination "based on affectional preference, not acts."[97] Thus, the court concluded: "From [Owens'] words it would be difficult to conclude that his Christianity supports discrimination based on preference rather than acts. Thus, the Minneapolis ordinance as applied in this case does not impose a burden upon Owens' free exercise of religion."[98]

Some of the more sophisticated judicial analyses of the burden that civil rights laws might place on religious beliefs are represented in the various opinions issued in *Gay Rights Coalition of Georgetown University Law Center v. Georgetown University.*[99] This case concerned the refusal of Georgetown University, a Jesuit school, to recognize gay student groups that had organized at the university and the law school.[100] The university administration permitted the gay student groups to exist and to use various school facilities.[101] However, the administration drew the line at "endorsing" the student groups. The administration asserted that if it allowed the groups to use the Georgetown name, receive university funds, and have access to subsidized office space, telephone service, office supplies, and equipment, it would be connoting its endorsement of the groups.[102] As the administration explained:

This situation involves a controversial matter of faith and the moral teachings of the Catholic Church. "Official" subsidy and support of a gay student organization would be interpreted by many as *endorsement of the positions taken by the gay movement on a full range of issues.* While the University supports and cherishes the individual lives and rights of its students, it will not subsidize this cause. *Such an endorsement would be inappropriate for a Catholic University.*[103]

Judge Pryor's concurrence provides a good example of a judge simply not accepting the allegations of a religious person (or, in this case, a religious institution):

> I do not understand Georgetown to argue that discrimination against any persons or groups is a tenet of its faith. Rather, it claims that providing the disputed facilities and services to the gay student organizations infringes the University's religious interest in embracing a particular doctrine of sexual ethics. Therefore, to require the University to make available its facilities and services in an evenhanded manner works, at most, an *indirect* infringement of its religious interest. For just as enforcement of the prohibition against discrimination on the basis of political affiliation does not signify endorsement of any particular political party, enforcement of the Human Rights Act's ban on discrimination on the basis of sexual orientation does not signify endorsement by the government or by the covered entity of any particular doctrine of sexual ethics.[104]

In contrast to Judge Pryor's concurrence, the plurality opinion in the *Georgetown* case parsed the situation somewhat differently—acknowledging that the District of Columbia's law did place some burden on the university, but nevertheless refusing to accept fully the university's allegations with regard to that burden. The plurality first interpreted the D.C. Human Rights Act (which prohibited discrimination based on sexual orientation) as not requiring that any covered entity, including Georgetown University, endorse a gay group.[105] The plurality concluded: "[T]he Human Rights Act does not require one private actor to 'endorse' the ideas or conduct of another."[106]

Instead, the plurality focused on the "mere" conduct required by the law:

> While the Human Rights Act does not seek to compel uniformity in philosophical *attitudes* by force of law, it does require equal *treatment*. Equality of treatment in educational institutions is concretely measured by nondiscriminatory provision of access to "facilities and services." . . . Georgetown's refusal to provide tangible benefits without regard to sexual orientation violated the Human Rights Act. To that extent only, we consider the merits of Georgetown's free exercise defense.[107]

Thus, the plurality held that the D.C. law required that the university simply engage in the conduct of providing funds, facilities, and services in an evenhanded manner to the gay student groups. The plurality then simply asserted that providing such funds, facilities, and services did not translate into an endorsement of the groups' beliefs on sexual ethics, despite the University's clear statement that it viewed precisely such actions as connoting endorsement.[108]

As was apparent in the *Georgetown* case, a classic mark of judges who downplay the burden on religious people who are forced to engage in certain conduct is an unwillingness to err on the side of accepting the allegation that conduct can impair belief. For those of us who believe that government should err on the side of accepting such allegations (whether the allegation is that engaging in certain conduct will impair a person's religiously based belief or secularly based belief), the Court's decision in *Rumsfeld v. Forum for Academic & Institutional Rights, Inc. (FAIR)*[109] was particularly troubling.

The core argument of the law schools and law faculty in *Rumsfeld v. FAIR* was that forcing the schools to act in a certain way burdened their freedom of speech and freedom of expressive association.[110] The cavalier manner in which the Court treated FAIR's allegations does not bode well for future claims made by those who feel their religious or secular beliefs are being burdened when they are forced to comply with neutral civil rights laws.[111]

In *FAIR*, the law schools and law faculty claimed that the government burdened their freedom of speech and their freedom of expressive association[112] by requiring that they treat military recruiters better than other recruiters who discriminate based on sexual orientation.[113] The schools and faculty argued that while military recruitment was a compelling government interest, forcing the schools to treat military recruiters similarly to other recruiters (with no symbolic or logistical differences to convey the schools' disapproval of the military's recruitment policy) was not narrowly tailored to fit the compelling government interest of military recruitment.[114]

What exactly was the burden about which the schools and faculty were complaining? Obviously, the government was not requiring that the law schools pronounce their support for the statutory policy of "Don't Ask, Don't Tell," which set the parameters of military recruitment and which prohibited the recruitment of openly gay law students as Judge Advocate General or JAG Corps officers. No such speech was being coerced. Nor was the government prohibiting schools from loudly expressing their belief that an appropriate legal recruitment policy would have placed no weight on the sexual orientation of law students. To the extent that a school viewed itself as creating an expressive community based on such a view of justice, the government was not standing in its way.

The "only" thing the government was requiring from the law schools was a simple act of *conduct*: it was requiring that schools *treat* military recruiters *equally* to all other recruiters, even though the law schools viewed the military recruiters as advancing, and possibly embodying, an unjust and perhaps immoral position. Where was the burden in requiring such conduct?[115]

As with some religious people's claims that the act of complying with a neutral civil rights law burdens their religious beliefs, the answer lies in the inherent entangling between conduct and practice *in some situations.*

In most situations, of course, conduct is not intended to convey expression. For that reason, we do not ordinarily feel that a requirement to engage in certain conduct (or not to engage in certain conduct) necessarily undermines our identity or beliefs. We engage in innumerable acts throughout the day. We might get on the subway in the morning, buy a newspaper, order lunch, give an exam or take an exam, fix a car, buy stock, or feed a baby. We rarely experience ourselves as expressing a belief system when we engage in these forms of conduct. Beliefs may underlie our actions (for example, public transportation is good; newspapers should be supported; babies should be cared for), but it is rare that we experience our conduct (or our lack of engaging in certain conduct) as inherently intertwined with our beliefs and identities.

But that is not always the case. Sometimes being forced to engage in certain conduct—or being precluded from engaging in certain conduct—*will* impinge on our beliefs or identities. This is not an overly difficult situation to perceive. It is certainly not beyond the sophistication of a legislature or a court to ascertain. It requires that an individual articulate a particular belief or identity, and then articulate how being forced to engage in an act (or how being prohibited from engaging in an act) will interfere with, or will undermine, that belief or identity.

This is precisely the situation that the law schools and law faculty faced in *FAIR.* The schools and faculty experienced the "mere" conduct of assisting military recruiters as undermining their expressive beliefs. The members of FAIR held two expressive beliefs: first, that law students should be hired without regard to their sexual orientation, and second, that aiding and abetting any recruiter who took sexual orientation into account in hiring was unjust. Thus, a mandate by the government that the schools assist military recruiters who did not hire openly gay law students was experienced by the schools as burdening that second belief. Because the belief itself related to *conduct* (*i.e.*, it is unjust to aid and abet a discriminatory recruiter), the mandate to engage in certain conduct (*i.e.*, treat military recruiters the same as other recruiters) necessarily burdened that belief.

The Supreme Court got around this difficulty by simply refusing to accept that the government's requirement that the law schools engage in certain conduct burdened their expressive beliefs—much as some judges simply refuse to accept that a requirement to engage in certain conduct burdens the religious beliefs of an individual or an institution. The Court first recast the schools' argument as a concern that assisting military recruiters would mean that students

would get confused and would not be able to differentiate the military recruiters' message from the schools' message. To that contrived concern, the
Court wryly responded: "We have held that high school students can appreciate the difference between speech a school sponsors and speech the school permits because legally required to do so, pursuant to an equal access policy. Surely
students have not lost that ability by the time they get to law school."[116]

The schools' *actual* concern—that simply engaging in the conduct of hosting the military recruiters undermines the schools' expressive belief in nondiscrimination—was simply dismissed by the Court in a conclusory manner:

> To comply with the [Solomon Amendment], law schools must allow military
> recruiters on campus and assist them in whatever way the school chooses to as-
> sist other employers. Law schools therefore "associate" with military recruiters
> in the sense that they interact with them. But recruiters are not part of the law
> school. Recruiters are, by definition, outsiders who come onto campus for the
> limited purpose of trying to hire students—not to become members of the
> school's expressive association. This distinction is critical. Unlike the public
> accommodations law in *Dale*, the Solomon Amendment does not force a law
> school "to accept members it does not desire."[117]

Thus, the Court asserted that the conduct of associating with military recruiters who are not members of the school did not undermine the law
schools' expressive beliefs. The fact that the law schools experienced the association as causing precisely that result was simply ignored by the Court and
dismissed.

Religious employers who do not want to provide health benefits to same-
sex couples and religious schools who do not want to provide funding for gay
rights groups might view themselves as far removed from law schools that do
not wish to assist military recruiters who discriminate against gay law students. But the parallels between the two groups are stark: In each case, an individual or an institution experiences the coerced conduct (the "equality
mandate") as burdening its beliefs. And in each case, the individual or institution runs the risk that the State and the courts will simply dismiss its experience of burden as not real.

C. Justifying the Burden on Belief Liberty
It may be cold comfort to those with strongly held beliefs regarding the immorality and sinfulness of homosexuality that I argue that the burden on their
belief liberty should be acknowledged. After all, as I noted in the beginning
of this chapter and as I hope to make clear in this section, I believe it will
rarely be the case that a court should use the Due Process Clause to insert an

exemption to an LGBT equality law in order to accommodate the belief liberty of those who are regulated by the law.[118]

As Justice Souter contended in his *Glucksberg* concurrence, a court should not intervene "merely to identify a reasonable resolution of contending values that differs from the terms of the legislation under review."[119] Rather, "[i]t is only when the legislation's justifying principle, critically valued, is so far from being commensurate with the individual interest as to be arbitrarily or pointlessly applied that the statute must give way."[120]

Under this approach, I find it difficult to envision any circumstance in which a court could legitimately conclude that a legislature that has passed a LGBT equality law, with no exceptions for individual religious people based on belief liberty, has acted arbitrarily or pointlessly. If the "justifying principle" of the legislation is to protect the liberty of LGBT people to live freely and safely in all parts of society, it is perfectly reasonable for a legislature not to provide any exemption that will cordon off a significant segment of society from the nondiscrimination prohibition. This may not be the result a particular judge might have reached were she in the legislature, but it is certainly a "reasonable resolution of contending values" for a legislature to have reached.

Nevertheless, I believe explicating the burden that such civil rights laws may place on some individuals' belief liberty is still worthwhile. While a court should not be permitted to re-strike a balance between competing liberties when the balance already struck by the legislature is reasonable, that does not mean the *legislature* should not choose to place certain exemptions in the law at the outset. The utility in acknowledging the burdens on belief liberty that might arise from the application of civil rights laws is that advocates of such laws might see their way to deciding that the legislature should protect belief liberty in a limited set of circumstances. Indeed, the best outcome would be for such decisions to be made in a negotiated setting with those whose beliefs will be adversely impacted by the law.

It probably seems dangerous to advocates of LGBT equality to acknowledge that a civil rights law might burden the liberty of those who are regulated by the law. This is because laws prohibiting discrimination based on sexual orientation that have been held to burden a constitutionally protected right have not fared well in Supreme Court jurisprudence thus far.[121] The Supreme Court's opinion in *Boy Scouts of America v. Dale*,[122] creating an exemption for the Boy Scouts of America to New Jersey's law prohibiting discrimination based on sexual orientation, is the classic example.

In *Dale*, the Court spent the bulk of its opinion explaining why it agreed with the Boy Scouts that forcing the organization to retain James Dale as an assistant scoutmaster, after Dale had acknowledged that he was gay, would "significantly burden"[123] the Boy Scouts' desire "to not promote homosexual conduct as a legitimate form of behavior."[124]

As can be deduced from what I have written thus far, I have only a small quarrel with the Court's analysis in that regard. It seems eminently reasonable to me that a group that wishes to convey the message that homosexual behavior is immoral, wrong, and unacceptable would not want one of its leaders to be a happy, well-adjusted, and ordinary-seeming gay person. My small quarrel with the Court's analysis is that the Boy Scouts failed to consistently and clearly convey such a message about homosexuality to its members. I have no difficulty accepting an organization's statement of its beliefs and then deferring to that organization's allegation that engaging in certain conduct will undermine those beliefs. Nevertheless, it does seem to me that the organization must clearly *state* its beliefs and then conform its actions to those beliefs in a logical fashion. The Boy Scouts' position was problematic on both fronts: first, the organization's public membership documents did not clearly state that homosexuality was inconsistent with the Boy Scouts' oath, and second, the organization did not consistently remove heterosexual scoutmasters who publicly stated that homosexuality was acceptable.[125]

But the fatal flaw in the Court's *Dale* opinion, from my perspective, was its failure to truly examine whether the burden on the Boy Scouts was *justified*. This would have required, first, a careful analysis of the state's interest in prohibiting discrimination based on sexual orientation in order to determine the importance of that interest. Next, it would have required an analysis of whether refusing to include an exemption in the law for entities whose expressive association beliefs would thereby be burdened was "so far from being commensurate with the individual interest as to be arbitrarily or pointlessly applied."[126]

If that analysis had been done, and if the Court had taken seriously the adverse impact on the identity liberty of gay people when a government fails to protect them from private discrimination, I believe the Court would have appropriately determined that a group as large and as broad-based as the Boy Scouts should not have been granted an exemption from the state law.

But the Court's analysis in *Dale* regarding whether New Jersey's interests in protecting gay people justified its burdening of the Boy Scouts' expressive association rights was neither thorough nor thoughtful. The Court's "analysis" consisted of the following three sentences:

> We have already concluded that a state requirement that the Boy Scouts retain Dale as an assistant scoutmaster would significantly burden the organization's

right to oppose or disfavor homosexual conduct. The state interests embodied in New Jersey's public accommodations law do not justify such a severe intrusion on the Boy Scouts' rights to freedom of expressive association. *That being the case*, we hold that the First Amendment prohibits the State from imposing such a requirement through the application of its public accommodations law.[127]

"*That being the case?*" The very lack of analysis in the Court's opinion—the simple reliance on these conclusory words—was a slap in the face of gay people. It was also an example of poor legal reasoning—or perhaps simply absent legal reasoning.[128]

The plurality in the *Georgetown* case did a better job of analyzing the compelling interest a government might have in prohibiting discrimination on the basis of sexual orientation. After delving extensively into the literature regarding sexual orientation, as well as exploring the legislative history of the D.C. Council's ordinance, the plurality noted the following:

> The Council determined that a person's sexual orientation, like a person's race and sex, for example, tells nothing of value about his or her attitudes, characteristics, abilities or limitations. It is a false measure of individual worth, one unfair and oppressive to the person concerned, one harmful to others because discrimination inflicts a grave and recurring injury upon society as a whole. To put an end to this evil, the Council outlawed sexual orientation discrimination in employment, in real estate transactions, in public accommodations, in educational institutions, and elsewhere. Such comprehensive measures were necessary to ensure that "[e]very individual shall have an equal opportunity to participate fully in the economic, cultural and intellectual life of the District, and to have an equal opportunity to participate in all aspects of life. . . ."[129]

The plurality also invoked the majestic sweep of the federal constitutional liberty interest in underscoring the importance of a state interest in prohibiting discrimination based on sexual orientation:

> The compelling interests, therefore, that any state has in eradicating discrimination against the homosexually or bisexually oriented include the fostering of individual dignity, the creation of a climate and environment in which each individual can utilize his or her potential to contribute to and benefit from society, and equal protection of life, liberty and property that the Founding Fathers guaranteed to us all.[130]

Ensuring that LGBT people can live honestly and safely in all aspects of their social lives requires that society set a baseline of nondiscrimination on the grounds of sexual orientation and gender identity. If individual business owners, service providers, and employers could easily exempt themselves from such laws by making credible claims that their belief liberty is burdened by the law, LGBT people would remain constantly vulnerable to surprise discrimination. If I am denied a job, an apartment, a room at a hotel, a table at a restaurant, or a procedure by a doctor because I am a lesbian, that is a deep, intense, and tangible hurt. That hurt is not alleviated because I might be able to go down the street and get a job, an apartment, a hotel room, a restaurant table, or a medical procedure from someone else. The assault to my dignity and my sense of safety in the world occurs when the initial denial happens. That assault is not mitigated by the fact that others might not treat me in the same way.[131]

Thus, for all my sympathy for the evangelical Christian couple who may wish to run a bed and breakfast from which they can exclude unmarried straight couples and all gay couples, this is a point where I believe an inevitable choice between liberties must come into play. In making that choice, I believe society should come down on the side of protecting the identity liberty of LGBT people. Once an individual chooses to enter the stream of economic commerce by opening a commercial establishment, I believe it is legitimate to require that they play by certain rules.[132] If the government tolerated the private exclusionary policies of such individuals in the commercial sector, such toleration would necessarily come at the cost of gay people's sense of belonging and safety in society. Just as we do not tolerate private racial beliefs that adversely affect African-Americans in the commercial arena, even if such beliefs are based on religious views, we should similarly not tolerate private beliefs about sexual orientation and gender identity that adversely affect the ability of LGBT people to live in the world.[133]

But that is not to say that we should not acknowledge that this societal choice *has* resulted in a burden on some individuals' belief liberties and that we should not be forced to articulate why such a burden is appropriate. A government's reasons for burdening liberty should be, as Professor Rebecca Brown argues, "accessible to all in a meaningful sense."[134] Brown defines these as reasons that "have some public and secular component to them and [do] not rest entirely on personal moral belief systems not universally shared."[135] While I am not sure I would use Brown's formulation of a "personal moral belief system[] not universally shared," I do believe that the reasons given by the state must "reflect the public good."[136] And ensuring that members of the public who have a morally neutral characteristic will be able to live without fear of or vulnerability to discrimination based on that characteristic certainly seems to be a reason that reflects the public good.

The question remains, however, whether there are limited situations in which a *legislature* might legitimately choose to protect the belief liberty of individuals or institutions over the identity liberty of LGBT people. I believe there are two situations that are worth exploring.

As a general matter, once a religious person or institution enters the stream of commerce by operating an enterprise such as a doctor's office, hospital, bookstore, hotel, treatment center, and so on, I believe the enterprise must adhere to a norm of nondiscrimination on the basis of sexual orientation and gender identity. This is essential so that an individual who happens upon the enterprise is not surprised by a denial of service and/or a directive to go down the street to a different provider. While I was initially drawn to the idea of providing an exemption to those enterprises that advertise solely in very limited milieus (such as the bed & breakfast that advertises only on Christian websites), I became wary of such an approach as a practical matter. The touchstone for any approach, I believe, needs to be whether LGBT people might be made vulnerable in too many locations across society. An "advertising exception" seemed potentially subject to significant abuse.

Nevertheless, I believe there might be a more limited exception that would be justified. There are enterprises that are engaged in by belief communities (almost always religious belief communities) that are specifically designed to inculcate values in the next generation. These may include schools, day care centers, summer camps, and tours. These enterprises are sometimes for-profit and sometimes not-for-profit. They are within the general stream of commerce, together with many other schools, day care centers, summer camps, and tours.

I believe a subset of these enterprises present a compelling case for the legislature to provide an exemption in a law mandating nondiscrimination based on sexual orientation. The criteria for an exemption should be as follows: the enterprise must present itself clearly and explicitly as designed to inculcate a set of beliefs; the beliefs of the enterprise must be clearly set forth as being inconsistent with a belief that homosexuality is morally neutral; and the enterprise must seek to enroll only individuals who wish to be inculcated with such beliefs.

The dignity of LGBT individuals would still be harmed by excluding such enterprises from the purview of a nondiscrimination law. But in weighing the interests between the groups, I believe the harm to the enterprise in having its inculcation of values to its members significantly hampered (as I believe it would be if it were forced to comply with such a law) outweighs the harm to the excluded LGBT members.

I am more hesitant regarding the second limited circumstance, but I offer it for analysis and critique.[137] I believe a legislature might legitimately offer an exemption for *leadership* positions in enterprises that are broadly represented in commerce. Many religious institutions operate the gamut of social services in the community, such as hospitals, gyms, adoption agencies, and drug treatment centers. These enterprises are open and marketed to the general public and often receive governmental funds. It seems quite appropriate to require that the services of these enterprises be delivered without regard to sexual orientation and that most employment positions in these enterprises be available without regard to sexual orientation.

But the balance of interests, it seems to me, shifts with regard to the *leadership* positions in such enterprises. Particularly for religiously affiliated institutions, I believe it is important that people in leadership positions be able to articulate the beliefs and values of the enterprise. If the identity and practice of an openly gay person would stand in direct contradiction to those beliefs and values, it seems to me that the enterprise would suffer a significant harm. Thus, in this limited circumstance, a legislature may legitimately conclude that the harm to the enterprise will be greater than the harm to the particular individuals who would be excluded from such positions. A legislature that came to this conclusion might legitimately provide a narrow exemption from a nondiscrimination mandate in employment for such leadership positions.

II. Conclusion

Professor Andy Koppelman, with whom I have been in dialogue on this issue for some time, correctly observes that my suggestions in this area are radical.[138] In one respect, this is true. My suggestion that there should be judicial and legislative acknowledgment of a "belief liberty" under the Due Process Clause that encompasses *any* sincerely held core belief can indeed be viewed as a radical departure from the more traditional judicial and legislative focus on solely religiously based beliefs.[139]

As I hope my analysis has made clear, however, such an acknowledgment need not bring the mechanisms of our complex society to a screeching halt. For a court to invalidate a law based on its burdening of belief liberty, the court must first find that the legislature could not have legitimately enacted the law as a "reasonable resolution of contending values."[140] By contrast, a legislature is permitted greater latitude and greater responsibility to consider and weigh these contending values when it enacts legislation in the first place—exactly as it should be in a democratic process.

My primary argument is that we gain something as a society if we acknowledge that a law requiring individuals to act in a certain way might burden some individuals' belief liberties. Such an acknowledgment is necessary if we wish to be respectful of the whole person. Protecting one group's identity liberty may, at times, require that we burden others' belief liberties. This is an inherent and irreconcilable reality of our complex society. But I would rather live in a society where we acknowledge that conflict openly, and where we engage in an honest dialogue about what accommodations might be possible given that reality, than to live in a society where we pretend the conflict does not exist in the first place.

But in dealing with this conflict, I believe it is essential that we not privilege moral beliefs that are religiously based over other sincerely held core moral beliefs. Laws passed pursuant to public policies may burden the belief liberty of those who adhere to either religious or secular beliefs. What seems of paramount importance to me is that we respect these core beliefs and do the best we can in this imperfect world of ours to protect both identity liberty and belief liberty to the greatest extent possible.

CHAPTER SIX

Marriage: Its Relationship to Religion, Law, and the State

Charles J. Reid, Jr.[1]

This chapter serves two essential purposes. First, it provides a historical context to contemporary debates involving the decoupling of the legal regulation of marriage from its roots in a Christian order. That order was given decisive shape in medieval and early modern Europe and adapted to American purposes by nineteenth-century judges and legislators. It was natural for early American jurists to look back to these sources, especially as mediated by the ecclesiastical law of England. Part I explores some examples of this sort of borrowing. Marriage was said by early American courts to be a matter of divine law and to reflect the law of God. This point was made in a general rhetorical way, but also given practical implementation through such vehicles as incest laws. Thus some courts in incest prosecutions looked to the definition in chapter eighteen of the Book of Leviticus. This history highlights the radical departure from tradition marked by decisions such as *Goodridge v. Department of Public Health*,[2] which distort this historical record.

Second, this chapter seeks to demonstrate the ultimate unworkability of a radical separation of religion and law on the subject of marriage. As a matter of anthropology, the human personality seeks to mark social transitions such as marriage with ritual and solemnity. As a matter of jurisprudence, the law teaches values through the behaviors it sanctions and those it prohibits. Part II lays bare some of the deeper incoherencies in a liberal theory of marriage that prizes as the ultimate value the continuing consent of parties, with no regard for other considerations.

I. Religion, Marriage, and the State: The Medieval Synthesis

A necessary first step must be definitional. Religion has been defined in various ways by philosophers, anthropologists, historians, and others, receiving different definitions depending on the faith commitments of the scholar proposing the definition. A particularly compelling definition has been offered by Judge John Noonan, describing religion as fundamentally about the relationship between persons and "a heart not known, responding to our own."[3] This unknown presence, who shapes us, stands with us, whom we trust with our deepest intimacies, is God. "[L]iving communication" characterizes this relationship, which must be approached with "empathy" and "imagination."[4] Religion, furthermore, is bound inextricably with the nature of the human person. Indeed, Noonan makes the point that religion is as ineradicable an aspect of the human experience as the sexual impulse.[5] Religion is about nothing less than the meaning of ultimate existence—"the problem of being and nonbeing, life and death."[6]

What is of interest to the legal scholar are the ways in which the collective insights into ultimate meaning formed by a particular society come to be translated into norms and rules for social existence. This chapter is concerned with one particular aspect of this much larger question—the nexus found at the confluence of three streams of human reality: religious belief, especially understood as collective social enterprise; the marital union; and the ways in which the state has used its authority and power to mediate and define the terms of the other two.

This chapter will have its center of gravity in American legal history of the last two hundred years. But American legal history is not fully explicable without an appreciation of what went before. Frederic William Maitland said regarding English legal history, "Such is the unity of all history that anyone who endeavors to tell a piece of it must feel that his first sentence tears a seamless web."[7] This insight applies as much to American law as to English law. Indeed, to tell the story of the interaction of religion, law, and the state in American history requires us to go back in time at least to the twelfth century. This starting point helps to reveal the powerful relationship that has prevailed in Western history between religious faith and the legal structure of marriage. The twelfth century witnessed a renaissance in learning.[8] The first universities were founded and set as their goal not merely the conservation of the collected wisdom of the past but the actual creation of knowledge through a dialectical method that questioned received authority.[9] This development was made possible by a general settling down of society and the emergence of complex institutional structures after a half millennium of transitory and failed experiments at political organization following the collapse of Roman power in the West. Indeed, it has been persuasively contended that the Western legal tradition itself came into being in the twelfth century as canon lawyers, many of them teaching and writing at the new universities, reduced to systematic juridic forms the mass of ecclesiastical learning of the previous one thousand years.[10]

Historically, going as far back in time as the twelfth century, marriage was defined in terms of legal categories that were shaped fundamentally by Christian theological insight. It was in the twelfth and thirteenth centuries that canon lawyers at the major European universities began to put into systematic legal form the theological heritage of the previous thousand years with a focus in particular on the thought of Augustine and other patristic writers of the era.

Augustine, who wrote at the end of the fourth century and the beginning of the fifth, conceived of marriage as serving three basic goods: procreation, permanence, and life long faithfulness or unity.[11] Medieval lawyers reduced these theological insights to legal categories and brought to their enforcement the coercive jurisdiction of the Church, which had at its disposal a variety of spiritual sanctions.[12] Where parties to a marriage affirmatively excluded one or more of these Augustinian goods from their exchange of consent, the union itself failed. The state, for its part, by and large ceded control of the marital relationship to the Church and contented itself with regulating some of the "incidents" that accompanied valid marriage. In the context of medieval England this involved such incidents as the exaction of feudal dues at the time of the marriage and the adoption of rules governing the inheritance of real, but not personal, property.[13]

Medieval canonists were vigorous in fleshing out a theory of marriage that assigned theological significance to nearly every attribute of the marital relationship. They stressed, for instance, that only the consent of the parties themselves sufficed to make a marriage and gave as a reason the theological insight that marriage was an enduring union of souls that required a freely chosen decision to enter precisely in order to convey its symbolic qualities to the world.[14] The canonists further distinguished between consent and consummation, and determined that while consent made a marriage, consummation conferred on it a special firmness that no human power might break.[15] Again, a theological explanation was offered as the basis of this rule. Consummation transformed a human relationship into a living, earthly representation of Jesus Christ's unfailing marriage to His Church.[16]

The medieval canonists developed yet more refinements for their theologically inspired analysis of marriage. They distinguished between grounds of nullity and grounds of divorce. This much was required by their theology of an unbreakable marital bond. Entry into a life-long commitment obviously required the observance beforehand of a high degree of freedom from coercion and an awareness of the nature of the contract and its obligations. Hence persons marrying one another had to be free of external coercion,[17] and they could not be the victims of fundamental error as to the person whom they were marrying.[18] Furthermore, they might be prevented from marriage with one another by any of a number of impediments that existed in the law.[19]

The recognition that a given marriage might be invalid, that it might be so radically flawed that it could be considered never to have come into existence, led the canonists to develop a judicial system empowered to investigate such claims. Success before the ecclesiastical courts led to the granting of an annulment; and those who obtained annulments of their putative marriages were thereby freed to move on to new partners. After all, they had not been married at all in the eyes of the Church.

On the other hand, parties whose marriages, although valid, failed for some fundamental reason such as adultery or a lapse into heresy, enjoyed the right to seek an ecclesiastical divorce, although such a decree carried no right of remarriage. In addition to adultery and heresy, one might also seek a decree of separation by reason of excessive violence and brutality (called *saevitia* by the canonists).[20] Again, what one sees at work here are the consequences of the doctrine of indissolubility—the marital bond was held to be enduring, even where the parties found it impossible to live together and were granted by competent authority the right to live apart. Since the bond endured for so long as both parties remained alive, remarriage was theoretically impossible during the lifetime of the other party.

Nor were these the only rules the medieval canonists developed. The canonists were truly prolific in defining and developing any number of the other elements of domestic relations law as it evolved from the middle ages to the twentieth century.

The English Reformation modified some aspects of the edifice constructed by the medieval canonists. The belief that marriage was a sacrament was abolished.[21] The Anglicans also followed the lead of their continental Protestant brethren in reposing ultimate authority in the male head of household while simultaneously diminishing the rights of women.[22]

But in other respects, the Anglican canonists did not greatly disturb the basic legal structure established by their medieval predecessors. English jurists continued to stress—as had the medieval canonists—that marriage was a contract that derived its efficacy from divine law. Thus John Ayliffe, writing in the early eighteenth century, noted that marriage "was first instituted by God himself in Paradise."[23] It was ordained by God "for the Propagation of Mankind."[24] Indeed, the "Law of Nature" and "right Reason itself" taught that the "Necessity of human Propagation" was the obvious and transcendent purpose for which marriage was brought into being.[25]

Ayliffe's contemporaries echoed these sentiments. Lord Stair in the late seventeenth century described marriage in similarly transcendent terms. Marriage, he wrote, "Was *iure divino*"—the product of divine law.[26] The marriage contract, Lord Stair added, "is not a human, but a divine, contract."[27] The basic rules of marriage were also the product of divine law. Lord Stair gave the specific example of the incest prohibitions. "[T]here is," he stressed, "a natural abhorrence of that promiscuous commixtion of blood."[28]

English Protestant lawyers thus shared with their medieval forebears a belief in the divine origin of marriage, even while they eschewed its sacramental character. And even though they no longer considered marriage a sacrament, they continued to retain the older canonistic rules governing marital indissolubility. A party seeking to take leave of his or her marriage might, like his or her medieval ancestors, choose either to have the marriage declared invalid (styled by the English lawyers divorce *a vinculo*), or to seek "a separation from bed and board" (divorce *a mensa et thoro*). A decree of nullity carried with it the right of remarriage, but separation from bed and board did not.[29] To obtain the right to marry following such an "ecclesiastical divorce," furthermore, one had to take the step of petitioning Parliament for permission, which in practice was rarely sought and even more rarely granted.[30]

Until 1857, the English ecclesiastical courts retained jurisdiction over marriage and its incidents.[31] In the centuries between the Reformation and the abolition of ecclesiastical jurisdiction, these courts had created an ornate structure of marriage law, which would prove to have significant impact on the law of the nineteenth-century United States.

While the great bulk of this chapter is concerned with exploring the relationship between religious belief and marriage in American law, it is necessary to understand the medieval and early-modern English background because it provides deep structure to the American law of marriage. American lawyers continued to operate, well into the twentieth century, in a juristic universe that used the language of divine and natural law to describe the marital relationship and its peculiar attributes. Many peculiarities of the law of domestic relations as found in the nineteenth- and early-twentieth-century America can only be explained by a knowledge of the canon law that had come before. In short, the frame of reference that lawyers relied upon to define and defend the obligations of parties to a marriage was essentially medieval. Sacramentality may have disappeared and secular courts may have come to regulate the marital relationship, but still the medieval thought-world persisted in some very interesting ways.

But while the ideas and language frequently remained identical with the vocabulary and thought-world of much older times, the North American legal context was, of course, entirely different from early modern England or late medieval Europe. Perhaps the most important difference is the fact that early American courts operated in a universe in which ecclesiastical jurisdiction had been abolished. While English lawyers had to wait until the late 1850s to see ecclesiastical jurisdiction over marriage abolished, the jurisdiction of church courts had almost entirely vanished from America before the founding of the new republic.

This, then, is the anomaly that informs the relationship between domestic relations law and the state in the context of American legal development—the anomaly of secular courts applying categories of thought that were given shape and substance by centuries of labor on the part of ecclesiastical canonists and courts. While I shall focus on the tripartite relationship described by my title—marriage, religion, and the state—it is a relationship defined not only by the use of religious categories to define marriage, but also by the fact that it was secular, not religious, courts that had to make use of these essentially religious categories. How this anomaly played out in American history is the subject of part II of this chapter. The normative question—does this historical record compel some sort of response?—is deferred until the chapter's final section.

II. Marriage and Religion in American Legal History

A. Preliminary Considerations

American domestic relations law has deep roots in the sort of medieval and early-modern Christianity discussed in part I. To draw upon this material as deeply as one might wish would require a book-length treatment. This part gives instead a brief and impressionistic survey of the subject, looking at a few representative samplings of the ways in which American courts invoked, adapted, and utilized a religious frame of reference in resolving matrimonial disputes.

The use of a legal vocabulary—distinctive turns of phrase or ideas—is traceable to medieval Christian or to Anglican canonistic antecedents. Tracing legal vocabulary has value in its own right as an intellectual history—an exercise that speaks not only to what early American courts thought about marriage, but also what they regarded as legitimate sources of law. Aside from its value as history, the investigation has value in widening the horizon of contemporary public policy debates that seem excessively dependent upon a variety of utilitarian calculations to the exclusion of larger questions about ultimate human goods.

As a preliminary matter, one must recognize how different from our own was the early American understanding of the sources of law. A modern American law student is trained to read cases to search for their holdings, to read statutes in search of their scope and application, and to consider carefully the language of particular constitutional provisions. These are now the formal sources of law to the exclusion of almost everything else. This intensely positivistic reading of the law, however, was simply not known to lawyers in the early American republic. One might take William Blackstone's account of the sources of law as representative of the ways in which early American lawyers viewed the most fundamental question a lawyer confronting the sources must ask, *i.e.*, what is law? (Blackstone's *Commentaries*, although English, was considered the obligatory starting point for legal study in the United States even decades after the Revolutionary War.[32])

In his hierarchy of sources, Blackstone began with "the law of nature," which is nothing less than "[the] will of [man's] maker," God.[33] This natural law included "the eternal, immutable laws of good and evil."[34] The eternal natural law, Blackstone stressed, was superior to human law; indeed, "no human laws are of any validity, if contrary to this."[35] Natural law, furthermore, consisted of two subcategories: that taught directly by God, through Scripture; and that deduced by the human person through the use of reason.[36] Blackstone followed this distinction by insisting once again, "[N]o human law should be suffered to contradict these."[37]

After establishing the primacy of divine and natural law, Blackstone then turned his attention to the "municipal law," by which he meant the law binding within particular kingdoms and realms ("'a rule of civil conduct prescribed *by the supreme power in a state*'").[38] The British Constitution, which consisted of the monarchy, the lords spiritual and temporal, and the House of Commons, Blackstone claimed, was uniquely well suited to exercise this authority.[39] Charged with lawmaking and law-interpreting powers, these constitutional offices oversee, conserve, and advance the municipal law of the realm—not the common law only, but also the "ecclesiastical," the "military," the "maritime," and the "academical law."[40] Common law, which is both written and unwritten, consists finally in customs, judicial interpretation, and statutory enactment.

Blackstone's writings reflected an essentially theistic understanding of the law with deep roots in medieval thought. The proposition that human law mirrors and must be in conformity with the divine and natural law can be found in many medieval sources.[41] The relative degree of deference he showed to the authority of the king and Parliament reflected, no doubt, the sort of recognition an eighteenth-century Anglican had to pay to the status of the king as supreme in church as well as state. But even with that qualification, it is clear that Blackstone understood the divine and natural law, whose main principles are knowable by human reason, to serve as an ultimate check on the potential arbitrariness of merely human rule.

Blackstone's *Commentaries* would prove immensely popular in the new United States and exercised a commanding authority over early American jurists. The study of Blackstone's *Commentaries* as an indispensable introduction to the study of law ensured that practitioners would acquire an awareness of the wholeness of the law and a sense of its jurisprudential foundations in a way that instruction from casebooks has failed to do, given the latter's tendency to move from doctrine to doctrine, all the while focused on narrow questions of law.[42]

And these jurisprudential foundations were self-consciously Christian. In particular, early American lawyers and judges picked up and developed Blackstone's teaching that "Christianity is a part of the laws of England."[43] This assertion became so ubiquitous in the nineteenth century that one modern historian wrote:

> Nineteenth-century American judges and lawyers often claimed that Christianity was part of the common law. From Kent and Story in the early part of the century, to Cooley and Tiedeman toward the end, the maxim that "Christianity is part and parcel of the common law" (or some variant thereof) was heard so often that later commentators could refer to it as a matter "decided over and over again," one which "text writers have affirmed."[44]

B. The Survival of a Religious Vocabulary in the American Law of Marriage

1. Marriage, the Divine Law, and the Law of God

It is jarring and unexpected to find references to divine law when reading the opinions of American courts that have undertaken to explain the foundations of the law of marriage. One might expect to see this sort of reasoning in a medieval discussion of marriage's sacramentality.[45] One might also expect to see such language in an early Anglican treatise on canon law, such as Ayliffe's, which insisted that the institution of marriage was a matter of

"Divine Will and Command."[46] And, of course, one still encounters this sort of language in the official teaching of the Catholic Church, as, for example, the Second Vatican Council's affirmation that marriage "is an institution confirmed by divine law."[47] But to find such assertions in American judicial opinions seems entirely out of place.

One is nevertheless confronted with a group of cases that declare exactly that. In 1876, in language that is, at least in part, eerily reminiscent of the privacy decisions of the mid-1960s United States Supreme Court, the Supreme Court of New Hampshire wrote of marriage that "it is the most intimate and confidential of all human relations, and has always been sanctioned and protected by both human and divine law."[48] The Supreme Court of Washington declared in 1892 that "the married state is a most commendable one, and ought to be encouraged in all legitimate ways, having, as it does, its origin in divine law."[49] The Supreme Court of Indiana rejected the proposition that a married woman over the age of twenty-one required a guardian as something that "would be a violation of all our ideas of secular and the divine law."[50] The Missouri Supreme Court spoke of marriage as a "sacred relation," held as much "in the common as in the Divine Law."[51]

This phraseology retained significance into the early and middle decades of the twentieth century. In 1958, the New York Supreme Court, Appellate Division, quoted with approval an earlier decision of the New Jersey Supreme Court that said, "The human race was created male and female with the manifest purpose of perpetuating the race. Marriage without sexual intercourse utterly defeats its purpose, as sexual intercourse except in the marital relation is contrary to the divine law . . . ."[52]

Perhaps the most interesting of these early- and middle-twentieth-century cases comes from Pennsylvania. At issue in *In re Enderle Marriage License*, decided in 1954, was a statute that prohibited marriage between cousins.[53] Frank, the petitioner, was adopted into the Enderle family and sought to marry his cousin by adoption, Adelheld.[54] The parties were not blood relations. The court determined that the statute in question was intended to prevent incest between blood relations only, and not those related by adoption, and so permitted the issuance of the marriage license. What is interesting, however, was the reasoning the court employed in reaching this conclusion. It offered two secular justifications for its reading of the statute, but gave primacy to an argument drawn explicitly from its understanding of the divine law:

> The purpose of the legislature in prohibiting marriages within certain degrees of consanguinity and affinity is at least threefold: (1) To maintain the Divine Law forbidding the marriage of close relatives; (2) for eugenic reasons, to preserve

and strengthen the general racial and physical qualities of its citizens by pre-venting inbreeding; and (3) to maintain the sanctity of the home and prevent the disastrous consequences of competition for sexual companionship between members of the same household or family.[55]

Fifty years removed from *Enderle*, we no doubt would find different lan-guage when analyzing this problem. The invocation of racial improvement and eugenics, thankfully, is no longer a part of our public discourse, although a general desire to prevent inbreeding is certainly still a legitimate public pol-icy. And a concern to limit sexual competition within a family unit would loom very large in our public justifications for the law. Divine law, however, would no longer be mentioned, let alone have the "D" and the "L" put in capital letters. What is remarkable, however, is how hardy such language has proven to be. The reasoning of the *Enderle* court would have been recogniz-able by thirteenth-century canonists and by seventeenth- and eighteenth-century Anglican divines alike. *Enderle*'s language moved, in other words, in a very ancient thought-world.

Analytically nearly identical to divine law is the linguistic formula, "the law of God." In addition to divine law, one encounters frequent invocations of "the law of God" in cases involving marriage and domestic relations. Thus one finds the Arkansas Supreme Court writing:

> [W]e ought to say that marriage is a divine institution. As a consequence thereof, it is ordained by the laws of God and man that children shall be brought into the world. The family throughout all Christendom is the primal unit of society.[56]

Invocations of "the law of God," like invocations of the divine law, are not found only in cases arising in the Bible Belt. One sees, for example, the Con-necticut Supreme Court upholding a lawyer's disbarment upon his adultery conviction because he chose "'to put his own ideas of law above what you might fairly call the laws of God and man.'"[57] The Supreme Judicial Court of Massachusetts denounced attempts at marriage that were "against the laws of God" and specifically referenced the incest provisions.[58] And a dissenting opinion from the Supreme Court of California described a man who chose to cohabit with a woman other than his wife as someone whose "relationship violates the laws of God and man."[59]

Like invocations of divine law, one finds references to the "laws of God" or "God's law" occurring with at least some frequency into the middle decades of the twentieth century. Thus a dissenting opinion in a 1947 case from Washington denounced a couple living in adultery as "insensible to the laws of God and man."[60] The Texas Court of Criminal Appeals, meanwhile, sustained a bigamy conviction as upholding "the laws of God and man."[61] Even Learned Hand, not a particularly religious judge,[62] invoked "God's law" in ruling that an immigrant couple consisting of an uncle and a niece were not guilty of any crime for having married one another in a foreign ceremony and thus were not subject to deportation.[63]

The question a historian must confront is how one should make sense of these cases. The following conclusions seem warranted: Many early American jurists seemed to think that marriage was something that had its origins in a natural law that in turn reflected a divine plan; this natural law exercised real power over human affairs even in the absence of the state or the state's laws. It fell to lawmakers and judges to interpret and apply this law, not to legislate out of whole cloth. More generally, one can also conclude that Christianity continued to exercise not only a cultural influence over the judiciary but a real intellectual and moral attraction. While I am restricting this chapter to marriage and domestic relations law, its thesis—that the jurisprudential foundations laid down by generations of medieval and early-modern lawyers continued to influence the shape of American judicial thought until only a couple of generations ago—seems capable of a broader application. I have explored some aspects of this influence in other work.[64]

This two-fold reading of the historical record, emphasizing both the general historical influence of Christianity and its specific applicability to the shape of American domestic relations law, is probably the most helpful explanation for the marital teaching of the early American jurist, Chancellor James Kent of New York. Kent declared that, "The primary and most important of the domestic relations is that of husband and wife. It has its foundation in nature, and is the only lawful relation by which Providence has permitted the continuance of the human race."[65]

2. The Book of Leviticus and the Early American Judiciary

General invocations of divine law or the law of God, a critic might insist, reveal nothing more than a decent respect for the common pieties of the age. It reveals little real influence of Christian principle on actual legal practices or doctrines. Proof of influence only comes with evidence that a particular contemporary legal institution has assumed a certain shape *precisely because of* some particular Christian teaching. The acknowledgments of divine law so far discussed, this critic might continue, really show only that some judges at least knew to appeal to popular Christian opinion in a more religious age.

Such a criticism would be invalid. In fact, one can point to particular instances of influence on particular legal institutions. At the most general level, the American law of marriage favored the fundamental values of procreation, permanence, and fidelity precisely because of ecclesiastical antecedents.[66] One might also consider more specific legal institutions, such as the prohibition of incest. As the *Enderle* case reveals, multiple justifications might be cited as support for the incest prohibition.[67] In fact, however, nineteenth-century legal commentators tended to look to the Bible when arguing against incest. Introducing the subject of incestuous marriage to his readers in 1891, Joel Prentiss Bishop, one of the most prolific of the nineteenth-century treatise writers,[68] declared "[t]he law of this subject [to be] a compound of natural law and theological dogma."[69] Bishop went on to trace the history of the rules regarding incest and marriage, as they had developed in the Anglo-American context. A statute of King Henry VIII— "which is common law in this country," Bishop assured his readers—"declared lawful the marriage of all persons not prohibited by God's law to marry; and that no reservation or prohibition, God's law except, shall trouble or impeach any marriage without the Levitical degrees."[70]

The Henrician statute's reference to the "Levitical degrees" proved especially fertile ground for nineteenth- and twentieth-century courts. Chapter eighteen of the book of Leviticus prohibited, among other liaisons, sexual intercourse between a parent and his or her children, between or among siblings, and, by implication, lineal descendants or ancestors in the parental line.[71] Leviticus also prohibited sexual relations between in-laws.[72] The term "consanguinity" was used generally in the law to describe those barred from marriage to one another by blood relationship, while "affinity" was used to describe those in-laws forbidden to marry one another. For much of American history, courts made regular use of the Levitical degrees and the categories they established as a source of guidance in resolving a number of disputed questions concerning domestic relations law.

The extent to which the Henrician statute with its biblical foundation was considered an applicable source of law can be gauged by an early Kentucky opinion that engaged in what might look to contemporary readers as a fairly tortured reasoning process. The Kentucky Supreme Court in *Jenkins v. Jenkins' Heirs* rejected an expansive reading of the statute that permitted all those not related in the Levitical degree to marry.[73] More was required to marry validly, the court insisted: Since marriage was a civil contract and, impliedly at least, was governed by the rules of contractual capacity, parties were required to enjoy the use of reason in order to consent.[74] Thus the court concluded not only close relatives but also the insane were prohibited from marriage.[75] It is clear that the court felt compelled to engage in this labored exegesis of biblical precedent and the natural-law grounds of contractual capacity because it was painting on a largely blank canvas; it does not appear that there was a statute on point. The court wished to make it clear that neither incest nor the marriages of the insane would be tolerated. And the rules established in Leviticus were the best source it could come up with for the incest prohibition.

Other courts accepted the Levitical degrees as a convincing foundation for the incest prohibition. The Supreme Judicial Court of Massachusetts in 1924 confronted the question whether parties related by the half-blood were prohibited from marriage.[76] The court reviewed the history of the Commonwealth's incest prohibition, beginning with the acceptance of the Levitical degrees as a source of law in sixteenth-century ecclesiastical law and on through a succession of ecclesiastical and secular sources.[77] The court concluded that it should accept the interpretation placed on the Levitical degrees by the English ecclesiastical courts when they prohibited marriages among those related by the half-blood.[78]

The Louisiana Supreme Court, for its part, acknowledged that incest lacked "a fixed and definite meaning," but that the Levitical degrees provided generally sound guidance.[79] In 1914, the Iowa Supreme Court justified its acceptance of the Levitical degrees by noting that their use in resolving incest questions was endorsed by a leading legal encyclopedia.[80] And in 1929, the Iowa Supreme Court reviewed the legal history of the Levitical degrees and their importance to domestic relations law in responding to an appeal of a criminal conviction for incest.[81]

The Levitical degrees figured prominently in a variety of contexts, such as judicial efforts to define or clarify what is meant by "incest;" the determination of appeals of criminal convictions for incest; and the resolution of sometimes vexing and complex problems involving wills, trusts, and inheritances. Examples of each will be considered.

The degree to which courts unreservedly consulted Leviticus for guidance on definitional questions in domestic relations law can be illustrated by the case of *Brotherhood of Locomotive Firemen and Enginemen v. Hogan*, decided in 1934 by a federal district court in Minnesota.[82] At issue was the legal definition of "affinity." "Affinity," the court wrote, "is generally defined by the relationship by marriage between a husband and his wife's blood relatives, or between a wife and her husband's blood relatives. Unlawful or forbidden marriages due to affinity are set forth in Leviticus, chapter 18."[83]

Courts also looked to the Levitical degrees as a means of justifying convictions for incest. *Lipham v. State* involved a prosecution under Georgia law of a husband who had sexual relations with his stepdaughter, the out-of-wed-lock child of his wife.[84] The Georgia Supreme Court sustained his conviction:

> If a man marry the mother of an illegitimate daughter, and take the daughter into his care and custody, he becomes charged with a duty towards her. His disregard of morality and decency in having sexual intercourse with her is a crime transcending a mere misdemeanor. The act has all the elements which constitute incest. As incest, it should be punished. "Thou shalt not uncover the nakedness of a woman and her daughter." Leviticus, 18:17.[85]

The New York Court of Appeals was confronted with an even more reprehensible version of the question *Lipham* presented. The defendant in *People v. Lake* had fathered an out-of-wedlock daughter and some years later, when she had "just grown into womanhood," hired her as his "bookkeeper."[86] He took advantage of her sexually and was charged and convicted of incest. The Court of Appeals sustained his conviction, relying for support in part upon its reading of English law and the Book of Leviticus: "It was early held to be unlawful for a bastard to marry within the Levitical degrees (*Hains v. Jeffel*, 1 Ld. Raymond 68); a doctrine which of necessity recognized relationships of consanguinity."[87] Since marriage was impossible by reason of incest, the court reasoned, the defendant's illicit relationship should also be deemed incestuous and so punishable.[88]

Courts finally looked to the Levitical degrees in establishing inheritance rights among close family members. This is especially evident in some lawsuits that sought to establish parental rights to inherit from illegitimate offspring or to represent their offspring's estates in wrongful-death actions. In these cases, those who opposed extending inheritance rights or the right to bring a cause of action tended to cite common law rules derived in part from a reading of the Levitical degrees. In essence, it was claimed that illegitimate children were bound to observe the Levitical degrees in their choice of marriage partners, but that this should be the only aspect of their relationship to their biological parents that should be given recognition by law. They should, on this reading of the sources, refrain from sexual intimacy with close blood relations but otherwise share none of the legal privileges that were derived from membership in the family. Courts tended to accept this argument unless statutory support could be found evincing a legislative intent to abolish the old common law disabilities of bastardy. Where the old disabilities had been done away with, on the other hand, courts tended to permit claims based on family relationships to go forward.[89]

3. One Flesh and Putting Asunder: The Common Law Reception of Biblical Ideals of Marital Unity

So far, we have considered the ways in which courts invoked the language and authority of divine law and the law of God in describing and defining the marital relationship; and the ways in which courts employed the book of Leviticus, sometimes but not invariably as mediated through the law of Henry VIII, to resolve a variety of questions on incest. Next, we shall consider judicial usage of a particular biblical teaching, *i.e.*, Jesus's declaration that marriage must be permanent, to address contemporary questions of separation and divorce.

The book of Genesis, in the poetic diction of the King James Bible, declared: "A man shall leave his father and his mother, and shall cleave unto his wife; and they shall be one flesh."[90] Close variations of this language and imagery were used by Jesus, as recorded in the Gospels of Matthew and Mark, to establish an ideal of unbreakable unity between husband and wife. In Matthew, Jesus declared:

> Have ye not read, that he which made them at the beginning, made them male and female? And he said, "For this cause a man shall leave father and mother, and shall cleave to his wife; and they twain shall be one flesh." Wherefore they are no more twain, but one flesh. What therefore God hath joined together, let not man put asunder.[91]

Mark's account of this teaching represented a largely verbatim summary of that found in Matthew.[92] Paul made use of similar imagery in Ephesians: "For we are members of his body, of his flesh, and of his bones. For this cause shall a man leave his father and his mother, and shall be joined unto his wife, and they two shall be one flesh."[93]

This group of closely-related biblical texts exerted wide influence on judicial thought regarding marriage and divorce for the nineteenth and much of the twentieth centuries. One can find different variations on these biblical themes in any number of judicial contexts. One of the most important of these usages, obviously, was the defense of the integrity of the marital unit itself. Marriage was a sacred relationship that should be free from attack by third parties and respected and preserved by those who are joined by its yoke.

In a world of limited, fault-based divorce, where a party seeking a divorce needed to demonstrate some sort of marital misconduct on the part of one's spouse, at least some petitioners claimed that they were entitled to a divorce because their partners had never achieved any real degree of emotional separation from their parents. To paraphrase Jesus's teaching, they did not leave their mother and father emotionally, and so were unable to cleave to their spouse and thereby become one flesh. This lack of independence, the claim went, so gravely disrupted the new household that it had no real chance of succeeding against the vicissitudes of fortune.

An Indiana case from 1897 illustrates the way this argument might be made and the way in which a court might quote the Bible in response. The case involved a claim for alienation of affection brought by the former husband against his ex-mother-in-law.[94] The mother-in-law, it was alleged, had sought "to deprive [husband] of the society and services of his wife, and cause her to separate from him."[95] The court responded with a mixture of biblical quotation and outright theology:

> Marriage is the most sacred and holy relation known to Divine or human law. It is an institution ordained of God, sanctioned by all the nations of the earth, and recognized the world over as the foundation of society and school of morals, and no one has a right to destroy and disrupt that relation, except for good and sufficient cause. It was early declared in the Mosaic law that a man should leave his father and mother, and cleave unto his wife, and that they should be one flesh. One of the disciples of the Great Teacher said: "But from the beginning of the creation God made them male and female. For this cause shall a man leave his father and mother, and cleave to his wife; and they twain shall be one flesh. What therefore God hath joined together let no man put asunder."[96]

While most cases do not engage in this level of scriptural exegesis or theological speculation, many cases invoke the imagery of the child leaving his or her parents and cleaving to the spouse whenever a dispute involving the parents or in-laws came to be litigated. Thus, the Vermont Supreme Court lectured a husband who would not move apart from his relatives in order to accommodate his wife's apparent strong desire for living arrangements independent of his old family ties:

> Any man who has proper tenderness and affection for his wife would certainly not require her to reside near his relatives if her peace of mind were thereby seriously disturbed. This would be very far from compliance with the Scriptural exposition of the duty of husbands: "For this cause, shall a man leave father and mother and cleave to his wife, and they twain shall be one flesh."[97]

Similarly, a Michigan case decided in 1928 pitted a husband who insisted that his mother reside in the family home and a wife who sought a divorce

---

on that account after separating from him.[98] Again, one sees a court invoking Scripture to admonish a husband to perform his husbandly duties:

> In this the plaintiff [husband] was wrong. In other circumstances, his devotion and loyalty to his mother would be commendable, but where the wife's interests intervene, his first duty is her welfare and happiness. "For this cause shall a man leave father and mother, and shall cleave to his wife; and they twain shall be one flesh."[99]

One, in fact, finds this sort of scripturally-grounded analysis as recently as the late 1940s. At issue in *Maricopa County v. Douglas* was a statute that required children to make contributions toward the needs of elderly and infirm parents.[100] The county attorney sought to enforce the statute against community property owned by the elderly parent's daughter and son-in-law. The couple asserted that such enforcement would run counter to the state's policy in favor of marriage. The court agreed, using Scripture for support:

> We must now decide which theory public policy favors most—the support of the aged or the maintenance of the community. We think the latter is more important. The Holy Scripture tells us "Therefore shall a man leave his father and his mother, and shall cleave unto his wife; and they shall be one flesh." Genesis 2:24.[101]

The integrity of the marriage might also be attacked not by outsiders but by one of the parties, either by seeking a divorce that was unjustified in the eyes of the court or by engaging in acts of misconduct—criminal or otherwise—at the expense of an innocent spouse. *Humber v. Humber*, a Mississippi case from 1915, involved a husband who alleged that his wife had been excessively cruel to him, thus warranting the granting of a divorce.[102] The court found the husband's allegations of cruelty insufficient to justify a divorce and looked to the Bible for justification for its determination:

> Marriage is a most solemn contract, provided for by the laws of the state and sanctified by the ceremonies of the church. The dissolution of its bonds is no light matter. The best sentiment of society is opposed to divorce. The law authorizing divorces for certain causes requires a strict compliance with its provisions. The church is guided by these words of eternal truth touching the subject:
> "From the beginning of the creation God made them male and female. For this cause shall a man leave his father and mother, and cleave to his wife; and

they twain shall be one flesh; so then they are no more twain but one flesh. What, therefore, God hath joined together, let not man put asunder."[103]

A much older case, *Logan v. Logan*, dating to 1841, reached a similar result in favor of the marriage, on a fact pattern the details of which the Kentucky Supreme Court delicately refrained from probing too explicitly.[104] In establishing the legal standard to be applied, the court looked to ecclesiastical law's understanding of cruelty. There must be true *"saevitia"*— "savagery"—the court wrote.[105] "Less severity than this will not authorize a court in this State to 'put asunder' those whom 'God hath joined together.' And were it otherwise, domestic quarrels might mischievously engross all the services of Courts of Justice."[106]

The use of the canonistic category of *saevitia* by an antebellum Kentucky Supreme Court would by itself be a remarkable demonstration of the deep and continuing influence of the canon law on American legal forms.[107] Focused as we are on scriptural influence, we might try to read *Logan* and *Humber* together as support for the proposition that when courts invoked biblical expressions like "one flesh" or "put asunder," they were generally willing to sustain the marriage in the face of a petition for divorce. *Lanier v. Lanier*, an 1871 Tennessee case, may or may not be seen as support for this hypothesis, depending upon the weight one assigns to the dissenting opinion filed in that case.[108]

The facts in *Lanier* can be described as extreme. The husband alleged that his wife had succeeded in poisoning him; that he became deathly ill thanks to the effects of the poison; and that she deserted him during his hour of illness and need.[109] Even if these facts were not literally true, the majority of the court agreed, the wife's desertion was sufficient to justify the granting of the divorce.[110]

This result caused Justice Peter Turney to dissent. Turney (1827-1903) had been a colonel in the First Tennessee Infantry, demonstrating remarkable bravery at Antietam and Fredericksburg. After the Civil War, he was elected to the Tennessee Supreme Court in 1870 and became Chief Justice in 1886. He would subsequently be elected governor of the state of Tennessee.[111] Turney's dissent put front and center the Christian character of marriage, including especially his biblically grounded understanding of its indissoluble character.

Sounding very much like Augustine, Turney wrote that marriage subsists first in friendship between the parties. Turney, however, wished to apply this first principle directly to the case at hand. Thus, he observed that marital friendship:

> thrives under constraint, and never rises to such a height as when any strong interest or necessity binds two persons together and gives them some common object of pursuit. We need not, therefore, be afraid of drawing the marriage knot, which chiefly subsists by friendship, the closest possible.[112]

Having built a foundation sufficient at least in his own mind to sustain further argument, Turney chose the last part of this sentence—on the drawing of the "closest possible" marital knot—for further comment.[113] There are good social reasons, Turney asserted, for rigorously enforcing the indissolubility of marriage. There was a public interest in the proper selection of marriage partners, and the enforcement of a rigorous standard of indissolubility, Turney believed, would concentrate the minds of young people contemplating marriage. "[W]e will find male and female not only more cautious, thoughtful and honorable in their affiances and marriages, but much of other crime will fail to publish itself through the Courts, because it shall have passed away."[114]

After reviewing the significance of human friendship to marriage and the social benefits derivable from a strict enforcement of indissolubility, Turney turned his attention to the question of religious faith:

> Every lawyer in the land has been taught not only that the Bible is law, but that it is the source of law. It is found in every complete law library as part thereof, and the standard work therein.[115]

Lawyers, judges, and officers of the court must all take an oath of office upon the Bible.[116] Turney emphasized that this is "so because the Bible is the supreme law."[117] And the Bible contained the fundamental rules that should govern marriage for all days and ages, including our own:

> In this authority, from which every well defined right of person and property is derived, we find—Matthew, chp. 19, verses 3 to 10, inclusive—the law of divorce stated in these words, by our Saviour:
>
> "The Pharisees also came unto him, tempting him and saying unto him, Is it lawful for a man to put away his wife for every case? And he answered and said unto them, Have ye not read, that he which made them at the beginning made them male and female, and said, for this cause shall a man leave father and mother and cleave to his wife; and they twain shall be one flesh.
>
> They said unto him, Why did Moses then command to give a writing of divorcement and to put her away?
>
> He saith unto them, Moses, because of the hardness of your hearts, suffered you to put away your wives; but from the beginning it was not so.
>
> And I say unto you, whosoever shall put away his wife, except it be for fornication, and shall marry another, commiteth adultery, and whoso marrieth her which is put away, doth commit adultery."[118]

Turney viewed the court as being put to a choice. The court must select between "a statutory regulation demoralizing in its every influence and tendency" and "an express divine law."[119] Turney made it clear that he opted for the Bible and God's law.[120]

This constellation of biblical phrases played a major role in justifying other distinctive aspects of the Anglo-American law of domestic relations. Judges and jurists were particularly keen to use the Bible to support arguments in favor of *feme covert*—the doctrine that held a woman's legal personality to be absorbed into that of her husband's at the time of marriage.[121] Another area of law that looked to this biblical doctrine of "two in one flesh" for justification was the doctrine of spousal immunity, by which husbands and wives might be prohibited from testifying against each other in judicial proceedings,[122] or otherwise forbidden from bringing any cause of action against one another.[123]

III. Marriage and the State

A. Marriage Is Religious

This review of the Christian sources of American marriage law reveals a remarkable consistency that has endured over centuries, from the twelfth century until the last two or three decades of the twentieth. From the twelfth century to the middle twentieth, it was acceptable for jurists to refer to marriage as something brought into being through divine inspiration or guidance. Marriage was a "divine institution." It belonged not only to the law of man to regulate but to the law of God, which brought it into being. From the twelfth century to the middle twentieth, legal writers were willing to look to Scripture for guidance, or at the very least nod in the direction of Scripture when rendering particular judgments. To be sure, some of this might have been rhetorical posturing or conventional piety. But the use of this body of words, phrases, imagery and ideas spoke to a set of shared cultural understandings that viewed marriage in an expressly Christian context. The presence in American judicial decisions of the nineteenth and early- and mid-twentieth centuries of this older vocabulary, in other words, bespoke a connectedness to a cultural reality that had been formed and nurtured through the rich deposit of historical Christianity.

But while this body of material is fascinating for its contribution to intellectual or cultural history, it also raises profound questions for contemporary lawyers who recognize that law is inevitably a historical process. We have been through upheavals in the last half century that make this particular body of case law and principles seem as odd and quaint as any museum piece in the Smithsonian. No judge, writing in her public capacity, would today speak of the divine institution of marriage although, obviously, religious traditions continue to subscribe to such beliefs and judges who belong to such traditions might privately acknowledge this belief.[124]

Why, then, should we recall this history today? What relevance does it have, outside of discrete and insular communities of believers? If we acknowledge the historical reality that Western lawyers for centuries quite automatically accepted the proposition that marriage had a religious grounding worthy of respect, one is led to ask another question: Is there something about marriage that is irreducibly religious? Does this larger Western historical experience, only abandoned within the lifetimes of many readers, connect to something more universal about the human person and the nature of marriage?

One might attempt an answer to this question by considering findings from the discipline of anthropology. Bronislaw Malinowski (1884-1952) is still widely considered to be among the most important of the founders of anthropological studies. Born to a Polish university professor and his wife and a member by birth of Poland's landed aristocracy,[125] Malinowski was at home throughout Europe, studying not only in his native Poland but also at Leipzig and teaching for most of his career at the University of London and the London School of Economics. He would, in fact, become a leader of English academic anthropology. He did important field work among the natives of Papua New Guinea and with the Trobriand Islanders, and even though details of this field work have been questioned, his larger conclusions—on questions like the necessary relationship between religion, ritual, and the great transitions of human life (birth, marriage, death)—remain persuasive today.

Malinowski's research program converged on two of the principal themes of this chapter—the centrality of religious belief for human society and the transcendent significance of marriage to society's perpetuation.

Malinowski was raised Catholic and graduated from Jagiellonian University, where his father taught.[126] His earliest published writings reflected on religious themes. One of his first essays proposed a definition of religion that would remain remarkably constant, with appropriate refinements, through his later work—"*Religion*: This is a system of traditions explaining and justifying the world, and a system of norms regulating our conduct."[127]

Although a confirmed agnostic, Malinowski's own work remained saturated with a kind of cultural Catholicism. He thought in terms of the faith of his youth no matter the time and space he put between himself and his childhood. He appreciated that all religious belief had in common a desire to put the believer in contact with the deity.[128] He used a distinctively Catholic vocabulary to describe the social phenomena he observed.[129] And when he witnessed a husband beating his wife while conducting field research in aboriginal Australia, he was moved to think of his own wife and recorded in his diary: "association: marriage and spiritual harmony."[130]

Malinowski was moved to address marriage as an outgrowth of his field-work. In his work, Malinowski encountered a great variety of "human mar-riage." Marriage might come in the form of "monogamy, polygyny, and polyandry; matriarchal and patriarchal unions; households with patrilocal and matrilocal residence."[131] Not every society taught that marriage was the sole legitimate outlet for human sexual expression. In many societies, "un-married boys and girls are free to mate in temporary unions, subject to the barriers of incest and exogamy, and of such social regulations as prevail in their community."[132] He acknowledged, "there are a number of communities in which the marriage bond is broken as regards the exclusiveness of sex with the consent of both partners and with the sanction of tribal law, custom, and morality."[133]

In all of this diversity, Malinowski recognized some common elements. Grounding his work on the insights of his old professor Edvard Wester-marck,[134] Malinowski asserted: "Even in its biological aspect, . . . 'marriage is rooted in the family rather than the family in marriage.'"[135] "Marriage," Ma-linowski continued, "on the whole is rather a contract for the production and maintenance of children than an authorization of sexual intercourse."[136] It is this agreement, Malinowski argued, that carried transcendent significance. Marriage, so understood, "has to be concluded in a public and solemn man-ner, receiving, as a sacrament, the blessings of religion and, as a rite, the good auspices of magic."[137]

Malinowski elaborated on this theme in a debate with Robert Briffault in the early 1930s, which was subsequently edited and published posthumously by Ashley Montagu in 1956.[138] Under the chapter heading "Marriage as a Religious Institution," Malinowski began:

> Marriage is regarded in all human societies as a sacrament, that is, as a sacred transaction establishing a relationship of the highest value to man and woman. In treating a vow or an agreement as a sacrament, society mobilises all its forces to cement a stable union.[139]

In using the term "sacrament," Malinowski did not intend to refer to the religious observances of the Catholic Church. His intention, rather, was to use this familiar language to make the larger point that historically and an-thropologically all societies have attached symbolic significance to the act of joining parties in marriage. In every society, Malinowski can be under-stood to have asserted, marriage carries some "sacramental," *i.e.*, religious, significance. Symbols freighted with meaning are used to signify the endur-

ing connection formed by the parties—rings, perhaps, or special garments.[140] The families of the parties are usually intimately involved in making the arrangements and planning the ceremonies.[141] Some level of community participation is also expected in solemnizing the special event.[142]
The parties utter special words signifying their commitment and thereby
magically transform the relationship.[143] These symbols, these ceremonies,
these exchanges of promises are intended to mark the union off as something of transcendent value, something that the larger society stands ready
to protect and preserve, indeed, something for which God or the gods can
and must serve as guarantors.

Malinowski, furthermore, admonished those in his own day who wished
to desacralize the marital relationship writing, "Are we to secularise marriage
completely and withdraw it from the control of religion, and perhaps even of
law, as is the tendency in the Soviet legislation and in the program of many
would-be reformers?"[144]

Malinowski warned against the danger inherent in an intense and complete
secularization of marriage. Marriage had been "sanctioned by religion, as well
as by law . . . throughout humanity."[145] Indeed, in Malinowski's mind, religion,
marriage, and law had always been interconnected in deep and almost primal
ways: "[T]he religious sanctions embrace the legal character of marriage, that
is, they make it binding, public, and enforced by the organized interests of
the community."[146]

Malinowski acknowledged that he himself did not belong to an identifiable religious persuasion.[147] He admitted that agnostics might dispute the
connections between religion and marriage, but even agnostics would acknowledge the importance of marriage to community order.[148] Even the agnostic, Malinowski asserted, "must endow the institution of marriage and the
family with new values, and so make them stable in his own fashion."[149]

The trend that Malinowski presciently anticipated in the early 1950s—
that marriage might be entirely desacralized—is seemingly coming to pass.
At the very least, the law is now rigorously committed to ensuring the success of this project of desacralization. While this is not the place for detailed
argument, it might suffice to point out that the social crises that we face—
such as divorce and the widespread incidence of out-of-wedlock births—may
in part result from this larger effort to reduce marriage from a sacred enterprise, blessed and sanctioned and sustained by communal ritual, into something much more mundane, even banal. The consequence has been the dis-
posability of human relationships themselves.

B. The Law Teaches Values

Not only is marriage in some irreducible sense religious; law, in some fundamental sense, inevitably teaches values. This is a major argument made by
Mary Ann Glendon in her book, *Rights Talk*.[150] Although Glendon did not
take up the subject of marriage in her book, she wrote more broadly about
rights and the ways in which American courts have miseducated the public on
the relationship of rights and duties. Her discussion of the judiciary's mistreat-
ment of the question of communal responsibility and rights bears some lessons
for the domestic relations materials we have already reviewed.

Americans are fond, Glendon observed, of seeing rights as divorced from
duties; when they invoke rights, it is usually because they want to satisfy some
individual preference with little thought to larger social consequences.[151] We
live, she writes, in "[t]he high season of rights."[152] Comparative law, Glendon
notes, quickly reveals how idiosyncratic American legal rhetoric is on the subject of rights. She compares and contrasts naturalization ceremonies in the
United States and Canada.[153] New citizens of each country are commonly addressed by the government official who swears them in. In the United States,
such a speech is likely to emphasize the transcendent significance of individual
rights,[154] while in Canada, in contrast, it is likelier that one will be called to
take up the responsibility of being a good neighbor to others.[155] Such a ceremony, Glendon notes, is likely to make a lasting impression on one's mind.[156]

An analysis of the no-duty-to-rescue rule and its impact on American legal and political thinking comprises a central core of Glendon's book.[157] She
traces the ways in which this anomaly of American law slowly migrated from
private law to constitutional law. Under the no-duty-to-rescue rule, citizens
generally do not owe to others the affirmative duty to come to their assistance in moments of crisis; the no-duty-to-rescue rule thus teaches lessons
not only about the narrow principles of tort law,[158] such as the distinction between acts and omissions as a matter of causation, but broader lessons about
the relationship of individualism to social responsibility.[159]

An important part of this larger discussion is Glendon's review of the lessons imparted by the United States Supreme Court case of *DeShaney v. Winnebago County Department of Social Services*.[160] *DeShaney* involved a tragic set
of facts: Joshua DeShaney was a ten-year-old boy who had been systematically
abused by his father and was ultimately diagnosed with severe brain trauma as
a result of the abuse.[161] Throughout the period he was abused, officials of the
county Department of Social Services stood by, documenting the abuse but
failing to take effective action even when Joshua's father failed to comply with
conditions he agreed to as the result of recommendations made by a "Child
Protection Team" that had investigated conditions in Joshua's home.[162]

Chief Justice William Rehnquist authored the majority opinion. Sharply distinguishing between negative and affirmative rights and declaring that the "Due Process Clauses [of the Fifth and Fourteenth Amendments] generally confer no affirmative right to governmental aid, even where such aid may be necessary to secure life, liberty, or property,"[163] the Chief Justice's opinion can be read very nearly as a constitutionalization of the no-duty-to-rescue rule.[164] Although the county's social service agency had commenced intervention in Joshua's home life, it was under no constitutional obligation to ensure a favorable outcome—it had, in other words, no constitutionally cognizable duty to rescue Joshua from his violent surroundings.

What makes this case relevant to our concerns is the method Glendon used to draw lessons from it. She criticized Rehnquist's opinion less on its substance than on the errors it was likely to teach the American public.[165] Supreme Court opinions have a wide audience. In addition to lawyers, journalists, intellectual and social historians, and a large number of literate laypersons now read Supreme Court opinions. And these readers are likely to understand *DeShaney* to stand for the proposition that there is a sharp separation between a public order, where government is responsible for policing its own business, and a world of private ordering, where "the weak [are] completely at the mercy of the strong."[166] And by implying that the no-duty-to-rescue rule governs the government's relationship to its citizens, "the *DeShaney* case miseducates the public about the American version of the welfare state, and about the role of citizens in shaping and reshaping it."[167] *DeShaney*, in other words, while perhaps correct as to its legal reasoning, is a failure because of the lessons the larger American public may derive from it.

Transposed to marriage, Glendon's methodology has much to offer us. If legal opinions necessarily educate, what are the lessons to be learned from the cases and material covered in this chapter? The first, most obvious lesson is the primacy of marriage in the ordering of society. Marriage was so important that it was consistently explained and justified by reference to the ultimate and divine. Marriage was a part of the divine plan for the world; it was a feature of the divine law; its particular attributes, such as the Levitical degrees, were a feature not only of the law of man but of the law of God. Proper marital conduct was not only a matter of one's relationship with the state, but with the deity. Marriage, one can conclude, was seen as supremely important to social well-being.

There are yet other lessons taught by these cases and materials. It can safely be said that America in the nineteenth century was still governed by a Protestant establishment, whose presence was felt *de facto*, if not always *de jure*. Christianity was accepted as a source of the common law and judges and jurists were not shy about drawing from conventional Christian sources to explain whole areas of law.[168] Christian, biblically grounded modes of discourse thus helped to cement this Protestant hegemony with respect to marriage law and transmit it forward in time to the next generation. And in a nation, most of whose citizens were also Protestant, this must have seemed like a natural mode of discourse. This Christian foundation, furthermore, was not something recent, made up by the courts in response to the exigencies of current events, but had deep roots in the distinctive legal tradition of medieval canon law, particularly as mediated through Anglicanism.

If the body of opinions and texts examined in this chapter taught one lesson with respect to marriage and its centrality to society and faith, it taught another lesson with respect to the authority of the state. To speak of divine law is to speak at the same time of a law placed above the positive enactments of the state. It was Peter, after all, who proclaimed to the Sanhedrin, "We must obey God rather than men."[169]

Marriage—seen as a matter of divine or natural law, understood as a matter of divine institution, explained as the product of divine command, explicated by the Jesus of the New Testament as conferring deep and solemn duties on its participants—necessarily stood to some extent beyond the state's authority to harm, destroy, or alter. Marriage was not a creation of the state; its existence predated the state. It was something state authorities were charged with conserving. The judicial invocations of divine law that accompanied so many domestic relations decisions can be understood as reinforcing these propositions and commitments to state officials—from governors, to legislators, to administrators, all the way to local justices of the peace and town clerks.

One can contrast the lessons these historical materials teach with the lessons one might derive from a passage in *Goodridge v. Department of Public Health*, the Massachusetts same-sex marriage case of 2003.[170] Regarding the relationship of marriage to the state, the court wrote, "Simply put, the government creates civil marriage. In Massachusetts, civil marriage is, and since pre-Colonial days has been, precisely what its name implies: a wholly secular institution."[171] This statement, like the majority opinion in *DeShaney*, miseducates the public. In light of the cultural and legal history set forth above, *Goodridge*'s claim can be seen to be patently false. Its temporal framework is bizarre. One struggles to make sense of the assertion that "civil marriage" has been a creation of the state since "pre-Colonial days." The court cannot mean to refer to the forms of marriage that prevailed among the Narragansett Indians who greeted the first European settlers, although that is what the court must literally be understood to say.

The *Goodridge* court's description of marriage is erroneous on at least two other counts. First, the sharp distinction between "civil" marriage and something else, which the *Goodridge* court never names but must presumably be religious marriage, similarly misrepresents the early sources we have reviewed. The nineteenth-century American law of domestic relations, even in Massachusetts, was heavily dependent upon Christian sources, especially canonistic sources. This chapter has reviewed a few of those sources. It is a distortion of the historical record to call marriage "a wholly secular institution."

Second, it is wrong to assert, as a matter of historical record, that the state "creates" civil marriage. As the evidence we have reviewed makes clear, this is not the way the nineteenth-century mind understood the origin of marriage. Indeed, in the forms of legal discourse we have been exploring, invocations of divine law or the law of God to explain particular features of the law of marriage were hardly unknown in Massachusetts. Like their contemporaries, Massachusetts jurists borrowed from Christian understandings of marriage, especially as mediated through the ecclesiastical courts, to explain the shape and content of their domestic relations law.[172]

Goodridge thus miseducates the public just as the *DeShaney* opinion did. Its history lesson, regrettably, will not be confined to the practicing bar of Massachusetts. Lawyers and literate lay people alike, all over the country, will understand it to be a roughly accurate depiction of historical truth, which it most emphatically is not.

On the other hand, this miseducation has—at least thus far—had a relatively minor impact on the broader historical and cultural understanding of the meaning of marriage that has prevailed in the United States since before its founding. As long as that traditional understanding prevails, it is unlikely that disjoining the legal definition of marriage from the traditional understanding will be well received, whether politically or judicially.

C. Law Has a Religious Dimension

At the outset of this chapter, I proposed a definition of religion borrowed from John Noonan, which had as its core the relationship of the believer with the divine presence.[173] Harold Berman, in his book, *The Interaction of Law and Religion*, has proposed a different definition that is also appropriate for analyzing the relationship of religion and law.[174] Religion, Berman writes, "is not only a set of doctrines and exercises; it is people manifesting a collective concern for the ultimate meaning and purpose of life—it is a shared intuition of and commitment to transcendent values."[175]

Law, Berman continues, must necessarily partake of religious values, understood in this broad, anthropological sense. Through the use of ritual, through appeal to tradition and authority, and through invocation of universal values, law attempts to concretize and apply a given society's set of beliefs about ultimate values.[176] Berman challenges those who would view law in purely secular terms. The great fallacy of a purely secular account of the law is its abandonment of ultimate values: "The law of the modern state, it is said, is not a reflection of any sense of ultimate meaning and purpose in life; instead, its tasks are finite, material, impersonal—to get things done, to make people act in certain ways."[177]

Berman further characterizes this understanding of law as "instrumentalist."[178] The lawgiver—whether legislator or judge—takes a narrow view of those subject to the law. Persons, the lawgiver surmises, will respond in certain predictable ways to laws intended to appeal to widely held notions of cost/benefit analysis. Laws are tailored accordingly, to place incentives on desirable conduct and to discourage the undesirable. Such efforts, furthermore, always carry with them a sense of tentativeness: The law comes to be seen as "experimental;" its values, its norms, its prohibitions and permissions, are seen as always subject to revision, based on the latest fashionable economic or political theory of what society should be about.[179]

The problem with this sort of instrumentalism, in Berman's estimation, is its failure to conform to human nature. Instrumentalists generally assume that law gains its force through its threat of coercive force.[180] This assumption has been part and parcel of modern legal positivism since John Austin first formulated his command theory of law in the early nineteenth century. Such a theory of law, however, ignores the human tendency to obey law not simply because of the threats that accompany disobedience, but also because of the belief that one does something affirmatively good by obeying the law. Berman notes, "[a]s psychological studies have now demonstrated, far more important than coercion in securing obedience to rules are such factors as trust, fairness, credibility, and affiliation."[181]

The sense of trust, furthermore, is enhanced by the very nature of law:

> Law itself, in all societies, encourages the belief in its own sanctity. It puts forward its claim to obedience in ways that appeal not only to the material, impersonal, finite, rational interests of the people who are asked to observe it, but also to their faith in a truth, a justice that transcends social utility—in ways, that is, that do not fit the image of secularism and instrumentalism presented by the prevailing theory.[182]

Berman concludes that instrumentalist understandings of law—theories of law that rest, fundamentally, not on a shared sense of right and wrong but only on second-order pragmatic principles—will ultimately prove unworkable.[183] To be successful, to command respect and allegiance, the law must embody what Berman terms "transrational" values, including a sense of tradition and authority. Neither, Berman asserts, can be explained exclusively in secular terms. Tradition necessarily carries a religious dimension as mythic significance is ascribed to past events,[184] while invocations of authority usually carry with them some sense of judgment about ultimate right and wrong.[185]

This understanding of the deep interconnectedness of law and religion helps to explain the survival of references to divine law and the law of God in early American judicial thought. Appeals to rules ordained by God, articulated in a world where ownership and knowledge of the King James Bible was perhaps the single strongest common bond among persons, can certainly be understood as an effort to inculcate in the populace a deeply internalized sense of proper and improper marital conduct.

Berman's insights also reveal the deep incoherence of contemporary philosophical liberalism, especially when applied to reform of the marriage law to accommodate the same-sex marriage movement. One might consider a recent essay by Linda McClain.[186] Her target was Congresswoman Marilyn Musgrave of Colorado's Fourth District, a Pentecostal and a principal sponsor of an amendment to the United States Constitution that would have the effect of enshrining in federal law the proposition that true marriage exists only between a male and a female. The particular focus of McClain's criticism was Musgrave's assertion, made in defense of the amendment, that it was needed to preserve "'God's created order.'"[187]

McClain rejected the premise on which these statements rested—that there is no tight boundary line separating religious from secular conceptions of marriage. Looking in part to *Goodridge*, McClain countered:

> [I]n a pluralistic constitutional democracy, citizens owe each other certain duties of civility and mutual respect concerning the forms of argument they make. Thus, government's interest in defining, regulating, and supporting the institution of civil marriage must be explained in terms of public reasons and political (or public) values that are accessible to other citizens regardless of whether they share each other's religious convictions.[188]

McClain is far from alone in advancing such claims. William Eskridge, a professor of law at Yale University and a leading advocate for same-sex marriage, relies on a robust theory of philosophical liberalism to argue that the Constitution was intended to create a liberal state agnostic to claims about fundamental goods or ends.[189] Like McClain and many others, Eskridge relies on claims about "public reason" that effectively prohibit the possibility of distinctively religious voices even entering the public square.[190]

The not-so-hidden danger in these claims is precisely the risk Berman warned against—the replacement of norms that reflect deeply held convictions of right and wrong with a series of second-order instrumentalist claims about the shape marriage law should take.

From a constitutional perspective, perhaps the most appropriate answer is Noonan's response that the believer who relies on religious belief to reach a particular public policy position does nothing different from "any conscientious citizen or politician who consults the source of truth he holds in highest regard."[191] What is protected by the Constitution, in Noonan's estimation, is the right of all persons to participate in the political process, not the right of the nonbeliever to be free of the annoyance of having to confront religious claims of truth.[192]

Were this a longer study, we might develop this point. We should content ourselves with the observation that if marriage is religious, not necessarily in a confessional but at least in a larger anthropological sense of that word, so then is the law of marriage. Correspondingly, legal reform that seeks to desacralize marriage—to make it subject to nothing more than ordinary contract rules, to separate its religious dimension from its civil effects—will probably fail. Indeed, the crisis over out-of-wedlock births, the levity with which the marital commitment is taken, and the easy availability of divorce might all be seen as outgrowths of this desacralization.

Complete desacralization of the law, however, may carry even deeper consequences. The separation of law from deeply cherished beliefs about right and wrong might lead to societal demoralization as the people become alienated from the law. The concluding pages of Alasdair MacIntyre's *After Virtue* draw a stark picture of the role alienation played in the collapse of the civil polity of the Western Roman Empire, as people turned their back on imperial rule:

> A crucial turning point in that earlier history occurred when men and women of good will turned aside from the task of shoring up the Roman *imperium* and ceased to identify the continuation of civility and moral community with the maintenance of that *imperium*. What they set themselves to achieve—often not recognizing fully what they were doing—was the con-

struction of new forms of community within which the moral life could be sustained . . . .[193]

Where the state and its law fail—where they have grown so out of touch with human needs and emotions that it ceases to command loyalty, one might read MacIntyre as saying—then it falls to the people to build their own communities responsive to their own values, independent of state authority.

The marriage debate may hold within it the seeds of this extreme form of alienation from the state. It remains the case that *governmental* efforts to strip clergy of the legal marriage function would likely fail in the foreseeable future, because civil society—even after *Goodridge* and the *Marriage Cases*[194]—largely continues to view its own (principally religious) concept of marriage as the primary phenomenon to which the law should conform. But if the impulse of the state to divert its legal definition of marriage from the traditional one spreads, civil society may separate *itself* from the state's theory and practice of marriage, in order better to preserve its own.

IV. Conclusion

This chapter has drawn on legal history, anthropology, and jurisprudence. The common thread is that the separation of marriage from religion, or from the state, is a much more difficult task than it might at first blush appear. For nearly two millennia within the Western tradition, marriage has been associated with—and predicated on—religious insight, particularly that drawn from or inspired by the Jewish and Christian holy books collectively called "The Bible." This chapter documents the relationship between this larger Western tradition and American domestic relations law.

Even apart from this historically peculiar feature of the West, all marriage has a religious dimension to it that is probably unavoidable. In all societies, marriage is signified by some form of symbolic action or exchange; it reflects commitments not only by the individuals involved, but also by larger communities, whether family, church, locality, or something larger or smaller than these groups. Marriage is a commitment that embraces not only the good of the parties, but points to something larger—society's sense of the ultimate.

Furthermore the lessons that lawgivers seek to inculcate in those subject to the law are also important. Law teaches values—this is an insight as true for the law of marriage as for any other area of the law. How society structures the laws governing coupling, commitment, child rearing, and other essential functions of the reproductive process teaches values about these aspects of daily life. The current debate over the future of marriage is in part a struggle over the proper lessons to be taught by the law.

Finally, law itself points to a larger substantive vision of the good. For this reason, some, like Harold Berman, argue that the law itself has a religious dimension that we deny at risk of imperiling the soundness of society's legal order. And this religious dimension of law—this sense that the law must embody some larger, more transcendent understanding of right and wrong—also animates much of the contemporary debate over marriage. Legislative or judicial attempts to sever the traditional bonds among marriage, religion, and law are, for these reasons, doomed to failure in the short and the long term.

Afterword
Douglas Laycock[1]

I. From Both Sides, the Puritan Mistake

From a civil libertarian perspective, this is a depressing book. All six contributors—religious and secular, left, center, and right—agree that same-sex marriage is a threat to religious liberty. Yet little of that threat is inherent in the concepts of religious liberty, gay rights, or same-sex marriage.

Religious minorities and sexual minorities could easily be on the same side. In resisting legal and social pressures to conform to majoritarian norms, they make essentially parallel and mutually reinforcing claims against the larger society. They claim that some aspects of human identity are so fundamental that they should be left to each individual, free of all nonessential regulation, even when manifested in conduct. No human being should be penalized because of his beliefs about religion, or because of his sexual orientation. And no human being should be penalized because of her religious practice, or because of her choice of sexual partners, unless her conduct is actually inflicting significant and cognizable harm on some other person. Both religious and sexual minorities need space in which to live their lives according to their own beliefs, values, and identity.

This view that religious and sexual liberty present parallel claims is not just theoretical. It is exemplified most clearly in the Equal Access Act,[2] which guarantees the right of student clubs to meet in the country's secondary schools. The Act's principal beneficiaries have been evangelical religion clubs and gay-rights clubs, each protected from the widespread propensity to censor anything controversial in American high schools.[3] The congruence of these claims is also exemplified, more theoretically and less practically, in the work of scholars who support both religious liberty and sexual liberty. I have devoted much of my career to defending the rights of religious minorities of many faiths, including evangelical Christians. I have been less actively involved in the struggle for gay rights—specialization is inevitable in the modern academy—but my support for gay rights has long been a matter of record. In an early article—early both in my career and in the modern gay-rights movement—I said that that the claim to constitutional protection for gay rights presented an "easy case."[4] Of course I did not have the prescience to be thinking about marriage in 1981; I was thinking mostly about criminal prohibitions and about discrimination in government employment. More recently, I have testified in Congress that we should enact gay-rights laws and also enact religious exemptions.[5] And I have defended in court, on religious liberty grounds, the right of a lesbian parent to take her child to a gay-friendly church over the father's objection.[6] Andrew Koppelman at Northwestern is a prominent example of a scholar more actively supporting both religious liberty and sexual liberty.[7]

Unfortunately, support for the equal liberty of both sides is a rare position, either inside or outside of the academy. Too many Americans continue to commit modern versions of the Puritan mistake. The Puritans came to Massachusetts for religious liberty, but only for themselves. So far as they were concerned, adherents of other faiths had the liberty to go anywhere in the world outside Massachusetts, and that was quite enough religious liberty for them. Contemporary Americans are not so flagrant about protecting only themselves, but they have a similar tendency to protect only those they can sympathize with. Too many Americans react to claims of religious or sexual liberty on the basis of what they think of the religious belief or sexual practice at issue. The appeal of liberty as such is often insufficient to override antipathy to the beliefs or practices of the group asserting its right to liberty.

When the competing claims are to religious liberty and sexual liberty, people feel even more free to protect only the liberty they rely on for themselves. Two different liberties are involved, and there is no unavoidable inconsistency in saying that one of these liberties is protected by the Constitution and one is not, or that one gets sweeping protection and the other gets protection so narrow that it is barely discernable. Religious conservatives tend to take the first position: that sexual liberty is nowhere mentioned in the Constitution. Gay-rights advocates tend to take the second position; unable to deny that the Constitution protects the free exercise of religion, they construe that protection down to the vanishing point. The same kind of dissembling can be applied to statutes. When a gay-rights club in Salt Lake City sued under the Equal Access Act, Senator Orrin Hatch said the Act was never intended to protect them.[8] He had cosponsored the Act, and he surely knew better, but that is what he thought his constituents wanted to hear, and he was unwilling to lead them on an issue of equal liberty for all. Few politicians on either left or right do any better.

The litigating organizations that defend civil liberties for religious conservatives and for gays and lesbians direct much of their firepower at each other. Religious liberty groups generally take the lead in opposing same-sex marriage, define opposition to same-sex marriage as part of their core mission, and emphasize it in their fundraising. Gay-rights groups have not similarly opposed religious liberty across the board, but they oppose religious liberty in any application that might affect gay rights, and they oppose religious liberty more generally whenever necessary to their more specific goals. Gay-rights groups organized the opposition that killed the proposed Religious Liberty Protection Act in the 105th[9] and 106th[10] Congresses, and I am told that they are organizing the opposition to the proposed Workplace Religious Freedom Act[11] today. On both sides, groups organized to defend liberty for their members devote much of their effort to opposing liberty for others.

It is all very frustrating, but in the real world, it seems utterly unavoidable. Each side sees the other as a genuine threat to its values and to its own liberty. Many of the activists on each side do and say things that lend credence to the other side's worst fears. A negotiated truce seems to be impossible, because each side is a loose coalition of many groups and millions of individuals, so that no one is empowered to make a deal even if anyone were so inclined. As in so many public debates, the fundraising advantage goes to the more extreme and flamboyant advocates on each side, so that agitating the conflict is encouraged and reasoned discourse is discouraged.

II. The Scope of the Conflict

This book is an oasis of reasoned discourse amidst all the conflict, but even so, conflict pervades the book. Marc Stern catalogs the conflicts that have already arisen between sexual liberty and religious liberty, affecting housing, employment, places of public accommodation, medical and pharmacy services, commercial licensing, government funding, access to government property, freedom of speech, and religion clubs in public schools and universities, to mention only the major categories. Douglas Kmiec and Jonathan Turley each focus on revocation of tax exemptions for churches and other tax-exempt organizations that refuse to accept same-sex marriage. Robin

Wilson, Chai Feldblum, and Charles Reid explore potential solutions to the conflict, offering radically different views of what a solution should look like.

Some of this conflict would be readily avoidable with a modicum of tolerance and good will on both sides, but these essays also make clear, to an extent that I had not appreciated, that some of this conflict is unavoidable.

A. The Avoidable Conflict

In principle we can create private spaces in which each side can live its own values. Such a commitment to live and let live is the essence of civil liberty. But both sides bitterly resist letting the other side live its own values; in fact, each side seeks to impose its own view of marriage on everybody else. Conservative religious believers are the most open about that; they have joined with many other voters in prohibiting same-sex marriages in most of the states and prohibiting any federal recognition of same-sex marriages in the states that permit them. These votes wrote into explicit law the practice of the ages, but for most of those ages, no one gave the question any serious thought. Long tradition cannot disguise the fact that prohibiting a person's choice of marriage partner is a deep intrusion into one of the most intimate and personal of human choices.

Supporters of same-sex marriage are more tolerant in the most obvious way; they do not propose to prohibit opposite-sex marriage. Of course they have no political choice about that, but their tolerance is also entirely genuine. They have no desire to ban opposite-sex marriage or to tell other people how to structure their families or their sex lives. That difference is no small thing.

But that difference is pretty much the limit for tolerance of traditional religious believers among gay-rights organizations. Supporters of same-sex marriage demand not just legal recognition for same-sex marriages, and not just tolerance from the private sector, but recognition and affirmative support from the public and private sector alike. In Robin Wilson's succinct formulation, they show every sign of seeking "to take same-sex marriage from a negative right to be free of state interference to a positive entitlement to assistance by others."[12]

Some of them seek far more. They seek to suppress all public expression of disagreement or disapproval, or at least all such expression for which they have any plausible legal theory for suppression. Harassment law can be invoked to suppress expression of traditional moral views in educational and employment settings; discrimination rules can be invoked to drive off campus any student club that maintains a statement of faith or standards of sexual morality for members or officers. The American understanding of freedom of speech is a substantial but uncertain bulwark against such efforts; Marc Stern describes how each of these issues is the subject of recurring litigation.[13]

Revocation of tax exemptions for all churches that refuse to perform same-sex marriage ceremonies, and for any other religious organization that in any way resists same-sex marriage, would place those churches and organizations at an enormous financial disadvantage as compared to churches and organizations that conform to the new teaching. The emerging effort to revoke tax exemptions is thus an attempt to drive these churches and their affiliates either out of existence or into coerced silence. In choosing to focus on the revocation of tax exemptions, Jonathan Turley and Doug Kmiec take their stand in what should be one of the last ditches for dissenters from same-sex marriage. (Professor Turley defends these dissenters out of a commitment to liberty and not because he agrees with them.) The Turley and Kmiec arguments against politicizing tax exemptions are important and fundamental. Courts would not find the issue easy if the executive branch ever disagreed with Professors Turley and Kmiec. But at least so long as large and historically important churches refuse to recognize gay marriages, it seems to me unlikely that the executive branch in any jurisdiction would try to revoke tax exemptions over the issue. Fortunately, this issue so far remains more potential than actual.[14]

The ultimate goal for those seeking to suppress dissent would be to use hate-speech laws to prohibit any public expression of traditional moral teachings on same-sex sexual relations. Disapproval of same-sex marriages would be like pornography, confined to private expression among audiences who seek it out—or perhaps prohibited even there, if we ever take our lead from the unsuccessful Swedish effort to prosecute a pastor for giving a sermon.[15] The use of hate-speech regulation to suppress dissent has had some success abroad, but so far little success in this country.

Of course not all gays and lesbians support these efforts at censorship. But they seem to lack any capacity to restrain their allies who do support such efforts. They are mostly unwilling to oppose others within their movement, even when core constitutional rights are at stake for their opponents outside the movement. Such unwillingness to criticize allies does not distinguish them from any other strong social or political movement in the United States.

If the right to same-sex marriage eventually seems secure across most American jurisdictions, we might hope for a reduction in hostilities on collateral issues. But that is not how the American culture wars have tended to progress. Securing important ground more often leads to new and escalated demands and to more aggressive efforts against remaining pockets of resistance, all continuing either until effective opposition is wiped out or until a backlash secures firm ground of its own and the two sides finally recognize that they have fought to a stalemate. It seems safe to assume—and I think all the contributors to this volume do assume—that legal recognition of same-sex marriage would lead to further efforts to secure affirmative support from both the public and private sectors and the elimination or narrow confinement of any right to conscientious objection to the new regime.

All of this may be inevitable in the world we inhabit, but it is not at all necessary in logic or policy. It is not even smart politically. It gives credence to the sense of existential threat among moral traditionalists, and thus it stiffens their resistance. The supporters of same-sex marriage are surely right that their marriages will not change or undermine other people's opposite-sex marriages. But even if they could persuade their opponents of that, and so far they have not, any political benefit is forfeited by the visible efforts of so many in the gay and lesbian community to drive all dissent from the public domain. Of course the same criticism applies to the other side. Claims to liberty by religious traditionalists would be more credible, and quite possibly more persuasive, if they did not devote so much of their energy to restricting the liberty of others.

This area of avoidable conflict covers a large domain: speech, association, religious teachings, marriage ceremonies, tax exemption, and probably more. If same-sex marriage were legalized, and if each side would refrain from raising any legal or political issues based merely on their feelings—feelings of being disgusted, offended, disapproved, disrespected, or opposed—large bodies of potential litigation would disappear.

B. The Unavoidable Conflict

Even in an ideal world, many other points of conflict would remain harder to avoid. Defining private spaces for each side is an important first step, but lines must also be drawn in public spaces. People with fundamentally different views of the meaning and limits of marriage inevitably interact in ways that have tangible impacts on both sides. Even if conflict were confined to issues where someone on each side experiences an immediate and tangible personal effect, the remaining areas of conflict would be substantial.

Same-sex marriage will require a range of governmental and commercial services, and for some couples, religious services. Marriage licenses must be issued and wedding ceremonies performed. Weddings in our culture generally require printers, tailors, dressmakers, photographers, florists, caterers, bridal shops, wedding registries, and other services. Married couples need a house or an apartment, lodging when they travel, mortgages, furniture, groceries, plumbers, and all the other services of a modern economy. They may need other private actors to recognize their marriage for many potential purposes: fringe benefits, insurance, adoption, child care, marriage counseling, medical care, litigation, and probably many less obvious situations.

For many items on this list, with transactions well removed from the wedding and not involving explicit reference to the marriage, same-sex couples will encounter few difficulties. To the extent that they deal with large and impersonal business enterprises, they will encounter few difficulties with any item on the list—at least not after same-sex marriage is firmly established legally. In large urban areas, where most gays and lesbians still live, any goods and services they desire will be widely available; the free market will overwhelm pockets of moral disapproval. But for services closely related to weddings or marriages, with small businesses and individual officials and entrepreneurs, and in smaller communities, same-sex couples will sometimes encounter reluctance or refusal to serve their needs.

As Marc Stern, Robin Wilson, and Chai Feldblum each discuss in their different ways, some small businesses will refuse to perform personal services closely related to the wedding itself, and some small landlords will refuse to rent apartments. Conceivably, some bed and breakfasts will refuse to rent rooms, although so far as I am aware, that possibility remains Professor Feldblum's hypothetical and not a litigated case. Some religious social service agencies will refuse services. These merchants and landlords and agencies will feel that they are being asked to promote or facilitate sin in a way that makes them personally responsible for the sin that ensues, or in the case of adoption agencies, that they are being asked to place children in a sinful environment. Sometimes these refusals of service may be an act of bigotry or social protest, but very often, the claim to feel personal moral responsibility, or even fear of divine punishment, will be in complete good faith. Similarly, some employees in the county clerk's office will feel personal moral responsibility for issuing same-sex marriage licenses. Many churches, and some judges, will refuse to perform same-sex weddings. These conflicts cannot be entirely avoided, even with considerably greater tolerance on both sides than either side has displayed so far.

There is a tendency on the gay-rights side to dismiss these feelings of moral responsibility on the religious side. In this view, the person providing services to a same-sex couple is not participating in the sexual conduct she considers immoral and cannot reasonably think of herself as responsible for it. But that is a mistake. Many religious traditions have a long history of theological teaching attempting to identify the point at which one who cooperates with another's wrongdoing, or even one who fails to sufficiently resist, becomes personally responsible for that wrongdoing.[16] Secular ethicists have also addressed the issue.[17] Both believers and nonbelievers have moral commitments, often intuitive, sometimes well developed, on the extent to which one can facilitate, condone, cooperate with, or profit from the wrongdoing of others.

Political and theological liberals have their own heated debates about the boundaries of such vicarious moral responsibility. An obvious and prominent example is recurring campaigns for disinvestment in businesses guilty of various unsavory practices. In the campaign against apartheid in South Africa, governments and universities were variously urged to divest themselves of all investments in any company with a place of business in South Africa that did not conform to the Sullivan Principles on fair treatment of black workers; any company with a place of business in South Africa (whether or not it complied with the Sullivan Principles); any company that sold goods in South Africa; or even any mutual fund that owned shares in any company doing business in South Africa.

The law addresses such issues of vicarious responsibility in the law of aiding and abetting, conspiracy, and nuisance, to mention only the most obviously relevant doctrines. California rejected the claims of landlords who felt moral responsibility for the sexual use of bedrooms they rented,[18] but California would have held those same landlords fully responsible if tenants had used those bedrooms for prostitution.[19] The state and the landlords did not disagree about the landlords' responsibility for their property; they disagreed about the moral implications of nonmarital, noncommercial sex. There is nothing unique, or even unusual, about traditional believers feeling personal moral responsibility if they facilitate, or help celebrate, what they consider to be a deeply immoral relationship.

So either the same-sex couple must find another merchant or another landlord, or the traditionally religious merchant or landlord must violate deeply felt moral obligations. These conflicts are thus unavoidable. Still, unavoidable conflict does not necessarily mean unmanageable conflict. For the most part, these conflicts are not zero-sum games, in which every gain for one side produces an equal and opposite loss for the other side. If legislators and judges will treat both sides with respect, harm to each side can be minimized. Of course that is a huge "if." The most likely political outcome is that if the gay-rights movement becomes strong enough to enact general recognition of same-sex marriage, it will simply roll over its opponents on all these collateral questions. Existing gay-rights legislation often includes no religious exemption at all apart from background rights under state and federal constitutions and Religious Freedom Restoration Acts, which gay-rights litigants then seek to minimize.[20]

But this pattern of all-or-nothing battles is neither universal today nor inevitable in the future,[21] and ending marriage discrimination is more controversial than ending other kinds of discrimination. The recent round of state constitutional amendments means that in many states, legalizing same-sex marriage will require a referendum. If the center can hold—if some significant block of votes will respect both sides—then the political outcome may be that protection of dissenters on these collateral questions is an essential part of the political bargain that enacts same-sex marriage. The most likely source for such a significant block of centrist votes would be theologically liberal believers, who might intuitively support gay rights and, if they stop to think about it, support religious liberty as well. More conservative believers who oppose same-sex marriage would do well to court these more liberal believers and make the case for protecting both sides. But of course that is not their current strategy.

III. Balancing Interests

Assuming that such a critical block of centrist voters can be brought into existence, and that it insists on laws that protect both sides to the extent possible, what would such a resolution look like? Robin Wilson, Chai Feldblum, and Charles Reid each propose solutions. An editor must respect all his authors equally, and I do; each argues well for his or her position. But their proposals are radically different, and no editor could *agree* with them all equally. To readers that have come this far, it must be obvious that my own views are far closer to those of Robin Wilson than to either of the others.

Wilson, Feldblum, and I agree that some balancing of conflicting interests is the only alternative to a total subordination of one side's interests to those of the other. But in Professor Feldblum's balancing, the gay-rights side nearly always wins. She finds tangible harm in any refusal of service, even if the same service is readily available next door and in a hundred other places around the city. Not only that; she finds that the insult of being refused service and the inconvenience of going elsewhere—mostly the insult, if I understand her correctly—almost universally outweighs the harm of forcing the merchant to violate a deeply held moral obligation. The only exceptions she would allow are programs to instruct youth in religious or moral values, and possibly—only possibly, so then again maybe not—for filling leadership positions in enterprises run by organizations committed to a particular set of religious or moral values.

This proposed balancing imposes the new moral values on essentially all public spaces, and also on many spaces I would have thought were private, within the domain of religious organizations. Whether a Catholic social-service agency must hire a spouse from a same-sex marriage as its executive director is for her a close case. And she clearly implies that that Catholic agency must be willing to hire same-sex spouses for all lesser positions, and to provide its services to same-sex couples with no mention of moral disapproval.

Robin Wilson proposes what seems to me a much more sensible balance: to protect the right of conscientious objectors to refuse to facilitate same-sex marriages, except where such a refusal imposes significant hardship on the same-sex couple. What follows may be either an elaboration or a modification of what Professor Wilson has in mind, but her suggestions and mine are at least similar.

The scope of any right to refuse service to same-sex couples must depend on comparing the harm to the couple of being refused service and the harm to the merchant or service provider of being coerced to provide service. What is most importantly at stake for each side is the right to live out core attributes of personal identity. In my view, the right to one's own moral integrity should generally trump the inconvenience of having to get the same service from another provider nearby. Requiring a merchant to perform services that violate his deeply held moral commitments is far more serious, different in kind and not just in degree, from mere inconvenience.

The larger problem for same-sex couples is the insult, the pointed reminder that some fellow citizens vehemently disapprove of what they are doing. But same-sex couples know that anyway, and the American commitment to freedom of speech ensures that they will be reminded of it from time to time. Hurt feelings or personal offense are so far not a basis for censorship of ideas in American law.[22] A refusal of service is more pointed, and it is conduct not speech, but I think the harm that it inflicts is substantially similar in kind.

There remains the issue of unfair surprise. When Professor Feldblum's same-sex couple arrives at the bed and breakfast at 10:00 p.m. after a long journey, going elsewhere to find lodging is no ordinary inconvenience. As Andrew Koppelman has pointed out, this case is a breach of contract quite independent of any gay-rights law,[23] and there is not likely to be a religious exemption to the voluntarily assumed obligations of contract.[24] Remedies for breach of contract are often undercompensatory in consumer cases, because they generally do not compensate frustration or emotional distress, although the specific example should be covered by an emerging exception for disrupted vacations.[25] I would have no objection to a requirement that merchants that refuse to serve same-sex couples announce that fact on their website or, for businesses with only a local service area, on a sign outside their premises. Whether the gay-rights side would want such a requirement is a harder question. An advertising requirement would avoid unfair surprise, and it would probably deter many merchants from refusing service at all, for fear that their public avowal of discrimination against same-sex couples might cost them business from sympathetic opposite-sex couples. On the other hand, gays and lesbians might fear that many such notices would reinforce resistance and embolden other merchants to post similar notices. I think the benefits would outweigh the costs, but this is not a confident prediction.

More generally, market share matters. In a community where many merchants refused to serve same-sex couples, a public notice requirement would be essential to avoid the burden of couples going from store to store searching for someone who would serve their needs. And at some point, even with a public notice requirement, the available choice of merchants might become so constrained that inconvenience would become significant hardship. Large businesses take up more market share, and an owner's claim of personal responsibility for everything that happens in his business grows more attenuated as the business expands, so a sensible legislative provision would be to put a limit on the size of businesses eligible to claim an exemption. But when legislators and activists tried to negotiate such a limit during congressional consideration of the proposed Religious Liberty Protection Act, the two sides had such radically different views of an appropriate limit that no agreement could be reached. And that negotiation addressed only landlords and the number of apartment units. A universally applicable cap for all businesses would be much more difficult to negotiate.

Hardship is obvious when there is only one or a few relevant merchants in a community and none of them will serve same-sex couples. In that case, I agree with Professor Wilson that the merchant's right to moral integrity is outweighed by the same-sex couples' right to live in the community in accordance with *their* moral commitments.

Professor Wilson raises the possibility of employees in the county clerk's office who refuse to issue marriage licenses to same-sex couples. Such an employee needs to have a co-worker immediately available to issue the license without anyone having to wait in another line. Government employees cannot have more than *de minimis* rights to refuse to perform their core job functions for all members of the public, and probably most courts would not even concede a *de minimis* right.

I have a different reaction to judges refusing to perform same-sex weddings. This reaction contains a large dose of intuition, but I think I can defend it. Weddings are not really part of a judge's job. A judge has the authority to marry people, but generally no obligation to marry anybody, and my sense is that most judges who do an occasional wedding do it as a personal favor for friends or acquaintances. There is no doubt that such a judge is exercising state authority, vested in him in his capacity as a judge, but that is not conclusive; under existing marriage law a clergyman performing a wedding is also exercising state authority. I think that even for the judge, there is such a strong element of personal discretion in presiding over a wedding that it is entirely appropriate to respect his feelings of moral responsibility for his role in doing so. A judge who holds himself out as willing to marry all comers would present a different case.

Finally, within the church itself, I think the protection for religious dissenters from same-sex marriage is substantially absolute. No one can have a legal right to a religious service or ritual; there can be no Catholic wedding or Baptist wedding except on terms acceptable to those responsible for Catholic or Baptist churches. In an important sense, a legally coerced Catholic wedding would not be a Catholic wedding at all. It would be a sham. Legally coerced religious services are utterly inconsistent with free exercise of religion.

This sketch of a solution designed to protect both sides is sure to be unsatisfactory to both sides. From the gay-rights perspective, discrimination gets a certain legitimacy, and in the worst case, the stream of commerce might be sprinkled with public notices of discriminatory intent. In more traditional communities, same-sex couples planning a wedding might be forced to pick their merchants carefully, like black families driving across the South half a century ago. All of this is true, and in some parts of the country it would be very real, but in most cities, such problems would be minimal.

From the religious perspective, Professor Wilson and I seem to say that outside the church itself, conscientious objectors to same-sex marriage can refuse to cooperate only when it doesn't really matter because someone else will provide the desired service anyway. But when a particular merchant's refusal to cooperate might actually delay or prevent the conduct he considers sinful, then he loses his rights and has to facilitate the sin.

Unfortunately, that is true, and if there is to be any protection for religious dissenters at all, this qualification is inevitable in the governmental and commercial sectors. Religious dissenters can live their own values, but not if they occupy choke points that empower them to prevent same-sex couples from living *their* own values. If the dissenters want complete moral autonomy on this issue, they must refrain from occupying such a choke point. Same-sex couples are citizens of the United States, entitled to live anywhere in the country that they choose. Their right to live and to acquire goods and services must be protected in the Bible Belt as well as in Greenwich Village, and that may mean that a religious merchant in the Bible Belt sometimes has fewer rights than a religious merchant in Greenwich Village. That may seem ironic, but it isn't; this whole proposal is about protecting minorities. The same-sex couple needs more legal protection in the Bible Belt, and the conservative believer needs more protection in Greenwich Village.

Spelling out the details of strong gay-rights legislation with strong religious exemptions does not make an entirely pretty picture, even to me. There are problems in both directions, sometimes giving offense to same-sex couples and sometimes overriding the deep moral convictions of religious dissenters. But these problems are preferable to completely trampling the core values of one side or the other—either prohibiting same-sex marriage entirely, or requiring religious dissenters to violate their deep moral convictions whenever asked, however modest or nonessential the benefit to same-sex couples. Either of those alternatives would be neater than attempting to let both sides live its own values to the extent possible, but neatness is not a moral good. Either of those alternatives would be far worse in terms of liberty, far worse in terms of respect for individual integrity, far worse in terms of emotional suffering, than the messiness of protecting each side's liberty as far as possible.

A third alternative with some legislative appeal would be to exempt all not-for-profit religious organizations and refuse to exempt any business or other for-profit entity. This would have the virtues of drawing a bright line and of protecting the core case of the churches and their affiliates. It would have the disadvantage of refusing protection in a substantial range of cases in which the hardship imposed by refusing to exempt conservative religious business people would far outweigh the hardship to same-sex couples of allowing exemptions.

The result would be to exclude from a range of occupations and professions many believers who are unwilling to violate their faith commitments. Such occupational exclusions have an odious history. The English Test Acts and penal laws long excluded Catholics from a range of occupations, including positions of responsibility in the civil and military service, solicitors, barristers, notaries, school teachers, and most businesses with more then two apprentices.[26] These occupational exclusions are one of the core historic violations of religious liberty, and of course this history was familiar to the American Founders. In light of this history, it is simply untenable to say—as some courts have[27]—that exclusion from an occupation is not a cognizable burden on religious liberty. Exclusion from one's chosen occupation is obviously a burden on religious liberty, and the only serious argument is about the reach of the asserted compelling interest in regulation.

IV. Separating Church and State in Marriage[28]

There is one other step that would go far to reduce conflict over same-sex marriage. That would be to clearly separate legal from religious marriage in law and in public understanding. Part of the reason the same-sex-marriage issue is so intractable is that it arises in the context of our most fundamental and long lasting breach of separation of church and state. Separation of church and state is an ambiguous and contested concept,[29] but nearly all Americans agree at least on *institutional* separation—that the institutions of the church should be distinct from the institutions of the state. Even the Puritans maintained a substantial degree of institutional separation. Yet in marriage, legal and religious institutions are thoroughly combined.

Marriage is a religious institution and a religious relationship. It is a sacrament in the Catholic faith and an important religious commitment in the Protestant and Jewish faiths. It is ordained in the Jewish and Christian Scriptures. "Therefore shall a man leave his father and his mother, and shall cleave unto his wife: and they shall be one flesh,"[30] according to the Torah. And in the Christian Gospels, Jesus quotes this passage from the Torah and continues, "What therefore God hath joined together, let not man put asunder."[31] Both Scriptures repeatedly condemn adultery.[32]

Marriage is also a legal institution and a legal relationship, the basis for a whole set of legal rights. The legal relationship defines property rights, mutual duties of support, inheritance rights, tax liabilities, evidentiary privileges, rights to sue for personal injury or file for bankruptcy, claims to pensions, social security, and insurance benefits, and much more. In the same-sex marriage litigation in Massachusetts, the Commonwealth said that "hundreds of statutes" create rules or authorize benefits on the basis of marriage.[33] Despite rising divorce rates, governments and employers use marriage as the principal indicator of long-term commitment and mutual dependence. Governments and employers offer long-term benefits to spouses because marriage defines long-term legal obligations.

Sex and sexual morality remain central to religious understandings of marriage, but sex has less and less to do with the law of marriage. In most states, adultery and fornication are no longer crimes and seducing another person's spouse is no longer grounds for a lawsuit. In states where these laws are still on the books, public opinion almost certainly would not tolerate prosecutions or damage judgments. Divorces are no longer based on adultery, because nearly all states have enacted no-fault divorce, so that "grounds" for divorce are no longer needed. Unconsented sex with one's wife is rape in most states, meaning that the fact of marriage no longer proves irrevocable consent to sex. Inability to have sexual intercourse is still a ground for annulment in many states, but only if the other spouse chooses to invoke that ground,[34] and often, only if the inability was not disclosed before the marriage,[35] the deceived spouse does not ratify the marriage after discovering the inability,[36] and/or the deceived spouse sues within a short statute of limitations.[37] Under statutes such as these, a couple can have a valid marriage without ever having sex.

No doubt legislators and judges still assume that sexual relations are central to marriage, and on the rare occasions when the issue arises, judges still say so.[38] But law does not require an exclusive sexual relationship in marriage, or do much to protect such a relationship. Religious traditionalists may be unhappy about this state of the law too, but it was driven by changes in heterosexual norms, and resistance to same-sex marriage will do nothing to restore the marriage law of the early twentieth century. Private sexual relationships have been largely deregulated both in and out of marriage. Once a license is issued, it is rare for any legal rule about sex to be the basis for any legal decision about marriage. The modern law of marriage is mostly about economic and financial matters.

Religious and legal marriage are thus distinct in concept as well as in origin. But in American law and in public understanding, the two institutions are thoroughly intertwined, jointly administered by church and state. The state deputizes clergy of all faiths to administer vows that create legal marriages as well as religious marriages. Most of our churches effectively deputize the state to grant divorces that dissolve religious marriages as well as legal marriages. And we have a single word—marriage—to describe both the religious relationship and the legal relationship. Lack of vocabulary thus makes it difficult to think about the two relationships separately.

Of course not everyone conflates the two relationships in every circumstance. Divorced Catholics need a church annulment before they can remarry, and Orthodox Jews need a *get*, a decree from a religious court. People awaiting their annulment or *get* are legally divorced but still religiously married. But my impression is that most Americans simply think of these people as divorced and having a problem with their church.

Much of the intensity of the same-sex marriage debate results from conflating the religious and legal relationships. When President Bush issued an official statement on the Massachusetts same-sex marriage decision, he said that marriage is "sacred" and that redefining marriage threatens its "sanctity."[39] "Sacred" and "sanctity" are religious concepts; each word is an approximate synonym for "holy" or "holiness," respectively. The President's statement assumed that the courts were redefining the religious institution. Many Americans share that assumption, and they are outraged.

A significant minority of Americans opposes same-sex marriage but supports same-sex civil unions, and state supreme courts have had to decide whether civil unions suffice or whether equality requires marriage.[40] Many observers have marveled at the high stakes attached to a label, to whether a single word may be used to describe the relationship. On the religious side, the stakes are precisely that marriage is a religious relationship, a sacred institution, not to be changed by secular officials in ways that believers consider to be immoral. On the gay-rights side, the stakes seem to be partly the symbolic value of full equality, and partly widespread reports that employers and bureaucrats still refuse to recognize civil unions for purposes of benefits linked to marriage.[41]

The two courts that have so far required same-sex "marriage," and not just civil unions, clearly understood that they have no right or power to redefine a religious institution. The Massachusetts court referred throughout its opinion to "civil marriage," not simply to marriage. The court described "civil marriage" as "a wholly secular institution" created by the government,[42] and it noted that never in its history had Massachusetts required a religious ceremony to create a civil marriage.[43] The court also said: "Our opinion in no way limits the rights of individuals to refuse to marry persons of the same sex for religious or any other reasons."[44] These points should have gotten more emphasis, and their significance should have been more explicitly stated, but their meaning is clear enough on careful reading: the court understood and intended that its ruling applies only to legal marriage and not to religious marriage.

The California court was more explicit. It said that "[f]rom the state's inception, California law has treated the legal institution of *civil* marriage as distinct from *religious* marriage."[45] And the court twice suggested that the legislature might choose a word other than marriage for all couples, "to emphasize and clarify that this civil institution is distinct from the religious institution of marriage."[46] The court emphasized that "no religion will be required to change its religious policies or practices with regard to same-sex couples, and no religious officiant will be required to solemnize a marriage in contravention of his or her religious beliefs."[47] Unaware of the many issues raised in this volume, the court said that this protection ensured that same-sex marriage "will not impinge upon the religious freedom of any religious organization, official, or any other person."[48]

However clear the distinction between legal marriage and religious marriage might have been to these two courts, the distinction has been lost on the public. To make such a distinction effective would probably require legislation and new vocabulary. The Massachusetts and California courts used the phrase "civil marriage." But "civil" is a word of many meanings; if we are going to try to solve the vocabulary problem with only an adjective, I think "legal marriage" better communicates the central point. Better yet, as any writing teacher will tell you, nouns are more important than adjectives. We should leave the word "marriage" to its religious meaning, and use the new phrase "civil union" to describe the relationship formerly known as civil or legal marriage. "Civil unions" should not be a second-class status for same-sex couples;

civil union should be the legal relationship created by the state for *straight* couples—and for gays and lesbians in states that choose to legally recognize committed same-sex relationships. "Marriage" should be reserved for private and religious relationships, and the state should have nothing to do with it.

Charles Reid argues eloquently in this volume against separating legal marriage from religious marriage. He says that the Anglo-American law of marriage is rooted in the Christian understanding of marriage and that the two cannot be separated without grave and destructive social consequences. I do not doubt his account of history; he knows far more about the history of marriage than I will ever learn. But I disagree with him about the current situation. Religious teaching still defines marriage for millions of Americans, but for millions of other Americans, that is no longer true. In a 2003 poll conducted shortly after the first Massachusetts decision on same-sex marriage, 53 percent of respondents viewed marriage as principally a religious matter, while 33 percent viewed it principally as a legal matter.[49] And no one should be surprised at the results of the next question. Those who viewed marriage as primarily a religious matter opposed same-sex marriage by lopsided margins. Those who viewed marriage as primarily a legal matter supported same-sex marriage by a modest majority.[50]

Even if Professor Reid is right that religious faith provides a better foundation for marriage than any secular account, any possible religious foundation for marriage is lost to those who find it impossible to believe the religious account. Once religious teachings seem unbelievable to a person, there is no going back by any act of will or by simply deciding that it would be better to believe. Many Americans might find it a more comfortable world if religious teachings seemed more plausible to them, but that yearning does not in itself make those teachings seem any more plausible to nonbelievers. In a religiously pluralistic society, we must have an account of legal marriage that works for believers and nonbelievers alike. Professor Reid's proposed solution to our current problems is really an appeal to reject same-sex marriage and return to the traditional understanding. That may yet happen, although the age structure of public opinion seems against it. Professor Reid's argument will not yield a solution for a world in which same-sex marriage has been generally legalized.

What would it mean to fully separate religious marriage from secular civil unions? Clergy could perform marriages within each faith tradition, but they could not perform civil unions. Civil unions would be created in a secular ceremony led by a judge, a notary public, or a clerk at city hall. Civil unions could be ended by civil courts that would sort out property rights, economic obligations, and child custody. Marriages could be ended only within the religious tradition that performed the marriage. Each faith could maintain its own rules and marriage tribunals for its adherents. Or if a church chose, it could defer to the state's decisions about any civil union between the same partners. But then it would have only itself to blame if it didn't like the state's decisions.

The important thing is that public attention would be focused on the independence of the two statuses. A couple could marry in church, civilly unite with the state, or both. They could divorce in church, dissolve their civil union with the state, or both. They could be married but not civilly united, civilly united but not married, or both, or neither. Maybe most couples would keep their religious and civil statuses synchronized. But that would be their choice, and they would be forced to think about the choice. With every new couple forced to think about the choice, some knowledge of the difference would become widespread. Forcing couples to attend to the choice is critical to public understanding, so separating the processes for creating and terminating religious and legal marriages is more important than the choice of vocabulary.

Separating secular civil unions from religious marriages, and focusing public attention on the separation, would not solve all the problems discussed in this book. Some same-sex couples will want religious ceremonies, and some churches and synagogues will choose not to provide them. And these couples may still encounter a merchant from a different faith who doesn't want to provide goods or services essential to the wedding celebration. Some merchants might still boycott even a wholly secular ceremony celebrating a purely secular civil union.

But there is reason to hope that clearly separating secular civil unions from religious marriages would take some of the emotional intensity out of this debate. Jonathan Turley has suggested that this simple vocabulary change would solve the whole problem.[51] I am not that optimistic, but I think it would help. Separate vocabulary, separate ceremonies, and separate dissolution proceedings would emphasize that the state is not attempting to change a religious institution, that marriage is fully restored to the control of religious organizations, and that conservative churches can define marriage as conservatively as they choose. The law of civil unions would not be about marriage at all, and it need not be about sexual morality at all. In a world of no-fault dissolution of civil unions, there would be no need to even mention sex in the law of civil unions. Civil unions would mostly be about financial benefits and obligations, things plainly within the state's power to regulate. Clarifying these distinctions would reduce the sense in the religious community that a sacred institution is under attack, and that would be a good thing in itself. And maybe, reducing the sense of attack would reduce the urge to counter attack, and thus reduce the number of merchants inclined to boycott same-sex couples, same-sex civil union ceremonies, and maybe even same-sex marriage ceremonies.

Many traditional religious believers will be unhappy with separating legal from religious marriage. Legal marriage, or civil unions, would carry all the temporal consequences—financial benefits and obligations and judicial enforceability. Religious marriage would be a voluntary institution, enforceable only in the next life, if at all. But of course all religious commitments are voluntary in a society with religious liberty and no established church, and if the claims of religion are true, the religious institutions address what is most important. Traditionalists might prefer a world in which their understanding of marriage is also the legal understanding—in which their understanding of marriage is, in effect, established. But that world is long lost. By tying religious marriage to legal marriage—most obviously by Protestant religious recognition of civil divorces—churches have suffered the negative consequences of establishment. The state may support religion or take charge of religion, but the state is not faithful to religious teaching. In states where legal marriage is extended to same-sex couples, religious marriage will be much safer if it is cleanly separated. The descendants of the Puritans voted overwhelmingly to give up their established church when Unitarians starting winning elections and taking over tax-supported Congregationalist churches.[52] Those churches and believers who still think of legal marriage as theirs are in the same position today. Whether they continue to oppose same-sex marriage or acquiesce, they will best protect their own religious liberty if they take refuge in the difference between religious and legal marriage.

Of course it is true today that churches do not have to recognize the state's definition of marriage. But everything about the way we administer marriage tends to conceal that fact. We have so combined a religious institution with a legal one that millions of Americans share the President's view that the "sanctity" of marriage somehow depends on law, not faith. To have any hope of separating the sanctity of religious marriage from the legal and policy debate over same-sex relationships, we have to cleanly and publicly separate the state from religious marriage.

V. Conclusion

The nature of marriage is a question with profound religious significance and fundamentally disputed answers. The state has no more business imposing a single answer to that question than to any other religious question. Marriage is for the churches; government should confine itself to civil unions. And then we should try as best we can to create rules that enable Americans with fundamentally different views of marriage to live in peace and equality in the same society.

Notes

Introduction: Anthony R. Picarello, Jr.

1. *See* Mark D. Stern, *Same-Sex Marriage and the Churches*, *infra*, notes 29–92 and accompanying text.

2. *See id.*, at notes 93–120, 223–240 and accompanying text.

3. *See id.*, at notes 125–274 and accompanying text.

4. *See id.*, at notes 275–311 and accompanying text.

5. 26 U.S.C. § 501(c)(3) (2000).

6. *See* Bob Jones University v. United States, 461 U.S. 574 (1983).

7. *See* Jonathan Turley, *An Unholy Union: Same-Sex Marriage and the Use of Governmental Programs to Penalize Religious Groups with Unpopular Practices*, *infra*, notes 15–45 and accompanying text.

8. *See* Boy Scouts of Am. v. Wyman, 335 F.3d 80 (2d Cir. 2003).

9. *See* Turley, *supra* note 7, at notes 46–65 and accompanying text.

10. *See id.*, at notes 61–65 and accompanying text.

11. *See id.*, at notes 66–77 and accompanying text.

12. *See* Robin Fretwell Wilson, *Matters of Conscience: Lessons for Same-Sex Marriage from the Healthcare Context*, *infra*, notes 44–88 and accompanying text.

13. *See id.*, at notes 34–38, 89–129 and accompanying text.

14. *See id.*, at notes 130–195 and accompanying text.

15. *See id.*, at notes 196–205 and accompanying text.

16. *See* Douglas W. Kmiec, *Same-Sex Marriage and the Coming Antidiscrimination Campaigns Against Religion*, *infra*, notes 36–103 and accompanying text.

17. *See id.*, at notes 104–108 and accompanying text.

18. *See id.*, at notes 110–116 and accompanying text.

19. *See id.*, at notes 80–97 and accompanying text.

20. *See* Chai R. Feldblum, *Moral Conflict and Conflicting Liberties*, *infra*, notes 28–30 and accompanying text.

21. *See id.*, at notes 118–140 and accompanying text.

22. Washington v. Glucksberg, 521 U.S. 702, 752-789 (1997) (Souter, J., concurring).

23. *See* Feldblum, *supra* note 20, at notes 39–77 and accompanying text.

24. *See id.*, at notes 78–117 and accompanying text.

25. *See id.*, at notes 134–137 and accompanying text.

26. *See* Charles J. Reid, Jr., *Marriage: Its Relationship to Religion, Law, and the State*, *infra*, notes 1–123 and accompanying text.

27. *See id.*, at notes 191–194 and accompanying text.

28. *See id.*, at notes 124–194 and accompanying text.

29. *See id.*, at notes 191–194 and accompanying text.

30. *See* Douglas Laycock, *Afterword*, *infra*, notes 12–21 and accompanying text.

31. *See id.*, at notes 22–27 and accompanying text.

32. *See id.*, at notes 28–52 and accompanying text.

Chapter One: Marc D. Stern

1. The views expressed here are my own, and not those of AJCongress.

2. Letter from Arnold Schwarzenegger to the Members of the California State Assembly, *available at* www.gov.ca.gov/pdf/press/vetoes_2005/AB_849_veto.pdf (last visited June 14, 2008).

3. Assemb. B. 849, 2005 Reg. Sess. (Cal. 2005).

4. Civil Marriage Act, ch. 33, S.C. 2005 (Canada).

5. *See* Chai R. Feldblum, *Moral Conflict and Conflicting Liberties*, *infra*, at notes 131–136 and accompanying text; Robin Fretwell Wilson, *Matters of Conscience: Lessons for Same-Sex Marriage from the Healthcare Context*, *infra*, at notes 182–183 and accompanying text; Douglas W. Kmiec, *Same-Sex Marriage and the Coming Antidiscrimination Campaigns Against Religion*, *infra*, at notes 78–103 and accompanying text.

6. Douglas Laycock, *Afterword*, *infra*, at notes 28–52 and accompanying text; Charles J. Reid, Jr., *Marriage: Its Relation to Religion, Law, and the State*, *infra*, at notes 45–123 and accompanying text; Kmiec, *supra* note 5, at notes 78–90 and accompanying text.

7. Religious Freedom Restoration Act, 42 U.S.C. §§ 2000bb *et seq.* (2000).

8. Black v. Virginia, 538 U.S. 343 (2003). The few courts that have considered campus "hate speech" codes invalidated them. However, the rule that hate speech is fully protected has eroded in the context of workplace harassment and in public schools. *See, e.g.*, *infra*, at notes 42–72 and accompanying text; Aguilar v. Avis Rent

A Car System, Inc., 980 P.2d 846 (Cal. 1999) (injunction against future racist remarks in the workplace).

9. For a recent compilation of the case law, *see* Gilles v. Davis, 427 F.3d 197 (3d Cir. 2005) (distinguishing between generalized criticism of homosexual activity and speech challenging the sexual choices of individual students). The Third Circuit indicated that the former was constitutionally protected. It was vague as to whether the latter constituted fighting words or remained protected speech.

10. John Hooper, *Anti Islamic Italian Author in New Legal Fight*, THE GUARDIAN (July 13, 2005), *available at* www.guardian.co.uk/world/2005/jul/13/books.italy (last visited June 14, 2008); *Trial Over Italian Islam 'Insult,'* BBC News (May 24, 2005), *available at* http://news.bbc.co.uk/2/hi/europe/4576663.stm (last visited June 14, 2008).

11. Hellquist v. Owens, 2002 Sask. Q.B. 506, *rev'd,* 2006 Sask. Ct. App. 41.

12. *Owens,* 2002 Sask. Q.B. 506, at pars. 19–20.

13. *Id.* at par. 23.

14. Hellquist v. Owens, 2006 Sask. Ct. App. 41.

15. R Albert Mohler, Jr., *The End of Religious Liberty in Canada* (Oct. 3, 2004), *available at* www.baptist2baptist.net/Issues/TenCommandments/MohlerMay242004 .asp (last visited June 14, 2008). The headline has so far proven wholly exaggerated.

16. Whatcott v. Sask. Human Rights Tribunal, 2007 Sask. Q.B. 450.

17. Trinity W. Univ. v. Coll. of Teachers, [2001] 1 S.C.R. 772 (Sup. Ct. Canada).

18. *Id.* at par. 57 (L'Heureux-Dubé, J., dissenting).

19. Lund v. Boissoin at par. 341, Human Rights Panel of Alberta (Nov. 30, 2007), *available at* www.albertahumanrights.ab.ca/LundDarren113007Pa.pdf (last visited July 23, 2008). For discussion of the case, see Daryl Slade, *Anti-Gay Letter Meant to Promote Debate: Alberta Pastor,* CANWEST NEWS SERVICE (July 17, 2007), *available at* http://rightssites.com/republicanparty/articles.inc.php?command=show&ID=11116 (last visited June 14, 2008).

20. Lund v. Boissoin, Human Rights Panel of Alberta (May 30, 2008), *available at* www.albertahumanrights.ab.ca/Lund_Darren_Remedy053008.pdf (last visited July 23, 2008).

21. Attis v. New Brunswick Sch. Dist. # 15, [1996] 1 S.C.R. 825, 856 (par. 41) (emphasis omitted)..

22. *Id.* at 856–57 (pars. 42–44) (quoting an earlier opinion).

23. Melzer v. Bd. of Educ., 336 F.3d 185 (2d Cir. 2003).

24. Sweden v. Ake Green (Sup. Ct. Sweden 2005). *See also Swedish Gay Hate Priest Launches Appeal,* THE LOCAL: SWEDISH NEWS IN ENGLISH (Jan. 19, 2005), *available at* www.thelocal.se/article.php?ID=862&date=20050119 (last visited June 14, 2008) (priest preached that homosexuality was a tumor that would lead, *inter alia,* to pedophilia); *Swedish Pastor's Hate Crime Conviction Overturned,* THE BECKET FUND (Feb. 11, 2005), *available at* www.becketfund.org/index.php/article/353.html (last visited June 14, 2008); *Swedish Court Reviews 'Hate' Case,* BBC NEWS (May 9, 2005), *available at* http://news.bbc.co.uk/2/hi/europe/4530209.stm (last visited June 14, 2008) (announcing the Supreme Court's decision to review the case). *See also* Keith

B. Richburg & Alan Cooperman, *Swede's Sermon on Gays: Bigotry or Free Speech*, WASH. POST A1 (Jan. 29, 2005).

25. *The Yogyakarta Principles: Principles on the Application of International Human Rights Law in Relation to Sexual Orientation and Gender Identity* (2007) (Principle 21) (emphasis added), *available at* www.yogyakartaprinciples.org/principles_en.pdf (last visited June 14, 2008).

26. *'Yogyakarta Principles' A Milestone for Lesbian, Gay, Bisexual, & Transgender Rights*, HUMAN RIGHTS WATCH (March 26, 2007), *available at* www.hrw.org/english/docs/2007/03/26/global15546.htm (last visited June 14, 2008).

27. *See Scholar's Group: Accrediting Agency Violating First Amendment*, N.Y. SUN (Nov. 4–6, 2005).

28. Kevin Freking, *Surgeon General Hopeful Denies Bias Against Gays*, BOSTON GLOBE (July 13, 2007), *available at* www.boston.com/news/nation/washington/articles/2007/07/13/surgeon_general_hopeful_denies_bias_against_gays/ (last visited June 14, 2008).

For a case holding that a person's views on homosexuality can disqualify him (or her) from certain public offices, *see* Lumpkin v. Brown, 109 F.3d 1498 (9th Cir. 1997). Legal issues are likely to arise only when government seeks to remove a person already appointed to government office; the appointing authority has total, or almost total, discretion over who to appoint in the first place. *See* Mayor v. Educ. Equal. League, 415 U.S. 605 (1974).

29. Krell v. Gray, 24 Cal. Rptr. 3d 764 (Cal. Ct. App. 2005).

30. *Id.* at 775 (quoting CAL. CONST., art. I, § 28). The court relied heavily on *Aguilar v. Avis Rent A Car System, Inc.*, 980 P.2d 846 (Cal. 1999).

31. Kelly Hayboer, *Reprimanded College Worker Has an Ally*, STAR LEDGER (NJ) (July 21, 2005), *available at* www.thefire.org/index.php/article/6132.html (last visited June 14, 2008); Letter from Peter C. Harvey (New Jersey Attorney General, signed by Cheryl R. Clark, Deputy Attorney General) to Greg Lukianoff, Director of Legal and Public Advocacy for Individual Rights in Education, Re: Jihad Daniels (July 15, 2005), *available at* www.thefire.org/pdfs/ad466e8b2d8a3cc2d57b2d903c9ff321.pdf) [hereinafter Harvey Letter] (last visited June 14, 2008). The policy says nothing of freedom of speech.

32. *See generally* Lewis v. United Parcel Serv., Inc., 2005 WL 2596448 (N.D. Cal. 2005).

33. Erznoznik v. City of Jacksonville, 422 U.S. 205 (1975). *See* the comprehensive listing of Supreme Court cases in Judge Fuentes' dissent in *Gilles v. Davis*, 427 F.3d 197 (3d Cir. 2005).

34. Harvey Letter, *supra* note 31.

35. Aguilar v. Avis Rent A Car System, Inc., 980 P.2d 846 (Cal. 1999).

36. Press Release, *Victory for Free Speech and Religious Liberty at William Paterson University* (Dec. 7, 2005), *available at* www.thefire.org/index.php/article/6552.html (last visited June 14, 2008).

37. Pittsburgh Press v. Pittsburgh Comm'n on Human Relations, 413 U.S. 376 (1973). *See also* United States v. Space Hunters, Inc., 429 F.3d 416 (2d Cir. 2005)

(acknowledging that the broad ban on harassment in the Fair Housing Act could raise First Amendment problems).

38. *Pittsburgh Press*, 413 U.S. at 391.

39. See *infra*, at notes 261–263 and accompanying text.

40. The Supreme Court has all but eliminated First Amendment protection for public employees speaking in an official capacity. Garcetti v. Ceballos, 547 U.S. 410 (2006). Nonofficial speech by public officials is judged by the standards of Connick v. Myers, 461 U.S. 138 (1983).

41. See Curay-Cramer v. Ursuline Acad., 344 F. Supp. 2d 923 (D. Del. 2004) (upholding right of Catholic school to fire teacher for publicly endorsing *Roe v. Wade*), *aff'd*, 450 F.3d 130 (3d Cir. 2006).

42. N.Y. EXEC. LAW § 296(11) (West Supp. 2008). *But see* Scheiber v. St. John's Univ., 638 N.E.2d 977 (N.Y. 1994) (noting that exemption is narrowly construed because it derogates the beneficent purposes of the civil rights laws). To qualify for the seemingly total exemption, a religious institution must show that the discrimination is related to its religious purposes.

43. See Doe v. Lutheran High Sch., 702 N.W.2d 322 (Minn. Ct. App. 2005).

44. See Ohio Civil Rights Comm'n v. Dayton Christian Sch., Inc., 477 U.S. 619 (1986).

45. See Hope Int'l Univ. v. Superior Court, 14 Cal. Rptr. 3d 643 (Cal. Ct. App. 2004).

46. NLRB v. Catholic Bishop, 440 U.S. 490 (1979).

47. *Cf.* Employment Div. v. Smith, 494 U.S. 872 (1990).

48. CARL ESBECK, STANLEY CARLSON-THIES, AND RONALD J. SIDER, THE FREEDOM OF FAITH BASED ORGANIZATIONS TO STAFF ON A RELIGIOUS BASIS (2004).

49. Dodge v. Salvation Army, 1989 WL 53857 (S.D. Miss. 1989).

50. Wilder v. Bernstein, 944 F.2d 1028 (2d Cir. 1991).

51. Religious Freedom Restoration Act, 42 U.S.C. §§ 2000bb *et seq.* (2000).

52. Lown v. Salvation Army, 393 F. Supp. 2d 223 (S.D.N.Y. 2005).

53. Catholic Charities v. Serio, 859 N.E.2d 459 (N.Y. 2006); Catholic Charities v. Superior Court, 85 P.3d 67 (Cal. 2004).

54. See Lutheran Soc. Serv. v. United States, 758 F.2d 1283 (8th Cir. 1985).

55. See Thomas J. Lueck, *State Court Rules Against Catholic Church on Insurance*, N.Y. TIMES B4 (Oct. 20, 2006).

56. Hall v. Baptist Mem'l Health Care Corp., 215 F.3d 618 (6th Cir. 2000).

57. See Marc D. Stern, *Covering Homosexuality in the Schools*, 8 RELIGION IN THE NEWS 14 (2005).

58. Harper v. Poway Unified Sch. Dist., 345 F. Supp. 2d 1096 (S.D. Cal. 2004), *aff'd*, 445 F.3d 1166 (9th Cir. 2006), *vacated as moot*, 127 S. Ct. 1484 (2006); Nixon v. N. Local Sch. Dist. Bd. of Educ., 383 F. Supp. 2d 965 (S.D. Ohio 2005). In *Poway*, a school official suggested that Harper leave his faith in his car.

59. More recently, another district court held that those protesting the day of silence could wear t-shirts with positive messages (*e.g.*, "be straight"), but not negative

ones ("homosexuality is a sin"). Zamecnik v. Indian Prairie Sch. Dist. No. 204 Bd. of Educ., 2007 WL 1141597 (N.D. Ill. 2007). The United States Court of Appeals for the Seventh Circuit has now reversed, granting an injunction, but leaving open the final result. 523 F.3d 668 (7th Cir. 2008).

60. Tinker v. Des Moines Indep. Cmty. Sch. Dist., 393 U.S. 503 (1969); Bethel Sch. Dist. No. 403 v. Fraser, 478 U.S. 675 (1986); Hazelwood Sch. Dist. v. Kuhlmeier, 484 U.S. 260 (1988).

61. The *Poway* appeals court reasoned that a ban on hate speech in the schools—embodied in California's education code—was a "neutral . . . state policy." The school claimed to allow only positive messages, not negative ones. Not only is this claim of neutrality incoherent, it is precluded by two Supreme Court decisions. Black v. Virginia, 538 U.S. 343 (2003); R.A.V. v. City of St. Paul, 505 U.S. 377 (1992).

62. Morse v. Frederick, 127 S. Ct. 2618 (2007).

63. *Id.* at 2627–28.

64. *Id.* at 2637 (Alito and Kennedy, JJ., concurring). Justice Thomas, in another concurrence, expressed the view that the Constitution offers no protection for student free speech.

65. For a comprehensive review, *see* Saxe v. State Coll. Area Sch. Dist., 240 F.3d 200 (3d Cir. 2001) (invalidating on overbreadth grounds a public school anti-hate-speech rule). Note, however, that Judge Alito, author of *Saxe*, elsewhere observed that religious speech advocating racial hatred could be barred from the public schools. C.H. ex rel. Z.H. v. Oliva, 226 F.3d 198, 212 (3d Cir. 2000). *See* D.B. ex rel Brodgon v. Lafon, 217 Fed. Appx. 519 (6th Cir. 2007).

66. 419 F. Supp. 2d 937 (E.D. Ky 2006), *aff'd on other grounds*, 521 F.3d 602 (6th Cir. 2008).

67. Mozert v. Hawkins County Bd. of Educ., 827 F.2d 1058 (6th Cir. 1987). More recently, *see* Fields v. Palmdale Sch. Dist., 427 F.3d 1197 (9th Cir. 2005). *Morrison* was appealed to the Sixth Circuit on the narrow question of whether a now abandoned part of the school's student conduct code impermissibly restricted speech critical of fellow students. The American Civil Liberties Union (which had represented gay students in the antecedent harassment case) joined with the Alliance Defense Fund in challenging the former speech code. The court refused to reach the issue. 521 F.3d 602 (6th Cir. 2008).

68. In *Mozert*, the Sixth Circuit rejected a right of excusal from "offensive" portions of the curriculum, but made it clear that students could not be punished for refusing to accept the school's views on any subject.

69. For a rare case making the point, see Holloman v. Harland, 370 F.3d 1252 (11th Cir. 2004).

70. Hansen v. Ann Arbor Sch., 293 F. Supp. 2d 780 (E.D. Mich. 2003).

71. *Compare Fields*, 427 F.3d 1197, *with* C.N. v. Ridgewood Bd. of Educ., 430 F.3d 159 (3d Cir. 2005). (These courts disagree on the exact scope of the bar to parents claiming that a school curriculum interfered with parental rights.)

72. Citizens for a Responsible Curriculum v. Montgomery County Pub. Sch., 2005 WL 1075634 (D. Md. 2005).

73. Equal Access Act, 20 U.S.C. §§ 4071 *et seq.* (2000).

74. *Id.*, 20 U.S.C. § 4071(b)(4).

75. *Id.*, 20 U.S.C. § 4071(d)(5).

76. *Id.*, 20 U.S.C § 4071(d)(7).

77. *Id.*, 20 U.S.C. § 4071(f).

78. Tinker v. Des Moines Indep. Cmty. Sch. Dist., 393 U.S. 503 (1969).

79. Hsu v. Roslyn Union Free Sch. Dist., 85 F.3d 839 (2d Cir. 1996). I discuss *Hsu* in more detail *infra*, at notes 166–170 and accompanying text.

80. Caudillo v. Lubbock Indep. Sch. Dist., 311 F. Supp. 2d 550 (N.D. Tex. 2004). The decision was not appealed.

81. Lawrence v. Texas, 539 U.S. 558 (2003).

82. Equal Access Act, 20 U.S.C. §4071(f) (2000).

83. Caudillo v. Lubbock Indep. Sch. Dist., 2003 WL 22670934, at *7 (N.D. Tex. 2003) (some citations omitted).

84. Okwedy v. Molinari, 333 F.3d 339 (2d Cir. 2003), *on appeal after remand*, 195 Fed. Appx. 7 (2d Cir. 2006).

85. *Okwedy*, 333 F.3d at 341–42.

86. The case was decided in two parts. The free speech issue was decided in *Okwedy, id.* The remaining issues, including a free exercise claim and a claim of an Establishment Clause preference for religious faiths, were decided in a separate unpublished order. Okwedy v. Molinari, 69 Fed. Appx. 482 (2d Cir. 2003). For comment on such cases, *see* Clyde Haberman, *All the Views Unfit to Print on a Billboard*, N.Y. TIMES B1 (Nov. 18, 2003); Naomi Schaeffer, *And There Shall Be a Sign*, WALL ST. J. W17 (May 19, 2000) (reporting on refusal of billboard companies to rent space for anti-abortion ad as too controversial). *See also* Am. Family Ass'n v. City of San Francisco, 277 F.3d 1114 (9th Cir 2002).

87. *Okwedy*, 333 F.3d at 344.

88. Okwedy v. Molinari, 69 Fed. Appx. 482, 484 (2d Cir. 2003) (citations omitted). The "*Lemon* test" refers to *Lemon v. Kurtzman*, 403 U.S. 602 (1971).

89. N.Y.C. Admin. Code, § 8–101 (2005).

90. City Defendant's Reply Memorandum of Law in Further Support of Motion for Summary Judgment, *Okwedy v. Molinari*, 00–Civ. 005426 (NG) at 5–6.

91. *Id.* at 5, citing *Loving v. Virginia*, 388 U.S. 1 (1967).

92. *Id.*

93. Moose Lodge v. Irvis, 407 U.S. 163 (1972).

94. *Id.* at 173.

95. *Id.* at 180 (Douglas, J., joined by Marshall, J., dissenting). Justice Brennan also dissented.

96. *See, e.g.*, Rendell-Baker v. Kohn, 457 U.S. 830 (1982); Blum v. Yaretsky, 457 U.S. 991 (1982).

97. In light of the long state sanction of two-gender marriage only, one cannot dismiss the possibility of an action being brought under a custom theory of state action. *See* Adickes v. S.H. Kress & Co., 398 U.S. 144 (1970). A statute that purported to allow private parties to continue a policy of limiting marriage to different gender couples might be vulnerable to such a challenge.

98. *Compare, e.g.,* Hyatt Corp. v. Honolulu Liquor Comm'n, 738 P.2d 1205 (Haw. 1987) (ban on race discrimination within Commission's power), *with* Davis v. Attic Club, 371 N.E.2d 903 (Ill. App. Ct. 1977) (ban on sex discrimination by private clubs *ultra vires*).

99. B.P.O.E. Lodge No. 2043 v. Ingraham, 297 A.2d 607, 616 (Me. 1972), *appeal dismissed*, 411 U.S. 924 (1973) (emphasis in original; citations omitted).

100. Benyon v. St. George Dixie Lodge No. 1743, 854 P.2d 513 (Utah 1993); Elks Lodge No. 719 v. Dep't of Alcoholic Beverage Control, 905 P.2d 1189 (Utah 1995).

101. *See, e.g., B.P.O.E. Lodge,* 297 A.2d at 611–13.

102. The results are generally consistent with a body of law developed in regard to private clubs by the Supreme Court. *See, e.g.,* N.Y. State Club Ass'n v. New York, 487 U.S. 1 (1988); *cf.* Human Rights Comm'n v. Benevolent & Protective Order of Elks, 839 A.2d 576 (Vt. 2003).

103. Boy Scouts v. Dale, 530 U.S. 640 (2000).

104. 17 ME. REV. STAT. ANN. § 1301-A (West 2006).

105. *B.P.O.E. Lodge,* 297 A.2d at 616–17.

106. *See, e.g.,* Corp. of the Presiding Bishop v. Amos, 483 U.S. 327 (1987).

107. *B.P.O.E. Lodge,* 297 A.2d at 616–17.

108. *See* Love In Action, Int'l v. Bredesen, 05-2724 (W.D. Tenn. 2005), for just such a challenge. The case ultimately settled with the state agreeing not to regulate counseling and Love in Action agreeing not to dispense medication. *See also Lown v. Salvation Army, Inc.,* 393 F. Supp. 2d 223 (S.D.N.Y. 2005).

109. CATHOLIC ANSWERS, SPECIAL REPORT: GAY MARRIAGE (2004), *available at* www.catholic.com/library/gay_marriage.asp (last visited June 14, 2008).

110. Maura Lerner, *St. Cloud State's Department Statement on Gays Causes Backlash,* MINNEAPOLIS STAR TRIBUNE 1A (June 1, 1993).

111. National Association of Social Workers, *Code of Ethics, available at* www.socialworkers.org/pubs/code/default.asp (last visited June 14, 2008).

112. W. Va. State Bd. of Educ. v. Barnette, 319 U.S. 624 (1943).

113. Kevin Duchschere, *Catholic Group Opposes Gay School Counselors,* MINNEAPOLIS STAR TRIBUNE 7B (Jan. 19, 1995).

114. *See* Larry Cohler-Esses, *Wanted—True Believers Only,* JEWISH WEEK 1 (Nov. 18, 2005), *available at* www.thejewishweek.com/viewArticle/c36_a8550/News/New_York.html (reporting that a social worker plaintiff claimed that the Salvation Army's rules on gays would create conflict between the Salvation Army's beliefs and her professional responsibilities). *See also* Brooker v. Bd. of Governors, 06-C10-3422 (W.D. Mo. 2006) (settling complaint that social work student was penalized for her religious views on homosexuality).

115. St. Agnes Hosp. v. Riddick, 748 F. Supp. 319 (D. Md. 1990). This specific result has been overturned by federal legislation. *See* Wilson, *supra* note 5, at notes 47–50, 81–88, and accompanying text].

116. Staver v. Am. Bar Ass'n, 169 F. Supp. 2d 1372 (M.D. Fla. 2001); Zavaletta v. Am. Bar Ass'n, 721 F. Supp. 96 (E.D. Va. 1989).

117. *Compare* NCAA v. Tarkanian, 488 U.S. 179 (1988).

118. American Bar Association, *2007-2008 ABA Standards for Approval of Law Schools*, Standard 211(c), *available at* www.abanet.org/legaled/standards/20072008 StandardsWebContent/Chapter%202.pdf (last visited June 18, 2008).

119. Wilson, *supra* note 5, at notes 211–215 and accompanying text.

120. *See, e.g.*, Elizabeth O'Brien, *Catholic Adoption Agency Will Close Before Giving Children to Homosexual Parents, Bishop States*, LIFESITENEWS.COM (July 30, 2007), *available at* www.lifesitenews.com/ldn/2007/jul/07073003.html (last visited June 14, 2008). *See also Catholic Charities Proposed Exemption from Anti-Discrimination Laws Cannot Pass Constitutional Muster* (statement of Jewish Alliance for Law & Social Action and Americans United for Separation of Church and State), *available at* http://releases.usnewswire.com/GetReleases.asp?id=62527 (last visited June 14, 2008). For a case raising similar issues in the context of an agency that placed adoptive children only with evangelical Christian parents, *see* Scott v. Family Ministries, 135 Cal. Rptr. 430 (Cal. Ct. App. 1976). A similar problem has arisen in Great Britain. *See* Robin Fretwell Wilson, *A Matter of Conviction: Moral Clashes Over Same-Sex Adoption*, 22 BYU J. L. & SOC. POL'Y 475 (2008).

121. Bellmore v. United Methodist Children's Home and Dep't of Human Resources (Fulton County Super. Ct.). For discussion, see *Bellmore v. United Methodist Children's Home and Dept. of Human Resources of Georgia*, LAMBDALEGAL (May 28, 2003), *available at* www.lambdalegal.org/our-work/publications/facts-backgrounds/bellmore-background.html (last visited June 14, 2008).

122. *Top 6 News Items – November 6, 2003*, MARRIAGEWATCH.ORG (Nov. 6, 2003), *available at* http://marriagelaw.cua.edu/News/news2003/110603.cfm (last visited June 14, 2008). (see item 4, *GA settlement: Faith-Based groups no tax $ if no GLBT*).

123. Executive Order 13279, published in 67 FED. REG. 77,141 (Dec. 16, 2002), *available at* www.whitehouse.gov/news/releases/2002/12/20021212-6.html (last visited June 14, 2008).

124. *See* Locke v. Davey, 540 U.S. 712 (2004); Rust v. Sullivan, 500 U.S. 173 (1991); Grove City Coll. v. Bell, 465 U.S. 555, 575–76 (1984).

125. Such cases have been litigated. *See* Hyman v. City of Louisville, 99 Civ. 597-S (W.D. Ky. 2001) (doctor's office; freedom of religion claim rejected); State by McClure v. Sports and Health Club, Inc., 370 N.W.2d 844 (Minn. 1985), *appeal dismissed*, 478 U.S. 1015 (1986) (freedom of religion claim rejected, recognizing compelling interest in banning discrimination). *Compare* Shahar v. Bowers, 70 F.3d 1218 (11th Cir. 1995), *same judgment entered en banc*, 114 F.3d 1097 (11th Cir. 1997) (upholding discharge of employee who entered into a purely religious same-sex marriage ceremony, accepting role mode argument because same-sex marriage violated the law, and plaintiff was an assistant state attorney general).

126. *See, e.g.*, Devlin v. City of Philadelphia, 862 A.2d 1234 (Pa. 2004).

127. The Unruh Civil Rights Act provides: "All persons within the jurisdiction of this state are free and equal, and no matter what their sex, race, color, religion, ancestry, national origin, disability, medical condition, marital status, or sexual orientation

are entitled to the full and equal accommodations, advantages, facilities, privileges, or services in all business establishments of every kind whatsoever." Cal. Civ. Code § 51(b) (West 2007).

128. *Id.; see also* Cal. Civ. Code § 51.5 (West 2007)

129. Mass. Civil Rights Act, Mass. Gen. Laws ch. 12, § 11H (2007).

130. *See* Willitts v. Roman Catholic Archbishops, 581 N.E.2d 475 (Mass. 1995); Redgrave v. Boston Symphony Orchestra, Inc., 502 N.E.2d 1375 (Mass. 1987) (both interpreting this statute).

131. Congress recently considered legislation that would have ended the ban on religious discrimination in hiring (but not in admissions) in Head Start programs operated by religious organizations. The proposal, known as the Boehner Amendment to H.R. 2123 in the 109th Congress, failed.

132. Fair Housing Act, 42 U.S.C. § 3607(a) (2000) (religious exemption).

133. *See, e.g.,* United States v. Space Hunters, 429 F.3d 416 (2d Cir. 2005); Scheiber v. St. Johns Univ., 638 N.E.2d 977 (N.Y. 1994).

134. Griggs v. Duke Power Co., 401 U.S. 424 (1971) (high school diploma requirement for simple blue collar jobs constituted illicit racial discrimination because it disproportionately excluded blacks without adequate showing of job relatedness).

135. Levin v. Yeshiva Univ., 754 N.E.2d 1099 (N.Y. 2001).

136. *Id. See also* Devlin v City of Philadelphia, 862 A.2d 1234 (Pa. 2004) (ban on sexual orientation discrimination will encompass discrimination against same-sex couples).

137. Harris v. Capital Growth Investors XIV, 805 P.2d 873 (Cal. 1991). There appears to be an exception for disability discrimination. Lentini v. Cal. Ctr. for the Arts, Escondido, 370 F.3d 837 (9th Cir. 2004).

138. Fair Housing Act, 42 U.S.C. § 3604(c) (2000) (discriminatory statements in connection with sale or lease of housing).

139. United States v. Space Hunters, Inc., 429 F.3d 416, 424 (2d Cir. 2005).

140. City of Boerne v. Flores, 521 U.S. 507 (1997).

141. Bob Jones Univ. v. United States, 461 U.S. 575 (1983).

142. Of course, if private schools are free to discriminate against gay couples because there is no state action, other non-state actors are free to insist on the equality of such couples, even where that insistence substantially hampers private religious observance of others in their establishments. This is the teaching of the case in which Orthodox Jewish students at Yale sought exemption from Yale's insistence that they live in co-ed dorms in the face of their religious opposition to that requirement. Hack v. President and Fellows, 237 F.3d 81 (2d Cir. 2000). Yale asserted its own academic autonomy in its defense. Those arguments presumably could be invoked by others seeking to operate dorms premised on a different moral vision.

143. While the courts have upheld private racial boycotts to advance an integrationist agenda, NAACP v. Claiborne Hardware Co., 458 U.S. 886 (1982), some courts have been less willing to tolerate boycotts advancing religious agendas, Jews

for Jesus v. Jewish Cmty. Relations Council, 968 F.2d 286 (2d Cir. 1992); *but see* Paul v. Watchtower Bible & Tract Soc'y, 819 F.2d 875 (9th Cir. 1987).

144. Religious Freedom Restoration Act, 42 U.S.C. §§ 2000bb *et seq.* (2000).

145. Equality Act, 2006, c. 3 (Eng.), *available at* www.opsi.gov.uk/acts/acts2006/pdf/ukpga_20060003_en.pdf (last visited June 14, 2008).

146. WOMEN AND EQUALITY UNIT, GETTING EQUAL: PROPOSALS TO OUTLAW SEXUAL ORIENTATION DISCRIMINATION IN THE PROVISION OF GOODS AND SERVICES (2006). A summary of this report is *available at* www.equalities.gov.uk/publications/sexo_con_summary.pdf (last visited June 14, 2008).

147. COMMUNITIES AND LOCAL GOVERNMENT, GETTING EQUAL: PROPOSALS TO OUTLAW SEXUAL DISCRIMINATION IN THE PROVISION OF GOODS AND SERVICES—GOVERNMENT RESPONSE TO CONSULTATION (March 2007), *available at* www.communities.gov.uk/archived/publications/corporate/gettingequaloutlaw (last visited June 13, 2008).

148. Jonathan Petre, *School Cannot Sack Head in 'Gay Marriage'*, TELEGRAPH (Aug 14, 2007), *available at* www.telegraph.co.uk/news/main.jhtml?xml=/news/2007/08/13/ngay113.xml (last visited June 14, 2008); Wilson, *supra* note 5, at note 215 and accompanying text.

149. Bob Jones Univ. v. United States, 461 U.S. 574 (1983).

150. Jonathan Turley, *An Unholy Union: Same-Sex Marriage and the Use of Governmental Programs to Penalize Religious Groups with Unpopular Practices*, *infra*, at notes 15–45 and accompanying text; Kmiec, *supra* note 5, at notes 18–77 and accompanying text; Wilson, *supra* note 5, at notes 89–129 and accompanying text.

151. 26 U.S.C. § 501(c)(3) (2000).

152. Associated Press, *Teens Suspected of Being Lesbians Sue Private School*, CONTRA COSTA TIMES F4 (Dec. 30, 2005). The suit is Mother Doe v. Cal. Lutheran High Sch. Ass'n, RIC 441819 (Cal. Super. Ct. 2007). An appeal is pending.

153. EEOC v. Southwestern Baptist Theological Seminary, 651 F.2d 277 (5th Cir. 1981).

154. N.Y. EXECUTIVE LAW § 296(11) (West Supp. 2008).

155. No such exemption was invoked in *Levin v. Yeshiva University*, 754 N.E.2d 1099 (N.Y. 2001), although it was obvious to all concerned that Yeshiva operated under Orthodox Jewish auspices.

156. Scheiber v. St. John's Univ., 638 N.E.2d 977 (N.Y. 1994) (Jewish vice president of student affairs). *St. John's* also holds that whether an institution is entitled to invoke § 296(11) depends on its functioning, not the formalities of its incorporation.

157. *St. John's*, 638 N.E.2d at 980.

158. *See Ontario Christian School—Lesbians Need Not Apply—Kids of Lesbians Need Not Apply*, in A PASSION FOR TEACHING SCHOOL AND OPINIONS (Sept. 23, 2005), *available at* http://ukiahcoachbrown.blogspot.com/2005/09/ontario-christian-school-lesbians-need.html (last visited June 14, 2008).

159. In Ontario, Canada, where Catholic schools are government schools, a preliminary injunction was issued requiring a Catholic school to permit a gay student to attend a prom with his male friend. Although the court relied in part on plaintiff's

representation that he would allow the case to be litigated to completion after the prom, several years later he voluntarily dismissed the complaint. *See* Hall v. Power, 59 O.R. (3d) 423 (Ont. Super. Ct. 2002).

160. Wilder v. Bernstein, 848 F.2d 1338 (2d Cir. 1988).

161. AJCongress's files.

162. Runyon v. McCrary, 427 U.S. 160, 167–68 (1976).

163. Norwood v. Harrison, 413 U.S. 455 (1973).

164. *Runyon*, 427 U.S. at 176 (quoting the opinion of the court of appeals).

165. Levin v. Yeshiva Univ., 754 N.E.2d 1099 (N.Y. 2001).

166. Hsu v. Rosyln Union Free Sch. Dist., 85 F.3d 839 (2d Cir. 1996). The Court discussed and distinguished *Hurley v. Irish-American Gay, Lesbian and Bisexual Group*, 515 U.S. 557 (1995). The Equal Access Act is codified at 20 U.S.C. §§ 4071 *et seq.* (2000).

167. *Hsu*, 85 F.3d at 857–58.

168. *Id.* at 870–71.

169. *Id.* (citations omitted; emphasis added); *cf.* Truth v. Kent Sch. Dist., 499 F.3d 999 (9th Cir. 2007) (upholding rule requiring that clubs protected by Equal Access Act not discriminate in membership on the basis of religion).

170. Hurley v. Irish-Am. Gay, Lesbian and Bisexual Group, 515 U.S. 557 (1995).

171. Christian Legal Soc'y v. Walker, 453 F.3d 853 (7th Cir. 2006).

172. Sara Lipka, *Arizona State U. Allows Christian Group to Bar Gay Members*, THE CHRONICLE OF HIGHER EDUC. (Sept. 16, 2005).

173. *E.g.*, ENCM-SDDS v. Achtenberg (S.D. Cal. 2005).

174. CAL. EDUC. CODE § 66292.1 (West Supp. 2008); *id.* at 66030 (West Supp. 2008).

175. Gay Rights Coalition v. Georgetown Univ., 536 A.2d 1 (D.C. 1987).

176. Employment Div. v. Smith, 494 U.S. 872 (1990).

177. The trial court had observed that Georgetown was free to note that it offered facilities to the gay club only under the force of D.C. law. The Court of Appeals left open the question of whether the club could insist on using the Georgetown name. The Court invoked *PruneYard Shopping Center v. Robins*, 447 U.S. 74 (1980), for the proposition that merely serving as a platform for speech with which one disagrees is not unconstitutional compelled speech. *PruneYard* has since been read to mean only that there is no First Amendment violation when the property owner can effectively disclaim responsibility for the speech. *Cf.* Rumsfeld v. FAIR, 547 U.S. 47, 64–65 (2006); Hurley v. Irish-Am. Gay, Lesbian and Bisexual Group, 515 U.S. 557, 576–77 (1995). For a recent discussion of this issue in an English context, *see United We Stand? A Report on Current Conflicts Between Christian Unions and Students' Union* (*Ekklesia*, no date, but either 2006 or 2007), *available at* www.ekklesia.co.uk/content/united_we_stand_report.pdf. (last visited June 18, 2008).

178. *Georgetown*, 536 A.2d at 50 (Ferrer, J., concurring and dissenting) (citations omitted).

179. Romeo v. Seton Hall Univ., 875 A.2d 1043 (N.J. Super. Ct. App. Div. 2005).

180. *Id.* at 1046.

181. *See also* Little v. Wuerl, 929 F.2d 944 (3d Cir. 1991) (same). *Romeo* collects other cases to the same effect.

182. *See* Drews v. State, 167 A.2d 341 (Md. 1961), *vacated on other grounds,* 378 U.S. 547 (1964); Garifine v. Monmouth Park Jockey Club, 148 A.2d 1 (N.J. 1959).

183. Civil Rights Act of 1964, 42 U.S.C. § 2000a(b) (2000) (public accommodations).

184. *Compare* Curran v. Mt. Diablo Council of the Boy Scouts, 952 P.2d 218 (Cal. 1998) (Boy Scouts not a business establishment under Unruh Civil Rights Act), *with* Matter of U.S. Power Squadrons v. State Human Rights Appeal Bd., 452 N.E.2d 1199 (N.Y. 1983) (yachting club a place of public accommodation).

185. *See, e.g.,* Welsh v. Boy Scouts, 993 F.2d 1267 (7th Cir. 1993); Seabourn v. Coronado Area Council, 891 P.2d 385 (Kan. 1995).

186. Boy Scouts v. Dale, 530 U.S. 640 (2000).

187. *Cf.* Runyon v. McCrary, 427 U.S. 160 (1976) (42 U.S.C. § 1981).

188. *See, e.g.,* Adams ex rel Harris v. Boy Scouts—Chickasaw Council, 271 F.3d 769 (8th Cir. 2001).

189. Stout v. YMCA, 404 F.2d 687 (5th Cir. 1968); Nesmith v. YMCA, 397 F.2d 96 (4th Cir. 1968); United States by Mitchell v. YMCA, 310 F. Supp. 79 (D.S.C. 1970).

190. United States v. Slidell Youth Football Ass'n, 387 F. Supp. 474 (E.D. La. 1974).

191. 775 Ill. Comp. Stat. Ann. 5/5-101(A)(6) (West Supp. 2008); Kan. Stat. Ann. § 44-1002(h) (2000).

192. *See* LaCava v. Lucander, 791 N.E.2d 358 (Mass. App. Ct. 2003); Pa. Human Relations Comm'n v. Alto-Reste Park Cemetery Ass'n, 306 A.2d 881 (Pa. 1973) (non-sectarian cemetery). *Cf.* Price v. Evergreen Cemetery Co., 357 P.2d 702 (Wash. 1960) (statute failed to indicate that it applied to private cemeteries).

193. *Compare* Matter of Cahill v. Rosa, 674 N.E.2d 274 (N.Y. 1996) (dental offices places of public accommodation, noting that it was inconceivable that dentists would defend a racial exclusion), with Duffy v. Ill. Dep't of Human Rights, 820 N.E.2d 1186 (Ill. App. Ct. 2004); Baksh v. Human Rights Comm'n, 711 N.E.2d 416 (Ill. App. Ct. 1999) (dental practices not places of public accommodation under Illinois statute).

194. Americans with Disabilities Act, 42 U.S.C. § 12187 (2000).

195. Roman Catholic Archdiocese v. Commonwealth, 548 A.2d 328 (Pa. Commw. Ct. 1988).

196. Gay Rights Coalition v. Georgetown Univ., 536 A.2d 1 (D.C. 1987).

197. *See* Ocean Grove Camp Meeting Ass'n v. Vespa-Papaleo, 2007 WL 3349787 (D.N.J. 2007).

198. *Cf.* State by McClure v. Sports & Health Club, Inc., 370 N.W.2d 844 (Minn. 1985) (employment).

199. That law bars discrimination against same-sex couples. Koebke v. Bernardo Heights Country Club, 115 P.3d 1212 (Cal. 2005).

200. Hart v. Cult Awareness Network, 16 Cal. Rptr. 2d 705 (Cal. Ct. App. 1993). *See* Clegg v. Cult Awareness Network, 18 F.3d 752 (9th Cir. 1994) (club without physical meeting place not covered under federal public accommodation law).

201. Many exemption statutes in various areas of the law assume that organizations providing religious services are formally part of a church. This may be true of the Catholic Church and some Protestant groups; it is rarely true for Jews.

202. *See* Paquette v. Regal Art Press, Inc., 656 A.2d 209 (Vt. 1994) (place of public accommodation refusing to print leaflets for Catholic pro-choice group; appeals court requires further fact finding: did printer refuse to print *all* pro-choice leaflets or *Catholic* pro-choice leaflets?). For a Canadian decision on point, *see* Brockie v. Ontario (Human Rights Comm'n), 165 O.A.C. 324 (Ont. Super. Ct. (Div. Ct.) 2002).

203. Cleveland v. Nation of Islam, 922 F. Supp. 56 (N.D. Ohio 1995).

204. Donaldson v. Farrakhan, 762 N.E.2d 835 (Mass. 2002). *See also* Smith v. Knights of Columbus, 2005 BCHRT 544 (Brit. Colum. Human Rights Tribunal).

205. *Donaldson*, 762 N.E.2d at 841 (citations omitted.)

206. Hurley v. Irish-Am. Gay, Lesbian and Bisexual Group, 515 U.S. 557 (1995).

207. *Id.* at 561.

208. *Id.* at 572–73.

209. *Id.* at 572.

210. *See, e.g.,* N.Y. State Club Ass'n v. City of New York, 487 U.S. 1 (1988); Roberts v. U.S. Jaycees, 468 U.S. 609 (1984).

211. Boy Scouts v. Dale, 530 U.S. 640 (2000).

212. Dale v. Boy Scouts, 734 A.2d 1196 (N.J. 1999), *rev'd*, 530 U.S. 640 (2000).

213. *Id.* at 1227.

214. *Id.* at 1226.

215. Boy Scouts v. Wyman, 335 F.3d 80 (2d Cir. 2003).

216. Barnes-Wallace v. Boy Scouts, 275 F. Supp. 2d 1259 (S.D. Cal. 2003) (nonexclusive lease of campground and aquatic center), *state-law questions certified to state court*, 530 F.3d 776 (9th Cir. 2008); Evans v. City of Berkeley, 129 P.3d 394 (Cal. 2006) (free use of berth in city marina). *Evans* can be read to hold that groups like the Scouts could be denied real property tax exemptions. The court of appeals' theory of standing in *Barnes-Wallace* is particularly worthy of note—that although plaintiffs are free to use the property, they are unwilling to do so because they would have to go through the Boy Scouts to make reservations.

217. In Re Guardianship of Kowalski, 478 N.W.2d 790 (Minn. Ct. App. 1991) (allowing lesbian partner to serve as guardian). *Cf.* Langan v. St. Vincent Hosp., 802 N.Y.S.2d 476 (N.Y. App. Div. 2005), *appeal dismissed*, 850 N.E.2d 672 (N.Y. 2006) (wrongful death action); Armijo v. Miles, 26 Cal. Rptr. 3d 623 (Cal. Ct. App. 2005) (same).

218. *Cf.* Stewart v. Schwartz Bros.-Jeffer Mem'l Chapel, Inc., 159 Misc. 2d 884 (N.Y. Sup. Ct. 1993) (leaving issue open) (funeral arrangements).

219. Gilmore v. City of Montgomery, 417 U.S. 556 (1974).

220. *Id.* at 574 (citations omitted; emphasis in original).

221. *Id.* at 575 (citations omitted).

222. For additional cases, *compare* Binet-Montessori, Inc. v. San Francisco Unified Sch. Dist., 160 Cal. Rptr. 38 (Cal. Ct. App. 1974), with Wilmington Christian Sch., Inc. v. Bd. of Educ., 545 F. Supp. 440 (D. Del. 1982) (right to buy or lease property and engage in religious discrimination) (conflicting results); 81 Cal. Atty. Gen. Ops. 189 (1998); Sherman v. Cmty. Consol. Sch. Dist. 21, 1993 WL 57522 (N.D. Ill. 1993) (access to public schools); Winkler v. Chicago Sch. Reform Bd. of Trustees, 382 F. Supp. 2d 1040 (N.D. Ill. 2005), *rev'd for want of standing sub nom.* Winkler v. Gates, 481 F.3d 977 (7th Cir. 2007) (assistance of army in hosting Boy Scouts Jamboree).

223. N. Coast Women's Care Med. Group v. Superior Court (Benitez, Real Party in Interest), 40 Cal. Rptr. 3d 636 (Cal. Ct. App.), *review granted,* 139 P.3d 1 (Cal. 2006)

224. The Unruh Civil Rights Act protects registered domestic partners from discrimination. Koebke v. Bernardo Heights Country Club, 115 P.3d 1212 (Cal. 2005).

225. Smith v. Fair Employment & Hous. Comm'n, 913 P.2d 909 (Cal. 1996).

226. Opinion of the Council on Ethical and Judicial Affairs, *CEJA Opinion 2-A-08, on Subject: E-10.05, Potential Patients, Amendment* (2008), *available at* www.ama-assn.org/ama1/pub/upload/mm/471/cejo2.doc (last visited June 18, 2008). *See also* American Psychological Association, *Ethical Principles of Psychologists and Code of Conduct* (2002), *available at* www.apa.org/ethics/code2002.html (last visited June 18, 2008). Principle E, one of a set of General Principles described as "aspirational in nature," says that psychologists "try to eliminate the effect on their work of biases . . . and they do not knowingly participate in or condone activities of others based upon such prejudices." Taken seriously, this principle would bar Orthodox Jewish, evangelical, and Catholic psychologists.

227. Wilson, *supra* note 5, at notes 44–88, 130–146, and accompanying text.

228. Shelton v. Univ. of Med. & Dentistry, 223 F.3d 220 (3d Cir. 2000). *Cf.* Endres v. Ind. State Police, 349 F.3d 922 (7th Cir. 2003) (police officer has no right to accommodation of belief against being assigned to protecting objectionable conduct, there gambling).

229. *See* Wilson, *supra* note 5, at notes 22–24, 130, 197, and accompanying text.

Robin Fretwell Wilson, *Essay: The Limits of Conscience: Moral Clashes over Deeply Divisive Healthcare Procedures,* 34 AM. J. OF LAW & MED. 31 (2008).

231. In the abortion referral context, *see* Mother & Unborn Baby Care, Inc. v. State, 749 S.W.2d 533 (Tex. App.—Forth Worth 1988) (finding that antiabortion counselors had no free speech or freedom of religion right to misrepresent their attitude toward abortion in advertisements designed to attract pregnant women for antiabortion counseling).

232. Wilson, *supra* note 5, at notes 22–23, 130.

233. For a complete list, see Congressional Research Service (Jody Feder), *Federal & State Laws Regarding Pharmacists Who Refuse to Dispense Contraceptives* (Oct. 7, 2005) (Order Code RS22293), *available at* http://assets.opencrs.com/rpts/RS22293-20051007.pdf (last visited June 18, 2008)

234. N.J. Stat. Ann. 45:14–66 (Supp 2008).

235. Rob Stein, *Pharmacists' Rights at Front of New Debate*, Wash. Post A1 (March 28, 2005) (reporting that the American Pharmacists Association was prepared to support a right of conscience if there was a compulsory duty of referral).

236. *Doyle Vetoes 'Conscience Protection Act,'* Peace Corps Online, (Oct. 17, 2005), *available at* http://peacecorpsonline.org/messages/messages/467/2036827.html (last visited June 14, 2008).

237. *Cf.* United States v. Ballard, 322 U.S. 78 (1944).

238. *See* Love in Action Int'l v. Bredesen, 05-2724 (W.D. Tenn.). The settlement is described *supra*, note 108.

239. Bruff v. N. Miss. Health Servs., Inc., 244 F.3d 495 (5th Cir 2001).

240. Lotosky v. Univ. of Rochester, 192 F. Supp. 2d 127 (W.D.N.Y. 2002); Hellinger v. Eckerd Corp., 67 F. Supp. 2d 1359 (S.D. Fla. 1999).

241. Fair Housing Act, 42 U.S.C. § 3602(b) (2000) (definition of covered housing).

242. Woods v. Foster, 884 F. Supp. 1169 (N.D. Ill. 1995) (sexual harassment).

243. Hovson's, Inc. v. Township of Brick, 89 F.3d 1096 (3d Cir. 1996).

244. *See, e.g.*, Essling's Homes Plus, Inc. v. City of St. Paul, 356 F. Supp. 2d 971 (D. Minn. 2004).

245. City of Edmonds v. Oxford House, Inc., 514 U.S. 725 (1995); Oxford House-C v. City of St. Louis, 77 F.3d 249 (8th Cir. 1996).

246. United States v. Hughes Mem'l Home, 396 F. Supp. 544 (W.D. Va. 1975).

247. Baxter v. City of Belleville, 720 F. Supp. 720 (S.D. Ill. 1989) (hospice for AIDS patients).

248. Fair Housing Act, 42 U.S.C. § 3604(a) (2000) (ban on religious discrimination).

249. Civil Rights Act of 1964, 42 U.S.C. § 2000e-2(a)(1) (2000) (discrimination in "terms, conditions, or privileges" of employment).

250. Dothard v. Rawlinson, 433 U.S. 321 (1977).

251. Civil Rights Act of 1964, 42 U.S.C. § 2000e-2(k)(1)(A)(i) (2000) (business necessity defense to disparate-impact employment discrimination).

252. Corp. of the Presiding Bishop v. Amos, 483 U.S. 327 (1987).

253. Chambers v. Omaha Girls Club, 834 F.2d 697 (8th Cir. 1987).

254. *Compare* Cline v. Catholic Diocese, 206 F.3d 651 (6th Cir. 2000); Ganzy v. Allen Christian Sch., 995 F. Supp. 340 (E.D.N.Y. 1998); *with* Boyd v. Harding Acad., Inc., 88 F.3d 410 (6th Cir. 1996). For a recent analogous Scottish case, see Percy v. Bd. of Nat'l Mission, [2005] H.L. 73 (House of Lords).

255. New York City and San Francisco require contractors to pay medical benefits for same-sex partners. They allow religious contractors to allow employees to select any household member for coverage, thus minimizing the problem (through use of a fig leaf) of explicit endorsement of same-sex relationships. *See* S.D. Myers, Inc. v. City of San Francisco, 336 F.3d 1174 (9th Cir. 2003).

256. Pittsburgh Press Co. v. Pittsburgh Comm'n on Human Relations, 413 U.S. 376 (1973).

257. United States v. Space Hunters, Inc., 429 F.3d 416 (2d Cir. 2005).

258. EEOC v. Townley Eng'g & Mfg. Co., 859 F.2d 610 (9th Cir. 1988).

259. One that AJCongress urged in an *amicus* brief in that case.

260. These issues have arisen in connection with efforts to strengthen Title VII's accommodation requirements. *See House Hearing Reveals Broad Support, But Some Opposition for Religious Bias Bill*, 74 U.S.L.W. 2300 (Nov. 22, 2005).

261. Civil Rights Act of 1964, 42 U.S.C. § 2000e(j) (2000) (religious accommodation in employment).

262. Trans World Airlines, Inc. v. Hardison, 432 U.S. 63 (1977).

263. Peterson v. Hewlett Packard Co., 358 F.3d 599 (9th Cir. 2004). *But see* Erdmann v. Tranquility, Inc., 155 F. Supp. 2d 1152 (N.D. Cal. 2001) (not all speech related to same-sex marriage constitutes harassment).

264. Tucker v. Cal. Dep't of Educ., 97 F.3d 1204 (9th Cir. 1996); Altman v. Minn. Dep't of Corrections, 251 F.3d 1199 (8th Cir. 2001). *But see* Good News Employee Ass'n v. Hicks, 223 Fed. Appx. 734 (9th Cir. 2007).

265. Moranski v. Gen. Motors Corp., 2005 WL 552419 (S.D. Ind. 2005), *aff'd*, 433 F.3d 537 (7th Cir. 2005).

266. Buonanno v. AT&T Broadband, LLC, 313 F. Supp. 2d 1069 (D. Colo. 2004).

267. *Altman*, 251 F.3d at 1203.

268. Virts v. Consol. Freightways Corp., 285 F.3d 508 (6th Cir. 2002); Weber v. Roadway Express, Inc., 199 F.2d 270 (5th Cir. 2000).

269. Trans World Airlines, Inc. v. Hardison, 432 U.S. 63 (1977).

270. Brady v. Dean, 790 A.2d 428 (Vt. 2001).

271. *See* Endres v. Ind. State Police, 349 F.3d 922, 928–30 & n.1 (7th Cir. 2003) (Ripple, J., dissenting from denial of rehearing en banc and collecting cases).

272. Garcetti v. Ceballos, 547 U.S. 410 (2006).

273. Fairchild v. Riva Jewelry Mfg., 2007 N.Y. Misc. Lexis 4912 (N.Y. Sup. Ct. 2007).

274. Smith v. Fair Employment & Hous. Comm'n, 913 P.2d 909 (Cal. 1996).

275. Civil Rights Act of 1964, 42 U.S.C. § 2000e-2(e)(2) (2000); 42 U.S.C. § 2000e-1(a) (2000) (religious exemptions from ban on employment discrimination). The Court upheld the exemption's constitutionality in *Corporation of the Presiding Bishop v. Amos*, 483 U.S. 327 (1987).

276. Fair Housing Act, 42 U.S.C. § 3607(a) (2000) (religious exemption).

277. *Id.* For a detailed description of how much religious control is sufficient to invoke the exemption, see United States v. Columbus Country Club, 915 F.2d 877 (3d Cir. 1990) (small country club renting summer homes, requiring letter of approbation for potential tenants from parish priest, and offering weekly mass, not religious).

278. Federal Unemployment Tax Act, 26 U.S.C. §§ 3301 *et seq.* (2000).

279. *See* St. Martin Evangelical Lutheran Church v. South Dakota, 451 U.S. 772 (1981). The unemployment tax exemption has since been amended to eliminate the distinctions among religious schools revealed in *St. Martin. See* 26 U.S.C. § 3309(b)(1)(C) (2000).

280. United States v. Lorantffy Care Ctr., 999 F. Supp. 1037 (N.D. Ohio 1998); United States v. Hughes Mem'l Home, 396 F. Supp. 544 (W.D. Va. 1975).

281. Thomas v. Anchorage Equal Rights Comm'n, 102 P.2d 937 (Alaska 2004); Swanner v. Anchorage Equal Rights Comm'n, 874 P.2d 274 (Alaska 1994).

282. Smith v. Fair Employment & Hous. Comm'n, 913 P.2d 909 (Cal. 1996).

283. Atty. Gen. v. Desilets, 636 N.E.2d 233 (Mass. 1994). For a comprehensive collection of the cases, see N.D. Fair Hous. Council, Inc. v. Peterson, 625 N.W.2d 551 (N.D. 2001).

284. The federal version is found at 42 U.S.C. § 3603(b)(2) (2000) (Mrs. Murphy exception to the Fair Housing Act). Note, however, that the exemption is no defense to an action for race discrimination under 42 U.S.C. § 1982 (2000) (derived from the Civil Rights Act of 1866).

285. *See, e.g.,* United States v. Space Hunters, Inc., 429 F.3d 416 (2d Cir. 2005).

286. Boy Scouts v. Dale, 530 U.S. 640 (2000).

287. Ocean Grove Camp Meeting v. Vespa-Papaleo, 2007 WL 3349787 (D.N.J. 2007). On one possible reading of the facts, the civil rights commission is being asked to order that a church be opened to same-sex marriages.

288. Civil Rights Act of 1964, 42 U.S.C. § 2000e-2(e)(2) (2000) (employment-discrimination exemption for religious educational institutions).

289. Pime v. Loyola Univ., 585 F. Supp. 435, 439–41 (N.D. Ill. 1984), *aff'd on other grounds,* 803 F.3d 351 (7th Cir. 1986). *See id.* at 357 (Posner, J., concurring).

290. Killenger v. Samford Univ., 113 F.3d 196 (11th Cir. 1997).

291. Hall v. Baptist Mem'l Health Care Corp., 215 F.3d 618, 625 (6th Cir. 2000). For a discussion of an analogous California exemption, which includes a defense against all claims, see *Kelly v. Methodist Hospital,* 997 P.2d 1169 (Cal. 2000).

292. *Hall,* 215 F.3d 618, 624 (citing Little v. Wuerl, 929 F.2d 944 (3d Cir. 1991) (divorced teacher married to lapsed Catholic fired; school exempt).

293.Civil Rights Act of 1964, 42 U.S.C. § 2000e-2(e)(2) (2000) (employment-discrimination exemption for religious educational institutions).

294. *Id.,* 42 U.S.C. § 2000e-1(a) (2000) (employment-discrimination exemption for religious organizations).

295. Corp. of the Presiding Bishop v. Amos, 483 U.S. 327 (1987).

296. Feldstein v. Christian Sci. Monitor, 555 F. Supp. 974 (D. Mass.1983).

297. EEOC v. Kamehameha Sch./Bishop Estate, 990 F.2d 458 (9th Cir. 1993). *Cf.* Kemmerer Vill., Inc. v. NLRB, 907 F.2d 661 (7th Cir. 1990) (children's institution founded by church, but in which church exercised no practical influence, not exempt from NLRA).

298. EEOC v. Fremont Christian Sch., 781 F.2d 1362 (9th Cir. 1986). *See also* Cline v. Catholic Diocese, 206 F.3d 651 (6th Cir. 2000); EEOC v. Pac. Press Publ'g Ass'n, 676 F.2d 1272 (9th Cir. 1982).

299. McClure v. Salvation Army, 460 F.2d 553 (5th Cir. 1972)

300. EEOC v. Roman Catholic Diocese, 213 F.3d 795 (4th Cir. 2000); *but cf.* Archdiocese v. Moersen, 925 A.2d 659 (Md. 2007) (organist not within the exception).

301. EEOC v. Catholic Univ., 83 F.3d 455 (D.C. Cir. 1996).

302. Scharon v. St. Luke's Episcopal Presbyterian Hosps., 929 F.2d 360 (8th Cir. 1991).

303. Weissman v. Congregation Shaare Emeth, 38 F.3d 1038 (8th Cir. 1994).

304. Employment Div. v. Smith, 494 U.S. 872 (1990).

305. EEOC v. Townley Eng'g & Mfg. Co., 859 F.2d 610 (9th Cir. 1988).

306. Religious Freedom Restoration Act, 42 U.S.C. §§ 2000bb *et seq.* (2000).

307. *Smith*, 494 U.S. 872.

308. Fraternal Order of Police v. City of Newark, 170 F.3d 359 (3d Cir. 1999) (Alito, J.).

309. *See, e.g.*, Axson-Flynn v. Johnson, 356 F.3d 1277. 1298 (10th Cir. 2004).

310. Atty. Gen. v. Desilets, 636 N.E.2d 233 (Mass. 1994).

311. Wilson, *supra* note 5, at notes 39–42, 172–176, and accompanying text; Feldblum, supra note 5, at notes 136–137 and accompanying text.

Chapter Two: Jonathan Turley

1. The author wishes to thank both the Becket Fund and the George Washington Law School for their support in the research and writing of this chapter.

2. *See* Jonathan Turley, *How to End the Same-Sex Marriage Debate*, USA TODAY 15A (April 3, 2006).

3. Lawrence v. Texas, 539 U.S. 558 (2003).

4. In re Marriage Cases, 183 P.3d 384 (2008).

5. Bruce Albert, *Troubled Senators Will Co-Sponsor Marriage Act*, TIMES PICAYUNE 2 (June 28, 2008) (noting the irony of Senators Larry Craig and David Vitter co-sponsoring the "Marriage Protection Act" despite their involvement in sex-related scandals). In California alone, almost a dozen state ballot initiatives have been put forward to reverse the decision. *See* John Wildermut, *11 State Ballot Measures Numbered, Ready to Go*, SAN FRANCISCO CHRONICLE B2 (June 28, 2008).

6. Bob Jones Univ. v. United States, 461 U.S. 574 (1983).

7. Boy Scouts v. Dale, 530 U.S. 640 (2000).

8. *Id.* at 647–48.

9. Roberts v. U.S. Jaycees, 468 U.S. 609 (1984).

10. Likewise, in *Hurley v. Irish-American Gay, Lesbian and Bisexual Group*, 515 U.S. 557 (1995), the Court upheld the right of the South Boston Allied War Veterans Council to exclude the Irish-American Gay, Lesbian, and Bisexual Group of Boston from its St. Patrick's Day parade.

11. Reynolds v. United States, 98 U.S. 145 (1878).

12. *See, e.g.*, Turley, *supra* note 2; Jonathan Turley, *Polygamy Laws Expose Our Own Hypocrisy*, USA TODAY 13A (Oct. 4, 2004); Jonathan Turley, *Of Lust and the Law*, WASH. POST (Sunday), Outlook B1 (Sept. 5, 2004).

13. Turley, *supra* note 2. Notably, the California Attorney General fought most aggressively in the recent decision to establish that even if same-sex couples were entitled to the legal benefits of marriage, they should not be allowed to use the noun "marriage":

> In defending the constitutionality of the current statutory scheme, the Attorney General of California maintains that even if the constitutional right to marry under the California Constitution applies to same-sex couples as well as to opposite-sex couples, this right should not be understood as requiring the Legislature to designate a couple's official family relationship by the term "marriage," as opposed to some other nomenclature.

In re Marriage Cases 183 P.3d 384, 43 Cal. 4th 757, 782 (2008).

14. Notably, after being denied tax-exempt status, Bob Jones University eventually abandoned its long-held policy.

15. Boy Scouts v. Dale, 530 U.S. 640, 647 (2000), quoting from Roberts v. U.S. Jaycees, 468 U.S. 609, 622 (1984).

16. Green v. Kennedy, 309 F. Supp. 1127 (D.D.C.), *appeal dismissed sub nom.* Cannon v. Green, 398 U.S. 956 (1970).

17. 26 U.S.C. § 501(c)(3) (2000).

18. Plessy v. Ferguson, 163 U.S. 537 (1896).

19. Brown v. Bd. of Educ., 347 U.S. 483 (1954).

20. This transition was noted by the Court in *Bob Jones University v. United States*, 461 U.S. 574, 592–93 (1983) ("Prior to 1954, public education in many places still was conducted under the pall of *Plessy v. Ferguson* . . . . This Court's decision in *Brown v. Board of Education* signalled an end to that era.") (citations omitted).

21. Green v. Kennedy, 309 F. Supp. 1127 (D.D.C.), *appeal dismissed sub nom.* Cannon v. Green, 398 U.S. 956 (1970).

22. Rev. Rul. 71-447, 1971-2 C.B. 230.

23. Bob Jones Univ. v. United States, 461 U.S. 574 (1983).

24. *Id.* at 594–96.

25. *Id.* at 586; *but see* Robert M. Cover, *The Supreme Court, 1982 Term: Forward: Nomos and Narrative*, 97 HARV. L. REV. 4, 63–64 (1983) ("Neither the text of the Code nor the legislative history before the IRS' 1970 ruling seemed to compel [the Court's] interpretation.").

26. *See generally* David A. Brennen, *Charities and the Constitution: Evaluating the Role of Constitutional Principles in Determining the Scope of Tax Law's Public Policy Limitation for Charities*, 5 FLA. TAX REV. 779, 796–802 (2002).

27. Evans v. City of Berkeley, 129 P.3d 394, 401 (Cal. 2006), quoting Rust v. Sullivan, 500 U.S. 173, 198 (1991).

28. *Id.* at 401.

29. Rumsfeld v. Forum for Academic & Institutional Rights, Inc., 547 U.S. 47 (2006). *See generally* Jonathan Turley, *An Issue of Hypocrisy*, NAT'L L.J. 34 (Jan. 9, 2006).

30. Walz v. Tax Comm'n, 397 U.S. 664, 674–75 (1970).

31. Trinidad v. Sagrada Orden de Predicadores, 263 U.S. 578 (1924).

32. Comm. for Pub. Educ. & Religious Liberty v. Nyquist, 413 U.S. 756, 794 (1973).

33. In *Texas Monthly, Inc. v. Bullock*, 489 U.S. 1 (1989), Justice Brennan again placed great emphasis on such blanket treatment of organizations as a whole without reference to their individual beliefs. Indeed, the secular purpose noted in reference to the *Walz* decision was a pluralistic society:

> W]e emphasized in *Walz* that in granting a property tax deduction, the State "has not singled out one particular church or religious group or even churches as such; rather, it has granted exemption to all houses of religious worship within a broad class of property owned by nonprofit, quasi-public corporations which include hospitals, libraries, playgrounds, scientific, professional, historical, and patriotic groups." The breadth of New York's property tax exemption was essential to our holding that it was "not aimed at establishing, sponsoring, or supporting religion," but rather possessed the legitimate secular purpose and effect of contributing to the community's moral and intellectual diversity and encouraging private groups to undertake projects that advanced the community's well-being and that would otherwise have to be funded by tax revenues or left undone.

Id. at 12, quoting Walz v. Tax Comm'n, 397 U.S. 664, 673–74 (1970) (citations omitted).

34. Bob Jones Univ. v. United States, 461 U.S. 574, 591–92 (1983).

35. *Id.* at 598; *see also id.* at 592 ("a declaration that a given institution is not 'charitable' should be made only where there can be no doubt that the activity is contrary to a fundamental public policy.").

36. *Id.* at 596–97 ("In the first instance . . . the responsibility for construing the Code falls to the IRS.").

37. Mueller v. Allen, 463 U.S. 388, 396 (1983), quoting Comm. for Pub. Educ. & Religious Liberty v. Regan, 444 U.S. 646, 662 (1980).

38. Christian Legal Soc'y v. Kane, 2006 WL 997217 (N.D. Cal. 2006), *appeal pending sub nom.* Christian Legal Soc'y v. Newton.

39. United States v. O'Brien, 391 U.S. 367 (1968).

40. Boy Scouts v. Dale, 530 U.S. 640 (2000).

41. In re Marriage Cases, 183 P.3d 384, 43 Cal. 4th 757, 840 (2008) ("Just as a statute that restricted marriage only to couples of the same sex would discriminate against heterosexual persons on the basis of their heterosexual orientation, the current California statutes realistically must be viewed as discriminating against gay persons on the basis of their homosexual orientation.").

42. Walz v. Tax Comm'n, 397 U.S. 664, 675 (1970).

43. Levin v. Yeshiva Univ., 754 N.E.2d 1099 (N.Y. 2001), discussed on Neal Conan, *Gay Rights Law Faces Legal, Religious Challenges*, Talk of the Nation, Nat'l

Pub. Radio (June 16, 2008), *available at* www.npr.org/templates/story/story.php?story Id=91554986.

44. Mother Doe v. Cal. Lutheran High Sch. Ass'n, RIC 441819 (Cal. Super. Ct. 2007), discussed on Conan, *supra* note 43.

45. N.Y. Times Co. v. Sullivan, 376 U.S. 254 (1964).

46. Boy Scouts v. Wyman, 335 F.3d 80 (2d Cir. 2003)

47. The Boy Scouts of Philadelphia faced eviction as a discriminatory organization under a local 1982 "fair practices" law. They were informed that either they must drop their discrimination against homosexuals or move out of the grand Beaux-Arts building they had rented from the city for $1 a year since 1928. The change pushed the rent from $1 a year to $200,000. Hans Zeiger, *Philly's Cold Shoulder; City Being Unbrotherly to Boy Scouts*, WASH. TIMES A19 (Jan. 22, 2008).

48. *Wyman*, 335 F.3d at 91.

49. These organizations included not just the Girl Scouts but gay-rights organizations and other religious organizations. *Id.* at 96 n.10.

50. Cornelius v. NAACP Legal Defense & Educ. Fund, Inc., 473 U.S. 788 (1985).

51. *Wyman*, 335 F.3d at 91.

52. Roberts v. U.S. Jaycees, 468 U.S. 609, 626 (1984).

53. This point was made by the Eighth Circuit in its ruling in favor of the Jaycees when Judge Richard Arnold noted that "[a]n organization of young people, as opposed to young men, may be more 'felicitous,' more socially desirable, in the view of the State Legislature, or in the view of the judges of this Court, but it will be substantially different from the Jaycees as it now exists." U.S. Jaycees v. McClure, 709 F.2d 1560, 1571 (8th Cir. 1983), *rev'd sub nom.* Roberts v. U.S. Jaycees, 468 U.S. 609 (1984). The internal quotation is from U.S. Jaycees v. McClure, 305 N.W.2d 764, 774 (Minn. 1981) (Sheran, C.J., dissenting).

54. *Roberts*, 468 U.S. at 621 (stressing that the Jaycee chapters were "neither small nor selective [and thus] lack the distinctive characteristics that might afford constitutional protection to the decision of its members to exclude women.").

55. Boy Scouts v. Dale, 530 U.S. 640, 668 (Stevens, J, dissenting). When the record was compiled in *Dale*, the Boy Scout Handbook defined "morally straight" in these terms: "To be a person of strong character, guide your life with honesty, purity, and justice. Respect and defend the rights of all people. Your relationship with others should be honest and open. Be clean in your speech and actions, and faithful in your religious beliefs. The values you follow as a Scout will help you become virtuous and self-reliant." Boy Scout Handbook, as quoted in *Dale*, 530 U.S. at 667 (Stevens, J., dissenting). The Boy Scouts insisted that such statements reflected values that were expanded on in practice to include a religious code that abhors homosexuality.

56. Boy Scouts v. Wyman, 335 F.3d 80, 91 (2d Cir. 2003).

57. *Id.* at 95 n.8.

58. For the purposes of full disclosure, I have publicly denounced the Boy Scouts policy while supporting its right to exercise its religiously based views. *See, e.g.*, Jonathan Turley, *Of Boy Scouts and Bigots*, CHI. TRIB. A27 (June 30, 2000).

59. *Cf.* Roberts v. U.S. Jaycees, 468 U.S. 609, 623 (1984) ("Infringements on [the right to association] may be justified by regulations adopted to serve compelling state interests, unrelated to the suppression of ideas, that cannot be achieved through means significantly less restrictive of associational freedoms.").

60. Hurley v. Irish-Am. Gay, Lesbian and Bisexual Group, 515 U.S. 557, 579 (1995) (citations omitted).

61. Karl N. Llewellyn, *Remarks on the Theory of Appellate Decision and the Rules or Canons About How Statutes Are To Be Construed,* 3 VAND. L. REV. 395, 401–06 (1950).

62. Indeed, in *Hurley,* the Court brushed aside the inconvenient public accommodation analysis by stating that "[a]lthough the state courts spoke of the parade as a place of public accommodation, once the expressive character of both the parade and the marching GLIB contingent is understood, it becomes apparent that the state courts' application of the statute had the effect of declaring the sponsors' speech itself to be the public accommodation." *Hurley,* 515 U.S. at 573.

63. Evans v. City of Berkeley, 129 P.3d 394 (Cal. 2006).

64. Barnes-Wallace v. Boy Scouts, 275 F. Supp. 2d 1259 (S.D. Cal. 2003), *state-law questions certified to state court sub nom.* Barnes-Wallace v. City of San Diego, 530 F.3d 776 (9th Cir. 2008).

65. Cuffley v. Mickes, 208 F.3d 702 (8th Cir. 2000).

66. Boy Scouts v. Dale, 530 U.S. 640, 648 (2000).

67. Roberts v. U.S. Jaycees, 468 U.S. 609 (1984).

68. This point was made most clearly in the trial decision in *Roberts* when the district court blissfully held that "[w]hile the Jaycees has a right to believe that its organization should only advance the interests of men, its practice of excluding women from equal benefits does not enjoy protection under the circumstances presented." U.S. Jaycees v. McClure, 534 F. Supp. 766, 771 (D. Minn. 1982), *rev'd,* 709 F.2d 1560 (8th Cir. 1983), *rev'd sub nom.* Roberts v. U.S. Jaycees, 468 U.S. 609 (1984).

69. *Roberts,* 468 U.S. at 623 ("We are persuaded that Minnesota's compelling interest in eradicating discrimination . . . justifies the impact that application of the statute to the Jaycees may have on the male members' associational freedoms.").

70. *Id.* at 628.

71. Bob Jones Univ. v. United States, 461 U.S. 574, 604 (1983), quoting Thomas v. Review Bd., 450 U.S. 707, 718 (1981) (citations omitted).

72. Walz v. Tax Comm'n, 397 U.S. 664, 669 (1970).

73. *Id.* at 691 (Brennan, J., concurring).

74. Peter Steinfels, *Advocates on Both Sides of the Same-Sex Marriage Issue See a Potential Clash with Religious Liberty,* N.Y. TIMES 11 (June 10, 2008).

75. Boy Scouts v. Wyman, 335 F.3d 80, 91 (2d Cir. 2003).

76. New York State Club Ass'n, Inc. v. City of New York, 487 U.S. 1, 13 (1988). *See also id.* ("effective advocacy of both public and private points of view, particularly controversial ones, is undeniably enhanced by group association, as this Court has more than once recognized by remarking upon the close nexus between the freedoms

of speech and assembly."), quoting NAACP v. Alabama ex rel. Patterson, 357 U.S. 449, 460 (1958).

77. Roberts v. U.S. Jaycees, 468 U.S. 609, 633 (1984) (O'Connor, J., concurring).

Chapter Three: Robin Fretwell Wilson

1. I am indebted to Johnny Rex Buckles, Naomi Cahn, Sam Calhoun, Doug Laycock, Jeffrey Kahn, Douglas Kmiec, John Lopatka, Pamela Melton, Anthony Picarello, and Jonathan Rauch for their careful reads and help. Garrett Ledgerwood, Richard Schlauch, and Joseph Mercer provided diligent, painstaking research assistance with the chapter.

2. Emergency contraceptives—such as "Plan B"—contain progestins that inhibit or delay ovulation and disrupt embryo transplant and implantation, although the precise mechanism by which they work is "not fully known." *Plan B facts and comparisons at Drug.com, available at* www.drugs.com/cdi/plan-b.html (last visited June 20, 2008).

Some see this as tantamount to abortion. Charisse Jones, *Druggists Refuse to Give Out Pill*, USA TODAY, Nov. 8, 2004, at 3A, *available at* www.usatoday.com/news/nation/2004-11-08-druggists-pill_x.htm (last visited June 6, 2008) (discussing the beliefs of some pharmacists that preventing the implantation of a fertilized egg is a form of abortion). Three million American women had used Plan B by 2003, while approximately one million had used Preven, an "older estrogen-progestin product" that acts in much the same way. *See* Sharon L. Camp et al., *The Benefits and Risks of Over-the-Counter Availability of Levonorgestrel Emergency Contraception*, 68 CONTRACEPTION 309, 309 (2003).

3. EUROPEAN UNION NETWORK OF INDEPENDENT EXPERTS ON HUMAN RIGHTS, OPINION NO. 4-2005: THE RIGHT TO CONSCIENTIOUS OBJECTION AND THE CONCLUSION BY EU MEMBER STATES OF CONCORDATS WITH THE HOLY SEE 14 (Dec. 14, 2005), *available at* http://europa.eu.int/comm/justice_home/cfr_cdf/doc/avis/2005_4_en.pdf (last visited June 6, 2008) [hereinafter *EU Network Opinion No. 4-2005*] (explaining that while individual clergy and clerks may object to participation in same-sex marriage if permitted by law, "it would be unacceptable [for] marriage [to be] unavailable to the couple concerned," which would result "from the refusal to celebrate a marriage between two persons of the same sex where this institution is recognized," and concluding that "public authorities should ensure in such circumstances that other officers will be available and willing to celebrate those unions").

Prompted by a draft treaty on abortion between the Vatican and the Slovak Republic, a member of the European Union (EU), the EU requested that the Network of Independent Experts on Human Rights examine legislative accommodations for refusals to participate in abortion. The Network expanded its review to include refusals to participate in other deeply divisive healthcare procedures, like euthanasia and the dispensing of birth control, as well as in the solemnizing of same-sex marriages. George Conger, *EU Ruling Worry For Clergy Over Same Sex Marriage*, CHURCH

OF ENGLAND NEWSPAPER, Jan. 13, 2006, *available at* www.adventbirmingham.org/arti-cles-print.asp?ID=2749 (last visited June 20, 2008).

4. *Socialist ideologue threatens Church: Be quiet or we'll silence you*, CATHOLIC NEWS SERVICES, *available at* www.catholicnewsagency.com/new.php?n=10073 (last visited June 20, 2008). The political figure, Professor Gregorio Peces-Barbra, explains that the Education for Citizenship program aims to "[C]over issues ranging from domestic violence to dangerous driving, which claims thousands of Spanish lives every year. But the course will also deal with issues like gender, sexuality and the family...." Victoria Burnett, *New secular civics class riling Catholic Church*, INTERNATIONAL HERALD TRIBUNE, *available at* www.iht.com/articles/2007/08/07/news.letter.php (last visited June 20, 2008). If the Church persists in its opposition to the program, Peces-Barbara threatened that "'the issue of the actions and situations of the Church and of estab-lishing new status, that puts her in her place and respects the autonomy of civil au-thority, should be taken up.'" *Socialist ideologue, supra.* Prime Minister Luis Rodríguez Zapatero agreed, stating that "no faith is above the law" and that it was society's role to "teach citizens the values of respect." *Id.*

5. Bill Graveland, *Alberta Allowing Same-Sex Marriage but Adding Protection to Op-ponents*, CANADIAN PRESS, July 12, 2005.

In addition to voluntary resignations, firings have also occurred. In the Nether-lands, a registrar was dismissed after refusing for religious reasons to solemnize the wedding of a same-sex couple, but later reinstated by the Commissie Gelijke Behan-deling, which enforces that country's General Equal Treatment Act. *EU Network Opinion No. 4-2005, supra* note 3. As the Commissie explained, insufficient reasons supported the refusal to renew the registrar's contract since "other public servants were prepared to celebrate same-sex marriages." *Id.*

6. Although many oppose it, religious leaders are not of a single mind about same-sex marriage. "[T]here are scholars in every major religious tradition that have pro-posed convincing alternatives to assumed anti-gay readings and traditions." *Articles of Faith: Reframing Issues of Religion, Public Policy and the Lesbian, Gay, Bisexual and Transgender Community*, TASK FORCE MEDIA, Feb 11, 2005.

7. Legislative accommodations appeared in both Canada's federal legislation and its provincial laws authorizing same-sex marriage. *See* The Civil Marriage Act, 2005 S.C., ch. 33, §3 (Can.) (specifying that under the Canadian Charter of Rights and Freedom, officials of religious groups may refuse to perform marriages that are not in accordance with their religious beliefs and that no person or organization may be sanctioned or deprived of any benefits for exercising their freedom of conscience and religious beliefs or for expressing their belief regarding marriage); Graveland, *supra* note 5 (observing that "Alberta will allow same-sex marriage but not force ministers . . . to perform the ceremonies if they don't want to").

Norway took a slightly different approach in its legislatively adopted recognition of same-sex marriage. It allows religious organizations to decide for themselves whether they will solemnize same-sex marriages. *See* Ministry of Children and Equal-ity, Information about Common Marriage Act for Heterosexuals and Homosexuals

(Mar. 14 2008), *available at* www.regjeringen.no/en/dep/bld/Topics/Homosexuality/ information-about-common-marriage-act-fo.html?id=509834 (last visited June 18, 2008).

8. Two jurisdictions in Canada, Yukon and Alberta, have said that they will not require their civil officials to marry same-sex couples. Memory McLeod, *Knights of Columbus aid commissioners who won't perform gay weddings: Service Club Pledges Support*, THE LEADER-POST, Apr. 17, 2007, *available at* www.canada.com/reginaleader-post/news/sports/story.html?id=ab7789c1-5988-421d-bd3b-1ade424e87b1 (last accessed June 20, 2008); Graveland, *supra* note 5 (reporting that marriage ministers will also be exempted). Legislation has been introduced in Canada to permit Justices of the Peace to refuse to marry a couple on the basis of religious convictions. John Ibbitson et al., *Tories plan to protect same-sex opponents*, GLOBE AND MAIL, Mar. 10, 2006, *available at* www.theglobeandmail.com/servlet/story/RTGAM.20061004.wsamesex03/ BNStory/National/home (last accessed June 20, 2008).

9. McLeod, *supra* note 8. Although the commissioner is not a government employee and receives no pay from the government, the complainant asked the tribunal to order him to pay her client $5000 in compensation; the tribunal has yet to issue its decision. *Id.*

See also Paul Sims, *Christian registrar 'threatened with sack' after refusing to conduct gay marriages*, DAILY MAIL, May 21 2008, *available at* www.dailymail.co.uk/news/article-1020809/Christian-registrar-threatened-sack-refusing-conduct-gay-marriages.html (last visited June 19, 2008) (discussing a British registrar's decision to sue her employer for discrimination after requesting to be excused from conducting same-sex marriages; the registrar alleges that after the request, she was bullied and her work environment deteriorated).

Similar questions arise in states that recognize civil unions. *See infra* note 194 and accompanying text (discussing a New Jersey Attorney General opinion requiring a public official who elects to be available generally for the purpose of solemnizing marriages, also to be available generally to solemnize civil unions).

10. *In re* Marriage Cases, 183 P.3d 384, 43 Cal. 4th 757, 783–785 (Cal. 2008) (concluding that the California Constitution protects the right to marry for same-sex couples as well as opposite-sex couples because "strict scrutiny" applies to California's statutes defining marriage and the "traditional definition of marriage [was] not a compelling state interest" under that test); Goodridge v. Dep't of Pub. Health, 780 N.E.2d 941 (Mass. 2003) (concluding that Massachusetts' limitation of marriage to heterosexual couples failed the lowest level of review, the "rational basis" test).

11. Adam Tanner & Mary Milikin, San Francisco mayor condemns refusal to marry gays, REUTERS, May 22, 2008, *available at* www.reuters.com/article/domesticNews/ idUSN223433420080523?pageNumber=1&virtualBrandChannel=0 (last visited June 19, 2008).

12. Katie Zezima, *Obey Same-Sex Marriage Law, Officials Told*, NEW YORK TIMES, April 26, 2004, at A15.

13. General Law of Massachusetts, Chapter 151B, § 5 (providing for civil penalties up to $50,000 when a party commits 2 or more discriminatory practices during a 7-year period preceding a complaint, and for smaller penalties in other instances).

14. *Relationship Recognition for Same-Sex Couples in the U.S.*, NATIONAL GAY AND LESBIAN TASK FORCE, *available at* www.thetaskforce.org/downloads/reports/issue_maps/relationship_recognition_2_08.pdf (last visited June 20, 2008) (noting that as of February 22, 2008, 10 states and the District of Columbia gives some relationship recognition for same-sex couples, through domestic partnership, reciprocal beneficiary, or civil union laws).

15. Barbara Bradley Hagerty, *Gay Rights, Religious Liberties: A Three-Act Story*, June 16, 2008, *available at* www.npr.org/templates/story/sory.php?storyID=91554986 (last visited June 19, 2008).

16. John Jalsevac, *U.S. Christian Camp Loses Tax-Exempt Status over Same-Sex Civil-Union Ceremony*, LIFESITE NEWS, Sept. 19, 2007, at *available at* www.lifesite.net/ldn/2007/sep/07091902.html (last visited June 19, 2008) (reporting that the New Jersey Department of Environmental Protection stripped the Ocean Grove Camp Meeting Association of its "tax-exempt status for part of its property" and that one homosexual advocacy group which believes the decision "doesn't go far enough" may press for "a bigger victory . . . by having the entire tax exemption removed"). The tax exemption arises under New Jersey's "Green Acres" program, which is "intended to preserve and enhance New Jersey's natural environment and its historic, scenic, and recreational resources for public use and enjoyment." Andy Humm, *Tax Break Denied to Jersey Anti-Gay Church*, Gay City News, Sept. 20, 2007, at *available at* www.gaycitynews.com/site/news.cfm?newsid=18838398&BRD=2729=2729&PAG=461&dept_id=5688648rfi=8 (last visited June 20, 2008). In February 2008, the tax assessor for the Township assessed approximately $20,000 in back taxes against Ocean Grove. *See* Bill Bowman, *$20G due in tax on boardwalk pavilion: Exemption lifted in rights dispute*, APP.COM (February 23, 2008), *available at* www.app.com/apps/pbcs.dll/article?AID=/20080223/NEWS/80223002/1004/NEWS 01 (last visited June 20, 2008).

Foreshadowing these actions, commentators have argued that tax exemption should be denied to organizations that will not serve same-sex couples. *See, e.g.*, Jonah M. Knobler, Letter to the Editor, *Mass. Should Revoke Church's Tax-Exempt Status*, Harvard Crimson, Mar. 17, 2006 (discussing the revocation of tax exemption for private adoption agencies who refuse to serve same-sex couples).

17. Harriet Bernstein et al., v. Ocean Grove Camp Meeting Assoc., No. PN34XB-03008 (NJ Dep't. of Law and Public Safety, filed June 19, 2007) (seeking damages and injunction against religious organization that denied complainants use of wedding pavilion for civil union ceremony). In response to those complaints, Ocean Grove filed suit in federal court seeking a declaration of its rights in regards to the pavilion. Jill P. Capuzzo, *Church Group Complains Of Pressure Over Civil Unions*, N.Y. TIMES, Aug. 14, 2007, at B4. The federal court dismissed the suit in light of pending

state litigation, which offered an ample opportunity for Ocean Grove "to raise its constitutional challenges." Camp Meeting Ass'n Of The United Methodist Church v. Papaleo, No. 07-3802, 2007 WL 3349787 (D. N.J. 2007). In January 2008, Ocean Grove sought to have the state-level complaints dismissed, without success. *See* Robert Schwaneberg, N.J. Rejects Request to Close Probe into Civil Unions Flap, Pew Forum on Religion and Public Life, *available at* http://pewforum.org/news/display.php?NewsID=14741 (last visited June 20, 2008) ("The association argued that forcing it to use its property for civil unions would violate its constitutional freedom of religion. . . . It was the Methodist group's second unsuccessful attempt to bring the investigation to a quick end.").

It is not clear how many same-sex couples are "having problems with civil unions in New Jersey," although six complaints concerning civil unions "were filed with the state Division of Civil Rights," two of which involved Ocean Grove. Michelle J. Lee, *One year later, N.J. civil unions stuck in "second-class status,"* PRESSOFATLANTIC CITY.COM (February 23, 2008), *available at* www.pressofatlanticcity.com/186/story/88685.html (last visited June, 20, 2008).

18. Anton N. Marco, *Same-Sex "Marriage:" Should America Allow "Gay Rights" Activists to Cross The Last Frontier?*, *available at* www.femdomale.com/samesex/marriage/index.html (last visited June 20, 2008) (asserting that "same-sex 'marriage' recognition would indeed 'legislate private tolerance' of 'gay rights' by religious organizations," and that "[t]he legal 'machinery' is already in place to compel . . . clergy to recognize and perform same-sex 'marriages' or forfeit licensure").

Scholars also worry about the implications of same-sex marriage for religious freedom. *See* Mary Ann Glendon, Editorial, *For Better or for Worse?*, WALL ST. J., Feb. 25, 2004, at A14:

Religious freedom, too, is at stake. As much as one may wish to live and let live, the experience in other countries reveals that once these arrangements become law, there will be no live-and-let live policy for those who differ. Gay-marriage proponents use the language of openness, tolerance and diversity, yet one foreseeable effect of their success will be to usher in an era of intolerance and discrimination the likes of which we have rarely seen before. Every person and every religion that disagrees will be labeled as bigoted and openly discriminated against. The ax will fall most heavily on religious persons and groups that don't go along. Religious institutions will be hit with lawsuits if they refuse to compromise their principles.

19. Butler v. Adoption Media, *LLC*, 486 F. Supp. 2d 1022, 1026 (N.D. Cal. 2007).

20. Transcript of Proceedings, United States District Court, Northern District of California, Butler v. Adoption Media LLC, Case No. C04-0135 PJH (JCS) (May 15, 2007). At the time of the refusal, California's Unruh Civil Rights Act did not prohibit discrimination based on sexual orientation or martial status. It has since been amended to cover both. *See* CAL. CIV. CODE §§ 51, 51.5 (2006).

21. Transcript of Proceedings, *supra* note 20, at 5 (on file with author).

22. *Health: Emergency Contraception*, BROADCAST NEWS, Dec. 14, 2005, 2005 WL 20105347.

23. MASS. GEN. LAWS ANN. ch. 111, § 70E(o) (West Supp. 2006) (providing that every female rape victim of childbearing age has the right to receive accurate written information about emergency contraception from any facility, including any private or state-run hospital, to be promptly offered the same, and to be provided with emergency contraception upon request). *See also* Scott Helman, *Romney Says No Hospitals Are Exempt from Pill Law: He Reverses Stand on Plan B*, BOSTON GLOBE, Dec. 9, 2005, at A1 (noting that Massachusetts Governor Mitt Romney overturned an initial ruling by the State Department of Public Health, which would have allowed privately run hospitals to opt out of the emergency contraception requirement if they objected on religious or moral grounds).

24. Julie Cantor & Ken Baum, *The Limits of Conscientious Objection: May Pharmacists Refuse to Fill Prescriptions for Emergency Contraception?*, 351 NEW ENG. J. MED. 2008, 2012 (2004) (arguing that "although health professionals may have a right to object, they should not have a right to obstruct," and asserting therefore that "[p]harmacists who object to filling prescriptions for emergency contraception should arrange for another pharmacist to provide this service to customers promptly").

25. Rob Stein, *For Some, There is No Choice*, WASHINGTON POST, July 16, 2006 A06, *available at* www.washingtonpost.com/wp-dyn/content/article/2006/07/15/AR2006071500790.html (last accessed June 20, 2008).

26. Questions of conscience in the marriage context have arisen since churches first struggled with what to do about remarriage. For instance, the British Parliament in 1857 addressed the obligation of clergymen to solemnize the marriage of remarried persons, a question hastened by Parliament's decision to permit once-married persons to marry again. It provided that "no Clergyman in Holy Orders of the United Church of *England* and *Ireland* shall be compelled to solemnize the Marriage of any Person whose former Marriage may have been dissolved on the Ground of his or her Adultery, or shall be liable to any Suit, Penalty, or Censure for solemnizing or refusing to solemnize the Marriage of any such Person" provided that "such Minister shall permit any other Minister in Holy Orders of the said United Church, entitled to officiate within the Diocese in which such Church or Chapel is situate, to perform such Marriage Service in such Church or Chapel." An Act to amend the Law relating to Divorce and Matrimonial Causes in England, 1857, 20 & 21 Vict., c. 85, §§ 57-58 (Eng.). More recently, Great Britain insulated clergy from having to perform marriages of people who have changed genders. *See* Gender Recognition Act, 2004, c. 7, 11, sched. 4 (U.K.), *available at* www.opsi.gov.uk/acts/acts2004/ukpga_20040007_en_7 (last visited June 20, 2008) (amending the Marriage Act of 1949, 1949, 12 & 13 Geo. 6, c. 76).

27. Roe v. Wade, 410 U.S. 113 (1973).

28. *See infra* notes 130–171 and accompanying text.

29. Roe v. Wade, 410 U.S. 113 (1973). Many see abortion as the one constitutional right that is virtually impervious to being overruled. *See The Supreme Court*, PBS RELIGION & ETHICS NEWSWEEKLY, Episode no. 410, Nov. 3, 2000, *available at* www.pbs.org/wnet/religionandethics/week410/feature.html (last visited June 20, 2008) (describing the decision in *Roe* as the "among the least likely to be overruled").

30. Griswold v. Connecticut, 381 U.S. 479, 486 (1965) (viewing decisions regarding reproduction as "intimate to the degree of being sacred" and holding that a married couple's decision to use contraception falls in a zone of privacy in which the state cannot interfere); *see also* Eisenstadt v. Baird, 405 U.S. 438, 453 (1972) (extending the right of contraceptive use to single persons because "[i]f the right of privacy means anything, it is the right of the *individual*, married or single, to be free from unwarranted governmental intrusion into matters so fundamentally affecting a person as the decision whether to bear or beget a child").

31. *See infra* note 195 and accompanying text (discussing whether the right to reproduce is a negative right or a positive one).

32. Church Amendment, 42 U.S.C. § 300a-7 (2000). Legislative accommodations outside healthcare date back to the 1950s and "program[s] of 'released time' religious instruction operated by the New York public schools," which the United States Supreme Court upheld against an Establishment Clause challenge. *See* Ira C. Lupu and Robert W. Tuttle, *Instruments of Accommodation: The Military Chaplaincy and the Constitution*, 110 W. VA. L. REV. 89, 101–02 (2007).

33. *Id.*

34. It is not surprising that questions of conscientious refusals were not decided by *Goodridge* and the *Marriage Cases*. Like *Roe* and *Griswold*, *Goodridge* and the *Marriage Cases* recognize a dramatically new right, at least for some persons. Unlike entitlements hatched in legislation, which lend themselves to accommodating the interests of third persons, civil rights cases are not well-suited to, and rarely accommodate, the interests of non-plaintiffs. Civil rights litigation generally produces an entitlement of the plaintiffs vis-à-vis the state, rather than entitlements of plaintiffs vis-à-vis other persons.

35. Indeed, there is a long history of litigation between secularists and religious institutions when the latter fulfills a traditional state role, as with education, adoption, and other social services. *See generally* Ira C. Lupu & Robert Tuttle, *The Distinctive Place of Religious Entities in our Constitutional Order*, 47 VILL. L. REV. 37 (2002) (outlining a history of important litigation defining the boundaries of the First Amendment Separation Clause).

36. *Liberal MPs Warn Parliament on Coming Religious Persecution from Liberal Gay "Marriage"*, LIFESITE, Mar. 22, 2005, *available at* www.lifesite.net/ldn/2005/mar/05032204.html (last visited June 20, 2008).

37. Alex Hutchinson, *Gay advocates fight churches' charity status Institutions fear losing tax breaks if the oppose same-sex unions; Rightly so, gay-rights group says*, THE OTTAWA CITIZEN, June 12, 2005, *available at* www.freerepublic.com/focus/f-news/1421544/posts (last visited June 20, 2008).

38. Bill Bowman, *Civil union denial spurs bias claim in Ocean Grove*, ASBURY PARK PRESS, Jun 21, 2007, *available at* www.app.com/apps/pbcs.dll/article?AID=/20070621/NEWS/70621003 (last visited June. 20, 2008).

Similar concerns over litigation have arisen in the European Union and Great Britain after the enactment of new rules prohibiting discrimination on the basis of sexual orientation. *See* David Byers, *British Jewish body expresses concern about new gay laws*, EUROPEAN JEWISH PRESS, Jan. 7, 2007, *available at* www.ejpress.org/article/news/uk/12708 (last visited June 20, 2008) ("Religious groups—including the Board of Deputies as well as elements of the British Christian and Muslim communities—are concerned that the rules will force religious groups to promote homosexual rights and, if they refuse, could persecute them on moral grounds.").

39. In August 2007, a district court in Iowa found Iowa's ban on same-sex marriage to be unconstitutional, a ruling now before the Iowa Supreme Court. *See Iowa court rules same-sex couples can marry*, *available at* www.cnn.com/2007/US/law/08/30/iowa.samesexmarriage/index.html (last visited June 20, 2008); Varnum v. Brien, No. CV5965, slip op. (Iowa Dist. Ct. Polk County Aug. 30, 2007), appeal docketed, No. 07-1499 (Iowa Sup. Ct. Aug. 31, 2007). The Supreme Court of Connecticut is also considering whether same-sex couples can marry. *See* Kerrigan v. State, 909 A.2d 89 (Conn. Super. Ct. 2006), appeal docketed, No. S.C. 17716 (Conn. Sup. Ct. July 28, 2006).

In June 2008, New York's Governor, David Paterson, announced that New York will give full faith and credit to legal same-sex marriages from other states. Governor Paterson instructed state agency heads to review state regulations and policy statements in order to make them comply. *See* Memorandum from David Nocenti to New York Agency Counsel (May 14, 2008), *available at* www.observer.com/2008/patersons-message-same-sex-marriage) (last visited June 19, 2008).

40. *See infra* notes 130–171 and accompanying text; Appendix.

41. United States Supreme Court precedence certainly discusses marriage as a fundamental right. Loving v. Virginia, 388 U.S. 1, 12 (1967) ("The freedom to marry has long been recognized as one of the vital personal rights essential to the orderly pursuit of happiness by free men.... Marriage is one of the 'basic civil rights of man,' fundamental to our very existence and survival." (quoting Skinner v. State of Oklahoma, 316 U.S. 535, 541 (1942))). *See also* Turner v. Safely, 482 U.S. 78 (1986) (concluding that a Missouri prison regulation requiring prior approval by the warden of any marriages between inmates or between an inmate and a civilian impermissibly burdened the constitutional right of prisoners to marry).

It remains to be seen whether same-sex marriage will be treated as a fundamental right under the United States Constitution. Academics are split on the question. *Compare* Toni Lester, *Adam and Steve vs. Adam and Eve: Will the New Supreme Court Grant Gays the Right to Marry*, 14 AM. U. J. GENDER SOC. POL'Y & L. 253, 307 (2006) (observing that while "it is difficult to predict with certainty what the ultimate decision will be when the Supreme Court next meets to consider a gay marriage claim, . . . if each member of the Court renders a decision that is in line with his or her views in the *Lawrence* decision, or in views expressed elsewhere as just discussed, the final decision will be that gay marriage is a fundamental right guaranteed under the [United States] Constitution") *with* Randy Beck, *The City of God and the Cities of Men: A Response to Jason Carter*, 41 GA. L. REV. 113, 150 (2006) (concluding that *Lawrence v. Texas*, which invalidated a state law against homosexual sodomy, does not imply "a constitutional right to same-sex marriage," and that urging that "if the Court ever faces a substantive due process argument for same-sex marriage, the abortion-funding decisions provide an adequate analogy to sustain governmental adherence to the traditional definition of marriage").

States are resolving the question under their own constitutions in different ways. Maryland's highest court concluded that there is no fundamental right to marry a person of one's own sex under Maryland's constitution, while the California Supreme Court found a "fundamental constitutional right to form a family relationship" under California's constitution. *Compare* Conaway v. Deane, 932 A.2d 571 (2007) *with In re* Marriage Cases, 183 P.3d 384, 43 Cal. 4th 757, 783–785 (Cal. 2008).

42. As part III explains, placing conscientious objections out of bounds even when a hardship will *not* occur would mean that public employees *must* provide a service despite religiously based objections, even though the service could be obtained easily from another public employee. Forcing people to act against their consciences when no one would otherwise lose needlessly treads on their religious beliefs, with no countervailing gain.

43. Jonathan Turley, *An Unholy Union: Same-Sex Marriage and the Use of Governmental Programs to Penalize Religious Groups with Unpopular Practices, supra*, note 2 and accompanying text.

44. *See* Katherine A. White, Note, *Crisis of Conscience: Reconciling Religious Health Care Providers' Beliefs and Patients' Rights*, 51 STAN. L. REV. 1703, 1703 (1999).

45. *See* Mark D. Stern, *Same-Sex Marriage and the Churches, supra*, notes 223–40 and accompanying text.

46. *See generally* Church of the Lukumi Babalu Aye, Inc. v. City of Hialeah, 508 U.S. 520 (1993); City of Boerne v. Flores, 521 U.S. 507 (1997).

47. St. Agnes Hospital, Inc. v. Riddick, 748 F. Supp. 319 (D. Md. 1990).

48. *See id.* at 330.

49. *See id.* at 333.

50. *See infra* notes 82–83 and accompanying text.

51. The popularity of this approach has not diminished. Advocates of increased access to emergency contraception have once more homed in on federal funding as a stick. In 2007, Senator Hilary Clinton (N.Y.) introduced a bill to enact the Compassionate Assistance for Rape Emergencies Act of 2007, which would withhold federal funding to any hospital that did not provide emergency contraception to sexual assault victims or provide victims with medically and factually accurate and unbiased information about emergency contraception, including an explanation that it does not cause an abortion. *See* S. 1240, 110th Cong. Sess.1 (2007) (read twice and referred to the Senate Committee on Finance). *See also* H. R. 464, 110th Cong, sess.1 (2007) (making nearly identical requirements; referred to the House Subcommittee on Health). Similar bills introduced in the 109th Congress were referred to the committee after introduction, and died there. *See, e.g.*, S. 1264 109th Cong. (2005) (read twice and referred to the Committee on Health, Education, Labor, and Pensions); H. R. 3326 109th Cong.(2005) (referred to the House Subcommittee on Health).

52. *See* Taylor v. St. Vincent's Hospital, 369 F. Supp. 948, 950 (D. Mont. 1973) (noting the court's injunction, which was ordered Oct. 27, 1972).

53. *Id.* at 949.

54. 42 U.S.C. § 1983 (2000).

55. *See* H.R. Rep. No. 93-227 (1973), *as reprinted in* 1973 U.S.C.C.A.N. 1464, 1473 (discussing the preliminary injunction granted by the federal district court in *Taylor*).

56. Hospital and Medical Facilities Amendments of 1964, Pub. L. No. 88-443, 78 Stat. 447 (codified at 42 U.S.C. § 291).

57. *See* H.R. Rep. No. 93-227, *supra* note 55, at 1473 (describing the federal district court's finding of "two other factors . . . that established a connection between the hospital and the State sufficient to support jurisdiction" in *Taylor*).

58. The Church Amendment appears in § 401 of the Health Programs Extension Act, which President Nixon signed into law in June 1973. Pub. L. No. 93-45, 87 Stat. 91, 95.

59. *Id.* The choice to provide protection to individuals *and* institutions is a costly one. Professor Minow argues that exemptions cumulate and, consequently, handing out exemptions to both organizations and individuals raises special considerations as to access. As she explains, "each additional exemption curtails the application of the overarching norm—and civil rights laws as a result can be too easily and thoroughly undermined." *See* Martha Minow, *Should Religious Groups Be Exempt from Civil Rights Laws?*, 48 B.C. L. Rev. 781 (2007) (noting that religious groups have long enjoyed protection from nondiscrimination statutes, although the level of protection varies with the nature of the discrimination. Discrimination involving sexual orientation by religious groups is implicitly exempt, while such groups enjoy fewer exemptions regarding gender discrimination and no exemptions regarding racial discrimination). In the emergency contraceptives context, I have argued that in an effort to ensure patient access, society should be more concerned for the conscience concerns of individual providers than institutions. *See, e.g.*, Robin Fretwell Wilson, *Essay: The Limits of Conscience: Moral Clashes over Deeply Divisive Healthcare Procedures*, 34 Am. J. of Law & Med. 31 (2008).

60. Church Amendment, *supra* note 58, at § 401.

61. Taylor v. St. Vincent's Hospital, 369 F. Supp. 948, 950–51 (D. Mont. 1973) (citing Pub. L. No. 93-45, 87 Stat. 91, Sec. 401(b); and quoting H.R. Rep. No. 93-227 (1973), *as reprinted in* 1973 U.S.C.C.A.N. 1464, 1553 [sic; actually 1473]).

62. *Id.* at 950. The court refused to examine the Church Amendment's constitutionality, finding that the issue was not before the court. *Id.* at 951. The court also rejected a challenge based on retroactive application. *See id.*

63. Chrisman v. Sisters of St. Joseph of Peace, 506 F.2d 308 (9th Cir. 1974).

64. *Id.* at 310.

65. *Id.*

66. *See, e.g.*, Greco v. Orange Mem'l Hosp. Corp., 513 F.2d 873 (5th Cir. 1975) (rejecting plaintiff's claim that hospital's refusal to allow abortions to be performed

was unconstitutional); Watkins v. Mercy Med. Ctr., 520 F.2d 894 (9th Cir. 1975) (rejecting plaintiff's claim that exclusion from staff privileges violated plaintiff's rights under First, Fifth, and Fourteenth Amendments); Doe v. Bellin Mem'l Hosp., 479 F.2d 756 (7th Cir. 1973) (rejecting plaintiff's claim that hospital's refusal to perform abortions violated 42 U.S.C. § 1983); Doe v. Charleston Area Med. Ctr., 529 F.2d 638, 643 (4th Cir. 1975) (rejecting plaintiff's claim that nonprofit hospital's refusal to perform abortions violated 42 U.S.C. § 1983).

67. Nyberg v. City of Virginia, 495 F.2d 1342 (8th Cir. 1974).

68. Id. at 1346.

69. Id. (alteration in original) (quoting Hathaway v. Worcester City Hosp., 475 F.2d 701, 706 (1973)).

70. Id.

71. Id. at 1343.

72. See Doe v. Hale Hosp., 500 F.2d 144 (1st Cir. 1974) (holding that a traditional public hospital owned by the city of Haverhill, Massachusetts could not forbid therapeutic abortions if it offers medically indistinguishable procedures); Friendship Med. Ctr., Ltd. v. Chicago Bd. of Health, 505 F.2d 1141 (7th Cir. 1974) (holding that the right to privacy included the right to be free from government regulation affecting the abortion decision during the first trimester of pregnancy, so that hospital corporation that sought to do abortions could not be limited in this by the Chicago Board of Health); Orr v. Koefoot, 377 F. Supp. 673 (D. Neb. 1974) (finding that a University Medical Hospital functions as a public hospital and therefore could not limit the number of nontherapeutic abortions performed per week to only those necessary to maintain a conservative medical teaching program). But see Roe v. Ariz. Bd. of Regents, 549 P.2d 150, 152 (Ariz. 1976) (upholding state's statutory prohibition on performance of abortions in a state university hospital and distinguishing Nyberg due to the availability of "adequate alternate facilities.").

73. Webster v. Reproductive Health Services, 492 U.S. 490 (1989).

74. Id. at 510.

75. Id. at 510, n.8.

76. Doe v. Bolton, 410 U.S. 179 (1973). State courts have reached similar results. In Roe v. Arizona Board of Regents, 549 P.2d 150 (Ariz. 1976), the Arizona Supreme Court upheld an Arizona statute allowing hospitals to refuse to admit patients seeking an abortion even as applied to a state university teaching hospital, reasoning that "[t]he sole and exclusive responsibility for the hospitalization and medical care of the indigent rests with the county. Pima County, where plaintiff resides, has established a county hospital. There is no suggestion that this facility would not have been available to the plaintiff for the abortion procedure."

77. Doe, 410 U.S. at 198 (concluding that "the interposition of the hospital abortion committee is unduly restrictive of the patient's rights and needs that, at this point, have already been medically delineated and substantiated by her personal physician. To ask more serves neither the hospital nor the State.").

78. Id. at 197.

79. *Id.* at 197–98 (emphasis added).

80. Watkins v. Mercy Med. Ctr., 364 F. Supp. 799, 803 (D. Idaho 1973), aff'd, 520 F.2d 894 (9th Cir. 1975). *See also* Doe v. Bellin Mem'l Hosp., 479 F.2d 756, 759–60 (7th Cir. 1973) ("There is no constitutional objection to the decision by a purely private hospital that it will not permit its facilities to be used for the performance of abortions.").

81. These conscience clauses expanded the scope of covered services, allowing providers to opt out of not only the abortion or sterilization service, but also out of providing counseling and referral for such services. For instance, in 1988, the Danforth Amendment of the Civil Rights Restoration Act of 1987 extended conscience protections to include "abortion-related services." *See* Pub. L. No. 100-259, § 909, 28 Stat. 28, 29 (codified at 20 U.S.C. § 1688) (providing that the receipt of monies under Title IX, which prohibits sex discrimination in federally-funded education programs, may not be construed to require an individual or entity to provide or pay for abortion-related services).

82. Danforth Amendment, 42 U.S.C. § 238n(a)(1) (2000).

83. *Id.*

84. Dep'ts of Labor, Health & Hum. Servs., and Educ., and Related Agencies Appropriations Act of 2004, Pub. L. No. 108-447, § 507, 118 Stat. 2809, 3164 (2004); Pub. L. No. 109-149, § 507, 119 Stat. 2833, 3164 (2005); Consolidated Appropriations Act, 2008, Pub. L. No 110-161, Div. G, § 507, 121 Stat. 1844, 2208 (2007).

85. Pub. L. No. 108-447, § 508(d)(1); Pub. L. No. 109-149, § 508(d)(1); Pub. L. No 110-161, § 508(d)(1).

86. Pub. L. No. 108-447, § 508(a) provides that:

The limitations established in the preceding section shall not apply to an abortion—(1) if the pregnancy is the result of an act of rape or incest; or (2) in the case where a woman suffers from a physical disorder, physical injury, or physical illness, including a life endangering physical condition caused by or arising from the pregnancy itself, that would, as certified by a physician, place the woman in danger of death unless an abortion is performed.

See also Pub. L. No. 109-149, § 508(a).

87. Pub. L. No. 108-447, § 508(d)(2). States have also expanded the range of entities covered by conscience clause protection. For instance, MO. ANN. STAT. § 376.1199 (West 2002) allows "Any health carrier which is owned, operated or controlled in substantial part by an entity that is operated pursuant to moral, ethical or religious tenets that are contrary to the use or provision of contraceptives" an exemption from having to include contraceptive coverage in its insurance policies. Additionally, in May 2004 the Michigan House of Representatives passed a bill that would exempt health insurers from covering healthcare items that violated ethical, moral or religious principles reflected in their bylaws or mission statements. *Michigan House Votes to Protect Conscience Rights in Health Care*, ST. & LOC. HEALTH L. WKLY., May 13, 2004. This bill passed the House but not the Senate. *See* Michigan Legislature, House Bill 5277, *available at* www.legislature.mi.gov/(ybf114vh2werx1iivuo40vqr)/mileg.aspx?page=Bills (last

visited June 20, 2008) (reporting the final status of H.B. 5277, 2003-2004 Sess. (Mich. 2004), as last "referred to the [Senate] Committee on Health Policy" on April 22, 2004).

88. Bob Egelko, *California Suit Hits Antiabortion Amendment*, S.F. CHRON. Jan. 26, 2005, at B3.

California challenged the constitutionality of the Weldon Amendment on the grounds that " the vague and sweeping nature of the Clause has the potential to dramatically curb women's access to reproductive health care information and services," *Press Release*, NATIONAL FAMILY PLANNING AND REPRODUCTIVE HEALTH ASSOCIA-TION, *available at* www.nfprha.org/site/apps/nl/content3.asp?c=ggLRIWODKtF&b= 1029145&ct=1390325 (last visited June 20, 2007). The challenge failed on standing grounds. National Family Planning and Reproductive Health Ass'n, Inc. v. Gonzales, 391 F.Supp.2d 200 (D.D.C. Sep. 28, 2005), *vacated and remanded* by National Family Planning and Reproductive Health Ass'n, Inc. v. Gonzales, 468 F.3d 826, 373 U.S.App.D.C. 346 (D.C.Cir. Nov 14, 2006) ("As plaintiff lacks standing to challenge the Weldon Amendment, the judgment below is vacated and the case remanded to the district court to dismiss for lack of jurisdiction."). California is the only state to have challenged the Weldon Amendment. Bob Egelko, *Abortion law challenge still in limbo*, SAN FRANCISCO CHRONICLE, February 6, 2008, *available at* www.sfgate.com/cgi-bin/article.cgi?f=/c/a/2008/02/06/BA7FUSFRK.DTL (last visited June 20, 2008).

89. *See infra* notes 91, 97 and accompanying text. Only the Internal Revenue Service can challenge an organization's qualification for federal tax exemption; third parties lack standing to sue the IRS with regard to determinations affecting other parties. *See* Allen v. Wright, 468 U.S. 737 (1984).

90. Massachusetts automatically qualifies as a tax-exempt organization "any religious corporation, trust, foundation, association or organization incorporated or established for religious purposes...." MASS. GEN. LAWS ANN. ch. 68, § 20 (West 2001). For a list of all Massachusetts statutes pertaining to tax-exempt/charitable organizations, see Office of the Mass. Attorney General, Charities: Statutes and Regulations, *available at* www.mass.gov/?pageID=cagoterminal&L=3&L0=Home&L1=Non-Profits+%26+Charities&L2=AG's+Oversight+%26+Enforcement+Role&sid=Cago&b=terminalcontent&f=nonprofit_statutes_and_regulations&csid=Cago (last visited June 20, 2008).

91. For instance, the General Laws of Massachusetts Title IX, Chapter 59, section 5 exempts from property taxes "houses of religious worship owned by, or held in trust for the use of, any religious organization." MASS. GEN. LAWS ANN. ch. 59, § 5, cl. 11 (West Supp. 2006).

92. In Massachusetts, "there is no statutory definition of a charity; the term is defined by case law." Generally, however, "charities share three characteristics: a) they are nonprofit organizations; b) they have a purpose which is primarily charitable; c) they benefit an indefinite class or number of people." Frequently Asked Questions, Office of the Massachusetts Attorney General, Nonprofit Charities Division, *avail-*

able at www.mass.gov/?pageID=cagoterminal&L=3&L0=Home&L1=Non-Profits+%26+Charities&L2=AG's+Oversight+%26+Enforcement+Role&sid=Cago&b=terminalcontent&f=nonprofit_general_faqs_about_charities&csid=Cago (last visited June 20, 2008). Religious organizations are exempt from registering and filing with the Nonprofit Charities Division. *Id.* The automatic extension of charitable status to religious organizations is routine in the United States. Patty Gerstenblith, *Associational Structures of Religious Organizations*, 1995 B.Y.U. L. Rev. 439, 469 (2005) ("[I]t is not necessary for a religious organization to adopt formally any legal structure in order to carry out its religious mission or even to attain favorable tax status.").

93. Martha Coakley, the Attorney General of Massachusetts, Remarks of Massachusetts Attorney General Martha Coakley to the Massachusetts Lesbian & Gay Bar Association's 22nd Annual Dinner, May 11, 2007; *Coakley warns anti-gay marriage law may be unconstitutional*, May 11, 2008, *available at* www.boston.com/news/local/massachusetts/articles/2007/05/11/coakley_warns_anti_gay_marriage_law_may_be_unconstitutional/ (last visited June 20, 2008).

94. A refusal to facilitate same-sex marriage by providing a reception hall or other services described in part III may violate state laws prohibiting discrimination on the basis of sexual orientation or otherwise breach the state's established public policy of recognizing same-sex marriages. Massachusetts may conclude, as New Jersey did, that duties of equal treatment extend to state officials and private persons, but not to religious organizations. *See infra* note 194 and accompanying text.

95. Jonah M. Knobler, Letter to the Editor, *Mass. Should Revoke Church's Tax-Exempt Status*, HARVARD CRIMSON, Mar. 17, 2006 (discussing the revocation of tax exemption for private adoption agencies who refuse to serve same-sex couples).

96. *See infra* note 125 (discussing different treatment of churches and religious organizations by federal tax regulators).

97. Section 501(c)(3) churches are exempt from federal income tax and federal unemployment tax. 26 U.S.C. § 501(a)-(c) (2000). Church contributions are also deductible by the contributor for income, estate, and gift purposes. Vaughn E. James, *Reaping Where They Have Not Sowed: Have American Churches Failed to Satisfy the Requirements for the Religious Tax Exemption?*, 43 CATHOLIC LAW. 29, 43 (2004). Churches may also issue tax-exempt bonds to finance activities, benefit from preferential postal rates, provide tax-deferred retirement plans, qualify for state and local tax exemption, and be exempt under "labor, bankruptcy, and other regulatory regimes." *Id.*

Despite these important benefits, federal tax exemption may benefit churches less than other exempt organizations. *See* Ellen P. Aprill, *Churches, Politics, and the Charitable Contribution Deduction*, 42 B.C. L. REV. 843 (2001) (arguing that churches are principally supported by lower-income taxpayers who may not itemize and, consequently, do not receive the benefit of Internal Revenue Code Section 170); Michael Hatfield, *Ignore the Rumors – Campaigning from the Pulpit Is Okay: Thinking Past the Symbolism of Section 501(c)(3)*, 20 NOTRE DAME J. L. ETHICS & PUB. POL'Y 125, 155-61 (2006) (arguing that receipts from charitable donations constitute excludible gifts, a benefit that would be available to churches in their capacity as charities even if they lost their exempt status under Section 501(c)(3)).

98. Section 501(c)(3) of the Internal Revenue Code (Code) provides federal tax-exempt status for organizations "organized and operated exclusively for religious, charitable, scientific, testing for public safety, literary, or educational purposes, or to foster national or international amateur sports competition ... or for the prevention of cruelty to children or animals." 26 U.S.C. § 501(c)(3) (2000). Exempt status under Section 501(c)(3) requires that "(1) the organization must be organized and operated exclusively for certain purposes; (2) there must not be private inurement to organization insiders; (3) there must be no more than an incidental private benefit to private persons who are not organization insiders; (4) no substantial part of the organization's activities may be lobbying; and (5) the organization may not participate or intervene in political activities." JOINT COMMITTEE ON TAXATION, HISTORICAL DEVELOPMENT AND PRESENT LAW OF THE FEDERAL TAX EXEMPTION FOR CHARITIES AND OTHER TAX-EXEMPT ORGANIZATIONS 7 (2005), *available at* www.house.gov/jct/x-29-05.pdf (last visited June 20, 2008). Once recognized by the IRS as tax exempt, a church generally will only jeopardize this tax-exempt status by violating one of the qualifying factors or taking other prohibited actions—chief among these is the restriction that "the organization's purposes and activities may not be illegal or violate fundamental public policy." INTERNAL REVENUE SERVICE, TAX GUIDE FOR CHURCHES AND RELIGIOUS ORGANIZATIONS 3 (2003), *available at* www.irs.gov/pub/irs-pdf/p1828.pdf (last visited June 20, 2008).

99. The only nondiscrimination provision in the Code permits the revocation of the tax-exempt status of social clubs that discriminate "on the basis of race, color, or religion." *See* 26 U.S.C. § 501(i) (2000).

100. Bob Jones University v. United States, 461 U.S. 574, 578 (1983).

101. *Id.* at 581, 583. The IRS relied on Revenue Ruling 71-447, which concluded that racially discriminatory policies in educational settings are "contrary to Federal public policy." Rev. Rul. 71-447, 1971-2 C.B. 230 (addressing whether a private school that otherwise meets the requirements of Section 501(c)(3) qualifies for exemption if it does not have a "racially nondiscriminatory policy as to students"). The IRS reiterated that "all charitable trusts, educational or otherwise, are subject to the requirement that the purpose of the trust may not be illegal or contrary to public policy." *Id.* at 3. The Revenue Ruling was the IRS's formalization of its revised policy on discrimination following the United States District Court for the District of Columbia's "preliminary injunction prohibiting the IRS from according tax-exempt status to private schools in Mississippi that discriminated as to admissions on the basis of race" in *Green v. Kennedy*, 309 F. Supp. 1127 (D.D.C. 1970). *Bob Jones*, 461 U.S. at 578-79.

Revenue Rulings are similar to legal opinions and "represent policy positions and, unlike private letter rulings, may be used as precedents." MICHAEL ROSE & JOHN CHOMMIE, FEDERAL INCOME TAXATION § 13.05 (3d ed. 1998). However, Revenue Rulings are not substantive authority or "binding on ... the courts." Stubbs, Overbeck

& Assocs., Inc. v. United States, 445 F.2d 1142, 1146-47 (5th Cir. 1971) (stating that a Revenue Ruling "is merely an opinion of a lawyer in the agency and must be accepted as such. It may be helpful in interpreting a statute, but it is not binding on . . . the courts. It does not have the effect of a regulation . . . . ").

102. *See Bob Jones*, 461 U.S. at 577.

103. *Id.* at 587.

104. *Id.* at 591.

105. *Id.* at 592.

106. *Id.* at 593. *See id.* at 593-95 (citing numerous examples of legislative, judicial, and executive branch expressions of the idea that racial discrimination in education violates public policy).

107. *Id.* at 593-94.

108. *Id.* at 603-04 ("Denial of tax benefits will inevitably have a substantial impact on the operation of private religious schools, but will not prevent those schools from observing their religious tenets."). Significantly, for purposes of its decision, the Court assumed the legitimacy of racial exclusivity as a religious tenet. *See Bob Jones*, 461 U.S. at 580 (noting that the sponsors of Bob Jones University "genuinely believe that the Bible forbids interracial dating and marriage").

109. *See* Douglas W. Kmiec, *Same-Sex Marriage and the Coming Antidiscriminiation Campaigns Against Religion, infra,* note 40 and accompanying text; *Bob Jones*, 461 U.S. at 604 n.29. Importantly, nothing in the decision clearly exempts churches from the public policy doctrine. The IRS does distinguish churches from other religious organizations and applies slightly different tax rules to each. this; INTERNAL REVENUE SERVICE, *supra* note 98, at 2. *See also* infra note 125 (discussing the treatment of churches).

110. I.R.S. Gen. Couns. Mem. 39792, at 11–12 (June 30, 1989) (holding that a perpetual charitable trust's racially restrictive provision "foster[ed] racial discrimination" and was "inconsistent with established public policy") (emphasis added). In that decision, the trust instrument provided "for the benefit and relief of worthy and deserving white persons. . .." and the trust provided goods and services to needy senior Caucasian citizens over the age of sixty. *Id.* at 5, 14. Since the trust denied eligibility based solely on race, it aggravated the "burdens placed on those who have traditionally been the subject of discrimination" and consequentially fostered racial discrimination. *Id.* The trust's activities were contrary to a "clearly defined federal public policy against racial discrimination" and did not fall within Section 501(c)(3) or Section 4947(a)(1). *Id.* at 15–16.

111. *Id.* at 8–9.

112. I.R.S. Priv. Ltr. Rul. 8910001 (Nov. 30, 1988) (holding that a privately administered trust for general goods and services with a governing instrument restricting beneficiaries to "worthy and deserving white persons" did not qualify for tax exemption under Section 501(c)(3) since the trust "aggravate[ed] the burdens placed on those who have traditionally been the subject of discrimination and thereby fosters racial discrimination" and, consequently, its activities were "contrary to a clearly defined public policy" against discrimination).

113. Church of Scientology v. Comm'r, 83 T.C. 381, 503 n.74 (1984), aff'd, 823 F.2d 1310 (9th Cir. 1987), cert. denied, 486 U.S. 1015 (holding that the Church of Scientology of California was not operated exclusively for religious purposes under Section 501(c)(3)).

114. At least one commentator reads IRS tax guidance as suggesting that conduct that would constitute a violation of law when performed by a state actor may be sufficient to revoke or deny a nonprofit's tax-exempt status. "[I]n the Bishop Estate technical advice memorandum, the IRS appears to maintain that activities that are unconstitutional if committed by the state also violate the public policy doctrine if committed by a private, charitable entity." Johnny Rex Buckles, Reforming the Public Policy Doctrine, 53 U. KAN. L. REV. 397, 420 (2005) (footnote omitted). In that memorandum, the IRS permitted the Bishop Estate, which admitted only Hawaiian descendents, to continue its tax exemption, finding that the Estate's policies were consonant with United States Supreme Court decisions upholding certain race-based governmental programs. Id. The IRS advised the Estate, however, to seek a private letter ruling on the memorandum's application following the then-pending Supreme Court decision in Rice v. Cayetano, 528 U.S. 495, 524 (2000), which struck down "Hawaii's law prohibiting persons of non-native ancestry from voting in an election for trustees of a state agency charged with bettering conditions for native Hawaiians." Buckles, supra, at 407 n.54. As Professor Buckles observed, the Bishop Estate ruling "arguably reflects the position of the IRS that actions by the state which are unconstitutional also violate the public policy doctrine when committed not by the state but by private charitable entities." Id.

115. See Buckles, supra note 114, at 432 ("[T]ax exempt charities need comply only with 'established' or 'fundamental' public policy").

116. Bob Jones, 461 U.S. at 593.

117. Id. at 592.

118. Church of Scientology v. Comm'r, 83 T.C. 381, 503 n.74 (1984).

119. I.R.S. Priv. Ltr. Rul. 8910001 (Nov. 30, 1988).

120. Rev. Rul. 71-447, 1971-2 C.B. 230 (concluding that a private school that otherwise meets the requirements of Section 501(c)(3) qualifies for exemption if it has a "racially nondiscriminatory policy as to students" since Titles IV and VI, The Civil Rights Act of 1964, Brown v. Board of Education, and numerous Federal court cases "demonstrate a national policy to discourage racial discrimination in education, whether public or private"). The IRS reiterated that "all charitable trusts, educational or otherwise, are subject to the requirement that the purpose of the trust may not be illegal or contrary to public policy." Id. at 3.

121. Buckles, supra note 114, at 427 (citing David A. Brennen, Charities and the Constitution: Evaluating the Role of Constitutional Principles in Determining the Scope of Tax Law's Public Policy Limitation for Charities, 5 FLA. TAX REV. 779, 841 (2002)).

122. Brennen, supra note 121, at 849. See id. at 848 (arguing that because the public policy doctrine "emanate[es] from Section 501(c)(3) of the ... Code" and is a statutory principle, "it is entirely inappropriate" for the IRS to look "almost exclu-

sively to constitutional law principles" rather than alternative sources such as state law to decide "when a charity violates established public policy"). *See also* Evelyn Brody, *Of Sovereignty and Subsidy: Conceptualizing the Charity Tax Exemption*, 23 J. CORP. L. 585 (1998) (conceptualizing exemption under Section 501(c)(3) as premised on the notion that charitable entities are "co-sovereigns" with the state); *but see* Buckles, *supra* note 114, at 430–33 (maintaining that limiting the public policy doctrine to federal public policy is a more rational approach).

123. Buckles, *supra* note 114, at 432. The public policy doctrine raises other questions as well. Is a pattern of behavior required or will a single violation suffice? Professor Buckles, who is critical of an expansive application of the public policy doctrine, speculates that "determining whether public policy is 'established' may be something like a game of darts":

> Acting in a manner that plainly violates (or causes another to violate) a statute, the Constitution, or an Executive Order is like hitting the "bull's eye"; it constitutes a breach of public policy. Acting in a manner that does not technically defy (or cause another to defy) any such authority is like hitting one of the concentric circles surrounding the bull's eye; one hit is not worth as much as striking the center-most point on the board, but multiple hits in one of the larger circles may equate to a single strike to the bull's eye.

Id. at 433. Also unclear is whether an organization that "commit[s] some illegal acts but still confer[s] an overall public benefit ... would violate the public policy doctrine. This judicial silence poses no small problem to those seeking clarity in the public policy doctrine." *Id.* at 410.

124. Even if punishing churches and religious organizations that oppose same-sex marriage is unlikely to be tax policy in the current administration, *see* Laura Spitz, *At the Intersection of North American Free Trade and Same-Sex Marriage*, 9 UCLA J. INT'L L. & FOREIGN AFF. 163, 178 & n.48 (2004) ("White House political adviser Karl Rove said after the November 2004 election that President Bush intends to continue seeking a constitutional amendment defining marriage as between a man and a woman.") (citations omitted), the public policy doctrine as constructed in *Bob Jones* does not foreclose future administrations from taking this position.

Of course, the federal Defense of Marriage Act (DOMA) will figure prominently in any public policy analysis. *See* 1 U.S.C. § 7; 28 U.S.C. § 1738C. It is conceivable, however, that the "clear public policy" of the state in which the organization operates will be marshaled in this analysis. *See* Buckles, *supra* note 114. It is also conceivable that the federal government's stance on same-sex marriage may change, either by judicial decision or legislation. *Compare* Larry Kramer, *Same-Sex Marriage, Conflict of Laws, and the Unconstitutional Public Policy Exception*, 106 Yale L.J. 1965 (1997) (predicting that DOMA will be found unconstitutional) *with* Mark D. Rosen, *Why the Defense of Marriage Act is not (Yet?) Unconstitutional:* Lawrence, *Full Faith and Credit, and the Many Societal Actors that Determine what the Constitution Requires*, MINN L. REV. 915, 999–1001 (concluding that the Defense of Marriage Act is constitutional). *See also* Michael R. Blood, *Dems iffy on gay marriage in debate*, LONG

BEACH PRESS-TELEGRAM, Aug 10, 2007, at 1A (reporting the stances on same-sex marriage of candidates for the Democratic nomination for president during a two-hour forum, the first time that major presidential candidates appeared on TV specifically to address gay issues).

125. Churches are automatically considered tax exempt; in contrast, religious organizations must apply to the IRS for recognition under Section 501(c)(3) unless their gross receipts do not normally exceed $5,000 annually. INTERNAL REVENUE SERVICE, *supra* note 98, at 3. While other Section 501(c)(3) entities must report their financial status, activities, and compensation paid to directors and officers on an Annual Information Report (Form 990), churches are exempt from filing annual informational returns. 26 U.S.C. § 6033 (a)(2) (2000). Congress imposed special limitations on how and when the IRS may audit churches. The IRS can only examine the church's religious activities to the extent necessary to determine whether the organization qualifies for church status, and may examine the church's records only to the extent necessary to determine whether it is liable for any additional internal revenue tax. *See* 26 U.S.C. § 7611(b)(1)(A) (2000); Reka Potgieter Hoff, *The Financial Accountability of Churches for Federal Income Tax Purposes: Establishment or Free Exercise*, 11 VA. TAX REV. 71, 75 (1991).

This hands-off approach for churches extends to deductions as well. For instance, the IRS has never challenged the right of a member of a church to deduct pew or synagogue fees even though there is a strong case for denying that deduction. *See* Douglas A. Kahn & Jeffrey H. Kahn, *"Gifts, Gafts, and Gefts"— The Income Tax Definition and Treatment of Private and Charitable "Gifts" and a Principled Policy Justification for the Exclusion of Gifts from Income*, 78 NOTRE DAME L. REV. 441 (2003).

126. *See* Johnny Rex Buckles, *Is the Ban on Participation in Political Campaigns by Charities Essential to Their Vitality and Democracy? A Reply to Professor Tobin*, 42 U. RICH. L. REV. (2008) (forthcoming).

127. Jason Felch and Patricia Ward Biederman, *Federal Probe Targets Political Activity at Churches, Nonprofits*, LOS ANGELES TIMES (November 8, 2005), 2005 WLNR 18004011.

128. *Id.*

129. *Id.*

130. Firings and other disciplinary actions against pharmacists who refuse to provide emergency contraceptives have dominated the news in recent years. *See, e.g.*, Rob Stein, *For Some, There is No Choice*, WASHINGTON POST, July 16, 2006 A06, *available at* www.washingtonpost.com/wp-dyn/content/article/2006/07/15/AR2006071500790 .html (last visited June 20, 2008); Leah Thorsen, *Druggists Suspended in Debate over Pill*, ST. LOUIS POST-DISPATCH, Nov. 30, 2005, at A1 (reporting that Walgreen's placed four Illinois pharmacists in the St. Louis area on unpaid leave for refusing to fill prescriptions for emergency contraception in violation of a rule imposed by Illinois Gov. Rod Blagojevich in April 2005 that requires Illinois pharmacies that sell contraceptives approved by the FDA to fill prescriptions for emergency birth control); Marilyn Gardner, *Pharmacist's Moral Beliefs vs. Women's Legal Rights*, CHRISTIAN SCI. MONITOR, Apr. 26, 2004,

at 11, *available at* www.csmonitor.com/2004/0426/p11s01-usju.html (last visited June 20, 2008) (reporting that a K-Mart pharmacist faced disciplinary hearings in Wisconsin after refusing to fill or transfer a woman's prescription for birth-control pills on the basis on the pharmacist's religious beliefs).

Some states explicitly protect the decision of a pharmacist or pharmacy to refuse to stock and/or dispense emergency contraceptives, following the traditional model of protecting a right of conscientious refusal. These include Arkansas, Georgia, Mississippi and South Dakota. *See* David A. Hyman & Robin Fretwell Wilson, *Health Care Regulation: The Year in Review, Searle Center on Regulation*, NORTHWESTERN UNIVERSITY SCHOOL OF LAW, *available at* www.law.northwestern.edu/searlecenter/papers/Hyman_Wilson_Annual_Rev_Final.pdf (last visited June 20, 2008). However, more states have mandated the provision of emergency contraceptives, either by statute, executive order, or pharmacy board regulation. *Id.* Over 20 states are still considering what action, if any, to take. *Id.*

131. *See* Appendix, Number 1.
132. *See* Appendix, Number 2.
133. *See* Appendix, Number 3.
134. *See* Appendix, Number 4.
135. *See* Appendix, Number 5.
136. *See* Appendix, Number 6.
137. *See* Appendix, Number 7.
138. *See* Appendix, Number 8.
139. *See* Appendix, Number 9.
140. *See* Appendix, Number 10.
141. *See* Appendix, Number 11.
142. *See* Appendix, Number 12.
143. *See* Appendix, Number 13.
144. *See* Appendix, Number 14.

145. Critics of conscience clauses lament that in many rural and traditionally conservative areas, the next closest pharmacy or hospital is miles away and not easily accessible. Adam Sonfield, *New Refusal Clauses Shatter Balance Between Provider "Conscience," Patient Needs*, THE GUTTMACHER REPORT (August 2004), *available at* www.guttmacher.org/pubs/tgr/07/3/gr070301.pdf (last visited June 20, 2008). I have argued elsewhere that these access claims lack sound empirical evidence, but that any concerns about barriers to access can be addressed with information-forcing rules, hardship exceptions to conscience clause protections, and prioritizing individual exemptions over institutional ones. *See* Wilson, *supra* note 59.

Recognizing that access issues are the dark underside of conscience clauses, some professional pharmacy groups believe we should do more to direct patients to willing providers. The American Pharmacists Association "recognizes the individual pharmacist's right to exercise conscientious refusal and supports the establishment of systems to ensure patient access to legally prescribed therapy without compromising the pharmacist's right of conscientious refusal." *American Pharmacists Ass'n, 2004 House of Delegates, Report of the Policy Review Committee, available at* www.pharmacist.com/AM/Template.cfm?section=About_AphA1&template=/MembersOnly.cfm&ContentID=2766 (last visited June 20, 2008).

146. *See* Appendix, Number 15.

147. Valley Hosp. Ass'n v. Mat-Su Coalition for Choice, 948 P.2d 963 (Alaska 1997).

148. *Id.* at 965, n.1.

149. *Id.* at 966.

150. *See infra* notes 157–161 and accompanying text (explaining why the hospital was quasi-public).

151. *Id.* at 965 n. 1 (quoting ALASKA STAT. § 18.16.010(b)).

152. *Id.* at 972.

153. *Id.* (quoting Brown v. Bd. of Educ., 349 U.S. 294, 300 (1955)).

154. *Id.*

155. *Id.*

156. *Id.* at 972, n. 20.

157. As part III explains, the scarcity of other providers should matter to the availability of conscience clause protection. In that instance, a compelling interest for positing a duty to assist then rests on proof of a real problem, not merely a theoretical problem. *Compare* Douglas Laycock, *Tax Exemptions for Racially Discriminatory Religious Schools*, 60 TEX. L. REV. 259, 274-276 (1982) (arguing that religious schools should be exempt from regulations prohibiting racial discrimination unless they educate such a large fraction of the local student body that they effectively substitute for the public school system or would preclude desegregation of the public schools); Douglas Laycock & Oliver S. Thomas, *Interpreting the Religious Freedom Restoration Act*, 73 TEX. L. REV. 209, 223 (1994) (arguing for similar exemptions with respect to refusals by landlords to rent to unmarried couples).

158. *Valley Hosp.*, 948 P.2d. at 970–71.

159. *Id.* at 970.

160. *Id.* at 971.

161. *See id.* at 966, 973 (affirming a superior court's order enjoining the hospital from "refusing to permit the facilities of Valley Hospital to be used for the performance of any lawful abortion procedure by qualified medical personnel").

162. 41 Iowa Op. Att'y Gen. 474, 478 (March 1, 1976).

163. *Id.* at 478.

164. Thomas v. Review Bd., 450 U.S. 707 (1981).

165. *Id.* at 709.

166. *Id.* at 710.

167. *Id.* at 712.

168. *Id.* at 715.

169. *Id.*

170. *Id.* at 717.

171. *See id.*

172. *See supra* notes 51–80 and accompanying text.

173. Presumably, the relationship between churches and individual clergy cannot be dictated by the government and, consequently, conscience clauses could not insulate individual clergy from repercussions at the hands of the church. *See infra* note 182 and accompanying text.

174. Chai R. Feldblum, *Moral Conflict and Conflicting Liberties, infra*, notes 131–132 and accompanying text.

175. *See infra* notes 196–215 and accompanying text (discussing how to balance competing moral claims and noting the value of information-forcing rules in avoiding a win-lose outcome).

176. Valley Hosp. Ass'n v. Mat-Su Coalition for Choice, 948 P.2d 963, 972 (Alaska 1997).

177. Bill Bowman, *Civil union denial spurs bias claim in NJ*, ASBURY PARK PRESS, June 21, 2007

178. Sarah Womack, *UK doctors seek opt-out in gay adoption cases*, LONDON TELE-GRAPH, July 2, 2007.

179. *Refusal to Artificially Inseminate 'Unmarried' Lesbian*, 47 NURSING LAW'S RE-GAN REPORT 7, (December 1, 2005). In this high-profile case, now before the California Supreme Court, specialists at North Coast Women's Health Center balked at artificially inseminating an existing patient of the practice, a lesbian woman, allegedly because of her sexual orientation. North Coast Women's Care Medical Group, Inc. v. Superior Court of San Diego County, 137 Cal. App. 4th 781 (2006). Benitez's doctors defended their refusal on religious grounds, claiming free exercise of religion as an affirmative defense. Benitez brought a motion to dismiss the defense, which the trial court granted. The appeals court reversed, concluding that there was a triable issue of fact as to whether the physicians' religiously motivated refusal was based solely on Benitez's marital status—a permissible grounds for refusal at the time—or whether it was based on her sexual orientation, in whole or in part. *North Coast*, at 647. Because the physicians assert an affirmative defense, the question before the California Supreme Court is whether there is "no triable issue of material fact as to the defense, and the moving party is entitled to judgment on the defense as a matter of law." North Coast Women's Care Medical Group, Inc. v. Superior Court of San Diego County, 134 Cal. App. 4th (2005), *reh'g granted.*

180. Simon Caldwell, *British cardinal says government is 'legislating for intolerance'*, CATHOLIC NEWS SERVICE, Mar. 29, 2007.

181. The state may not inquire into or review the internal decision making or governance of a religious institution. *See* Jones v. Wolf, 443 U.S. 595, 602 (1979); Serbian E. Orthodox Diocese v. Milivojevich, 426 U.S. 696 (1976).

182. Black v. Snyder, 471 N.W.2d 715, 720 (Minn. Ct. App. 1991). Similarly, a pastor's appointment and discharge were not reviewable because adjudication of the pastor's claims "would require an evaluation of scripture, doctrine, and moral principles." Singleton v. Christ the Servant Evangelical Lutheran Church, 541 N.W.2d 606, 611-12 (Minn. Ct. App. 1996). Likewise, individuals fired by church-owned

corporations because of nonaffiliation with the church's particular religion received no protection from dismissal. Corp. of Presiding Bishop of Church of Jesus Christ of Latter-Day Saints v. Amos, 483 U.S. 327 (1987).

183. For example, in addition to religious officials, Maryland state law allows a marriage ceremony to be performed by a clerk, a deputy clerk designated by the county administrative judge of the circuit court for the county, or a judge. MD. CODE ANN., FAM. LAW § 2-406(a)(2) (LexisNexis 2003).

184. See supra note 63–66 and accompanying text (discussing Chrisman v. Sisters of St. Joseph of Peace).

185. Feldblum, supra note 174, at notes 8, 132–133 and accompanying text.

186. Patricia Wen & Frank Phillips, Bishops to Oppose Adoption by Gays, BOSTON GLOBE, Feb. 16, 2006, at A1.

187. It is unclear whether the adopting parent was actively participating in a same-sex relationship. Compare Patricia Wen, Catholic Charities Stuns State, Ends Adoptions, BOSTON GLOBE, Mar. 11, 2006, at A1, available at www.bostonglobe.com/news/local/articles/2006/03/11/catholic_charities_stuns_state_ends_adoptions/ (last visited June 24, 2008) (finding that "approximately 13 children had been placed by Catholic Charities in gay households"), with Jerry Filteau, Catholic Charities in Boston Archdiocese to End Adoption Services, CATHOLIC NEWS SERVICE, Mar 13, 2006, available at www.catholicnews.com/data/stories/cns/0601456.htm (last visited June 24, 2008) (indicating that Catholic Charities "had arranged the adoption of 13 children by same-sex couples over the past 20 years"). After reports surfaced publicly about Catholic Charities's placement of thirteen children with lesbian or gay parents, the state's bishops directed Catholic agencies not to place children with gay or lesbian parents. Wen, supra. Catholic Charities' board had voted unanimously to continue to place children with lesbian and gay parents, but were overruled by the bishops, prompting eight members of the 42-member Catholic Charities board to resign. Patricia Wen, In Break from Romney, Healey Raps Gay Adoption Exclusion, BOSTON GLOBE, Mar. 3, 2006, at B4.

It is not surprising that an organization's leadership might veto an existing practice when it comes to their attention. Once the decision not to place children with same-sex couples was made, the question of an exemption arose.

188. 102 MASS. CODE REGS. § 1.03 (1) (2007) (requiring that adoption agencies "not discriminate in providing services to children and their families on the basis of race, religion, cultural heritage, political beliefs, national origin, marital status, sexual orientation, or disability").

189. Patricia Wen, Bishops Dealt Setback in Pursuit of Gay Adoption Exemption, BOSTON GLOBE, Feb. 17, 2006, at B3. But see Patricia Wen & Frank Phillips, Romney Shifts on Adoption by Gays, BOSTON GLOBE, Mar. 1, 2006, at B1 (noting that the governor "signaled new openness" to consider the bishops' request).

190. Wen, supra note 187. The Catholic bishops initially issued a public statement that they would seek relief from Massachusetts's regulatory requirements. See Statement of the Massachusetts Catholic Conference on Behalf of Archbishop Sean

P. O'Malley (Boston), Bishop George W. Coleman (Fall River), Bishop Timothy A. McDonnell (Springfiled), and Bishop Robert J. McManus (Worcester), *available at* www.thebostonpilot.com/articlearchives.asp?ID=2946 (last visited June 26, 2008). When relief was not forthcoming, however, the Catholic bishops discontinued Catholic Charities's adoption services altogether instead of engaging in a legal battle. *See* Minow, *supra* note 59, at 847.

191. One would think that this question would have arisen after *Loving v. Virginia* since interracial marriage was as divisive then as same-sex marriage is now. *See* Angela Williams, *Religious Influences in American Legislation:* Lawrence v. Texas, *The Right to Privacy, The Right to Choice, and The "Right to be Let Alone!"*, 7 J. L. Soc'y 196, 198–199 (2006). Interestingly, the experience after *Loving* provides little guidance to us here. There appear to be no cases after *Loving v. Virginia* in which clerks refused to issue licenses to, or judges refused to marry, interracial couples; nor are there any law reviews articles exploring how such refusals would be treated. In a single 1994 news report, an interracial couple threatened to sue Chester County, Tennessee, when county officials refused to marry them. *Interracial Couple Settles Over Rebuff on Marriage Rites*, MEMPHIS COMMERCIAL APPEAL, May 7, 1994, at A15. Chester County ultimately settled with the couple before they could bring suit. *Id.*

192. Memory McLeod, *Knights of Columbus aid commissioners who won't perform gay weddings: Service Club Pledges Support*, THE LEADER-POST, Apr. 17, 2007, *available at* www.canada.com/reginaleaderpost/news/sports/story.html?id=ab7789c1-5988-421d-bd3b-1ade424e87b1 (last accessed June 20, 2008) (reporting the statements of the Chief of Staff with Minister of Justice Frank Quennell's office).

193. *See* TEX. FAM. CODE ANN. § 2.203(a) (Vernon 2007) ("On receiving an unexpired marriage license, an authorized person *may* conduct the marriage ceremony as provided by this subchapter.") (emphasis added).

Some authorized celebrants may not want to marry couples for all sorts of reasons not having to do with their sexual orientation. For instance, they may believe that couples should receive pre-marital counseling before marrying. Any refusal to wed a same-sex couple may then raise factual questions about why the refusal occurred, leading to yet more litigation. *See* Hyman & Wilson, *supra* note 130.

194. The opinion was written partially in response to concerns by clergy that "'they might be put in the situation of performing civil unions against their will." Tina Kelley, *New Jersey Says Clerics Aren't Required to Unite Gay Couples*, N.Y. TIMES, Jan. 12, 2007, at B2. It exempts religious figures from this duty because of concerns about excessive entanglement between church and state. *Id.*

195. *See* Maureen K Bailey, *Contraceptive Insurance Mandates and Catholic Charities v. Superior Court of Sacramento: Towards a New Understanding of Women's Health*, 9 TEX. REV. L. & POL. 367, 370–371 (2005) (stating that the rights established in *Roe v. Wade* and *Griswold v. Connecticut* are negative rights); *but see* Elizabeth Price Foley, *Human Cloning and the Right to Reproduce* 65 ALB. L. REV. 625, 627–628 (2002) (acknowledging that many scholars believe a positive right to reproduce can be inferred from the case law).

196. *See supra* notes 181–82 and accompanying text.

197. *See* 68 Ill. Admin. Code 1330.91(k) (2006).

198. Jesse McKinley, *"I Do"? Oh No. Not Here You Don't*, N.Y. TIMES, June 13, 2208, *available at* www.nytimes.com/2008/06/13/us/13marriage.html (last visited June 24, 2008) (indicating that Kern County, California, will no longer solemnize any wedding vows for administrative and budgetary reasons, although couples in the county will still be able to acquire marriage licenses; County Clerk Ann K. Barnett "fully expects to be sued" for stopping the weddings); Marisa Lagos, *2 Counties to Halt All Weddings, Gay or Not*, S. F. CHRON., June 11, 2008, at A1 (reporting that Butte County, California, would no longer solemnize wedding vows, citing budgetary reasons, but stating that the decision was made long before the California Supreme Court's same-sex marriage decision came down; Merced County also announced a halt, but subsequently backed off the decision).

199. Neither is it inconceivable that a critical mass of clerks in a given office would exercise a conscientious refusal if provided the chance by the state. This may be especially true when the office of the clerk is an elected one.

Despite the possibility of hardship, locales in which everyone or nearly everyone will claim a moral objection should not occur very often. In urban areas, significant barriers to access are not likely to arise almost by definition; if opinion runs that strongly against same-sex marriage or civil unions, the state will simply put off-limits the recognition of these relationships. *See, e.g.*, Joshua K. Baker, SAME-SEX MAR-RIAGE: RECENT TRENDS IN PUBLIC OPINION, iMAPP POLICY BRIEF (April 29, 2005), *available at* www.marriagedebate.com/pdf/iMAPP.2005opinionupdate.pdf (last visited June 20, 2008) (tracing drops in public opinion supporting same-sex marriage after *Goodridge* to increasing support for legislative and constitutional bans on same-sex marriage). This, then, leaves pockets of resistance among voters that largely support same-sex marriage, which might occur in "red" minority areas in "blue" states, like upstate New York or Orange County, California.

200. *Compare* S.C. CODE ANN. REGS. § 20–1–220 (2006) ("No marriage license may be issued unless a written application has been filed ... at least twenty-four hours before the issuance of the license.") *with* WIS. STAT. § 765.08 (2007) ("no marriage license may be issued within 5 days of application for the marriage license.").

201. For instance, the requisite waiting period for same-sex couples could be measured from the time they present at the office, rather than when the application is completed and filed.

202. Conscientious objectors may also assert their own constitutional claims of free exercise, which are discussed at length elsewhere in this volume, while same-sex couples may assert a violation of the Establishment Clause. Legislative exemptions from certain laws for religious organizations have survived Establishment Clause attacks. In *Amos*, for example, the United States Supreme Court concluded that an exception for religious organizations in a law prohibiting religious discrimination in the workplace did not violate the Establishment Clause. Corp. of Presiding Bishop of Church of Jesus Christ of Latter-Day Saints v. Amos, 483 U.S. 327, 336 (1987). *See*

also Maher v. Roe, 432 U.S. 464 (1977) (concluding over Establishment Clause challenges that Title XIX of the Social Security Act does not require the funding of non-therapeutic abortions as a condition of participation in the joint federal-state Medicaid program).

203. *See e.g.*, *Marriage Commissioners*, THE EVANGELICAL FELLOWSHIP OF CANADA, *available at* www.evangelicalfellowship.ca/NetCommunity/Page.aspx?&pid=1268&srcid=732 (last accessed June 20, 2008) (reporting that a marriage commissioner in Saskatchewan, who was summoned before a Human Rights Tribunal for refusing to marry a same-sex couple, had been marriage commissioner for almost 25 years before he was approached to do the marriage).

204. Likewise, the decision by the county clerks in Butte and Kerr counties in California not to solemnize marriage for any couples, whether heterosexual or same-sex couples, also raises a barrier to marriage. *See supra* note 198.

205. How remote in time and place the willing celebrant can be and still be considered "available" is a question legislatures will have to decide.

206. Of course, a well-defined body of employment law may address this kind of refusal, in part. Title VII of the Civil Rights Act of 1964 exempts religious employers from the prohibition on religion-based discrimination "with respect to the employment of individuals of a particular religion to perform work connected with the carrying on by such corporation, association, educational institution, or society of its activities." *See* Lupu & Tuttle, *supra* note 32, at n. 22.

207. *See* Robin Fretwell Wilson, *A Matter of Conviction: Moral Clashes Over Same-Sex Adoption*, 22 BYU J. L & SOC. POL 475 (2008); *infra* note 211–215 and accompanying text.

208. Nancy K. Ota, *Queer Recount*, 64 ALB. L. REV. 889 (tallying the number of states that as of 2001 provided "legal protection from discrimination based on sexual orientation in public accommodations, education, housing, extension of credit, and union practices").

209. Anita Bernstein, *For and Against Marriage: A Revision*, 102 MICH. L. REV. 129, 141, 146, 149, 180 (2003).

210. States could, of course, choose another touchstone for the receipt of these benefits. Given the significant empirical evidence, however, that "marriage produces real differences in investment and outcomes for children in marital households," with similar gains for the adults, reducing state support of marriage would be precipitous and unwise. *See* Robin Fretwell Wilson, *Evaluating Marriage: Does Marriage Matter to the Nurturing of Children?*, 42 SAN DIEGO L. REV. 847, 879 (2005).

211. Adoption placement agencies do serve a public function, as do hospitals and healthcare providers.

212. *See* Michael Levenson, *Workers rush to fill void left by Boston agency's decision*, BOSTON GLOBE (March 11, 2006), *available at* www.boston.com/news/local/articles/2006/03/11/workers_rush_to_fill_void_left_by_boston_agencys_decision/ (last visited June 20, 2008). The Boston Globe reported that "Catholic Charities found more homes for foster children than any other private agency in Massachusetts"—many of

them the "most troubled foster children, including those with HIV and AIDS, mental and emotional problems, and histories of abuse," and therefore the "hardest children to adopt." The twenty-eight children placed by Catholic Charities in 2005 "was more than any of the other seven agencies under contract with DSS." Catholic Charities also "played another important role in helping children find homes: [counseling] workers at other agencies, in desperate need of advice on how to handle a difficult child or find a suitable family."

213. *See id.* (predicting that after Catholic Charities' exodus, "[f]oster children could face longer waits in an already backlogged system, and specialists say other agencies will have to scramble to pick up the Catholic Charities' caseload. Whether they can replace its network of seasoned, caring social workers is another question").

214. *See id.* The adoption director for one Massachusetts placement agency called the outcome "a shame because it is certainly going to mean that fewer children from foster care are going to find permanent homes." *Id.* The president of the Massachusetts Society for the Prevention of Cruelty to Children called it "a tragedy for kids." *Id.*

215. Jonathan Petre, *Church pulls out of Catholic agencies over 'gay equality' adoption law*, DAILY MAIL, May 24, 2008, *available at* www.dailymail.co.uk/news/article-1021721/Church-pulls-Catholic-agencies-gay-equality-adoption-law.html (last visited June 19, 2008).

Chapter Four: Douglas W. Kmiec

1. Transcript of Oral Argument, Rumsfeld v. Forum for Academic and Institutional Rights, Inc., No. 04-1152, 2005 WL 3387694 (U.S., argued Dec. 6, 2005) [hereinafter *FAIR Transcript*].

2. Bob Jones Univ. v. United States, 461 U.S. 574 (1983).

3. *FAIR* Transcript, 2005 WL 3387694, at 42.

4. Bob Jones Univ. v. United States, 461 U.S. 574 (1983) [hereinafter *Bob Jones*].

5. Linda Greenhouse, *Justices Weigh Military's Access to Law Schools*, THE NEW YORK TIMES, Dec. 7, 2005, at 1 (discussing the oral argument in *FAIR*).

6. The Court in a unanimous (8-0) decision upheld the requirement of equal access, rejecting FAIR's speech and association claims. Rumsfeld v. Forum for Academic and Institutional Rights, Inc. (FAIR), 547 U.S. 47 (2006).

7. Eugene Volokh, *Same-Sex Marriage and Slippery Slopes*, 33 HOFSTRA L. REV. 1155, 1178 (2005).

8. Larry W. Yackle, *Parading Ourselves: Freedom of Speech at the Feast of St. Patrick*, 73 B.U. L. REV. 791, 792 (1993).

9. Douglas W. Kmiec, *The Procreative Case Against Same-Sex Marriage*, 32 HASTINGS CONST. L. Q. 653 (Fall 2004 / Winter 2005). The Maryland Supreme Court has fully accepted the procreative case against same-sex marriage, rejecting claims premised upon fundamental right/due process or equal protection (gender or sexual orientation). *See* Conaway v. Deane, 401 Md. 219, 932 A.2d 571 (2007).

10. Nicholas A. Mirkay, *Is It 'Charitable' to Discriminate? The Necessary Transformation of Section 501(c)(3) into the Gold Standard for Charities*, 2007 WIS. L. REV. 45 (2007).

11. Regan v. Taxation with Representation of Washington, 461 U.S. 540 (1983). The Court reasoned that the Congress need not subsidize lobbying activity with an exemption from taxation and a related nonprofit could retain deductibility of contributions as well if it limited itself to nonlobbying activity.

12. Employment Div. v. Smith, 494 U.S. 872 (1990).

13. Eugene Volokh, *Freedom of Expressive Association and Government Subsidies*, 58 STAN. L. REV. 1919 (2006) (finding generally that tax exemptions can be denied if sexual orientation is added to the prohibited categories of discrimination, on the theory that government has no duty to subsidize constitutionally protected association).

14. Religious Freedom Restoration Act, 42 U.S.C. § 2000bb-1 (2000); invalidated as to state laws only in City of Boerne v. Flores, 521 U.S. 507 (1997); applied validly to federal law in Gonzales v. O Centro Espirita Beneficente Uniao Do Vegetal, 546 U.S. 418 (2006).

15. *But see In re* Marriage Cases, 183 P.3d 384 (Cal. 2008) (declaring sexual orientation to be a suspect, highly protected class as a matter of state *constitutional* interpretation in California; that constitutional status makes it immune from state statutes shielding religious freedom). Recall as well that the United States Supreme Court had already settled that Congress lacks federal constitutional authority to protect religious freedom generally vis-à-vis the states by means of federal statute. *See* City of Boerne v. Flores, 521 U.S. 507 (1997) (holding Congress exceeded its enforcement power under Section Five of the Fourteenth Amendment in enacting the Religious Freedom Restoration Act of 1993).

16. Associated Press, *Obama wants 'don't ask' repealed*, April 10, 2008, *available at* www.cnn.com/2008/POLITICS/04/10/obama.gay.ap/index.html (last visited June 29, 2008).

17.The conference was held on December 15, 2005. *See* Scholars' Conference on Same-Sex Marriage and Religious Liberty, May 4, 2006, *available at* www.becketfund.org/index.php/article/494.html (last visited June 29, 2008).

18. 26 U.S.C. § 501(a) (passed 1/11/06). This Section states: "An organization described in subsection (c) or (d) or section 401(a) [26 U.S.C. § 401(a)] shall be exempt from taxation under this subtitle [26 U.S.C. §§ 1 et seq.] unless such exemption is denied under section 502 or 503 [26 U.S.C. § 502 or 503]."

19. 26 U.S.C. § 501(c)(3).

20. *Id.*

21. *Id.*

22. 26 U.S.C. § 170(a), (c). Section 170 outlines charitable contributions and gifts. Section 170(a) states that the general rule is that "There shall be allowed as a deduction any charitable contribution . . . " Section 170(c) defines a charitable contribution as

"a contribution or gift to or for the use of . . . [a] corporation, trust, or community chest, fund, or foundation . . . organized and operated exclusively for religious, charitable, scientific, literary, or educational purposes, or to foster national or international amateur sports competition (but only if no part of its activities involve the provision of athletic facilities or equipment), or for the prevention of cruelty to children or animals . . . no part of the net earnings of which inures to the benefit of any private shareholder or individual."

23. *Bob Jones, supra* note 4.

24. *Id.* at 586. The IRS had maintained this position long before it litigated in *Bob Jones. See* Green v. Connally, 330 F. Supp. 1150, 1179-80 (D.D.C. 1971) (enjoining the Service from granting exempt status to racially discriminatory private schools in Mississippi, as the schools' violation of the public policy against discrimination prevented them from being "charitable"); Rev. Rul. 71-447, 1971-2 C.B. 230 (stating that "a school . . . must be a common law charity in order to be exempt" under § 501(c)(3)).

25. *Bob Jones*, 461 U.S. at 586.

26. *Id.* at 591; *see also* Restatement (Second) of Trusts § 377 (1959) ("A charitable trust cannot be created for a purpose which is illegal.").

27. *Bob Jones*, 461 U.S. at 591 n.18.

28. *Id.* at 593.

29. Brown v. Board of Educ., 347 U.S. 483 (1954).

30. *Bob Jones*, 461 U.S. at 592–96.

31. *Id.* at 604 n.29 (citing Bob Jones Univ. v. United States, 468 F. Supp. 890, 894 (1978)).

32. *Id.* at 604.

33. *Id.* at 604 n. 30 (quoting McGowan v. Maryland, 366 U.S. 422 (1961), and citing Harris v. McRae, 448 U.S. 297, 319–20 (1980)).

34. *Id.* at 597–98.

35. *Id.* at 605. The Court reached an identical result in the companion case to *Bob Jones. See* Goldsboro Christian Sch., Inc. v. United States, 461 U.S. 574 (1983) (denying a tax exemption to a school that maintained racially discriminatory admissions policies for its kindergarten through high school program).

36. Robin Fretwell Wilson, *Matters of Conscience: Lessons for Same-Sex Marriage from the Healthcare Context, supra*, note 111 and accompanying text (citing I.R.S. Priv. Ltr. Rul. 891001 (Nov. 30, 1988)).

37. Chevron, U.S.A., Inc. v. NRDC, Inc., 467 U.S. 837 (1984).

38. United States v. Mead Corp., 533 U.S. 218 (2001).

39. In Hospital Corp. of America & Subsidiaries v. Comm'r., 348 F.3d 136 (6th Cir. 2003), the court observed:

In *Mead Corporation*, the Court found that Congress had not implicitly delegated law-interpreting authority through the 10,000 to 15,000 tariff rulings made each year by forty-six different Customs offices without notice and comment procedures. The Court made clear, however, that while most of the Supreme Court cases applying *Chevron* involved notice-and-comment rulemaking or formal adjudication, "the want of such procedure . . . does not decide the case, for we have sometimes found reasons for *Chevron* deference even when no such administrative formality was required and none was afforded." The temporary regulations involved in this case were arrived at centrally by the Treasury Department after careful consideration. They were issued pursuant to statutory authority to "prescribe" needful rules and regulations. The regulation was "interpretive" in the same sense that the regulation in *Chevron* was interpretive—it gave content to ambiguous statutory terms. Congress clearly intended that the Treasury Department do so, and *Chevron* deference is therefore appropriate.

Hospital Corp., 348 F. 3d at 144–45 (citations omitted).

40. The racial discrimination limit also did not emerge suddenly in *Bob Jones*, and it seemed at first to draw a distinction between so-called benign and hurtful uses of race. For example, six years before *Bob Jones*, the IRS ruled that exempt status could be granted to a trade school exclusively for American Indians. Rev. Rul. 77–272, (1977). This type of "affirmative action" admission practice was not the "type of racial restriction that is contrary to Federal public policy," as it was "designed to implement certain statutorily defined Federal policy goals that are not in conflict with Federal public policy against racial discrimination in education." *Id.* at 4; *see* Adult Indian Vocational Training Act of 1956, Pub. L. No. 84-959, § 1, 70 Stat. 986, 986 (1956) (codified as amended at 25 U.S.C. § 309 (2004), providing for federal funds to be used to finance job training programs for adult American Indians). By contrast, shortly before *Bob Jones*, the United States Court of Appeals for the District of Columbia sustained the denial of exemption eligibility for an organization that sought to demonstrate the inferiority of minorities to white Americans of European ancestry. National Alliance v. United States, 710 F.2d 868 (D.C. Cir. 1983).

41. Pre-*Bob Jones*, the IRS denied an exemption to a world peace group since it sponsored demonstrations "in which demonstrators are urged to commit violations of local ordinances and breaches of public order." Rev. Rul. 75-384 (1975). The IRS commented that "the generation of criminal acts increases the burdens of government, thus frustrating a well recognized charitable goal, *i.e.*, relief of the burdens of government." *Id.*

42. Church of Scientology of Cal. v. Commissioner, 83 T.C. 381, 503 (1984), *aff'd*, 823 F.2d 1310 (9th Cir. 1987) (limited on other grounds).

43. *Id.* at 505.

44. Tech. Adv. Mem. 89-10-001 (Mar. 20, 1989); PLR 8910001 (PLR 1988). Note that pursuant to Section 6110(j)(3) of the Internal Revenue Code, "[t]his [private ruling] may not be used or cited as precedent."

45. Tech. Adv. Mem. 89-10-001, *supra* note 44, at 7.

46. *See generally* Oliver S. Thomas, *The Power to Destroy: The Eroding Constitutional Arguments for Church Tax Exemption and the Practical Effect on Churches*, 22 CUMB. L. REV. 605 (1992); David A. Brennen, *Charities and the Constitution: Evaluating the Role of Constitutional Principles in Determining the Scope of Tax Law's Public Policy Limitation for Charities*, 5 FLA. TAX. REV. 779, 840 (2002); and Kenneth C. Halcom, *Taxing God*, 38 MCGEORGE L. REV. 729 (2007).

47. Gen. Couns. Mem. 39,800 (Oct. 25, 1989) (IRS GCM 1989). Note that "[t]his [private ruling] document is not to be relied upon or otherwise cited as precedent by taxpayers."

48. *Id.* at 10.

49. *See* Cooper v. Aaron, 358 U.S. 1 (1958).

50. *Bob Jones*, 461 U.S. at 596 n.21.

51. *Id.* at 598.

52. Lawrence v. Texas, 539 U.S. 558 (2003).

53. Bowers v. Hardwick, 478 U.S. 186 (1986).

54. *Lawrence*, 539 U.S. at 571.

55. 1997 FSA LEXIS 478 (April 23, 1997) (Note, "[t]his document is not to be relied upon or otherwise cited as precedent").

56. *Id.* at 2.

57. Wilson, *supra* note 36, at note 88.

58. Lawrence v. Texas, 539 U.S. 558 (2003).

59. Goodridge v. Dep't of Pub. Health, 798 N.E.2d 941 (Mass. 2003).

60. *In re* Marriage Cases, 183 P.3d 384 (Cal. 2008).

61. Twenty-seven states have constitutional amendments explicitly barring the recognition of same-sex marriage. By statute, forty-one states restrict marriage to two persons of the opposite sex; six of these forty-one states recognize unions between same-sex partners but call them something other than "marriage." *See* Christine Vestal, Calif. Gay Marriage Ruling Sparks New Debate (June 12, 2008), *available at* www.stateline.org/live/details/story?contentId=310206 (last visited July 24, 2008).

62. Unitarian Universalist Association, "States Facing Constitutional Amendments Banning Same-Sex Marriage," *available at* www.uua.org/news/2004/freedomtomarry/state_ballot_initiatives.html (last visited June 29, 2008) (listing states that added constitutional amendments on the 2004 ballot, including Arkansas, Georgia, Kentucky, Louisiana, Michigan, Mississippi, Missouri, Montana, North Dakota, Ohio, Oklahoma, Oregon, and Utah).

63. Defense of Marriage Act, 28 U.S.C. § 1738C (2003) ("No State, territory, or possession of the United States, or Indian tribe, shall be required to give effect to any public act, record, or judicial proceeding of any other State, territory, possession, or tribe respecting a relationship between persons of the same sex that is treated as a marriage under the laws of such other State, territory, possession, or tribe, or a right or claim arising from such relationship.").

64. Boy Scouts of Am. v. Dale, 530 U.S. 640 (2000).

65. Walz v. Tax Comm'r, 397 U.S. 664 (1970).

66. *Id.* at 675.

67. *Id.* at 690.

68. South Dakota v. Dole, 483 U.S. 203 (1987).

69. Rumsfeld v. FAIR, 547 U.S. 47 (2006).

70. When the government disburses funds to convey a governmental message, it may take steps to ensure that its message is not garbled, distorted, or in the case of

the law schools, ignored by a grantee. Rust v. Sullivan, 500 U.S. 173, 196–200 (1991).

71. Boris I. Bittker, *Churches, Taxes, and the Constitution*, 78 YALE L. J. 1285, 1290 (1969) ("A[n] . . . analysis of the income of religious organizations might lead to the conclusion that the beneficiaries [of the parish] are too diffuse for a satisfactory imputation of the group's income to individuals, and so divergent in economic status that it would be difficult to establish a fair average rate at which to tax the church as their surrogate.").

72. *Id.* at 1290–91.

73. Jonathan Turley, *An Unholy Union: Same-Sex Marriage and the Use of Governmental Programs to Penalize Religious Groups with Unpopular Practices, supra,* note 72 and accompanying text.

74. *Bob Jones*, 461 U.S. at 609 (Powell, J., concurring).

75. *Id.*

76. *Id.* at 592 n.18 (majority opinion).

77. *Id.* at 592.

78. Recently, the *New York Times* reported that a Methodist association lost its state tax exemption when it denied the use of a meeting house for a lesbian civil union ceremony. The matter is in litigation, but the taxing authorities have taken the position that if the property is not open to all, it is not worthy of a subsidy. The association has raised a free exercise objection in federal court, but in the meantime, the association's tax bill may increase by $500,000. The taxing authorities showed little or no cognizance of the subsidy/exemption distinction referenced in the text. Jill P. Capuzzo, *Group Loses Tax Break Over Gay Union Issue,* THE NEW YORK TIMES, *available at* www.nytimes.com/2007/09/18/nyregion/18grove.html (last visited June 29, 2008).

79. Professor Turley aptly notes that eliminating altogether the public policy exception for tax exemption "requires an element of courage . . . [since] it means that racist and anti-Semitic citizens can form tax-exempt organizations. . . ." Turley, *supra* note 73, at note 78 and accompanying text. The analysis offered in the text of this chapter assumes this level of courage to be politically unlikely. For this reason, while it might be analytically tidy to eliminate any temptation to allocate tax exemptions on viewpoint grounds, it is unnecessary to achieve that full step in order to protect the church. The church fits the common law definition of a charity, and there is no common law support for same-sex marriage. There is no tenable basis to deny the church's tax exemption. Thus, churches should be unaffected even if the government retains the ability selectively to deny a tax exemption to organizations on the basis of hateful conduct. Refusing to sanction a conception of marriage unknown to most of American, if not western, history is hardly the equivalent of sexual harassment or the racial targeting of a person for criminal assault. *Compare* Wisconsin v. Mitchell, 508 U.S. 476 (1993) (distinguishing a government penalty enhancement for unpopular or even hateful expression from a penalty enhancement aimed at conduct that is not protected by the First Amendment).

80. *Bob Jones,* 461 U.S. at 591.

81. David Boaz has intriguingly argued for "privatizing" marriage by allowing couples to form their own contracts or participate in the religious ceremonies of their choice without state license. *See* David Boaz, *Privatize Marriage: A simple solution to the gay-marriage debate,* SLATE, *available at* http://patriot.net/~crouch/act/boaz.html (last visited June 29, 2008). State involvement would be limited to enforcement as with any other private contract. The Boaz proposal fails to recognize the extent to which marriage is not merely a private matter but the assumption of duty to community, and a promise to educate responsibly and care for offspring—matters in which the public has a profound interest well beyond other matters of private contract. *See generally* Douglas W. Kmiec, *Marriage and Family, in* NEVER A MATTER OF INDIFFERENCE (Peter Berkowitz ed., 2003).

82. A state-by-state compilation of these laws can be found at: www.sevenplanes.org/laws1.htm (last visited June 29, 2008). In California, for example, any priest, minister, or rabbi of any religious denomination, of the age of 18 years or over, may perform marriages. Ministers must complete the marriage license and return it to the county clerk within 4 days after the marriage.

83. Opinion No. 81-210, 64 Ops. Cal. Atty. Gen. 409 (Cal.A.G. 1981).

84. *See, e.g.,* Ligonia v. Buxton, 2 Me. 102 (1822) (holding that a marriage was void where it had been solemnized by a minister who had been ordained by an unincorporated religious society, and was not an ordained minister of the gospel within the meaning of a pertinent act. Furthermore, the court pointed out that the marriage was invalid because a ceremony had taken place at the home of a minister, which home was in a town in which neither party resided, in direct contravention of controlling laws); Ravenal v. Ravenal, 72 Misc. 2d 100 (N.Y. 1972) (invalidating a marriage performed by the mail-order minister of the Universal Life Church which the court noted did not have an actual church or meeting place, and it was not presided over by a minister or other person who was authorized to perform marriages, baptisms, and the like); State v. Lynch, 272 S.E.2d 349 (N.C. 1980) (marriage performed by Catholic layman invalid).

85. Burton v. Wilmington Parking Authority, 365 U.S. 715 (1961), as modified by American Mfrs. Mut. Ins. Co. v. Sullivan, 526 U.S. 40 (1999) (holding that Burton's "joint participation test" has been refined by legal developments that "established that privately owned enterprises providing services that the State would not necessarily provide," such as utilities, workers' compensation, and nursing, "even though they are extensively regulated, do not fall within the ambit of *Burton,*" internal citations omitted).

86. Edmonson v. Leesville Concrete Co., Inc., 500 U.S. 614 (1991).

87. Rendell-Baker v. Kohn, 457 U.S. 830 (1982) (private school not state actor because schooling is not exclusive function of the government).

88. West v. Atkins, 487 U.S. 42 (1988) (private prison doctor considered a state actor in light of the limited choice of the prison population for medical care).

89. Rendell-Baker v. Kohn, 457 U.S. 830 (1982) (practice of a private school to provide education for special needs students did not make it a state actor since there was no tradition of public provision of special education).

90. Meister v. Moore, 96 U.S. 76 (1877).

91. Brentwood Acad. v. Tenn. Secondary Sch. Ath. Ass'n, 531 U.S. 288 (2001).

92. *Id.* at 296.

93. Norwood v. Harrison, 413 U.S. 455 (1973).

94. *See id.* at 469–70.

95. Lown v. Salvation Army, Inc., 393 F. Supp. 2d 223, 236 (S.D.N.Y.2005).

96. Boy Scouts of America v. Till, 136 F. Supp. 2d 1295 (S.D. Fla. 2001) (school board can refuse to endorse or embrace the participation of the scouts in the schools, but it may not exclude the scouts from the school as a limited public forum), *but see* Evans v. City of Berkeley, 129 P.3d 394 (Cal. 2006) (holding that a citywide policy of excluding from a public subsidy groups that discriminate based on sexual orientation did not constitute targeting of a certain viewpoint, because its purpose was not to punish a private speaker's message but to protect individuals from discrimination).

97. *See supra* notes 14–15 and notes 65–79 and accompanying text (discussing the application of federal RFRA as well as the discussion of the difference between an exemption and a subsidy).

98. Serbian Eastern Orthodox Diocese v. Milivojevich, 426 U.S. 696, 713 (1976).

99. Rockwell v. Roman Catholic Archdiocese of Boston, 2002 WL 31432673 (D.N.H. 2002) (unpublished).

100. Employment Div. v. Smith, 494 U.S. 872 (1990).

101. E.E.O.C. v. Roman Catholic Diocese of Raleigh, N.C., 213 F.3d 795 (4th Cir. 2000) ("All circuits to have addressed the question have recognized the continuing vitality of the [ministerial] exception after the Supreme Court's decision" in *Smith*); Combs v. Central Texas Annual Conf. of United Methodist Church, 173 F.3d 343 (5th Cir. 1999); Gellington v. Christian Methodist Episcopal Church, Inc., 203 F.3d 1299 (11th Cir. 2000); *see also* Bryce v. Episcopal Church in the Diocese of Colorado, 289 F.3d 648, 656–57 (10th Cir. 2002) (dicta).

102. Allen v. Wright, 468 U.S. 737 (1984).

103. Roman Catholic Archbishop of Los Angeles v. Superior Court, 131 Cal. App. 4th 417, 433 (Cal. App. 2005).

104. Russell J. Upton, *Bob Jonesing Baden-Powell: Fighting the Boy Scouts of America's Discriminatory Practices By Revoking Its State-Level Tax-Exempt Status*, 50 AM. U. L. REV. 793 (2001) [hereinafter Upton].

105. *Id.* at 817 (citing Walz v. Tax Comm'n, 397 U.S. 664 (1970)).

106. Simon v. Eastern Kentucky Welfare Rights Org., 426 U.S. 26 (1976) (no standing to challenge favorable tax treatment given to nonprofit which did not supply the level of indigent non-emergency support desired by the complainant).

107. *Dale*, 530 U.S. at 661.

108. Boy Scouts of Am. v. Wyman, 335 F.3d 80 (2d Cir. 2003) (scouts excluded from charitable fund-raising campaign).

109. Regan v. Taxation with Representation of Washington, 461 U.S. 540 (1983).

110. *Wyman*, 335 F.3d at 91–93.

111. RAV v. City of St. Paul, 505 U.S. 377, 385 (1992).

112. Madsen v. Women's Health Ctr., 512 U.S. 753, 762–63 (1994).

113. *Cf.,* Vatican's statement including homosexuals in seminary training if chastity maintained for three or more years.

114. *Upton, supra* note 104, at 848–850, discussing the various private penalties exacted against the BSA.

115. *Id.* at 857–858.

116. Employment Div. v. Smith, 494 U.S. 872 (1990).

117. Douglas Laycock, *Tax Exemptions for Racially Discriminatory Religious Schools,* 60 TEX. L. REV. 259, 272–73 (1982).

118. Bruce N. Bagni, *Discrimination in the Name of the Lord: A Critical Evaluation of Discrimination by Religious Organizations,* 79 COLUM. L. REV. 1514, 1549 (1979).

119. James Madison, *Memorial and Remonstrance Against Religious Assessments, in* THE SUPREME COURT ON CHURCH AND STATE 18–19 (Robert A. Alley ed., 1988).

120. Hence, the longstanding religious exemption from Title VII's prohibition against discrimination in employment. 42 U.S.C. § 2000e-1(a). Following a 1972 amendment, the exemption applies to a religious organization whether or not it is engaged in religious activities. The exemption has been upheld as constitutional against an Establishment Clause challenge. Corporation of the Presiding Bishop of the Church of Jesus Christ of Latter-Day Saints v. Amos, 483 U.S. 327 (1987). Likewise, Congress exempted religious organizations from an nondiscrimination provision of the District of Columbia as it related to homosexuals. District of Columbia Appropriations Act of 1990, Pub. L. No. 101-168, 103 Stat. 1267, 1284 (1989). The exemption resulted from litigation against Georgetown, which refused to formally recognize a gay student group. The court held that formal recognition was not required, but extension of similar benefits as given other student groups was required. Gay Rights Coalition of Georgetown University Law Center v. Georgetown Univ., 536 A.2d 1 (D.C. 1987). *Cf.,* Dayton Christian Schs. v. Ohio Civ. Rts. Comm'n., 766 F.2d 932 (6th Cir. 1985) (Christian school dismissed teacher who had young children at home; civil rights commission asserted authority to resolve dispute). Reversing the trial court, the United States Court of Appeals for the Sixth Circuit in *Dayton* found for the school's right not to employ a teacher who disobeyed church teaching and jeopardized the school's ability to transmit that teaching to students. The United States Supreme Court reversed the Sixth Circuit on the grounds that the court should not have intervened in an on-going state proceeding, thereby leaving the freedom of religion issue unaddressed. Ohio Civ. Rts. Comm'n v. Dayton Christian Schs., 477 U.S. 619 (1986). *But see* Ganzy v. Allen Christian Sch., 995 F. Supp. 340, 348 (E.D.N.Y. 1998); Dolter v. Wahlert High Sch., 483 F. Supp. 266 (N.D. Iowa 1980) (denials of motions for summary judgment, limiting the ability of religious schools to dismiss unmarried, pregnant teachers on the characterization that such was gender discrimination).

121. For a thoughtful critique of unthinkingly favoring nondiscrimination laws over civil liberties, see DAVID E. BERNSTEIN, YOU CAN'T SAY THAT!: THE GROWING THREAT TO CIVIL LIBERTIES FROM ANTIDISCRIMINATION LAWS (Cato Institute 2003).

Professor Bernstein argues for keeping the nondiscrimination categories limited and broadening religious exemptions. *Id.* at 163.

Chapter Five: Chai R. Feldblum

1. An earlier version of this chapter was presented at a symposium at Brooklyn Law School and is published at 72 BROOKLYN L. REV. 61 (2006). This chapter was also delivered, in an abbreviated draft form, at a Becket Fund for Religious Liberty meeting in 2005. I am indebted to the research assistance of Amy Simmerman and Alyssa Rayman-Read for this version of the chapter.

2. *See, e.g.*, Everson v. Bd. of Educ., 330 U.S. 1, 8–14 (1947) (discussing historical reasons for the First Amendment, including the early Americans' desire to escape the "bondage" of European laws that compelled citizens to attend and support government-favored religions, and the colonial governments' practice of taxing citizens to pay for, among other things, ministers' salaries and the construction of churches).

3. As a practical matter, of course, current constitutional doctrine would provide minimal protection to any individual who experienced a civil rights law as burdening his or her religious beliefs or practices. Under the United States Supreme Court's decision in *Employment Division v. Smith*, 494 U.S. 872 (1990), a neutral law that burdens religious beliefs will be sustained as long as it is rationally related to a legitimate governmental purpose. But my argument is not designed simply to offer religious people a "second bite at the apple" post-*Smith*. Rather, as I hope to make clear in this chapter, I believe it is more *appropriate* to analyze religious belief claims as belief liberty claims, and not to elevate religious beliefs over beliefs derived from nonreligious sources.

4. Washington v. Glucksberg, 521 U.S. 702, 752–89 (1997) (Souter, J., concurring).

5. Among the law review articles and notes that have been written on this issue (all from the perspective of free exercise claims), some have suggested a balancing of interests, while others have focused on justifying either the religious interest or the nondiscrimination perspective. Surprisingly to me, I found a limited number of articles on the subject overall. *See, e.g.*, Richard F. Duncan, *Who Wants to Stop the Church: Homosexual Rights Legislation, Public Policy, and Religious Freedom*, 69 NOTRE DAME L. REV. 393, 438, 444 (1994) (arguing that nondiscrimination legislation based on sexual orientation is not a compelling interest like gender or race because homosexuality is still "morally controversial" and government should not legislate a particular view of sexual morality); Marie A. Failinger, *Remembering Mrs. Murphy: A Remedies Approach to the Conflict Between Gay/Lesbian Renters and Religious Landlords*, 29 CAP. U. L. REV. 383, 425–28 (2001) (proposing a remedies approach under which a landlord would be held liable for discrimination based on religious beliefs, but under which damages would be limited, so as to recognize and honor the landlord's religious beliefs, discourage frivolous claims challenging those religious beliefs, and strike a balance between the parties' "consciences"); Harlan Loeb & David Rosenberg, *Fundamental Rights in Conflict: The Price of a Maturing Democracy*, 77 N.D. L.

REV. 27, 49 (2001) (suggesting individual religiously based exemptions that could be overridden by a state's compelling interest in limited circumstances); Maureen E. Markey, *The Landlord/Tenant Free Exercise Conflict in a Post-RFRA World*, 29 RUTGERS L.J. 487, 549–52 (1998) (suggesting proposals for a modification or replacement of the compelling state interest test in free exercise cases that have the hallmarks of voluntary commercial activity and third party harm); Maureen E. Markey, *The Price of Landlord's "Free" Exercise of Religion: Tenant's Right to Discrimination-Free Housing and Privacy*, 22 FORDHAM URB. L.J. 699, 702–03 (1995) (arguing against individual religiously based exemptions from civil rights laws because allowing free exercise claims to trump civil rights laws could be the death knell for civil rights); Stephanie Hammond Knutson, Note, *The Religious Landlord and the Conflict Between Free Exercise Rights and Housing Discrimination Laws—Which Interest Prevails?*, 47 HASTINGS L.J. 1669, 1726–31 (1996) (noting difficulty in weighing civil rights interests and religious interests and proposing a religious exemption for small landlords); Alvin C. Lin, Note, *Sexual Orientation Antidiscrimination Laws and the Religious Liberty Protection Act: The Pitfalls of the Compelling State Interest Inquiry*, 89 GEO. L.J. 719, 748–51 (2001) (arguing against individual religiously based exemptions from civil rights laws because they inject a troubling "morality" inquiry into civil rights laws that are not based on morality concerns); Shelley K. Wessels, Note, *The Collision of Religious Exercise and Governmental Nondiscrimination Policies*, 41 STAN. L. REV. 1201, 1231 (1989) (urging protection for religious groups when the group looks "inward" to itself as a religious community, but not when the group "turns outwards" in providing services to others in the community); Martha Minow, *Should Religious Groups Be Exempt from Civil Rights Laws?*, 48 B.C.L. Rev. 781 (2007) (arguing that the different religiously based exemptions to civil rights laws vary depending on whether the discrimination is aimed at race, gender, or sexuality and can be understood as a byproduct of the social movements that advocated for the creation of nondiscrimination provisions); Rebecca Wistner, Note, *Cohabitation, Fornication, and the Free Exercise of Religion: Landlords Seeking Exemptions from Fair Housing Laws*, 46 Case W. Res. 1071 (1996) (concluding that the "compelling interest" test codified in the Religious Freedom Restoration Act does not require religious exemptions to fair housing laws that prohibit discrimination on the basis of marital status).

6. Nat'l Conference of State Legislatures, Same-Sex Marriage, *available at* www.ncsl.org/programs/cyf/samesex.htm (last visited June 23, 2008).

7. *Id.*

8. Nat'l Gay & Lesbian Task Force, State Nondiscrimination Laws in the U.S., *available at* www.thetaskforce.org/downloads/reports/issue_maps/non_discrimination_1_08.pdf (last visited June 23, 2008).

9. From 1988 to 1990, I was a staff attorney with the American Civil Liberties Union (ACLU) AIDS Project and the ACLU Lesbian & Gay Rights Project. In 1993, I was the Legal Director of the Campaign for Military Service, an enterprise to help lift the ban on the service of gay people in the military. From 1993 to 1998, I worked as a consultant to the Human Rights Campaign, a political organization ded-

icated to advancing gay rights. In that capacity, I served as a lead lawyer drafting and negotiating a federal bill to prohibit discrimination in employment on the basis of sexual orientation. From 1999 to 2006, I was an advisor and consultant to the National Gay & Lesbian Task Force, another political organization dedicated to advancing lesbian, gay, bisexual, and transgender equality. I have written amicus briefs on behalf of civil rights organizations, religious organizations, and gay-rights organizations in constitutional cases seeking to establish equality for gay people, including the United States Supreme Court cases of *Romer v. Evans*, 517 U.S. 620 (1996), and *Lawrence v. Texas*, 539 U.S. 558, 578 (2003), and in several lower court cases challenging the military's ban on gay service members.

10. *See* KARLYN BOWMAN & ADAM FOSTER, AMER. ENTER. INST., ATTITUDES ABOUT HOMOSEXUALITY AND GAY MARRIAGE, *available at* www.aei.org/publications/ filter.all,pubID.14882/pub_detail.asp (last visited June 23, 2008). I do not purport to be an expert in polling data nor do I assert that every survey I cite in the following paragraphs and footnotes is necessarily free from methodological errors. My sole assertion is that I believe Bowman's compilation indicates a trend towards the public caring *less* about homosexuality as a morally problematic issue. That trend is sufficient to make me think it is at least probable that civil rights laws protecting the liberty of LGBT people might be enacted over the coming decades and that the passage of such laws might then burden the liberty of those who believe that homosexuality is morally problematic.

11. *Id.* at 2. The NORC survey found that 70 percent of respondents in 1973 thought that a married person having sex outside of his or her marriage was "always wrong." *Id.* at 47. That number stayed consistently in the 70 percent range every year the survey was conducted until 2004, when 80 percent of respondent thought extramarital sex was "always wrong." *Id.* at 47–48.

12. *Id.* at 3.

13. *Id.* The subgroup analysis also looked at sex, race, education, church attendance, region, party, ideology, and family income. *Id.* The significant changes among younger people are apparent in other surveys as well. In a University of California at Los Angeles Cooperative Institutional Research Program survey of college freshman, 47 percent of respondents in 1976 answered that "[i]t is important to have laws prohibiting homosexual relationships." *Id.* at 6. By 2005, that number had decreased to 25 percent. *Id.*

14. For example, a February 2006 survey by Princeton Survey Research Associates (PSRA)/Pew Research Center found that 50 percent of respondents believe that "homosexual behavior" is "wrong," and a May 2006 Gallup poll found that 51 percent of respondents believe that "homosexual behavior" is "morally wrong." *Id.* at 4. A *Los Angeles Times* survey in 2000 found that 51 percent of respondents believed that "sexual relations between adults of the same gender" is "always wrong." *Id.* By contrast, a February 2004 Harris/CNN/*Time* poll found that only 38 percent of respondents considered "homosexual relationships" to be "not acceptable," while 49 percent considered them acceptable for others but not themselves, and 11 percent considered them

acceptable both for others and for themselves. *Id.* at 5. A May 2006 Gallup poll found that 54 percent of respondents felt that "homosexuality should be considered an acceptable alternative lifestyle," while 41 percent felt it should not. *Id.* at 6. And the percentage of people who believe that "homosexuality is a way of life that should be discouraged by society" has remained below 50 percent (ranging from 41 percent to 45 percent) in responses to a PSRA/Pew Research Center survey in 1999, 2000, 2003, and 2004. *Id.* at 8.

15. In a PSRA/*Newsweek* poll in 1985, only 22 percent of respondents said they had a "friend or close acquaintance" who was gay or lesbian. *Id.* at 16. In a 2000 PSRA/*Newsweek* poll, 56 percent of respondents said they had a "friend or close acquaintance" who was gay or lesbian. *Id.* In a July 2003 Gallup poll, 32 percent of respondents indicated they had "become more accepting of gays and lesbians" over the past few years, 59 percent said their attitudes had not changed, and 8 percent said they had become less accepting. *Id.* at 10.

16. *Id.* at 16.

17. *Id.*

18. For example, in a February 2006 survey by PSRA/Pew Research Center, 33 percent of respondents stated that "homosexual behavior" was "not a moral issue," while 12 percent called such behavior "acceptable." *Id.* at 4. In the May 2006 Gallup question, in which respondents were given only the options of "homosexual behavior" being "morally wrong" or "morally acceptable," 44 percent of respondents said it was morally acceptable. *Id.* It seems likely to me that the Pew data are more consistent with a significant segment of the public's view—*i.e.*, that homosexuality is not something to be agitated about, but is also not something they would call "morally acceptable."

19. *Id.* at 7.

20. *Id.*

21. *Id.* A 2004 Harris/CNN/*Time* poll reflects similar indifference. In that poll, respondents were asked whether they would be more or less likely to vote for a candidate who favored legalizing gay marriage, or whether it would make no difference. *Id.* at 15. Forty-eight percent of respondents said they would be less likely to vote for such a candidate, 10 percent said they would be more likely to vote for such a candidate, and 39 percent said it would make no difference to them. *Id.*

22. *Id.* at 21–24 (noting various polls showing consistent 50 percent to 65 percent disapproval of marriage for same-sex couples when respondents are given the opportunity to note solely their approval or disapproval of marriage for same-sex couples).

23. For example, in a 2003 Gallup/CNN/USA *Today* poll, respondents were asked whether "allowing two people of the same sex to legally marry will change our society for the better, will it have no effect, or will it change our society for the worse?" Forty-eight percent thought it would change our society for the worse, 10 percent thought it would change our society for the better, and 40 percent thought it would have no effect on our society. *Id.* at 25.

24. *Id.* at 27–28 (reviewing one poll from 2000, and fifteen polls from 2004, that gave respondents the option between marriage, civil unions, and no legal recognition for same-sex couples).

25. *Id.* What is particularly fascinating is that people *report* more moral disapproval of homosexuality among the American public than the polls indicate there actually *is*. In a 2001 Gallup poll, when asked, "What is your impression of how most Americans feel about homosexual behavior—do most Americans think it is acceptable or not acceptable?," 74 percent responded that most Americans believe homosexual behavior is not acceptable, while 21 percent responded that most Americans believe homosexual behavior is acceptable. *Id.* at 7. In fact, a May 2001 Gallup poll found that 40 percent of respondents considered "homosexual behavior" to be "morally acceptable," while 53 percent found it to be "morally wrong." *Id.* at 4. And in the NORC survey of 2002, 55 percent said homosexual behavior was "always wrong" and 5 percent said it was "almost always" wrong, 33 percent said it was "not wrong," and 7 percent said it was "only sometimes" wrong. *Id.* at 2.

26. *See, e.g.*, Amer. Psychiatric Ass'n, Gay Lesbian and Bisexual Issues, *available at* http://healthyminds.org/glbissues.cfm (last visited June 23, 2008) (quoting a 1992 American Psychiatric Association (APA) statement: "Whereas homosexuality per se implies no impairment in judgment, stability, reliability, or general social or vocational capabilities, the [APA] calls on all international health organizations and individual psychiatrists in other countries, to urge the repeal in their own country of legislation that penalized homosexual acts by consenting adults in private. And further the APA calls on these organizations and individuals to do all that is possible to decrease the stigma related to homosexuality wherever and whenever it may occur."); Amer. Psychological Ass'n, Being Gay Is Just as Healthy as Being Straight, *available at* www.psychologymatters.org/hooker.html (last visited June 23, 2008); Child Welfare League of America, LGBTQ Youth Issues: About the Program, *available at* www.cwla.org/programs/culture/glbtqabout.htm (last visited June 23, 2008) (noting the Child Welfare League of America's "full support for all young people, regardless of sexual orientation"); Child Welfare League of America, Position Statement on Parenting of Children by Lesbian, Gay, and Bisexual Adults, *available at* www.cwla.org/programs/culture/glbtqposition.htm (last visited June 23, 2008) ("The Child Welfare League of America . . . affirms that lesbian, gay, and bisexual parents are as well suited to raise children as their heterosexual counterparts.").

27. What many of these people do, with regard to public policy, is engage in "moral bracketing." Moral bracketing, a basic component of liberal political theory, allows people to say both that homosexuality is wrong *and* that antigay discrimination is wrong. Under this liberal view, as long as gay people do not harm anyone else, the State should be tolerant of them. *See* Chai R. Feldblum, *Gay Is Good: The Moral Case for Marriage Equality and More*, 17 YALE J.L. & FEMINISM 139, 147–50 (2005) [hereinafter Feldblum, *Gay Is Good*] (describing moral bracketing). The advantages and disadvantages of moral bracketing have intrigued me for over a decade. *See generally* Chai R. Feldblum, *The Federal Gay Rights Bill: From Bella to ENDA*, in CREATING

CHANGE: SEXUALITY, PUBLIC POLICY, AND CIVIL RIGHTS 149 (John D'Emilio, et al. eds., 2000) [hereinafter Feldblum, *Federal Gay Rights*]; Chai R. Feldblum, *The Limitations of Liberal Neutrality Arguments in Favour of Same-Sex Marriage, in* LEGAL RECOGNITION OF SAME-SEX PARTNERSHIPS: A STUDY OF NATIONAL, EUROPEAN AND INTERNATIONAL LAW 55 (Robert Wintemute and Mads Andnæs eds., 2001); Chai R. Feldblum, *The Moral Rhetoric of Legislation,* 72 N.Y.U. L. REV. 992 (1997) [hereinafter Feldblum, *Moral Rhetoric*]; Chai R. Feldblum, *A Progressive Moral Case for Same-Sex Marriage,* 7 TEMP. POL. & CIV. RTS. L. REV. 485 (1998); Chai R. Feldblum, *Sexual Orientation, Morality, and the Law: Devlin Revisited,* 57 U. PITT. L. REV. 237 (1996) [hereinafter Feldblum, *Sexual Orientation*]. My personal belief is that we will be able to achieve full liberty for LGBT people only if we directly engage in a moral discourse about sexuality, sexual orientation, and gender in the public domain. The Moral Values Project, an enterprise I launched in 2005, is designed to reach people who believe homosexuality is immoral but who also believe gay people should not be discriminated against. One goal of the Moral Values Project is to move people from the second view of gay sex I describe above to the third view of gay sex. For purposes of this chapter, however, I am simply postulating a trend towards more legal protection and equality for LGBT people, regardless of whether it is achieved through moral bracketing (as some people believe it can be) or through a direct engagement with moral discourse (as I believe is necessary).

28. I explain what I mean by "belief liberty," as well as what I consider "identity liberty" and "bodily liberty" *infra* at notes 68–75 and accompanying text.

29. For example, current polling data show that while the majority of Americans (58 percent) say marriage for same-sex couples should not be permitted, a much larger 85 percent of self-identified conservative Republicans and evangelical white Protestants say that marriage for gay couples should be illegal. Gary Langer, *Most Oppose Gay Marriage; Fewer Back an Amendment,* ABC NEWS, June 5, 2006, *available at* http://abcnews.go.com/US/Politics/story?id=2041689&page=1 (last visited June 23, 2008).

30. Employment Div. v. Smith, 494 U.S. 872, 879 (1990) (holding that "the right of free exercise does not relieve an individual of the obligation to comply with a 'valid and neutral law of general applicability on the ground that the law proscribes (or prescribes) conduct that his religion prescribes (or proscribes)'" (quoting United States v. Lee, 455 U.S. 252, 263 n.3 (1982) (Stevens, J., concurring))).

31. *See* BRUCE A. ACKERMAN, SOCIAL JUSTICE IN THE LIBERAL STATE 349–78 (1981); RONALD DWORKIN, TAKING RIGHTS SERIOUSLY 90–100 (1977); John Rawls, *The Priority of Right and Ideas of the Good, in* POLITICAL LIBERALISM 173–211 (1996); *see generally* Feldblum, *Gay Is Good, supra* note 27, at 143–50 (describing liberal neutrality approach); Feldblum, *Sexual Orientation, supra* note 27, at 245–46 (same). Carlos Ball has written extensively on liberal neutrality in the context of gay rights. *See* CARLOS BALL, THE MORALITY OF GAY RIGHTS (2002).

32. Tamara Metz, *Why We Should Disestablish Marriage, in* MARY LYNDON SHANLEY, JUST MARRIAGE 99, 101 (Joshua Cohen and Deborah Chasman eds., 2004).

33. *Id.* at 102.

34. *See, e.g.,* Feldblum, *Federal Gay Rights, supra* note 27 (documenting moral bracketing throughout introduction of recurring gay rights bills); Feldblum, *Moral Rhetoric, supra* note 27, at 996–1004 (deconstructing moral bracketing done by various Members of Congress during a hearing on Employment Non-Discrimination Act).

35. *See* Michael W. McConnell, *The Problem of Singling Out Religion*, 50 DePaul L. Rev. 1, 43–44 (2000).

36. *Id.* at 44.

37. *Id.* (emphasis added). As McConnell concludes:

> Such an approach would produce many of the same advantages for this cultural conflict that the First Amendment produces for religious conflict. This approach would provide the basis for civic peace on an issue where the nation is dangerously divided, it would provide maximum respect for individual conscience, it would depoliticize an issue that many of us believe is private and not political in character, and it would help to restore the public-private distinction.

Id. at 44–45.

38. *Id.* at 44.

39. The era was named after the substantive due process case of *Lochner v. New York*, 198 U.S. 45 (1905).

40. For just a small sample, see Randy E. Barnett, Restoring the Lost Constitution: The Presumption of Liberty (2004); Rebecca L. Brown, *Liberty, the New Equality*, 77 N.Y.U. L. Rev. 1491 (2002) [hereinafter Brown, *Liberty*]; Robert C. Post, *Foreword: Fashioning the Legal Constitution: Culture, Courts, and the Law*, 117 Harv. L. Rev. 4 (2003); Laurence H. Tribe, *Foreword: Toward a Model of Roles in the Due Process of Life and Law*, 87 Harv. L. Rev. 1 (1973); Laurence H. Tribe, Lawrence v. Texas: *The "Fundamental Right" That Dare Not Speak Its Name*, 117 Harv. L. Rev. 1893 (2004) [hereinafter Tribe, *Lawrence*]; Robin West, *Reconstructing Liberty*, 59 Tenn. L. Rev. 441 (1992).

41. Washington v. Glucksberg, 521 U.S. 702, 752–89 (1997) (Souter, J., concurring).

42. *Id.* at 759 (noting that the standard of reasonableness or arbitrariness under the Due Process Clause is "fairly traceable to Justice Bradley's dissent in the *Slaughter-House Cases*, in which he said that a person's right to choose a calling was an element of liberty . . . and declared that the liberty and property protected by due process are not truly recognized if such rights may be 'arbitrarily assailed'" (citation omitted)).

43. *Id.* at 761. Justice Souter begins his historical overview by reminding us that one of the first instances in which the Court applied the Due Process Clause was "the case that the [Fourteenth] Amendment would in due course overturn, *Dred Scott v. Sandford.*" *Id.* at 758 (citation omitted).

44. In *Allgeyer v. Louisiana*, 165 U.S. 578 (1897), the Court said that Fourteenth Amendment liberty includes

> the right of the citizen to be free in the enjoyment of all his faculties, to be free to use them in all lawful ways, to live and work where he will, to earn his livelihood by any lawful

calling, to pursue any livelihood or avocation, and for that purpose to enter into all contracts which may be proper, necessary and essential to his carrying out to a successful conclusion the purposes above mentioned.

Id. at 589. Justice Souter's observation of *Allgeyer* is the following: "Although this principle was unobjectionable, what followed for a season was, in the realm of economic legislation, the echo of *Dred Scott.*" *Glucksberg*, 521 U.S. at 760 (Souter, J., concurring).

45. While the ability to pursue one's calling can fall within the identity liberty I describe below, one must admit that the Court's assessment that one needs perfect economic freedom in doing so (including the freedom to agree to wretched work conditions), *see, e.g.*, Lochner v. New York, 198 U.S. 45, 59–61 (1905), was yet another failing of reasoning in many of the *Lochner*-era cases.

46. Scholars have correctly pointed out that the opinion authored by Justices O'-Connor, Kennedy, and Souter in *Planned Parenthood of Southeastern Pennsylvania v. Casey*, 505 U.S. 833 (1992), focused on a similar liberty spectrum. *See, e.g.*, Randy E. Barnett, *Justice Kennedy's Libertarian Revolution: Lawrence v. Texas*, 2002–2003 CATO SUP. CT. REV. 21, 33 (2003). Barnett notes that the discussion of the liberty right in *Casey* is commonly attributed to Justice Kennedy. *Id.* Assuming that is true, there are two Justices on the current Court, Justices Kennedy and Souter, who appear to be deeply invested in a flexible liberty analysis. *See* Post, *supra* note 40, at 85–96 (noting flexibility in the early evolution of modern substantive due process and describing the rigidity articulated by the *Glucksberg* majority).

47. Poe v. Ullman, 367 U.S. 497, 543 (1961) (Harlan, J., dissenting) (citations omitted). Justice Souter began his substantive analysis in his *Glucksberg* concurrence as follows:

My understanding of unenumerated rights in the wake of the *Poe* dissent and subsequent cases avoids the absolutist failing of many older cases without embracing the opposite pole of equating reasonableness with past practice described at a very specific level. That understanding begins with a concept of "ordered liberty," comprising a continuum of rights to be free from "arbitrary impositions and purposeless restraints."

Glucksberg, 521 U.S. at 765 (Souter, J., concurring) (citations omitted) (quoting *Poe*, 367 U.S. at 543, 549).

48. *Casey*, 505 U.S. at 851.

49. *Glucksberg*, 521 U.S. at 767 (Souter, J., concurring).

50. As Justice Souter put it:

Justice Harlan thus recognized just what the Court today assumes, that by insisting on a threshold requirement that the interest (or, as the Court puts it, the right) be fundamental before anything more than rational basis justification is required, the Court ensures that not every case will require the "complex balancing" that heightened scrutiny entails.

Id. at 767 n.9.

51. *Id.* at 768.

52. *Id.* In a footnote to this sentence, Justice Souter observed,

Our cases have used various terms to refer to fundamental liberty interests, and at times we have also called such an interest a "right" even before balancing it against the government's interest. Precision in terminology, however, favors reserving the label "right" for instances in which the individual's liberty interest actually trumps the government's countervailing interests; only then does the individual have anything legally enforceable as against the state's attempt at regulation.

Id. at 768 n.10 (citations omitted).

53. Indeed, he repeats that standard in various citations in his concurrence. *Id.* at 766–67.

54. *Id.* at 768 (emphasis added).

55. As Justice Souter put it:

Skinner, that is, added decisions regarding procreation to the list of liberties recognized in *Meyer* and *Pierce* and loosely suggested, as a gloss on their standard of arbitrariness, a judicial obligation to scrutinize any impingement on such an important interest with heightened care. In so doing, it suggested a point that Justice Harlan would develop, that the kind and degree of justification that a sensitive judge would demand of a State would depend on the importance of the interest being asserted by the individual.

Glucksberg, 521 U.S. at 762 (Souter, J., concurring) (citing *Poe,* 367 U.S. at 543). *See also id.* at 767 (stating that a court is "to assess the relative 'weights' or dignities of the contending interests").

56. *See id.* at 719–28 (majority opinion).

57. *Id.* For fascinating and excellent analyses of the development of substantive due process, and the effort by the *Glucksberg* majority to radically change the trajectory of that development, see Post, *supra* note 40, at 86–96 and Tribe, *Lawrence, supra* note 40, at 1921–25.

58. Lawrence v. Texas, 539 U.S. 558 (2003).

59. Post, *supra* note 40, at 96.

60. Tribe, *Lawrence, supra* note 40, at 1924–25.

61. *Id.* at 1931–32.

62. Nan D. Hunter, *Living with* Lawrence, 88 MINN. L. REV. 1103, 1117 (2004).

63. Chai R. Feldblum, *The Right to Define One's Own Concept of Existence: What* Lawrence *Can Mean for Intersex and Transgender People,* 7 GEO. J. GENDER & L. 115, 120 (2006) [hereinafter Feldblum, *Right to Define*] (describing liberty analysis in *Lawrence*). *See also* Chai Feldblum, Professor, Georgetown Univ. Law Ctr., Comments at From *Griswold* to *Lawrence* and Beyond: The Battle over Personal Privacy and the New Supreme Court (Mar. 2, 2006) (transcript *available at* http://pewforum.org/ events/index.php?EventID=95) (last visited June 23, 2008).

64. *See* Brown, *Liberty, supra* note 40.

65. *Id.* at 1498.

66. *Id.* at 1545–49.

67. This categorization also permits us to think more logically about whether such liberties are inherently and solely negative liberties that prohibit the government from restraining some action on our parts, or whether they are also inherently positive liberties that require some affirmative action on the part of the government to allow for their full expression. Obviously, the Supreme Court, for the moment, has come down clearly on the side that the liberty protected by the Substantive Due Process Clause is solely a negative liberty. *See, e.g.,* DeShaney v. Winnebago County Dep't of Soc. Servs., 489 U.S. 189, 195 (1989). But in many circumstances, the only way to achieve real liberty for some individuals will be for the government to take affirmative steps to bring about that liberty—even if such steps might then interfere with the liberty of others. *See, e.g.,* ROBIN L. WEST, RE-IMAGINING JUSTICE: PROGRESSIVE INTERPRETATIONS OF FORMAL EQUALITY, RIGHTS, AND THE RULE OF LAW 6–7 (2003) (describing the need for government to affirmatively support the ability of individuals to give and receive care and to feel safe); Feldblum, *Right to Define, supra* note 63, at 127–39 (noting affirmative steps government should take to protect the liberty of intersex and transgender people); West, *supra* note 40, *passim* (describing affirmative steps to be taken by government to ensure the liberty of women).

68. *See, e.g.,* Rochin v. California, 342 U.S. 165 (1952); Jacobson v. Massachusetts, 197 U.S. 11 (1905).

69. *Compare Jacobson,* 197 U.S. at 26–27 (holding compulsory vaccination to be constitutional), *with Rochin,* 342 U.S. at 172–74 (holding unconstitutional the forcible administration of emetic solution to induce vomiting in the course of drug investigation).

70. Planned Parenthood of S.E. Pa. v. Casey, 505 U.S. 833, 851 (1992). *See also* Lawrence v. Texas, 539 U.S. 558, 574 (2003) (relying on and quoting *Casey* when finding unconstitutional laws criminalizing consensual homosexual sex).

71. *See Lawrence,* 539 U.S. at 588 (Scalia, J., dissenting) ("And if the Court is referring not to the holding of *Casey,* but to the dictum of its famed sweet-mystery-of-life passage ('At the heart of liberty is the right to define one's own concept of existence, of meaning, of the universe, and of the mystery of human life'): That 'casts some doubt' upon either the totality of our jurisprudence or else (presumably the right answer) nothing at all. I have never heard of a law that attempted to restrict one's 'right to define' certain concepts; and if the passage calls into question the government's power to regulate *actions based on* one's self-defined 'concept of existence, etc.,' it is the passage that ate the rule of law.").

72. Feldblum, *Right to Define, supra* note 63, at 139. Larry Tribe's project on liberty, with its focus on self-government and relational rights, captures incredibly well what I call identity liberty. Tribe, *Lawrence, supra* note 40, at 1941–44.

73. Meyer v. Nebraska, 262 U.S. 390, 399 (1923) (emphasis added).

74. *Id.*

75. *Id.*

76. As Justice Souter was at pains to argue in his concurrence, "the kind and degree of justification that a sensitive judge would demand of a State would depend on the importance of the interest being asserted by the individual." Washington v. Glucksberg, 521 U.S. 702, 762 (1997) (Souter, J., concurring) (citing Poe v. Ullman, 367 U.S. 497, 543 (1961) (Harlan, J., dissenting)). *See also id.* at 767 ("[A] court [is] to assess the relative 'weights' or dignities of the contending interests . . . ."). There is no reason to presume that this same analysis could not be applied to the relative weights of beliefs. Thus, although Justice Souter makes no claim regarding belief liberty in his concurrence, I believe my approach is consonant with his analysis.

77. Prince v. Massachusetts, 321 U.S. 158, 164–65 (1944) (citations omitted). In *Prince*, the appellant was seeking a higher degree of protection for her religious beliefs than would have been accorded secular beliefs under the First Amendment. *See id.* at 164.

78. West Virginia v. Barnette, 319 U.S. 624, 642 (1943) ("If there is any fixed star in our constitutional constellation, it is that no official, high or petty, can prescribe what shall be orthodox in politics, nationalism, religion, or other matters of opinion or force citizens to confess by word or act their faith therein. If there are any circumstances which permit an exception, they do not now occur to us.").

79. The Supreme Court has often observed that while there is an absolute right to hold religious beliefs, *see, e.g.,* Wisconsin v. Yoder, 406 U.S. 205, 214, 219 (1972); Cantwell v. Connecticut, 310 U.S. 296, 303 (1940), religiously grounded conduct is not absolutely protected, *see, e.g.,* Bowen v. Roy, 476 U.S. 693, 699 (1986); *Yoder,* 406 U.S. at 220; Braunfeld v. Brown, 366 U.S. 599, 603 (1961).

80. *See, e.g.,* Texas v. Johnson, 491 U.S. 397, 405–06 (1989) (stating that flag burning as a political statement constitutes expressive conduct); Spence v. Washington, 418 U.S. 405, 409–10 (1974) (stating that the display of a flag bearing a peace symbol is constitutionally protected expressive conduct); United States v. O'Brien, 391 U.S. 367, 376–77 (1968) (recognizing that symbolic conduct is constitutionally protected).

81. Bowers v. Hardwick, 478 U.S. 186 (1986).

82. *See* Feldblum, *Sexual Orientation, supra* note 27, at 290–96 (detailing cases in which the "status-conduct" distinction has been used). As I noted in that article:

> Instead of countering the ramifications of *Hardwick* by decoupling sodomy and homosexual conduct, many gay rights attorneys have implicitly accepted the equivalence between homosexual conduct and homosexual sodomy and have instead sought to decouple homosexual *orientation* from homosexual *conduct*. This approach has produced victories in court for a few individual gay and lesbian plaintiffs, but at a cost to equal protection for gay people generally, and at a potential cost to the development of a more effective paradigm for equal rights for gay people.

Id. at 290.

83. *See id.* at 290–96; Chai Feldblum, *Based on a Moral Vision: The Majority in Romer v. Evans Could—and Should—Have Engaged the Dissent Directly on the Role of Popular Morality in Making Laws,* LEGAL TIMES, July 29, 1996, at S31; Chai R. Feldblum, *Keep the Sex in Same-Sex Marriage,* 4 HARV. GAY & LESBIAN REV. 23 (1997).

84. McClure v. Sports & Health Club, 370 N.W.2d 844, 846 (Minn. 1985) (*en banc*).

85. ·Blanding v. Sports & Health Club, 373 N.W.2d 784, 787 (Minn. Ct. App. 1985), *aff'd*, 389 N.W.2d 206 (Minn. 1986).

86. Smith v. Fair Employment & Hous. Comm'n, 913 P.2d 909, 912 (Cal. 1996).

87. *Id.* at 918–19. As I note in the text, the woman in this case was afraid she would not see her husband in the hereafter if she rented to the unmarried couple. The court used the formulation of a "significant burden" because it was applying the standard set forth in the Religious Freedom Restoration Act. *Smith*, 913 P.2d at 919.

88. *Id.* at 926. The court was contrasting the burden on a religious person who lost his or her job because of a refusal to work on the Sabbath and who then sought unemployment compensation:

> T]he degree of compulsion involved is markedly greater in the unemployment-compensation cases than in the case before us. In the former instance, one can avoid the conflict between the law and one's beliefs about the Sabbath only by quitting work and foregoing compensation. To do so, however, is not a realistic solution for someone who lives on the wages earned through personal labor. In contrast, one who earns a living through the return on capital invested in rental properties can, if she does not wish to comply with an antidiscrimination law that conflicts with her religious beliefs, avoid the conflict, without threatening her livelihood, by selling her units and redeploying the capital in other investments.

Id.

89. *Id.* at 926.

90. *Id.*

91. Donahue v. Fair Employment & Hous. Comm'n, 2 Cal. Rptr. 2d 32 (Cal. Ct. App. 1991). For subsequent appellate history of this case, see *infra* note 94.

92. *Id.* at 49 (Grignon, J., dissenting).

93. *Id.*

94. *Id.* (quoting Pines v. Tomson, 160 Cal. App. 3d 370, 389 (Cal. Ct. App. 1984)) (alterations in original) (citations omitted). The *Donahue* majority found a burden on the couple's free exercise of religion, as prohibited by the state constitution, and that the State did not have a sufficiently compelling interest in prohibiting marital status discrimination to override that exercise of religion. *Id.* at 46 (majority opinion). The opinion in *Donahue* was superseded by an order granting review, 825 P.2d 766 (Cal. 1992); the review was then dismissed and the case remanded, 859 P.2d 671 (Cal. 1993). The case of *Smith v. Fair Employment & Hous. Comm'n*, 913 P.2d 909, 912 (Cal. 1996), was decided three years after *Donahue* was remanded.

95. Blanding v. Sports & Health Club, 373 N.W.2d 784, 791 (Minn. Ct. App. 1985), *aff'd*, 389 N.W.2d 206 (Minn. 1986).

96. *Id.*

97. *Id.*

98. *Id.* In other words, because the state's civil rights law prohibited discrimination solely on gay "status," and not on gay "conduct," the obligation on the owners

not to discriminate on the basis of "affectional preference" could logically have no impact on their belief that homosexual *conduct* was immoral. In fact, according to the court, the state's law was perfectly matched to the owners' beliefs with regard to loving the sinner, but hating the sin. Of course, the fact that most of the gay men frequenting the sports and health club were presumably *also* having gay sex at some point was ignored by the court. Thus, the court's analysis, while offering an ironic twist on the status-conduct distinction, seems as riddled with illogic as when that distinction is applied in gay rights cases.

99. Gay Rights Coal. of Georgetown Univ. Law Ctr. v. Georgetown Univ., 536 A.2d 1 (D.C. 1987).

100. *Id.* at 8–14.

101. *Id.* at 10.

102. *Id.* at 11–12.

103. *Id.* (quoting Memorandum from Dean W. Schuerman, Georgetown Univ., to the Student Government, Georgetown Univ. (Feb 6, 1979) (emphasis added by the court).

104. *Id.* at 45 (Pryor, J., concurring) (footnote omitted).

105. *Id.* at 16 (plurality opinion).

106. *Id.* at 17.

107. *Id.* at 5 (quoting D.C. CODE § 1–2520 (1987)).

108. The plurality, unlike Judge Pryor, then accepted that there was a burden on the school in forcing the university to provide tangible benefits to the student groups (albeit a less minor burden than a forced endorsement would have been), and that the burden was outweighed by the State's compelling interest in prohibiting discrimination based on sexual orientation. *Id.* at 38.

109. Rumsfeld v. Forum for Academic and Institutional Rights, Inc. (FAIR), 547 U.S. 47 (2006).

110. *Id.* at 52.

111. Indeed, it was precisely the fear that people who wished to discriminate on the basis of sexual orientation or gender or race would use the argument that complying with a civil rights law burdened their freedom of expression that made so many gay-rights and civil rights advocates welcome the result in the *FAIR* decision. *See, e.g.,* Brief of Prof. William Alford et al. as Amici Curiae Supporting Respondents at 21–22, *FAIR,* 547 U.S. 47, *available at* www.law.georgetown.edu/solomon/documents/FAIRamicusHarvard.pdf (last visited June 23, 2008) (urging the Court to decide the case on statutory rather than constitutional grounds, to avoid providing constitutional shelter to those seeking to evade nondiscrimination laws); Jack Balkin, *All's FAIR in Law and War,* BALKINIZATION, Mar. 15, 2006, *available at* http://balkin.blogspot.com/2006/03/alls-fair-in-law-and-war.html (last visited June 23, 2008) (discussing the problems the law schools' possible success in *FAIR* would pose for the enforceability of nondiscrimination laws); Dale Carpenter, *Balkin on Solomon,* THE VOLOKH CONSPIRACY, Mar. 15, 2006, *available at* www.volokh.com/posts/1142448786.shtml (last visited June 23, 2008) (same). As I explain further *infra* at

notes 112–117 and accompanying text, I believe the result in *FAIR* was both wrong
and unfortunate. Moreover, I do not believe a contrary result would have given *carte
blanche* to those who wish to discriminate on the basis of sexual orientation, gender,
race, or any other ground. It would, however, have ensured that the burdens that
neutral civil rights laws place on those who disagree with the premises of such laws
would have been made more transparent, would have been accorded some recognition, and would have been justified in the legal process.

112. *See* Brief for the Respondents at 16–33, FAIR, 547 U.S. 47 (2006), [here-
inafter *Brief for the Respondents in FAIR*].

113. As a general matter, law firms and law organizations that do not attest to the
fact that they do not discriminate on the basis of sex, race, religion, national origin,
disability, or sexual orientation are not provided assistance by law schools in the recruitment process. *See* Assoc. of Am. Law Sch., Executive Comm. Regulations, Reg.
6–3.1, *available at* www.aals.org/about_handbook_regulations.php#6 (last visited June
23,2008) (requiring, in order to enforce the Association of American Law Schools'
(AALS) nondiscrimination by-laws, employers who recruit at law schools to provide
written assurance that they do not discriminate on any of the grounds prohibited in
AALS's bylaws); *see also* Brief of Nat'l Ass'n for Law Placement et al. as Amici Curiae Supporting Respondents at 2, 5, *available at* www.law.georgetown.edu/
solomon/documents/FAIRamicusNALP.pdf (last visited June 23, 2008) (discussing
same policy).

114. *See Brief for the Respondents in FAIR, supra* note 112, at 18, 44–48.

115. As the Supreme Court put it: "The Solomon Amendment neither limits
what law schools may say nor requires them to say anything. . . . As a general matter,
the Solomon Amendment regulates conduct, not speech. It affects what law schools
must *do*—afford equal access to military recruiters—not what they may or may not
say." *FAIR*, 547 U.S. at 60. Although the manner in which the government obtained compliance from the law schools was via the threat of withholding funds, the
Court concluded that the government could have demanded such compliance directly without violating the Federal Constitution. *Id.* For that reason, it was irrelevant that the government used the method of conditioning conduct on the receipt
of spending. *Id.* ("This case does not require us to determine when a condition placed
on university funding goes beyond the 'reasonable' choice offered in *Grove City [Col-
lege v. Bell]* and becomes an unconstitutional condition. It is clear that a funding condition cannot be unconstitutional if it could be constitutionally imposed directly. Because the First Amendment would not prevent Congress from directly imposing the
Solomon Amendment's access requirement, the statute does not place an unconstitutional condition on the receipt of federal funds." (citation omitted)).

116. *Id.* at 65 (citations omitted).

117. *Id.* at 69 (quoting Boy Scouts of Am. v. Dale, 530 U.S. 640, 648 (2000)) (internal quotation marks omitted).

118. To the extent that any equality law regulated belief directly, it should be held
invalid under the First Amendment. To the extent that forced compliance with an

equality mandate burdened an individual's belief liberty, my argument in this part is that such a burden is likely to be justified.

119. Washington v. Glucksberg, 521 U.S. 712, 768 (1997) (Souter, J., concurring).

120. Id.

121. Indeed, I believe it is precisely because this argument has so consistently failed that proponents of LGBT equality believe they must retreat to the position of denying the existence of any burden on a possible constitutional right to begin with. However, the same optimism that fuels my belief that the legal landscape will ultimately change for LGBT people also makes me believe that courts will begin to accept the compelling interest that government has in ensuring that LGBT people can live lives of honesty and safety.

122. Boy Scouts of Am. v. Dale, 530 U.S. 640 (2000).

123. Id. at 659.

124. Id. at 653 (internal quotation marks omitted).

125. On the importance of the latter point, see Nan D. Hunter, *Accommodating the Public Sphere: Beyond the Market Model*, 85 MINN. L. REV. 1591, 1611–13 (2001).

126. *Glucksberg*, 521 U.S. at 768 (Souter, J., concurring).

127. *Dale*, 530 U.S. at 659 (emphasis added).

128. For additional cases finding that a civil rights law may not be applied in a manner that burdens the religious beliefs of an individual or organization because of the lack of a compelling state interest, see Thomas v. Anchorage Equal Rights Comm'n, 165 F.3d 692, 716 (9th Cir. 1999), *vacated*, 220 F.3d 1134 (9th Cir. 2000) (no compelling government interest in protecting unmarried cohabiting heterosexual couples); Walker v. First Orthodox Presbyterian Church of San Francisco, No. 760–028, 1980 WL 4657, at *1 (Cal. Super. Ct. Apr. 3, 1980) (interest of City of San Francisco in its gay rights ordinance was not compelling).

129. Gay Rights Coalition of Georgetown Univ. Law Ctr. v. Georgetown Univ., 536 A.2d 1, 32 (1987) (citations omitted) (alterations in original).

130. Id. at 37.

131. As the court observed in *Smith v. Fair Employment Housing Commission*, "[T]o permit Smith to discriminate would sacrifice the rights of her prospective tenants to have equal access to public accommodations and their legal and dignity interests in freedom from discrimination based on personal characteristics." 913 P.2d 909, 925 (Cal. 1996). *Cf.* Heart of Atlanta Motel, Inc. v. United States, 379 U.S. 241, 250 (1964) ("[T]he fundamental object of [federal civil rights legislation] was to vindicate 'the deprivation of personal dignity that surely accompanies denials of equal access to public establishments.'" (quoting S. REP. NO. 872, at 16–17 (1964))).

132. A number of writers have made the argument that entering the stream of commerce should legitimately subject an enterprise to civil rights laws. *See, e.g.*, Mark Hager, *Freedom of Solidarity: Why the Boy Scout Case Was Rightly (But Wrongly) Decided*, 35 CONN. L. REV. 129, 157 (2002) (contending that "[o]rganizations engaged in commerce should not be cloaked with fundamental or First Amendment

freedom to exclude members on any bases they see fit"); Maureen E. Markey, *The Landlord/Tenant Free Exercise Conflict in a Post-RFRA World*, 29 RUTGERS L.J. 487, 549–52 (1998) (suggesting that the government need not show a compelling state interest test for nondiscrimination laws in free exercise cases in which religious people have engaged in voluntary commercial activity); Shelley K. Wessels, Note, *The Collision of Religious Exercise and Governmental Nondiscrimination Policies*, 41 STAN. L. REV. 1201, 1231 (1989) (urging protection for religious groups from civil rights laws when the group looks "inward" to itself as a religious community, but not when the group "turns outwards" in providing services to others in the community).

133. For cases finding that the government interest in prohibiting racial discrimination was sufficiently compelling to justify a burden on religious beliefs, see Bob Jones Univ. v. United States, 461 U.S. 574 (1983); Newman v. Piggie Park Enters, 256 F. Supp. 941 (D.S.C. 1966), *rev'd*, 377 F.2d 433 (4th Cir. 1967), *aff'd*, 390 U.S. 400 (1968). For an eloquent articulation of the dignity interests underlying the ability of a group of people to live in the world, see Jacobus tenBroek, *The Right to Live in the World: The Disabled in the Law of Torts*, 54 CAL. L. REV. 841 (1966).

134. Brown, *Liberty*, *supra* note 40, at 1547.

135. *Id.*

136. *Id.* Brown draws significantly on the work of political theorists to argue that "[a] major contribution of deliberative democracy theory to constitutional theory is its insight that a commitment to equality of all citizens gives rise to an obligation to justify laws with reasons that are accessible to all." *Id.* at 1548 (citing LAWRENCE C. BECKER, RECIPROCITY 73–144 (1986)); AMY GUTMANN AND DENNIS THOMPSON, DEMOCRACY AND DISAGREEMENT 55–59, 65, 84–85 & 377 n.43 (1996)).

137. My thoughts in this area are shaped by the thirteen years that I represented Catholic Charities USA (from 1993 through 2006) in the federal legislative arena as Director of the Federal Legislation Clinic at Georgetown University Law Center.

138. Andrew Koppelman, *You Can't Hurry Love: Why Antidiscrimination Protections for Gay People Should Have Religious Exemptions*, 72 BROOKLYN L. REV. 125 (2006).

139. As Koppelman observes, however, some members of the Supreme Court have, at times, been quite expansive with what they consider to be a "religiously based" belief. *See Welsh v. United States*, 398 U.S. 333, 340 (1970).

140. *Glucksberg*, 521 U.S. at 768 (Souter, J., concurring).

Chapter Six: Charles J. Reid, Jr.

1. This chapter is dedicated to Fr. John Lynch of the Catholic University of America in honor of his many years as a teacher, writer, administrator, and pastor of souls and scholars at the Catholic University of America. An earlier version of this chapter is published in THE JURIST. *See* Charles J. Reid, Jr., *Marriage: Its Relationship to Religion, Law, and the State*, 68 THE JURIST 252 (2008).

2. Goodridge v. Dep't of Pub. Health, 798 N.E.2d 941 (Mass. 2003).

3. JOHN T. NOONAN, JR., THE LUSTRE OF OUR COUNTRY: THE AMERICAN EXPE-RIENCE OF RELIGIOUS FREEDOM 2 (1998).

4. *Id.*

5. *Id.*

6. Edwin McDowell, *Professor Mircea Eliade, 79, Writer and Religious Scholar,* NEW YORK TIMES, at B6 (Apr. 23, 1986) (quoting Mircea Eliade).

7. F.W. MAITLAND AND FREDERICK POLLOCK, A HISTORY OF ENGLISH LAW BEFORE THE TIME OF EDWARD I (quoted in HAROLD J. BERMAN, LAW AND REVOLUTION: THE FORMATION OF THE WESTERN LEGAL TRADITION 49 (1983)).

8. *See generally* CHARLES HOMER HASKINS, THE RENAISSANCE OF THE TWELFTH CENTURY (1927).

9. Hastings Rashdall notes that Bologna and Paris, both established "during the last thirty years of the twelfth century," should be accounted the first universities. Bologna grew famous for its instruction in Roman and canon law; Paris for its theo-logical and philosophical investigations. 1 HASTINGS RASHDALL, THE UNIVERSITIES OF EUROPE IN THE MIDDLE AGES 17 (F.M. Powicke and A.B. Emden, eds., 1936).

10. *See generally* Berman, *supra* note 7.

11. Two of Augustine's most important works on this subject now appear in a sin-gle volume—the new edition with facing translation prepared by P.G. Walsh. *See* DE BONO CONIUGALI, DE SANCTA VIRGINITATE (2001).

12. I have summarized some of these developments in Charles J. Reid, Jr., *The Au-gustinian Goods of Marriage: The Disappearing Cornerstone of the American Law of Mar-riage,* 18 BYU J. PUB. L. 449, 451–56 (2004).

13. For the role played by the Crown and its law in medieval and early-modern Eng-land, see T.F.T. PLUCKNETT, A CONCISE HISTORY OF THE COMMON LAW 535–37 (5th ed.) (1956) (feudal incidents of marriage); *id.* at 528–30 (the emergence of primogen-iture as the means of regulating the inter-generational transfer of land in England).

14. CHARLES J. REID, JR., POWER OVER THE BODY, EQUALITY IN THE FAMILY: RIGHTS AND DOMESTIC RELATIONS IN MEDIEVAL CANON LAW 43–44 (2004).

15. JAMES A. BRUNDAGE, LAW, SEX, AND CHRISTIAN SOCIETY IN MEDIEVAL EUROPE 236 (1987) ("Consummation transformed the union into a 'sacrament' and hence made it indissoluble.").

16. The development of this idea is one of the themes of the book by Seamus Heaney, THE DEVELOPMENT OF THE SACRAMENTALITY OF MARRIAGE FROM ANSELM OF LAON TO THOMAS AQUINAS (1963).

17. On the freedom to marry, see Reid, *supra* note 14, at 37–50.

18. Error as to the person as well as the person's status (free or servile) invalidated consent. *See* JOHN T. NOONAN, JR., POWER TO DISSOLVE: LAWYERS AND MARRIAGES IN THE COURTS OF THE ROMAN CURIA 36 (1972).

19. For a list of the basic impediments, see RICHARD H. HELMHOLZ, MARRIAGE LITIGATION IN MEDIEVAL ENGLAND 36 (1974).

20. The grounds for divorce are discussed in Reid, *supra* note 14, at 135–49. The ground of violence developed as a kind of equitable estoppel, as American lawyers

would term it: the defendant wife would raise as a defense the husband's violence as a justification for her decision to separate, and the court would refuse to grant the husband's petition for reconciliation. *Id.*

21. JOHN WITTE, FROM SACRAMENT TO CONTRACT: MARRIAGE, RELIGION, AND LAW IN THE WESTERN TRADITION 140–53 (1997).

22. This diminution of the wife's rights is well expressed in the common-law doctrine of coverture, by which the wife's legal personality was merged with that of her husband to create a single legal entity with the husband empowered to act in its name. Blackstone described the consequences of this doctrine: "By marriage, the husband and wife are one person in law; that is, the very being or legal existence of the woman is suspended during the marriage, or at least is incorporated and consolidated into that of the husband: under whose wing, protection, and *cover*, she performs every thing; and is therefore called in our law-french a *feme-covert*." 2 WILLIAM BLACKSTONE, COMMENTARIES ON THE LAWS OF ENGLAND 430 (1979) (reprint of the 1766 edition). The ways in which the Bible was used by American courts to justify this doctrine are discussed *infra* at notes 32–123 and accompanying text.

23. JOHN AYLIFFE, PARERGON JURIS CANONICI ANGLICANI 359 (1734).

24. *Id.* at 359–60.

25. *Id.* at 360.

26. JAMES VISCOUNT OF STAIR, THE INSTITUTIONS OF THE LAW OF SCOTLAND 105 (David M. Walker ed., 1981).

27. *Id.*

28. *Id.* at 106.

29. LAWRENCE STONE, ROAD TO DIVORCE: ENGLAND, 1530–1987, at 301–06 (1990).

30. *See generally* Harvey Crouch, *The Evolution of Parliamentary Divorce*, 52 TUL. L. REV. 513 (1978).

31. A good account of the Marital Causes Act of 1857, which removed jurisdiction over domestic relations from the ecclesiastical courts and placed it instead in the hands of royal judges, appears in chapter five of STEPHEN CRETNEY, FAMILY LAW IN THE TWENTIETH CENTURY: A HISTORY 161–95 (2003).

32. An important study of the influence of Blackstone on early American legal education is Steve Sheppard, *Casebooks, Commentaries, and Curmudgeons: An Introductory History of Law in the Lecture Hall*, 82 IOWA L. REV. 547–64 (1997).

33. 1 BLACKSTONE, *supra* note 22, at 39.

34. *Id.* at 40.

35. *Id.* at 41.

36. *Id.* at 42.

37. *Id.* Closely related to these two types of natural law is a third branch of the law, the "law of nations" (*ius gentium*), which Blackstone understood as essentially derivative of these other laws. Blackstone explained the relationship: "Hence arises a third kind of law to regulate this mutual intercourse [among states], called 'the law

of nations;' which . . . depends entirely upon the rules of natural law, or upon mutual compacts, treaties, leagues, and agreements . . . ." *Id.* at 43.

38. *Id.* at 46.

39. *Id.* at 50.

40. *Id.* at 84. Blackstone treats the "civil and canon laws" as a branch of these laws subordinate to the common law, which is the most exalted law of the English nation. *Id.*

41. One might consult the opening passages of Gratian's *Decretum.* Gratian begins with the observation that humankind is governed by "law" and "customs." And by law, Gratian means the *ius naturae* found in the Gospels and in Jesus Christ's Golden Rule, "Do unto others as you would have them do unto you." D. 1, pr. Gratian followed this with an excerpt from Isidore of Seville that commenced: "*Omnes leges aut divinae sunt, aut humanae* ("All laws are either divine or human"). D. 1. 1. Blackstone's own definition of law clearly fits within this larger tradition originating in the twelfth century.

42. *See* Harold J. Berman and Charles J. Reid, Jr., *The Transformation of English Legal Science,* 45 EMORY L. J. 437 (1996).

43. Stuart Banner, *When Christianity Was Part of the Common Law,* 16 LAW & HIST. REV. 27, 30 (1998).

44. *Id.* at 27.

45. *See supra* note 15–20 and accompanying text.. See also, for example, the discussion of the divine plan for marriage as it applies to believers and nonbelievers in a canonist like Rufinus. RUFINUS, SUMMA DECRETORUM 442–43 (Heinrich Singer, ed.) (Aalen: Scientia Verlag, 1963).

46. Ayliffe, *supra* note 23, at 360.

47. *Gaudium et Spes,* para. 48. I am here following the translation of AUSTIN FLANNERY, O.P., VATICAN COUNCIL II: THE CONCILIAR AND POST-CONCILIAR DOCUMENTS 950 (1975).

48. Drew's Appeal, 57 N.H. 181, 182–83 (1876). The privacy cases, of course, retained the language about human intimacy but stripped away references to divine law.

49. *In re* Estate of McLaughlin v. McLaughlin, 30 P. 651, 658 (Wash. 1892).

50. *Ex parte* Post, 47 Ind. 142, 143 (1874).

51. Nichols v. Nichols, 48 S.W. 947 (Mo. 1908).

52. Diemer v. Diemer, 6 A.D.2d 822, 823 (N.Y. App. Div. 1958) (quoting Raymond v. Raymond, 79 A. 430, 431 (N.J. Ch. 1909)).

53. *In re* Enderle Marriage License, 1 Pa. D. & C.,2d 114 (Orphans' Ct. 1954).

54. *Id.*

55. *Id.* at 120. *Enderle's* invocation of Divine Law was repeated with apparent approval by at least two subsequent Pennsylvania decisions. In *Adameze v. Adameze,* the court, relying on language in *Enderle,* determined, on its reading of the Book of *Leviticus,* that marriage between first cousins related by blood was not prohibited by divine law. *See* Adameze v. Adameze, 47 Pa. D. & C.2d 445, 449 (Ct. Com. Pl.

1969). And in Marriage of M.E.W. and M.L.B., 4 Pa. D. & C.3d 51, 58 (Ct. Com Pl. 1977), the court cited without discussion or disapproval *Enderle's* use of divine law.

56. Pryor v. Pryor, 235 S.W. 419, 420-21 (Ark. 1922).

57. Grievance Comm. of Hartford County of Bar v. Broder, 152 A. 292, 295 (Conn. 1930) (quoting the sentencing judge at the time of the disciplined lawyer's conviction).

58. Sutton v. Warren, 51 Mass. 451, 452 (1845).

59. Moore Shipbuilding Corp. v. Indus. Accident Comm'n, 196 P. 257, 261 (Cal. 1921) (Oliver, J., dissenting). The language of Justice Oliver was subsequently repeated and endorsed by the Indiana Court of Appeals. *See* Russell v. Johnson, 42 N.E.2d 392, 398 (Ind. App. 1942).

A California appellate tribunal made a similar statement in a case with unusual facts. A wife alleged that her ex-husband's parents tortiously interfered with their marriage, causing it to fail. The court responded, "It is not unlikely in moments of resentment they said harsh and unkind things about her; but that fact alone does not justify an inference that they violated the laws of God and society by trying to break up the marriage relation of these young people." Bourne v. Bourne, 195 P. 489, 495 (Cal. Ct. App. 1919).

60. Norman v. Norman, 176 P.2d 349, 355 (Wash. 1947) (Simpson, J., dissenting).

61. Harrison v. State, 69 S.W. 500, 502 (Tex. Crim. App. 1902).

62. For most of his seventy years of public life, Learned Hand maintained agnosticism on matters of religious belief, although once, at the age of fourteen, he wrote a letter passionately invoking the mercy of Christ at the time of his father's death. In advancing old age, he would joke about what the ideal heaven would look like: He would hit a grand slam home run in a baseball game in the morning, return a punt for a touchdown in the afternoon, and be named after-dinner speaker ahead of such luminaries as Socrates and Voltaire. All of this, however, was in jest. *See* GERALD GUNTHER, LEARNED HAND: THE MAN AND THE JUDGE 22–23, 679–680 (Knopf 1995).

63. United States v. Francioso, 164 F.2d 163 (2d Cir. 1947). After noting that marriages between uncles and nieces were not forbidden under New York law until 1893, Hand asserted, "To be sure, its legality does not finally determine its morality, but it helps to do so, for the fact that disapproval of such marriages was so long in taking the form of law, shows that it is condemned in no sense as marriages forbidden by 'God's law.'" *Id.* at 164.

64. *See* Charles J. Reid, Jr., *The Disposal of the Dead: And What It Tells Us About American Society and Law, in* FIGURES IN THE CARPET: FINDING THE HUMAN PERSON IN THE AMERICAN PAST 428 (Wilfred M. McClay ed., 2007).

65. 2 CHANCELLOR JAMES KENT, COMMENTARIES ON AMERICAN LAW 74 (1836).

66. *See* Reid, *supra* note 12.

67. *See In re* Enderle Marriage License, *supra* note 53.

68. On Bishop's career and the great influence he enjoyed with his contemporaries, see Stephen A. Siegel, *Joel Bishop's Orthodoxy*, 13 LAW & HIST. REV. 215 (1995).

69. JOEL PRENTISS BISHOP, NEW COMMENTARIES ON MARRIAGE, DIVORCE, AND SEPARATION 316 (1891).

70. *Id.* at 318.

71. See Leviticus 18:6–18 for the entire list.

72. *Id.*

73. Jenkins v. Jenkins' Heirs, 32 Ky. 102 (1834).

74. *Id.* at 104–05.

75. *Id.*

76. Commonwealth v. Ashey, 142 N.E. 788 (Mass. 1924).

77. *Id.* at 788.

78. *Id.*at 788.

79. State v. Smith, 30 La. Ann. 846, 849 (1878).

80. State v. Andrews, 149 N.W. 245, 247 (Iowa 1914).

81. State v. Lamb, 227 N.W. 830, 831 (Iowa 1929).

82. Bhd. of Locomotive Firemen and Enginemen v. Hogan, 5 F. Supp. 598 (D. Minn. 1934).

83. *Id.* at 604–05.

84. Lipham v. State, 53 S.E. 817 (Ga. 1906).

85. *Id.* at 818.

86. People v. Lake, 17 N.E. 146, 146 (N.Y. 1888).

87. *Id.*at 147.

88. *Id. Cf.* Morgan v. State, 11 Ala. 289, 291 (1847) (sexual relations between a parent and child "at variance with the laws of God and man" and a violation of the Henrician statute "prohibit[ing] all marriage within the Levitical degrees"); State v. Bartley, 263 S.W. 95, 96 (Mo. 1924) (relying on Joel Prentiss Bishop and its own reading of the Henrician statute to condemn "marriages between persons related by blood or marriage within the Levitical degrees").

89. *See, e.g.,* Marshall v. Wabash R.R. Co., 25 S.W. 179, 181 (Mo. 1894) (distinguishing the common-law rule with its reliance on the Levitical degrees to deny marital or inheritance rights and state statutory reform that reaches a contrary result respecting inheritance); Brisbin v. Huntington, 103 N.W. 144, 147 (Iowa 1905) (relying on language similar to *Marshall* to reach the same result); Wheeler v. Southern Ry. Co., 71 So. 812, 814 (Miss. 1916) (the harshness of the common-law rules repealed by statute); L.T. Dickason Coal Co. v. Liddil, 94 N.E. 411, 412 (Ind. App. 1911) (relying in part on the result in *Marshall* to reach a similar conclusion); Williams v. McKeene, 193 Ill. App. 615, 618 (App. Ct. 1915) (describing the law of Henry VIII as "God's law" but recognizing the possibility of statutory amendment where inheritance rights were concerned).

90. Genesis 2:24 (King James).

91. Matthew 19:5–6.

92. Mark 10:6–9 ("But from the beginning of creation God made them male and female. For this cause shall a man leave his father and mother, and cleave to his wife. And they twain shall be one flesh, so then they are no more twain, but one flesh. What therefore God hath joined together, let not man put asunder.").

93. Ephesians 5:30–31.

94. Jonas v. Hirshberg, 48 N.E. 656 (Ind. App. 1897).

95. *Id.* at 662.

96. *Id.*

97. Powell v. Powell, 29 Vt. 148, 150 (1856).

98. DeMauriac v. DeMauriac, 220 N.W. 786 (Mich. 1928).

99. *Id.* at 787.

100. Maricopa County v. Douglas, 208 P.2d 646 (Ariz. 1949).

101. *Id.* at 651. The word "community," standing alone as a noun in this quotation, is an interesting and perhaps deliberately ambiguous choice of words. In the context of a suit over the extent to which the state might invade community property, the court clearly intended to say that the couple's property rights might not be so seized. But a more extensive reading of this noun is also possible. One might thus understand the court to be protecting not the community property alone, but the "community" formed by the unity of husband and wife. Such a reading is supported by the court's subsequent invocation of Genesis 2:24.

102. Humber v. Humber, 68 So. 161 (Miss. 1915). The court described the substance of the husband's claims thus:

> From the proof adduced by appellant it appears his purpose to show that the cruel and inhuman treatment complained of consisted of the conduct of his wife in a number of incidents, during their travels, in which she displayed temper and dissatisfaction with him and his provisions for her comfort and entertainment, and wherein she was inconsiderate of his feelings, abusive to him, discourteous and rude to his friends and kinsfolk, and generally disagreeable in her demeanor.

Id. at 161.

103. *Id.* at 164.

104. Logan v. Logan, 41 Ky. 142 (1841). The court's delicacy is remarkable:

> As might have been expected, [the couple] lived together in apparent harmony and happiness until early February, 1838, when, for the first time, so far as we are informed, their domestic peace was disturbed by intemperate complaints and upbraidings on her part for alleged grievances, neither satisfactorily established nor explained by proof; and by responsive conduct upon his part, sometimes neither conciliatory nor the most prudent, and which tended rather to exasperate than to soothe the deeply moved feelings of his discontented and irritated wife. Their discord, soon becoming clamorous, attracted public observation which instead of stifling, seemed only to inflame her heated passions. The intervention of friends, in and out of the church, invoked by Mr. Logan ostensibly for pacification, having failed and only added fuel to the flame, the prospect of cordial reconciliation became almost hopeless; and the irritability and wretchedness of the parties seemed so fixed and extreme as to indicate either the existence of some untold and deep-rooted grief or a destitution of that love and confidence which alone can happily cement the conjugal union, and without which wedlock is a curse.

Id. at 143.

105. *Id.* at 147.

106. *Id.*

107. *Saevitia* is briefly discussed above at *supra* note 20 and accompanying text.

108. Lanier v. Lanier, 52 Tenn. 462 (1871).

109. *Id.* at 463–64.

110. *Id.* at 464–65.

111. Daniel M. Robinson, *Tennessee Politics and the Agrarian Revolt, 1886–1896,* 20 MISSISSIPPI VALLEY HISTORICAL REVIEW 365, 373–78 (1933) provides a useful thumbnail sketch of Turney's career in Tennessee's gubernatorial politics. Because of Turney's interest in prison reform, a correctional institution for young offenders was later named in his honor.

112. Lanier v. Lanier, 52 Tenn. 462, 466 (Turney, J., dissenting). Turney continued, "The amity between the persons, where it is solid and sincere, will rather gain by [constraint]; and where it is wavering and uncertain, this is the best expedient for fixing it." *Id.* at 466–67.

113. *Id.* at 467–468.

114. *Id.* at 468.

115. *Id.* at 470.

116. *Id.*

117. *Id.* at 471.

118. *Id.* at 471–72.

119. *Id.* at 472.

120. Another instance in which divine law is invoked is the *sui generis* case of *Armstrong v. Berwick Borough Overseers,* 10 Pa. C.C. 337 (Ct. Com. Pl. 1891). At issue was an attempt by overseers of a poor house to separate a husband and wife. The court rejected this possibility, reasoning that "[t]he common law declares against it, and the divine law says that after marriage, they are no longer twain but one flesh, and what therefore God hath joined together let no man put asunder." *Id.*

121. *See, e.g.,* Bear's Administrator v. Bear, 33 Pa. 525, 526 (1859) ("The doctrine of the common law was, that the husband and wife are one person, the twain have become one flesh."); Jaques v. Trustees of the Methodist Episcopal Church in New York, 17 Johns. 548, 582 (N.Y. Sup. Ct. 1820) (Platt, J., concurring and dissenting) ("I confess that I love and venerate the primeval notion of that mystical and hallowed union of husband and wife: when 'they twain become one flesh.'"); Byrd v. Vance, 124 S.E. 705, 707 (Ga. 1924) (looking to the biblical language of "the twain are one flesh" to justify wife's legal disabilities); Madden v. Hall, 132 P. 291, 294 (Cal. Dist. Ct. App. 1913) ("The oneness constituted by the marriage relation at common law doubtless is based upon the statement of the Christ, 'For this cause a man will leave his father and his mother and cleave unto his wife, and they twain become one flesh.'" (quoting Warr v. Honeck, 29 P. 1117, 1118 (Utah 1892)); Pelzer, Rodgers & Co. v. Campbell & Co. 15 S.C. 581, 588 (1881) ("To speak in general terms, husband and wife are a unity, or, as it was expressed by the great law-giver, 'they twain shall be one flesh.'"); Drake v. E. M. Birdsall & Co., 10 Ohio Dec. Reprint 56 (Ct. Com. Pl. 1887) (speaking of a legislative act that had the effect of limiting the common-law disability placed on wives' contractual capacity, the court wrote, "[I]t is not to be assumed . . . that the Ohio Legislature has undertaken to annihilate nature,

nullify science, enact as law that which is condemned by the Divine Law, by human reason, by the common law which is the 'perfection of reason.'"). *Cf.* Corn Exch. Ins. Co. v. Babcock, 42 N.Y. 613, 645 (1870) (rejecting "[t]he old religious idea of a mystic union in marriage, by which 'they twain shall become one flesh,'" and the doctrine of *feme covert* consequent upon this teaching).

122. John Wigmore, in his treatise on the law of evidence, asserted that the oldest justification for the spousal testimonial immunity was Sir Edward Coke's (1552–1634) declaration that "[i]t hath been resolved by the justices that a wife cannot be produced either for or against her husband, *quia sunt duae animae in carne sua.*" 2 JOHN HENRY WIGMORE, EVIDENCE IN TRIALS AT COMMON LAW 857 (rev. by James H. Chadbourn, 1979) (quoting SIR EDWARD COKE, COMMENTARY UPON LITTLETON 6b (1628)). Older cases, generally quoting Coke's Latin, echoed this sentiment. Thus, *Smith v. Boston and Maine Railroad* asserted that Coke's maxim reflected a broader public policy "which regards as of vital importance the preservation of domestic peace and harmony, and the promotion of the unreserved confidence between the husband and wife which the sanctities of that relation require." 44 N.H. 325, 334 (1862). In *Handlong v. Barnes*, a New Jersey court also defended *in carne una* "upon the broad ground of the importance of preserving the sanctity of the marriage relation." 30 N.J.L. 69, 171 (1862). *Cf.* Reeves v. Herr, 59 Ill. 81, 83–84 (1871) (concurring in the same general proposition). On the other hand, Judge Charles Edward Clark, principal draftsman of the Federal Rules of Civil Procedure, wrote in 1949: "Admittedly the common-law principle that 'a wife cannot be produced either for or against her husband, *quia sunt duae animae in carne una*' . . . is gone; indeed, there is none now so poor as to do it reverence." United States vs. Walker, 176 F.2d 564, 569 (2d Cir. 1949) (Clark, J., dissenting). *Cf. In re Grand Jury Matter*, 673 F.2d 688 (3d Cir. 1982) which presented the question whether an offer of prosecutorial immunity overrode the spousal privilege. The court's majority ruled that the spousal immunity continued to serve important social goods, such "marital harmony." *Id.* at 693. Writing in dissent, Judge Arlin Adams reviewed the history of the privilege, beginning with Coke, to conclude that it should be strictly construed when applicable at all. *Id.* at 696–99 (Adams, J., dissenting).

123. The history of spousal immunity from suit, including its foundation in the scriptural interpretation of the early common lawyers as well as early case law, is reviewed in Carl Tobias, *Interspousal Tort Immunity in America*, 23 GA. L. REV. 359, 361–441 (1989) (a thoroughly researched argument for the abolition of the immunity that cites many early materials). Stephen Kelson, *The Doctrine of Interspousal Immunity: Does It Still Exist in Utah?* 3 JOURNAL OF LAW AND FAMILY STUDIES 161, 161–63 (2001) and Laura Wannamaker, *Note: Waite v. Waite: The Florida Supreme Court Abrogates the Doctrine of Interspousal Immunity*, 45 MERCER L. REV. 903, 904–10 (1994) are shorter studies that also look to the religious origins of the doctrine. Reliance on "one flesh" has now largely disappeared, but the philosophy that it expressed—a desire for harmony and unity between the spouses—can still be found in some cases. Thus, the Virginia Supreme Court wrote in 1975:

We are not concerned with the outmoded fiction that a husband and wife are of "one flesh." We are concerned . . . with a policy and with a rule of law that are designed to protect and encourage the preservation of marriages. Interspousal immunity is only a part of a whole system of laws and policies which recognizes the mutual obligations arising from a marriage and which encourages both marital and family harmony.

Korman v. Carpenter, 216 S.E.2d 195, 197 (Va. 1975).

124. The 1983 Code of Canon Law of the Catholic Church, c. 1059, declares that Christian marriages are regulated by divine law and canon law.

125. Grazyna Kubica, *Malinowski's Years in Poland, in* MALINOWSKI BETWEEN TWO WORLDS: THE POLISH ROOTS OF AN ANTHROPOLOGICAL TRADITION 88–90 (Roy Ellen, Ernest Gellner, Grazyna Kubica, and Janusz Mucha eds., 1988).

126. MICHAEL W. YOUNG, MALINOWSKI: ODYSSEY OF AN ANTHROPOLOGIST, 1884–1920, at 73–86 (2004).

127. Bronislaw Malinowski, *Religion and Magic: The Golden Bough, in* THE EARLY WRITINGS OF BRONISLAW MALINOWSKI 118 (Robert J. Thornton and Peter Skalnik, eds., Ludwik Krzanowski, tr., 1993).

128. BRONISLAW MALINOWSKI, FREEDOM AND CIVILIZATION 209 (1944) ("In all revealed dogma there is always one pragmatic truth: it not only tells us that totems, spirits, saints, and gods exist, it also demonstrates how by prayer, sacrifice, sacrament, and moral communion we can reach the Divinity.").

129. See, for instance, his use of "sacrament" to describe marriage. *See infra* note 137 and accompanying text.

130. BRONISLAW MALINOWSKI, A DIARY IN THE STRICT SENSE OF THE TERM 176 (1989). Malinowski's daughter recalled, regarding her parents' faith and their marriage: "It was a civil, not a religious, wedding, because neither of them were Christian believers. Bron[islaw], like most Poles, had been brought up in all the rites and beliefs of the Roman Catholic Church but lost his faith at an early age, an instance where his devout mother's influence failed." Helena Wayne, *Bronislaw Malinowski: The Influence of Various Women on His Life and Works*, 12 AMERICAN ETHNOLOGIST 529, 535 (1985).

131. BRONISLAW MALINOWSKI, SEX, CULTURE, AND MYTH 3 (1962).

132. *Id.* at 4.

133. *Id.* at 7.

134. On Malinowski's relationship to Westermarck, see Michael W. Young, *Introduction, in* THE ETHNOGRAPHY OF MALINOWSKI: THE TROBRIAND ISLANDS, 1915–1918, at 4 (Michael W. Young, ed., 1979).

135. Malinowski, *Sex, Culture, and Myth, supra* note 30, at 3.

136. *Id.* at 4.

137. *Id.* at 3.

138. MARRIAGE PAST AND PRESENT: A DEBATE BETWEEN ROBERT BRIFFAULT AND BRONISLAW MALINOWSKI (M.F. Ashley Montagu, ed., 1956).

139. *Id.* at 64.

140. *Id.* at 65.

141. *Id.*

142. *Id.*

143. *Id.* at 68.

144. *Id.* at 66.

145. *Id.* at 67.

146. *Id.* at 70.

147. *Id.* at 71.

148. *Id.* at 72.

149. *Id.*

150. Mary Ann Glendon, Rights Talk: The Impoverishment of Political Discourse (1991).

151. *Id.* at 3–4.

152. *Id.* at 4.

153. *Id.* at 12–13.

154. *Id.* at 12.

155. *Id.* at 13.

156. *Id.* ("Like the words of the marriage ritual, they etch themselves on our memory").

157. This is chapter four, entitled "The Missing Language of Responsibility." *Id.* at 76–108.

158. *Id.* at 83.

159. *Id.* at 89 (discussing *Jackson v. City of Joliet*, 715 F.2d 1200 (7th Cir. 1983)). In *Jackson*, a federal court, influenced by the no-duty-to-rescue rule, denied recovery to the families of two automobile accident victims where the suit had been brought against a police officer who, having happened upon the accident scene, failed to check for victims or summon assistance, such as paramedics or an ambulance. Citing specifically to *Yania v. Bigan*, 155 A.2d 343 (Pa. 1959), Judge Richard Posner announced in *Jackson* that the Constitution was intended to safeguard negative liberties and was not meant to provide protection for affirmative rights, even the right to be aided by an officer of the law.

160. DeShaney v. Winnebago County Dept. of Soc. Servs., 489 U.S. 189 (1989).

161. *Id.* at 193. Joshua suffered "a series of hemorrhages causes by traumatic injuries to the head inflicted over a long period of time." *Id.*

162. *Id.* at 192.

163. *Id.* at 196.

164. Glendon, *supra* note 150, at 97.

165. *Id.* at 94–97.

166. *Id.* at 95.

167. *Id.* at 97.

168. An important study of some these themes is Michael V. Hernandez, *A Flawed Foundation: Christianity's Loss of Preeminent Influence on American Law*, 56 Rutgers L. Rev. 625 (2004).

169. Acts 5:29.

170. Goodridge v. Dep't. of Pub. Health, 798 N.E.2d 941 (Mass. 2003).

171. *Id.* at 954.

172. *See, e.g.*, Martin v. Commonwealth, 1 Mass. 347, 398 (1805) (addressing the obligations of women married to British sympathizers during the Revolutionary War and declaring that "they owed [a duty of obedience] to their husbands," "by the law of God," and were thus under no obligation to abandon them as a condition of retaining property rights in Massachusetts); Sutton v. Warren, 51 Mass. 451, 452 (1845) (declaring incestuous marriages invalid as "against the laws of God"); Pratt v. Pratt, 32 N.E. 747, 748 (Mass. 1892) (declaring an intention to incorporate into Massachusetts divorce law the rules governing "collusion, connivance, condonation or recrimination, all of which we have adopted into our procedure from the canon and ecclesiastical law of England").

173. *See supra* note 3 and accompanying text.

174. Harold J. Berman, The Interaction of Law and Religion (1974).

175. *Id.* at 24.

176. *Id.* at 25.

177. *Id.* at 26–27.

178. *Id.* at 27.

179. *Id.* at 27–28.

180. *Id.* at 28.

181. *Id.*

182. *Id.* at 29. Berman adds: "Even Joseph Stalin had to reintroduce into Soviet law elements which would make his people believe in its inherent rightness—emotional elements, sacred elements; for otherwise the persuasiveness of Soviet law would have totally vanished, and even Stalin could not rule solely by threat of force." *Id.*

183. *Id.* at 30.

184. *Id.* at 34.

185. *Id.* at 34–35.

186. Linda C. McClain, *"God's Created Order," Gender Complementarity, and the Federal Marriage Amendment*, 20 BYU J. Pub. L. 313 (2006).

187. *Id.* at 314 (quoting Marilyn Musgrave). Musgrave was not alone in the 2006 congressional debate over same-sex marriage to make such a claim. McClain also identifies Congressmen Steven King of Iowa and Mike Pence of Indiana, who made similar claims. *Id.* at 317–19. In her House testimony, Musgrave declared:

> The self-evident differences and complementary design of men and women are part of [the] created order. We were created as male and female, and for this reason a man will leave his father and mother and be joined with his wife, and the two shall become one in the mystical, spiritual, and physical union we call "marriage."

House Judiciary Committee, Subcommittee on the Constitution, Hearing Testimony, May 13, 2004, 108th Congress (statement of Marilyn Musgrave, Chairwoman). Musgrave's Senate testimony for the most part tracks closely her House statement, although she added: "[M]arriage is a sacred institution, designed by the Creator [as] the union of a man and a woman." Senate Judiciary Committee Hearing on Same-Sex Marriage, June 22, 2004 (2004 W.L. 1413039 (F.D.C.H.)).

188. McClain, *supra* note 186, at 328–29. *See also* Linda C. McClain, *The Relevance of Religion to a Lawyer's Work*, 66 FORDHAM L. REV 1241 (1998).

189. WILLIAM N. ESKRIDGE, JR., EQUALITY PRACTICE: CIVIL UNIONS AND THE FUTURE OF GAY RIGHTS 129–31 (2002).

190. *Id.* at 129.

191. John T. Noonan, Jr., *The Bishops and the Ruling Class: The Moral Formation of Public Policy, in* RELIGION, SCIENCE, AND PUBLIC POLICY 138, 141 (Frank T. Birtel, ed., 1987).

192. Noonan continues, "Every public policy is an imposition on some persons, some groups. Pluralist democracy does not mean freedom from such impositions, but freedom to participate in the process. The Church, through the actions of Catholics, is free to be a participant." *Id.*

193. ALASDAIR MACINTYRE, AFTER VIRTUE 263 (2d ed. 1984).

194. *In re* Marriage Cases, 183 P.3d 384 (Cal. 2008).

Afterword: Douglas Laycock

1. I am grateful to Bruce Frier, Andrew Koppelman, Anthony Picarello, and Robin Fretwell Wilson for prompt and helpful comments on an earlier draft, to Madeline Kochen for references in the Talmud, and to my Texas student Charles Sanders for research assistance.

2. Equal Access Act, 20 U.S.C. §§ 4071 *et seq.* (2000).

3. For a brief survey of the litigation, see Todd A. DeMitchell & Richard Fossey, *Student Speech: School Boards, Gay/Straight Alliances, and the Equal Access Act*, 2008 B.Y.U. EDUC. & L.J. 89.

4. Douglas Laycock, *Taking Constitutions Seriously*, 59 TEX. L. REV. 343, 376 (1981).

5. Statement of Douglas Laycock, *Religious Liberty Protection Act of 1999*, Hearing before the Subcomm. on the Constitution of the House Comm. on the Judiciary 100, 103 (May 12, 1999) ("The goal here is for people with fundamentally different beliefs and values to be able to live together in peace in the same society. And the way to make that happen is with strong gay rights legislation and strong religious liberty legislation, and sort out case by case the relative reach of those two statutes."); *see also id.* at 120 ("There should be legal protection for gays and lesbians and also legal protection for persons with religious commitments to traditional sexual morality. There should be a general gay rights law, and there should be religious exemptions."). I gave similar testimony to the Senate Judiciary Committee in September 1999.

6. Brief *Amici Curiae* of the American Jewish Congress, the National Council of the Churches of Christ in the USA, the Universal Fellowship of Metropolitan Community Churches, and American Friends Service Committee, In the Interest of WKG, No. 02-99-00143 (Tex. App.–Fort Worth 1999). Marc Stern and I were the principal authors of this brief. The court's opinion is unpublished.

7. *See, e.g.*, ANDREW KOPPELMAN, THE GAY RIGHTS QUESTION IN CONTEMPORARY AMERICAN LAW (2002); Andrew Koppelman, *Is It Fair to Give Religion Special Treatment*, 2006 U. ILL. L. REV. 571 (answering that it is); Andrew Koppelman, *The Decline and Fall of the Case Against Same-Sex Marriage*, 2 ST. THOMAS L.J. 5 (2005). On the conflict between the two, see Andrew Koppelman, *Why Antidiscrimination Protections for Gay People Should Have Religious Exemptions*, 72 BROOK. L. REV. 125 (2006) [hereinafter Koppelman, *Antidiscrimination*].

8. James Brooke, *To Be Young, Gay and Going to High School in Utah*, N.Y. TIMES 8 (Feb. 26, 1996).

9. H.R. 4019, 105th Cong. (1998).

10. H.R. 1691, 106th Cong. (1999).

11. H.R. 1431, 110th Cong. (2007).

12. Robin Fretwell Wilson, *Matters of Conscience: Lessons for Same-Sex Marriage from the Healthcare Context, supra*, at note 34 and accompanying text.

13. Marc D. Stern, *Same-Sex Marriage and the Churches, supra*, at notes 29–72, 166–181 and accompanying text.

14. A Methodist association in New Jersey has lost its tax exemption for an outdoor pavilion because it refused to permit same-sex civil-union ceremonies there. See Wilson, *supra* note 12, at notes 16–18, 38, and accompanying text; Jill P. Capuzzo, *Group Loses Tax Break Over Gay Union Issue*, N.Y. TIMES B2 (Sept. 18, 2007). But judging by press accounts, the tax exemption at issue is not a religious tax exemption or a general non-profit tax exemption; it is apparently an exemption for preserving open space under the state's Green Acres Program. *Id.* And the revocation applies only to the pavilion and the land immediately under it, not to the whole church and not even to the association's surrounding property. *Id.*

15. Sweden v. Ake Green (Sup. Ct. Sweden 2005), discussed in Stern, *supra* note 13, at note 24 and accompanying text.

16. The Catholic doctrine of "cooperation" is carefully explained in 3 GERMAIN GRISEZ, THE WAY OF THE LORD JESUS: DIFFICULT MORAL QUESTIONS 871–97 (1997). For a Jewish example, see BABYLONIAN TALMUD, *Tractate Baba Kamma*, Folios 117a–117b (discussing whether persons with custody of another's property sufficiently resisted, or implicitly cooperated with, thieves attempting to take the property).

17. *See* CHRISTOPHER KUTZ, COMPLICITY: ETHICS AND LAW FOR A COLLECTIVE AGE (2000).

18. *See* Smith v. Fair Employment & Hous. Comm'n, 913 P.2d 909 (Cal. 1996) (state agency arguing successfully that religious landlord must rent to unmarried couple).

19. *See* Red Light Abatement Law, CAL. PENAL CODE § 11225 (West 2000) (condemning as a nuisance "every building or place in or upon which acts of illegal gambling . . . lewdness, assignation, or prostitution, are held to occur," and making the owner subject to injunction and damages); People v. Bhakta, 37 Cal. Rptr. 3d 652 (Cal. Ct. App. 2006) (enforcing the act against owners of a motel).

20. *See, e.g.,* CAL. CIV. CODE § 51 (West 2007) (the Unruh Civil Rights Act, pro-hibiting discrimination on the basis of sexual orientation in "all business establish-ments of every kind whatsoever," with no religious exceptions); N.Y. CIV. RIGHTS LAW § 40-c (West 1992) (prohibiting discrimination against any person "in his or her civil rights" by "any other person or by any firm, corporation or institution," with no religious exceptions).

21. *See, e.g.,* CAL. GOV'T CODE § 12926 (West 2005) (defining employer for pur-poses of employment discrimination laws not to include "a religious association or corporation not organized for private profit"). Marc Stern more fully describes the "crazy quilt pattern" of religious exemptions in antidiscrimination statutes. See Stern, *supra* note 13, at notes 274–305 and accompanying text.

22. *See, e.g.,* Hustler Magazine v. Falwell, 485 U.S. 46, 55 (1988) ("An 'outra-geousness' standard thus runs afoul of our longstanding refusal to allow damages to be awarded because the speech in question may have an adverse emotional impact on the audience."); FCC v. Pacifica Found., 438 U.S. 726, 745 (1978) ("But the fact that society may find speech offensive is not a sufficient reason for suppressing it. In-deed, if it is the speaker's opinion that gives offense, that consequence is a reason for according it constitutional protection."); Street v. New York, 394 U.S. 576, 592 (1969) ("It is firmly settled that under our Constitution the public expression of ideas may not be prohibited merely because the ideas are themselves offensive to some of their hearers.").

23. Koppelman, *Antidiscrimination, supra* note 7, at 136 n.51.

24. *Compare* Cohen v. Cowles Media Co., 501 U.S. 663 (1991) (holding, over four dissents, that First Amendment does not protect newspaper from suit for breach of a contract not to disclose the name of a source).

25. See 3 DAN B. DOBBS, LAW OF REMEDIES: DAMAGES – EQUITY – RESTITUTION § 12.5(1) at 113 (2d ed. 1993).

26. *See, e.g.,* An Act to Prevent the further Growth of Popery, 2 Geo. I, c. 10 (1715) ("No papist in trade shall keep more than two apprentices at a time, except in the hempen and flaxen manufacture"); An Act for enlarging the Time for taking the Oath of Abjuration, 1 Ann., stat. 2, c. 21 (1702) ("all ecclesiastical persons, mas-ters, head, and fellows of the university of Dublin, school-teachers, and barristers, at-torneys, solicitors, proctors, and notaries in Ireland" must take anti-Catholic oath); An Act for the Abrogating the Oath of Supremacy in Ireland and Appointing Other Oaths, 3 Wm. & Mary, c. 2 (1691) ("all persons in Ireland having any employment or office eecclesiastical, civil or military, the heads and fellows of the University of Dublin, master of any hospital or school, barrister, clerk in chancery, attorney, and professor of law, Physick or other science" must take anti-Catholic oath); An Act for preventing Dangers which may happen from Popish Recusants, 25 Car. II, c. 2 (1673) ("every person or persons as well Peeres as Commoners that shall beare any Office or Offices Civill or Military or shall receive any Pay, Salary, Fee or Wages by reason of any Patent or Grant from his Majestie or shall have Command or Place of Trust from, or under his Majestie or from any of his Majestyes Predecessors or by his or their au-

thority, . . . or in his Majestyes Navy . . . or shall be of the Household or in the Service of imployment of his Majestie" must take anti-Catholic oath).

27. *See, e.g.*, Smith v. Fair Employment & Hous. Comm'n, 913 P.2d 909, 926 (Cal. 1996) ("the landlord in this case does not claim that her religious beliefs require her to rent apartments; the religious injunction is simply that she not rent to unmarried couples. No religious exercise is burdened if she follows the alternative course of placing her capital in another investment.").

28. This section elaborates an idea that I have been urging in less formal venues for several years, starting on the ReligionLaw listserve in late 2003 (*see* http://lists.ucla.edu/pipermail/religionlaw/2003-December/016053.html (last visited July 24, 2008)), and then in a debate on March 24, 2005, sponsored by the Texas Journal of Civil Liberties and Civil Rights, (video available at http://realaudio.cc.utexas.edu:8080/asxgen/law/depts/media/Reels/TJCLCR3-24.wmv (last visited July 24, 2008)). I presented the argument orally at the 2005 conference on which this book is based. Conflicting obligations, including an unexpected interstate move, made it appear impossible for me to produce a written version of that presentation. Delays in the other contributions and the need for a concluding essay led to the possibility of this shorter version.

29. *See, e.g.*, Douglas Laycock, *The Many Meanings of Separation*, 70 U. Chi. L. Rev. 1667 (2003).

30. Genesis 2:24.

31. Matthew 19:6.

32. *See, e.g.*, Exodus 20:14; Matthew 19:18.

33. Goodridge v. Dep't of Pub. Health, 798 N.E.2d 941, 955 (Mass. 2003).

34. *See* Cal. Fam. Code § 2210(f) (West 2004); N.Y. Dom. Rel. Law § 7.3 (West 1999). Each of these statutes makes such a marriage voidable, not void, which means the marriage is valid until and unless the offended spouse sues to void the marriage.

35. *See, e.g.*, 750 Ill. Comp. Stat. Ann. 5/301(2) (West 1999).

36. *See, e.g.*, N.J. Stat. Ann. § 2A:34-1.c (West Supp. 2008); Tex. Fam. Code § 6.106 (West 2006).

37. *See, e.g.*, 13 Del. Code Ann. § 1506(a)(2) (Michie 1999) (one year); Ky. Rev. Stat. § 403.120(1)(b) (Michie 1999) (90 days).

38. Favrot v. Barnes, 332 So.2d 873, (La. Ct. App.), *rev'd on other grounds*, 339 So.2d 843 (La. 1976) (holding, prior to enactment of no-fault divorce in Louisiana, that prenuptial agreement to have sex only once a week was not effective to change marital obligations concerning sex, and thus did not make it a fault to request sex more often than agreed); M.T. v. J.T., 355 A.2d 204 (N.J. Super. Ct., App. Div. 1976) (holding that marriage between male and post-operative male-to-female transsexual was valid where evidence showed that transsexual was capable of normal sexual intercourse). The Louisiana case probably could not arise today. Louisiana enacted no-fault divorce in 1990, *see* La. Civ. Code § 102, Revision Comments—1990 (West 1999), so alleged fault on either side would now be irrelevant except in a covenant marriage, and in a covenant marriage, the fault alleged in *Favrot* would be irrelevant.

Louisiana now authorizes couples to enter into covenant marriages with more stringent requirements for divorce, LA. REV. STAT. ANN. §9:272 (West Supp. 2008), but only two to three percent of Louisiana couples actually do so. Katherine Shaw Spaht, *Covenant Marriage Seven Years Later: Its As Yet Unfulfilled Promise*, 65 LA. L. REV. 605, 618 (2005). Refusing sex is not as such a ground for divorce in a covenant marriage, but "abandoning the marital domicile" for one year and "constantly" refusing to return is a ground, and "living separately and apart continuously without reconciliation" for two years is a ground. LA. REV. STAT. ANN. § 9:307 (West Supp. 2008).

39. President's Statement on Massachusetts Church Ruling (Feb. 4, 2004), *available at* www.whitehouse.gov/news/releases/2004/02/20040204-9.html. The brief statement is quoted, substantially in full, in Richard W. Stevenson, *Bush Expected to Endorse Amendment on Marriage*, N.Y. TIMES A27 (Feb. 5, 2004).

40. In re Marriage Cases, 183 P.3d 384 (Cal. 2008) (requiring marriage); In re Opinions of the Justices to the Senate, 802 N.E.2d 565 (Mass. 2004) (requiring marriage); Lewis v. Harris, 908 A.2d 196 (N.J. 2006) (leaving choice of marriage or some substitute to the legislature). A similar case is pending in the Connecticut Supreme Court as this is written. Kerrigan v. State, 909 A.2d 89 (Conn. Super. Ct. 2006), *appeal pending*.

41. Alison Leigh Cowan, *Gay Couples Say Civil Unions Aren't Enough*, N.Y. TIMES B1 (March 17, 2008); Tina Kelley, *Civil Union Law Is Flawed, Says Panel in New Jersey*, N.Y. TIMES B5 (Feb. 20, 2008).

42. Goodridge v. Dep't of Pub. Health, 798 N.E.2d 941, 954 (Mass. 2003).

43. *Id.*

44. *Id.* at 965 n.29.

45. In re Marriage Cases, 183 P.3d 384, 43 Cal. 4th 757, 793 n.11 (2008). The court cited a provision of the California Constitution of 1849 providing that "No contract of marriage, if otherwise duly made, shall be invalidated by want of conformity to the requirements of any religious sect." CAL. CONST. art. XI, § 12 (1849), now codified as CAL. FAM. CODE § 420(c) (West 2004).

46. *Marriage Cases*, 43 Cal. 4th at 782, 830.

47. *Id.* at 855.

48. *Id.* at 854–55.

49. Katherine Q. Seelye & Janet Elder, *Strong Support Is Found for Ban on Gay Marriage*, N.Y. TIMES 11 (Dec. 21, 2003).

50. *Id.*

51. Jonathan Turley, *How to End the Same-Sex Marriage Debate*, USA TODAY 15A (Apr. 3, 2006).

52. See MARK DEWOLFE HOWE, THE GARDEN AND THE WILDERNESS: RELIGION AND GOVERNMENT IN AMERICAN CONSTITUTIONAL HISTORY 34-41 (1965).

APPENDIX TO CHAPTER 3

Excerpts From Selected State Statutes

1. STATES PROVIDING NO CONSCIENCE CLAUSE PROTECTION
Three states provide no conscience clause protection at all: Alabama, New Hampshire and Vermont.

2. STATES WHICH PERMIT AN OBJECTION ONLY IF INVOKER SHOWS PROOF OR STATES REASONS FOR OBJECTING IN WRITING

ARIZ. REV. STAT. ANN. § 36-2151 (2003):
A physician, or any other person who is a member of or associated with the staff of a hospital, or any employee of a hospital, doctor, clinic, or other medical or surgical facility in which an abortion has been authorized, who shall state in writing an objection to such abortion on moral or religious grounds shall not be required to participate in the medical or surgical procedures which will result in the abortion.

CAL. HEALTH & SAFETY CODE § 123420(a) (West 2006):
No employer or other person shall require a physician [or other health care provider] to directly participate in the induction or performance of an abortion, if the employee or other person has filed a written statement with the employer or the hospital, facility, or clinic indicating a moral, ethical, or religious basis for refusal to participate in the abortion.

Colo. Rev. Stat. Ann. § 18-6-104 (West 2004):

A person who is a member of or associated with the staff of a hospital or any employee of a hospital in which a justified medical termination has been authorized and who states in writing an objection to the termination on moral or religious grounds is not required to participate in the medical procedures which result in the termination of a pregnancy . . . .

Ga. Code Ann. § 16-12-142 (2007):

[A]ny person who states in writing an objection to any abortion or all abortions on moral or religious grounds shall not be required to participate in procedures which will result in such abortion . . . .

Idaho Code Ann. § 18-612 (2004):

Any [physician or person employed or controlled by a hospital] shall be deemed to have sufficiently objected to participation in [abortion] procedures only if he or she has advised such hospital in writing that he or she generally or specifically objects to assisting or otherwise participating in such procedures.

720 Ill. Comp. Stat. Ann. 510/13 (West 2003):

No physician, hospital, ambulatory surgical center, nor employee thereof, shall be required against his or its conscience declared in writing to perform, permit or participate in any abortion . . . .

Ky. Rev. Stat. Ann. § 311.800 (LexisNexis 2007):

No physician [or other health care provider], who shall state in writing to such hospital or health care facility his objection to performing . . . [an] abortion on moral, religious or professional grounds, shall be required to, or held liable for refusal to, perform, participate in, or cooperate in such abortion.

Mass. Gen. Laws Ann. ch. 112, § 12I (West 2003):

A physician [or other health care provider in a facility where an abortion is scheduled,] . . . who shall state in writing an objection to such abortion or sterilization procedure on moral or religious grounds, shall not be required to participate in the medical procedures which result in such abortion or sterilization . . . .

N.Y. Civ. Rights Law § 79-i (McKinney 1992):

When the performing of an abortion . . . is contrary to the conscience or religious beliefs of any person, he may refuse to perform or assist in such abortion by filing a prior written refusal setting forth the reasons therefor with the appropriate and responsible [institution or person] . . . .

43 PA. CONS. STAT. ANN. § 955.2 (West 1991):

No physician, [or other health care provider], who shall state in writing to [his or her] hospital or health care facility an objection . . . on moral, religious, or professional grounds, shall be required to or held liable for refusal to, perform, participate in, or cooperate in such abortion . . . .

VA. CODE ANN. § 18.2-75 (2004):

Any person who shall state in writing an objection to any abortion or all abortions on personal, ethical, moral or religious grounds shall not be required to participate in procedures which will result in such abortion . . . .

For a variation on this, Rhode Island provides an exception for scheduled abortions only. *See* **R.I. GEN. LAWS § 23-17-11 (2001):**
A physician or [other health care provider] or any employee of a health care facility in which an abortion . . . is scheduled, and who shall state in writing an objection to the abortion . . . on moral or religious grounds, shall not be required to participate in the medical procedures which result in the abortion . . . .

3. STATES WITH MINIMAL BURDENS ON REFUSALS, REQUIRING ONLY NOTICE TO THE PATIENT BEFOREHAND

CAL. HEALTH & SAFETY CODE § 123420(c) (West 2006):

Any such facility or clinic that does not permit the performance of abortions on its premises shall post notice of that proscription in an area of the facility or clinic that is open to patients and prospective admittees.

NEB. REV. STAT. § 28-337 (1995):

No [health care] facility in this state shall be required to admit any patient for the purpose of performing an abortion nor required to allow the performance of an abortion therein, but the [health care] facility shall inform the patient of its policy not to participate in abortion procedures.

OR. REV. STAT. § 435.475 (2007):

[The statute provides that no] hospital is liable for its failure or refusal to participate in such termination if the hospital has adopted a policy not to admit patients for the purposes of terminating pregnancies. However, the hospital must notify the person seeking admission to the hospital of its policy.

In a variation on this, some states allow physicians to refuse to give patients information about an abortion, but the physician must let the patient know about the refusal. *See, e.g.,* OR. REV. STAT. § 435.485 (2007):

No physician is required to give advice with respect to or participate in any termination of a pregnancy if the refusal to do so is based on an election not to give such advice or to participate in such terminations and the physician so advises the patient.

4. STATES PERMITTING THE OBJECTORS TO OBJECT

These statutes allow providers to tell patients "to find someone else:"

ARK. CODE ANN. § 20-16-601(a) (2005):
No person shall be required to perform or participate in medical procedures which result in the termination of pregnancy.

CONN. AGENCIES REGS. § 19-13-D54(f) (2005):
No person shall be required to participate in any phase of an abortion that violates his or her judgment, philosophical, moral or religious beliefs.

DEL. CODE ANN. tit. 24, § 1791 (2005):
No person shall be required to perform or participate in medical procedures which result in the termination of pregnancy.

FLA. STAT. ANN. § 390.0111(8) (West 2007):
No person who is a member of, or associated with, the staff of a hospital, nor any employee of a hospital or physician in which or by whom the termination of a pregnancy has been authorized or performed, who shall state an objection to such procedure on moral or religious grounds shall be required to participate in the procedure which will result in the termination of pregnancy.

HAW. REV. STAT. ANN. § 453-16(d) (LexisNexis 2005):
Nothing in this section shall require any hospital or any person to participate in such abortion nor shall any hospital or any person be liable for such a refusal.

IND. CODE ANN. § 16-34-1-4 (LexisNexis 1993):
No physician or [other health care employee] shall be required to perform an abortion or to assist or participate in the medical procedures resulting in or

intended to result in an abortion, if that individual objects to such procedures on ethical, moral, or religious grounds.

Iowa Code Ann. § 146.1 (West 2005):

An individual who may lawfully . . . participate in medical procedures which will result in an abortion shall not be required against that individual's religious beliefs or moral convictions to . . . participate in such procedures.

Kan. Stat. Ann. § 65-443 (2002):

No person shall be required to . . . participate in medical procedures that result in the termination of a pregnancy, and the refusal of any person to . . . participate . . . shall not be a basis for civil liability to any person.

Me. Rev. Stat. Ann. tit. 22, §§ 1591, 1592 (2004):

No physician, nurse or other person who refuses to perform or assist in the performance of an abortion, and no hospital or health care facility that refuses to permit the performance of an abortion upon its premises, shall be liable to any person . . . .

Mich. Comp. Laws Ann. § 333.20181 (West 2001):

A hospital, clinic, institution, teaching institution, or other health facility or a physician, member, or associate of the staff, or other person connected therewith, may refuse to perform, participate in, or allow to be performed on its premises an abortion.

Minn. Stat. Ann. § 145.414 (West 2005):

No person and no hospital or institution shall be coerced, held liable or discriminated against in any manner because of a refusal to perform, accommodate, or assist or submit to an abortion for any reason.

N.M. Stat. Ann. § 30-5-2 (LexisNexis 2003):

A person who is a member of, or associated with, the staff of a hospital, or any employee of a hospital . . . who objects . . . on moral or religious grounds shall not be required to participate in medical procedures which will result in the termination of a pregnancy . . . .

N.C. Gen. Stat. § 14-45.1(e), (f) (LexisNexis 2007):

Nothing in this section shall require a physician licensed to practice medicine in North Carolina or any nurse who shall state an objection to abortion on moral, ethical, or religious grounds, to perform or participate in medical procedures which result in an abortion.

N.D. CENT. CODE § 23-16-14 (2002):

No hospital, physician, nurse, hospital employee, nor any other person is under any duty, by law or contract, nor may such hospital or person in any circumstances be required to participate in the performance of an abortion, if such hospital or person objects to such abortion.

OHIO REV. CODE ANN. § 4731.91 (LexisNexis 2004):

No person is required to perform or participate in medical procedures which result in abortion, and refusal to perform or participate in the medical procedures is not grounds for civil liability nor a basis for disciplinary or other recriminatory action.

18 PA. CONS. STAT. ANN. § 3213(d) (West 2000):

Except for a facility devoted exclusively to the performance of abortions, no medical personnel or medical facility, nor any employee, agent or student thereof, shall be required against his or its conscience to aid, abet or facilitate performance of an abortion or dispensing of an abortifacient and failure or refusal to do so shall not be a basis for any civil, criminal, administrative or disciplinary action, penalty or proceeding, nor may it be the basis for refusing to hire or admit anyone.

S.D. CODIFIED LAWS § 34-23A-11 (2004):

No counselor, social worker, or anyone else who may be in such a position to where the abortion question may appear as a part of [the] workday routine, shall be liable . . . for damages arising from advising or helping to arrange for or for refusal to arrange or encourage abortion.

S.D. CODIFIED LAWS § 34-23A-12 (2004):

No physician, nurse, or other person who refuses to perform or assist in the performance of an abortion shall be liable to any person for damages arising from that refusal.

TENN. CODE ANN. § 39-15-204 (2006):

No physician shall be required to perform an abortion and no person shall be required to participate in the performance of an abortion. No hospital shall be required to permit abortions to be performed therein.

WYO. STAT. ANN. § 35-6-106 (LexisNexis 2007):

No person shall . . . be required to perform or participate in any abortion . . . .

These statutes tend not to distinguish between private and public hospitals; instead they insulate any hospital. *See, e.g.,* **ARIZ. REV. STAT. ANN.** § 36-2151 (2003):
No hospital is required to admit any patient for the purpose of performing an abortion.

5. STATES REQUIRING DOCTOR/FACILITY TO FACILITATE PATIENT'S ABILITY TO GET SERVICE FROM ANOTHER PROVIDER

The New England Journal of Medicine's Sounding Board recommended that with respect to emergency contraceptive, the objecting pharmacist must find a willing provider. *See* Julie Kantor & Ken Baum, *The Limits of Conscientious Objection—May Pharmacists Refuse to Fill Prescriptions for Emergency Contraception?*, 351 NEW ENGLAND JOURNAL OF MEDICINE 2008, 2008–12 (2004).

At least one state specifically rejects such a duty. *See* **MD. CODE ANN., HEALTH-GEN.** § 20-214 (LexisNexis 2005):
A licensed hospital . . . may not be required to permit, within the hospital, the performance of any medical procedure that results in artificial insemination, sterilization, or termination of pregnancy; or to refer to any source for these medical procedures.

6. STATES WITH PROTECTION SIMILAR TO THE CHURCH AMENDMENT

WIS. STAT. ANN. § 253.09(4) (West 2004):
[No individual or entity may be required to participate in or make its facilities available for abortion contrary to religious beliefs or moral convictions because of the receipt of] any grant, contract, loan or loan guarantee under any state or federal law.

7. STATES THAT INSULATE PROVIDERS FROM PUNISHMENT BY STATE AND LOCAL GOVERNMENTS

LA. REV. STAT. ANN. § 40:1299.33 (2001):
No [health care] facility, whether public or private, shall ever be denied governmental assistance . . . for refusing to permit its facilities, staff or employees to be used in any way for the purpose of performing an abortion.

MASS. GEN. LAWS ANN. ch. 112, § 12I (West 2003):
Conscientious objection to abortion shall not be grounds for . . . refusal to grant financial assistance under any state aided project . . . .

Mo. Ann. Stat. § 197.032 (West 2004):

No person or institution may be denied . . . any public benefit . . . on the grounds that they refuse to undergo an abortion, to advise, consent to, assist in or perform an abortion.

Mont. Code Ann. § 50-20-111 (2007):

[The] refusal by any hospital or health care facility or person [to provide advice] shall not be grounds for loss of any privileges or immunities . . . or for the loss of any public benefits.

8. States In Which Employees Hired For Express Purpose Of Performing Specific Service Or Employed By Facilities Which Exclusively Provide Abortions Are Not Exempted

745 Ill. Comp. Stat. Ann. 70/13 (West 2002):

Nothing in this Act shall be construed as excusing any person, public or private institution, or public official from liability for refusal to permit or provide a particular form of health care service if . . . the person, public or private institution or public official has entered into a contract specifically to provide that particular form of health care service; or . . . the person, public or private institution or public official has accepted federal or state funds for the sole purpose of, and specifically conditioned upon, permitting or providing that particular form of health care service.

Ky. Rev. Stat. Ann. § 311.800(5)(c) (LexisNexis 2007):

It shall be unlawful discriminatory practice for . . . [a]ny [person or institution] to discriminate against any person . . . on account of the willingness or refusal of such [person] to . . . participate in abortion or sterilization . . . if that health care facility is not operated exclusively for the purpose of performing abortions.

18 Pa. Cons. Stat. Ann. § 3213 (West 2000):

Except for a facility devoted exclusively to the performance of abortions, no medical personnel or medical facility, nor any employee, agent or student thereof, shall be required against his or its conscience to aid, abet or facilitate performance of an abortion or dispensing of an abortifacient and failure or refusal to do so shall not be a basis for any civil, criminal, administrative or disciplinary action, penalty or proceeding, nor may it be the basis for refusing to hire or admit anyone.

9. STATES WHICH LIMIT ENCROACHMENT BASED ON RESULTING UNDUE HARDSHIP

MO. ANN. STAT. § 188.105 (West 2004):

[Discrimination against one who has an objection] shall not be unlawful if there can be demonstrated an inability to reasonably accommodate an individual's refusal to participate in abortion without undue hardship on the conduct of that particular business or enterprise, or in those certain instances where participation in abortion is a bona fide occupational qualification reasonably necessary to the normal operation of that particular business or enterprise.

10. STATES WHICH PROHIBIT EMPLOYERS FROM ASKING PROSPECTIVE EMPLOYEES ABOUT REFUSAL TO PARTICIPATE

745 ILL. COMP. STAT. ANN. 70/7 (West 2002):

It shall be unlawful for any public or private employer, [or other such entity], . . . to place any reference in its application form concerning, to orally question about . . . any applicant . . . on account of the applicant's refusal to . . . participate in any way in any form of health care services contrary to his or her conscience.

11. STATES WITH RENEGADE PHYSICIAN PROTECTION

CAL. HEALTH & SAFETY CODE § 123420 (West 2006):

No such employee of a hospital, facility, or clinic that does not permit the performance of abortions, or person with staff privileges therein, shall be subject to any penalty or discipline on account of the person's participation in the performance of an abortion in other than the hospital, facility, or clinic.

MICH. COMP. LAWS ANN. § 333.20184 (West 2001):

A hospital . . . or other health facility which refuses to allow abortions to be performed on its premises shall not deny staff privileges or employment to an individual for the sole reason that the individual previously participated in . . . a termination of pregnancy.

TEX. OCC. CODE ANN. § 103.002 (b) (Vernon 2004):

A hospital or health care facility may not discriminate against a physician, nurse, staff member, or employee because of the person's willingness to participate in an abortion procedure in another facility.

12. STATES WHICH EXTEND RIGHT TO REFUSE BEYOND RELIGION/ MORALITY

43 PA. CONS. STAT. ANN. § 955.2 (West 1991):
No physician, nurse, staff member, or employee of a . . . health care facility, who . . . object[s] . . . on moral, religious, or professional grounds, shall be required to, or held liable for refusal to, perform, participate in, or cooperate in such abortion.

N.Y. CIV. RIGHTS LAW § 79-i (McKinney 1992):
When the performing of an abortion . . . is contrary to the conscience or religious beliefs of any person, he may refuse to perform or assist in such abortion. . . .

13. STATES WHICH LIMIT RIGHT TO REFUSE ONLY TO PRIVATE OR DENOMINATIONAL HOSPITALS

IND. CODE ANN. § 16-34-1-3 (LexisNexis 1993):
No private or denominational hospital shall be required to permit its facilities to be utilized for the performance of abortions.

IOWA CODE ANN. § 146.2 (West 2005):
A hospital, which is not controlled, maintained, and supported by a public authority, shall not be required to permit the performance of an abortion.

KY. REV. STAT. ANN. § 311.800 (3) (LexisNexis 2007):
No private hospital or private health care facility shall be required to . . . permit the performance of abortion contrary to its stated ethical policy.

OR. REV. STAT. § 435.475(3) (2007):
No hospital operated by this state or by a political subdivision in this state is authorized to adopt a policy of excluding or denying admission to any person seeking termination of a pregnancy.

S.C. CODE ANN. § 44-41-40 (2002):
No private or nongovernmental hospital or clinic shall be required to admit any patient for the purpose of terminating a pregnancy, nor shall such institutions be required to permit their facilities to be utilized for the performance of abortions.

TEX. OCC. CODE ANN. § 103.004 (Vernon 2004):

A private hospital or private health care facility is not required to make its facilities available for the performance of abortion unless a physician determines that the life of the mother is immediately endangered.

UTAH CODE ANN. § 76-7-306(2) (2003):

Nothing in this part shall require any private and/or denominational hospital to admit any patient for the purpose of performing an abortion.

WASH. REV. CODE ANN. § 9.02.150 (West 2003):

No person or private medical facility may be required by law or contract in any circumstances to participate in the performance of an abortion if such person or private medical facility objects to so doing.

WYO. STAT. ANN. § 35-6-105 (LexisNexis 2007):

No private hospital, clinic, institution or other private facility in this state is required to admit any patient for the purpose of performing an abortion nor to allow the performance of an abortion therein.

In other jurisdictions, case law limits application of the statutory exemption to denominational hospitals. *See* N.J. STAT. ANN. § 2A: 65A-2 (West 2000): No hospital or other health care facility shall be required to provide abortion . . . services or procedures.

New Jersey's Supreme Court held these provisions unconstitutional as applied to nonsectarian, nonprofit hospitals. *See* Doe v. Bridgeton Hosp. Ass'n, 366 A.2d 641 (N.J. 1976).

14. STATES WHICH HAVE EXPANDED THE RIGHT TO REFUSE TO INSURERS AND OTHER ENTITIES

MINN. STAT. ANN. § 145.414 (West 2005):

[N]o health plan company . . . or health care cooperative . . . shall be required to provide or provide coverage for an abortion.

MO. ANN. STAT. § 376.1199(1) (West 2002):

Nothing in this subsection shall be construed to require a health carrier to perform, induce, pay for, reimburse, guarantee, arrange, provide any resources for or refer a patient for an abortion [unless necessary to] prevent the death of the female upon whom the abortion is performed.

15. States Which Limit Right To Refuse To Nonemergencies

Mo. Ann. Stat. § 376.1199(1) (West 2002):
Nothing in this subsection shall be construed to require a health carrier to perform, induce, pay for, reimburse, guarantee, arrange, provide any resources for or refer a patient for an abortion. [unless necessary to] prevent the death of the female upon which the abortion is performed.

Nev. Rev. Stat. Ann. § 449.191 (LexisNexis 2004):
A hospital or other medical facility . . . which is not operated by the state or a local government or an agency of either is not required to permit the use of its facilities for the induction or performance of an abortion, except in a medical emergency.

S.C. Code Ann. §§ 44-41-40, -50 (2002):
No private or nongovernmental hospital or clinic shall be required to . . . permit their facilities to be utilized for the performance of abortions; *provided*, that no hospital or clinic shall refuse an emergency admittance.

Tex. Occ. Code Ann. § 103.004 (Vernon 2004):
A private hospital or private health care facility is not required to make its facilities available for the performance of abortion unless a physician determines that the life of the mother is immediately endangered.

Index

About the Editors and Contributors

Douglas Laycock is the Yale Kamisar Collegiate Professor of Law at The University of Michigan. He is a prolific scholar on religious liberty, other constitutional law issues, and the law of remedies. He is also an experienced appellate litigator, including before the Supreme Court of the United States, and has played a key role, in public and behind the scenes, in developing state and federal religious liberty legislation. He has represented clients across the political and theological spectrum. He is a graduate of Michigan State University and The University of Chicago Law School, a Fellow of the American Academy of Arts and Sciences, and a member of the Council of the American Law Institute. Before moving to Michigan, he taught at The University of Chicago and The University of Texas at Austin. Professor Laycock may be reached at laycockd@umich.edu.

Anthony R. Picarello, Jr. is General Counsel for the United States Conference of Catholic Bishops in Washington, DC. He organized the conference documented in this volume over the course of 2005 while serving as Vice President and General Counsel for the Becket Fund for Religious Liberty, a nonprofit, public-interest law firm dedicated to protecting the free expression of all religious traditions. He has lectured extensively on religious freedom law at conferences, seminars, and law schools across the country, and has published articles in the *First Amendment Law Review* and the *George Mason Law Review*. In January 2007, Mr. Picarello was named to *The American Lawyer* magazine's list of the top fifty litigators under age forty-five. Mr. Picarello may be reached at apicarello@usccb.org.

Robin Fretwell Wilson is the Law Alumni Faculty Fellow and professor of law at Washington & Lee University School of Law, where her scholarship focuses on family law, children and violence, and healthcare law. She is the editor of *Reconceiving the Family: Critical Reflections on the American Law Institute's Principles of the Law of Family Dissolution* (Cambridge University Press, 2006); and co-editor of *The Handbook of Children, Culture & Violence* with Nancy Dowd and Dorothy Singer (Sage Publications, 2006), and *Health Law and Bioethics: Cases in Context* with Sandra Johnson, Joan Krause, and Richard Saver (Aspen Publishers, 2008). Her work on family law and healthcare law has appeared in the *Cornell Law Review*, the *Emory Law Journal*, the *North Carolina Law Review*, the *San Diego Law Review*, the *Washington & Lee Law Review*, and numerous peer-reviewed journals. Professor Wilson may be reached at wilsonrf@wlu.edu.

Contributors

Chai R. Feldblum is a professor of law at Georgetown University Law Center, where she has taught in the areas of sexuality, gender and the law, legislation and administrative law, and disability law, and where she directs the Federal Legislation Clinic. She is the author of numerous articles and monographs including *The Moral Values Project: Deploying Moral Discourse for LGBT Equality* (2006); "Gay is Good: The Case for Marriage Equality & More" (2005), and "Rectifying the Tilt: Equality Lessons from Religion, Disability, Sexual Orientation and Transgender" (2003). She has served as a legislative lawyer consultant to the Human Rights Campaign and the National Gay & Lesbian Task Force, and has been a key drafter and negotiator on the Employment Non-Discrimination Act. Professor Feldblum may be reached at feldblum@law.georgetown.edu.

Douglas W. Kmiec is Caruso Family Chair and Professor of Constitutional Law, Pepperdine University. He served as head of the Office of Legal Counsel (U.S. Assistant Attorney General) for Presidents Ronald Reagan and George H.W. Bush, a position previously held by the late Chief Justice Rehnquist (for Nixon) and Justice Scalia (for Ford). Professor Kmiec's colleague and adjoining office mate during his service was yet another member of the Supreme Court, Samuel Alito. He is the former dean and St. Thomas More Professor of the law school at The Catholic University of America. Before that, for nearly two decades, Professor Kmiec was a member of the law faculty at the University of Notre Dame. At Notre Dame, he directed the Thomas White Center on Law & Government and founded the *Journal of Law, Ethics & Public Policy*. Professor Kmiec has been a White House Fellow, a Distinguished Fulbright Scholar on the Constitution (in Asia), the inaugural Visiting Distinguished Scholar at the National Constitution Center, and the recipient of numerous honors and honorary degrees. His published work is wide-ranging, including three books on the American Constitution, several legal treatises and related books, and hundreds of published articles and essays.

Charles J. Reid, Jr., is professor of law at the University of St. Thomas (Minnesota) where he teaches courses on jurisprudence, canon law, and great books. He is the author of *Power Over The Body, Equality In The Family: Rights And Domestic Relations In Medieval Canon Law* (2004). In addition, he has written many articles on the history of marriage and domestic relations law, in time periods ranging from the Christianizing Roman Empire of the fourth and fifth centuries to the nineteenth-century American frontier.

Marc D. Stern, Assistant Executive Director of the American Jewish Congress and Co-Director of its Commission on Law and Social Action, is one of the most respected lawyers in the United States on church-state and religious liberty issues. He is consulted widely by numerous Jewish and non-Jewish organizations interested in maintaining the separation of church and state. Instrumental in helping the American Jewish Congress successfully resist attempts to weaken First Amendment protections, Mr. Stern has been named one of the "Forward Fifty" most influential leaders of the American Jewish community. Mr. Stern has written numerous briefs, monographs, legislative testimony, and articles on civil liberties issues, including "Jews and Public Morality" in *Tikkun Olam: Social Responsibility in Jewish Law and Thought*; and "Anti-Semitism and the Law" in *Anti-Semitism in America Today*.

Jonathan Turley is the J.B. and Maurice Shapiro Professor of Public Interest Law at George Washington University. He is a nationally recognized legal scholar who has written extensively in areas ranging from constitutional law to legal theory to tort law. After a stint at Tulane Law School, Professor Turley joined the GW Law faculty in 1990, and in 1998, became the youngest chaired professor in the school's history. Professor Turley has served as counsel in some of the most notable cases in the last two decades, including his representation of the Area 51 workers at a secret air base in Nevada; the nuclear couriers at Oak Ridge, Tennessee; the Rocky Flats grand jury in Colorado; Dr. Eric Foretich, the husband in the Elizabeth Morgan custody controversy; and four former U.S. Attorneys General during the Clinton impeachment litigation. Professor Turley also has served as counsel in a variety of national security and terrorism cases, and has been ranked as one of the top 10 lawyers handling military cases.